Writing True

Writing True

THE ART AND CRAFT OF CREATIVE NONFICTION

Sondra Perl   **Mimi Schwartz**

Houghton Mifflin Company
Boston   New York

Publisher: *Patricia A. Coryell*

Editor in Chief: *Suzanne Phelps Weir*

Assistant Editor: *Anne Leung*

Editorial Associate: *John McHugh*

Senior Project Editor: *Kathryn Dinovo*

Senior Manufacturing Buyer: *Renee Ostrowski*

Senior Marketing Manager: *Cindy Graff Cohen*

Cover image: Three Worlds. Lithograph, December 1955. Escher, Maurits Cornelis (1898–1972). Photo Credit: Art Resource, N.Y.

Acknowledgments appear on page 388, which constitutes an extension of the copyright page.

Printed in the U.S.A.

Library of Congress Control Number: 2005926851

ISBN: 0-618-37075-7

56789-QUE-09 08

BRIEF CONTENTS

Contents

PREFACE

Creative Nonfiction is a new name for an old impulse: to write about the *real* world with grace, power, and personal commitment. There have been other names — *belles lettres,* literary nonfiction, New Journalism — but this name stuck. The term, first used in the early 1980s by the National Endowment for the Arts, has turned into a full-scale movement. According to Lee Gutkind, who launched the magazine *Creative Nonfiction* in 1991, there are now more than two dozen graduate programs in creative nonfiction; over 300 college courses; over 100 books on the subject; and increasing numbers of conferences with sessions on teaching and writing creative nonfiction. The result is an ever-expanding interest in memoir, personal essay, travel writing, and literary journalism, all part of a genre that gives writers permission to write creatively about the nonfiction world as they experience it.

The power of the genre is its invitation to *all* writers, no matter who they are, to speak out and be heard as individuals. Expert and novice, young and old, famous and never-heard-before, all have the legitimacy to say: "Here's my point of view. Here's how I see my world." And if they write well enough, with authority and artistry, they can convince readers, as Joan Didion says, "To see it my way!" This book provides strategies for making creative nonfiction come alive, whether one is focusing on personal experience or the world at large.

At the heart of all good writing is a compelling voice: one that demonstrates, with confidence and authority, that words matter, that they have the power to persuade, explain, illuminate, evoke, depict, and inspire. Creative nonfiction makes it easier to find our voices by encouraging us to explore what we most care about. We begin with a question or puzzlement, and with the help of memory, research, reading, interviews, speculation, imagining — whatever it takes — we attempt to capture the complexity of our subject. It's the struggle with complexity, more than "the big answer," that challenges creative nonfiction writers and defines what *Writing True* is all about. For "writing true," as we see it, is an act to shape the nonfiction world as writers experience it in a way that makes readers nod knowingly and read on.

We, Sondra and Mimi, the authors of this book, came to know the power of this genre by writing, teaching, and publishing it. Like many who started as academics, it took us time to discover that *all* nonfiction writing can be both informative *and* engaging. Ever since, our challenge has been to use voice to be both, whether we are composing personal essays, academic articles, or textbooks. And we pass that challenge on to our students — often with good results. Many tell us that after a creative nonfiction course, they feel more relaxed as writers, their writing voices are more varied and more fluent, and their written work, even on essay exams or dissertations, is more effective. Creative nonfiction, it seems, has a ripple effect across genres and disciplines.

Features

Why? Because this genre attempts to repair the rift between "straight nonfiction" and "creative nonfiction" that has artificially separated the attributes of good writing. In *Writing True*, we bring them back together, showing how fact *and* point of view, research *and* voice, can work in tandem to produce nonfiction writing that is strong, bold, evocative, interesting — and true. To help writers infuse their nonfiction work with creativity, we focus on the following:

- *The Role of Voice:* The right voice (or voices) for a given subject harnesses commitment and understanding for writer and reader.

- *The Use of Research:* First-hand experiences, memories, interviews, notes from readings, and fact-finding investigations, when incorporated seamlessly, make creative nonfiction relevant *and* interesting.

❧ *The Value of Storytelling:* Anecdotes, dialogue, scenes, suspense, character development, descriptions of place — all contribute to the power of creative nonfiction by showing, not just telling, what's important.

❧ *The Need for Point of View:* It's not enough to provide facts, quotations, or scenes that say, "Here reader, figure it out yourself." The writer must engage in the struggle to make sense of the subject.

❧ *The Possibilities of Form and Language:* "Creative" in nonfiction means finding the form and language that best match one's meaning.

Organization

Part I: Writing Creative Nonfiction

Writing True is organized to help writers find the topics that matter most to them — and offers strategies for turning first thoughts into finished work. We have found that our approach works with novice and experienced writers alike, whether enrolled in freshman composition, advanced essay workshops, graduate classes in creative nonfiction, memoir courses for adults — or simply writing on their own. Through examples and exercises, we demonstrate how memory, observation, reflection, voice, research, storytelling, and the writer's point of view are the heart of good nonfiction writing. So, too, is revision, which we emphasize in its "creative" sense, showing writers how to re-enter their drafts imaginatively — with the help of time, rereading, and feedback from others.

Chapters 1–4 focus on ideas for getting started, moving from initial jottings to full first drafts. Chapter 1 makes the case for why "creative" infuses vitality into nonfiction work, and it defines its subgenres and their benefits for writer and reader. Chapter 2 emphasizes how the notebook, also called a journal or daybook, is a key tool for creative nonfiction writers who discover their themes by writing first and figuring out "why" afterwards. Using our exercises, writers find the creativity in themselves by learning how to experiment with language and form, fault-free. Chapter 3 offers ten extended exercises for developing a draft. Some build on ideas that began in the notebook; others offer fresh imaginative triggers. Chapter 4 shows how to find the shape of promising fragments and turn them into full drafts by fleshing out what may only be half there on the page.

Chapters 5–7 focus on shaping drafts into polished work. In Chapter 5, the emphasis is on finding the voice or voices needed to write with authenticity from the inside out, providing the energy that makes readers pay attention. In Chapter 6, we show how to read a draft — one's own and others' — and how to give and receive feedback on works-in-progress. Active listening, one of the important skills we introduce in this chapter, shows even the most sophisticated writers how to become more adept at responding to the work of others. Chapter 7 focuses on revision—not just editing, but "creative" revision that involves "facing your dragons," finding "the story in the situation," and cutting what doesn't serve the text.

Chapter 8 deals with ways to add a lighter touch, even on what are often serious topics. It includes examples of humor, graphic memoir, collage, and other alternatives for approaching subjects in new ways. Chapter 9 presents strategies for engaging in the kind of research that enriches a text, whether one is writing a memoir or literary journalism. And Chapter 10 covers the controversies involved in writing creative nonfiction, discussing how writers handle such questions as: Where is the line between fact and fiction? What is the difference between factual and emotional truth? What are the ethics of creative nonfiction? What are the legal ramifications? How can we best handle writing about people we know?

At the end of each chapter we offer what we call Ways In: exercises for practicing the ideas and strategies we have presented. Each chapter can also stand alone *and need not be used sequentially.* The order will depend on interest and writing experience. For example, those who haven't used notebooks before might linger on Chapter 2, enjoying the act of writing as discovery without the additional pressure of making work public or sharing it with an audience. Veteran notebook or journal keepers may peruse this chapter and move on more quickly. The same holds true for Chapter 6 on "workshopping." Those new to group feedback will want to spend time on reading and practicing workshopping techniques; those experienced in the process may read for extra tips. Some chapters, like Chapter 3, Idea Generators, work well for use over time — trying one new technique, perhaps, each week.

Part II: Reading Creative Nonfiction

We offer an anthology of creative nonfiction to be read for pleasure and for technique. We chose these pieces, first, because we love them; second, because they offer a range of voices, experiences, and points of view; and third, because they reflect a variety of forms from traditional to avant-garde. To make studying these forms easier, we've divided the works into categories: *Memoir, Personal Essay, Portrait, Essay of Place,* and *Literary Journalism.* We also include *Stories of Craft,* in which writers of creative nonfiction discuss the genre, and *Short Shorts* that highlight the possibilities of form and language in two- to four-page essays. Our labels are somewhat arbitrary, as many works fall into more than one category. Feel free to mix and match at will.

Supplements for *Writing True*

On Our Website

On the website, you will find additional writing by authors we highlight in our text as well as interviews with a few about the craft of writing. You will find writing by students from different parts of the United States who have tried our exercises and met with success. You will find supplemental readings that show the "crossover" possibilities of creative nonfiction — into literary criticism and academic research, for example. Finally, we offer web links to creative nonfiction journals and additional resources that writers of creative nonfiction should know about — for reading and publishing opportunities. To visit our website, go to http://college.hmco.com/english.

Instructor's Resource Manual

Teachers of writing can download a range of suggestions for using *Writing True* in both their creative nonfiction and composition classes. Our Instructor's Manual includes favorite assignments, syllabi for different courses, and tips for using each of our ten chapters and the readings. They are based on the classroom experiences of instructors who have used this book in a range of courses whose names are as varied as The Creative Nonfiction Workshop, Advanced Essay Writing, Freshman Composition, Graduate Seminar in Writing, From Memory to Memoir, The Art of the Personal Essay, and Nonfiction Essay Writing.

Acknowledgments

No book is a solitary effort. The traces of colleagues, like-minded others, distant teachers, and important thinkers can be seen throughout. *Writing True* is no exception. We have been fortunate to be surrounded by colleagues and friends who have responded generously to our queries and whose thinking has helped us shape this book. Some offered feedback on specific chapters, others on the entire text, and a few in spirited late-night conversations about the nature of truth and the slipperiness of memory.

In particular, we wish to thank our field testers from around the country and their many students who experimented with the book in its early stages and gave us pages and pages of challenging commentary that helped us shape the chapters into their current form: Rita Eastburg, College of Lake County; Marlene Eby, College of Lake County; Sandy Jensen, Lane Community College; Joyce Greenberg Lott, South Brunswick High School; Heather Parker, California State University, Stanislaus; Jenny Spinner, Marymount University; Ann Tabachnikov, Fashion Institute of Technology, SUNY, and Lehman College, CUNY; and Karen S. Uehling, Boise State University.

We are also indebted to the outside reviewers who read generously and offered valuable suggestions both on the initial proposal and on the final manuscript: Lynn Z. Bloom, University of Connecticut,

Storrs; John Boe, University of California, Davis; Chas S. Clifton, Colorado State University, Pueblo; Dolores Johnson, Marshall University; Joe Mackall, Ashland University; Marie C. Paretti, Virginia Tech; Stephanie Paterson, California State University, Stanislaus; Michael Petracca, University of California at Santa Barbara; Lad Tobin, Boston College; and Robert Vivian, Alma College.

We thank our students who kept us honest by working with the manuscript in draft form. This includes graduate students in creative nonfiction seminars at Lehman College, CUNY; undergraduates in the Creative Nonfiction Workshop at Richard Stockton College of New Jersey; and adult writers in memoir courses at The Writer's Voice in Manhattan, the Cape May Writers Getaway in New Jersey, the Vermont College's Post-Graduate Summer Writers Conference, and the Hollyhock Retreat Center in British Columbia.

We also wish to thank the members of the New York City Writing Project who responded to our many queries to the listserve, Catherine Perry-Hourmati who assisted us with background research, Shawn Reischmann who helped with manuscript preparation, and Caleb Paull who introduced us to the power of digital storytelling.

Heartfelt thanks goes to our supportive team at Houghton Mifflin who asked hard questions and offered good advice while always respecting our vision for the book. A special thanks to Laura Barthule, our developmental editor; Anne Leung, our assistant editor; and Suzanne Phelps Weir, colleague, editor, and friend.

Most of all, we are grateful to those readers whose opinions we seek no matter what we are writing. They read and responded with the kind of care and attention that only close friends who happen to be great readers can give: Penelope Dugan, Richard Stockton College of New Jersey; Barbara Hurd, Frostburg State University; Lynn Powell, Oberlin College; Nancy Sommers, Harvard University; Maureen Stanton, freelance writer; and Nancy Wilson, Lehman College, CUNY.

Writing projects like this one often have a way of spilling into home lives, so finally we thank our families and friends for putting up with days of collaborative meetings, hour-long phone calls, and an endless preoccupation with revisions and deadlines. And we thank each other—for offering that vital second voice and perspective so needed when trying to write true.

Sondra Perl
Lehman College
and The Graduate Center
of The City University of New York

Mimi Schwartz
Professor Emeritus,
Richard Stockton College
of New Jersey

About the Authors

Sondra Perl is Professor of English and Urban Education at Lehman College and the Graduate Center of the City University of New York. An acclaimed teacher, in 1996, Sondra received the Professor of the Year Award from the Carnegie Foundation for the Advancement of Teaching, and in 2005, she received the Lehman College Award for Excellence in Research, Scholarship, and Creative Work. Sondra's articles have appeared in such journals as the *Harvard Educational Review, College Composition and Communication,* the *ADE Bulletin,* and *Writing on the Edge.* Her books include *Through Teachers' Eyes: Portraits of Writing Teachers at Work,* co-authored with Nancy Wilson; *Landmark Essays on Writing Process; Felt Sense: Writing with the Body;* and *On Austrian Soil: Teaching Those I Was Taught to Hate,* a memoir that tells the story of what happened to Sondra when she found herself teaching Austrian teachers whose parents had been Nazis. A Guggenheim Fellow, Sondra has been leading writing workshops in North America and Europe for over 20 years.

Mimi Schwartz is the author of *Thoughts from a Queen-Sized Bed,* a memoir about life in a long marriage: what you get and give up for it (American Lives Series, University of Nebraska Press). Other books include *Writing for Many Roles* and *Writer's Craft, Teacher's Art, Teaching What We Know.* Her short creative nonfiction has appeared in *Fourth Genre, Creative Nonfiction, Brevity, Tikkun, Calyx, Florida Review, Puerto del Sol, The New York Times, The Philadelphia Inquirer,* and *The Writer's Chronicle,* among others. Five of her essays have been chosen as Notables in *Best American Essays.* Her academic writing has appeared in *College English, College Composition and Communication, Writ-*

ing on the Edge, Journal of Teaching Writing and *Chronicles of Higher Education.* She is Professor Emeritus at Richard Stockton College of New Jersey, has been a MacDowell Fellow, Princeton Faculty Fellow, and Geraldine R. Dodge Fellow, and teaches memoir and creative nonfiction at writers' conferences nationwide. For more information, go to Mimi's website at http://www.MimiSchwartz.net.

PART ONE

Writing Creative Nonfiction

CHAPTER 1

Why Creative Nonfiction?

There are two worlds: the world that we can measure with line and rule, and the world that we feel with our hearts and imagination. To be sensible of the truth of only one of these is to know truth by halves.

— LEIGH HUNT

Creative. Nonfiction. Until recently, "creative" in writing has meant poetry, drama, and fiction; "nonfiction" has meant journalism, business writing, academic scholarship, and car manuals. So why combine them? Because creative nonfiction offers an invitation to writers that nonfiction, as understood today, often does not. "Nonfiction" has a no-nonsense ring to it, an emphasis on objectivity and logic. "Creative," on the other hand, is synonymous with "original, productive, inventive, not imitative." There's the promise of play in the word "creative"—and the possibility of adventure, discovery, the soar of language.

Put together, "creative" plus "nonfiction" produce a synergy that attracts fiction and nonfiction writers alike. At a recent writers conference, every session on creative nonfiction was packed with novelists, journalists, editors, poets, and educators all drawn to the power of these paired words that invite the poet's attention to language, the fiction writer's power of storytelling, the journalist's pursuit of fact, and the scholar's reliance on research.

Would-be writers from many disciplines also seem drawn to the possibilities of the genre. On the first day of teaching creative nonfiction at our respective colleges, we ask, "What is the appeal of creative nonfiction?" and hear this from the future chemists, poets, literary scholars, accountants, and journalists who sign up:

- "It's writing from the inside out."

- "Sounding like me in a t-shirt, not a shirt and tie."

- "Being free from the rules."

- "Capturing what matters."

- "Telling a good, true story—and not being boring."

These writers sense what is at the heart of the genre: a delicious freedom to write, struggle with, and recreate one person's vision of the real world and what's personally important in it. It's a freedom hard to find in today's academia or workplace, which often stresses impartial, generalizable answers. Surveys, reviews of the literature, and footnoted sources are the norm; writing in the first person is not. When used, the "I" often becomes "We" (as in "We discovered") or hides in the passive voice ("It is understood" instead of "I understood").

Such anonymity was not always expected. Look how freely Charles Darwin, writing over one hundred years ago, uses "I" in his famous scientific treatise, *The Origin of the Species*. In the middle of his theory of evolution he writes, comfortably, about his pet pigeons:

> Believing that it is always best to study some special group, I have, after deliberation, taken up domestic pigeons. I have kept every breed which I could purchase or obtain, and have been most kindly favored with skins from several quarters of the world. . . . I have associated with several eminent fanciers, and have been permitted to join two of the London Pigeon Clubs. The diversity of the breeds is something astonishing.

In Darwin's day and before, credibility was less tied to the voice of objectivity. Scientific theory and personal anecdote existed side by side, the subjective not incompatible with reasoned argument. But in our specialized age, many nonfiction writers feel more pressure to separate the world we measure by "line and rule," using writer Leigh

Hunt's terms, from the world "we feel with our hearts and imagination." To publish in scientific journals, today's Darwin would need a more anonymous and formal persona, or editors would write: "Too subjective. Too much 'I.' Your pet pigeons are irrelevant!" This may be true *if* readers say, "Who cares?" But what if readers *do care?* If the pigeon anecdote makes the treatise and Darwin more interesting, why not include it?

Creative nonfiction, then, is a new term for an old tradition of letting the objective and subjective work together to describe the real world. The aim is to make readers experience that world, using the "I" as a guide. Sometimes the "I" is the main subject of the text—and very active; at others, it's a bit player presenting a larger subject. Either way, creative nonfiction assumes that a lively intelligence is always there, behind the words, speaking in a voice that, say, if we heard it at a party, would make us want to stay awhile and meet the speaker.

Nonfiction Plus

The world of creative nonfiction is not invented. Events actually took place; characters are real people. The writer, who is handed the facts, must find the story in them and tell it true, ambiguities and all. In fiction, you can change, pretend, and invent—whatever it takes to be interesting. In creative nonfiction, you must locate and shape what is interesting in the messiness of real life. And interesting is key. It's not enough to report, summarize, and analyze the facts; creative nonfiction also values storytelling, voice, and evocative language to illuminate those facts, making readers connect experientially—as if they were there.

Surprising is also key—for as Robert Frost reminds us, "No surprise for the writer, no surprise for the reader." Discovering new thoughts through the act of writing enables writers to leap beyond what's verifiable by "line and rule" so that "creative" kicks in. You can't force it, but new truths emerge if you are open to imaginative play, as this writer is in a two-part name exercise that begins with the objective (I) and moves toward the subjective (II):

I. My name is Robyn. It is spelled with a "y" and not an "i" and has one "n." It has five letters, and spelled backwards it is nybor. It begins with "r," has two syllables, and is easy to say. It is a female as well as a male name. It is the name of a bird. It is a name my mother liked.

II. My name is Robyn, and I am like a bird. I have skinny legs and a round belly, little eyes, and I sing when happy. I'd rather live in a tree anyway and peck worms for food, live in a soft rush basket and lay my blue eggs. I'd rather sing than talk and be able to shiver in tiny waves, like a bird with its little heart beating fast. I am named for this bird. How did my mother know to do that?

The first records facts about the name "Robyn." No surprises here. The second moves beyond to capture the subjective experience of being Robyn. It is Robyn's name, as Robyn feels it at the moment—not just intellectually, but in the gut. Both versions are rooted in the real world; both offer information; but only the second is "creative," as in "original," "inventive," "not imitative."

Move beyond exercises, and the objective is often a springboard for the subjective, as you can see in Brian Doyle's essay, "Being Brians" (Chapter 12, Personal Essay). His opening paragraph is filled with facts that any Brian Doyle could have written:

There are 215 Brian Doyles in the United States, according to a World Wide Web site called *Switchboard*.

But the piece ends in a lyricism only one Brian Doyle could write:

. . . he was fascinated as a small boy sitting at his grandmother's knee and watching her sew a lace doily, the word *doily* squirming in his mouth, his tongue tumbling over Doyle and doily for days afterward. . . .

That's creative nonfiction, full of surprises for writer and reader, written in an individual voice that openly says, "See this world *my* way!"

These are requisites, we argue in this book, whether your subject is personal or not. Suppose, for example, New York City is the subject. If your aim is to *tell* readers what they need to know, it's nononsense nonfiction. But if you recreate the feeling of the New York experience, *showing* what it is like, it's nonfiction with "creative" in front of it. The line can blur because good writing—straight nonfiction and creative nonfiction—always attends to the craft of language, but creative nonfiction has that extra zing that comes from an engaging voice, a special way with language, a new slant. Which is which below?

> A child who grows up eleven stories in the air has a peculiar relationship with the outdoors. From the bedroom window, it was the sky that was my landscape, not the ground. The trees—saplings when I was a child, now six stories high—were seen from above, their trunks invisible under a great territory of leaves. It was as easy to touch a cloud as the earth below.
>
> —CORRINE DEMAS, *Eleven Stories High:*
> *Growing up in Stuyvesant Town, 1948–1968*

> Be alert at all times. The traffic density of streets in Manhattan is probably the highest in the country. . . . When driving in the other boroughs a street index and map are necessities. Note: Drivers should keep car doors locked at all times.
>
> —*AAA Tour Book—New York*

> A map of the city, colored to designate nationalities, would show more stripes than on the skin of a zebra, and more colors than any rainbow.
>
> —JACOB A. RIIS, *How the Other Half Lives*

> This is the geographic center of the Village. Around the park's central water fountain you'll see street musicians, ventriloquists, comedians, crack Frisbee throwers, skateboarding youngsters, magicians, jump roping, unicyclists and disco roller skaters. The Washington Square Arch (1892) is Stanford White's copy of a wood arch he made three years earlier to commemorate the centennial of George Washington's inauguration.
>
> —GAULT/MILLAU, *The Best of New York*

> They step down the grooved steps, clutching items, and the attendant lugs the bags out of the bin, looking for handles. They

get excited and jostle: is someone going to steal their bags? They
have all heard the stories. One of them has a cousin who came
here once and was a victim of a street crime. He had to have
money wired so he could get home and that was the last time
their clan went to New York. There is a thing called three-card
Monte out to get you. They have all heard the stories and they
all come anyway. The bags thud on concrete and get taken.

—Colson Whitehead, "The Port Authority" in
The Colossus of New York: A City in Thirteen Parts

How we say something makes all the difference. We can talk in
general terms or in specifics. We can theorize or tell stories. We can
sound formal or informal, personal or detached. Here are three
definitions that struck us by how differently they tackle the same task:
defining creative nonfiction. All are nonfiction, but only one is creative nonfiction in that it not only *tells* us, but also *shows* us what the
term means.

I.   [In creative nonfiction] . . . reality is mediated and narrativized; . . .
     the particular subjectivities of authors are crucial and should be
     textually embodied rather than effaced; . . . language and form
     must have a surface and texture that remind readers the work is
     artificed; . . . even though some readers are considerably more
     adept and enculturated, the work is not reserved for a narrow
     specialist audience.

II. Creative nonfiction uses storytelling techniques (i.e., dialogue,
     narrative description, figurative language, and character develop-
     ment) to tell true stories as the writer experienced them. Creative
     nonfiction shares the following attributes: topics based on actual
     people, places, and events; emphasis on personal voice; graceful
     and memorable language; strong sensory detail; use of memory,
     facts and research to shape point of view; and emphasis on lively
     prose that appeals to a broad audience.

III. The vertical-striped cushions in early '70s green and brown are
     hard and don't give much after three hours, yet there's something
     nostalgic about the couch where I have sat for so many writing
     courses—and how it triggers memories. . . .

     The couch is real. I've scribbled in the inked grooves of the
     wooden armrest to my right, written "Hi Joe!" to a friend who sits

here in another class. I've run my fingers over the cloth and felt the fabrics worn away by time and other young writers. Creative Nonfiction is real, or at least most of it. In my portfolio, Celeste really drove the pick-up at age eight, and my mother believed the TR-7 would flip if she drove on uneven pavement. But as with any literary genre, my view is limited, the details chosen and molded to bring out something more than just what happened.

What girl may have sat where I sit now, once crushed by comments to her poem? Perhaps a new mother napped on this couch, exhausted with her schoolwork and new child. There are so many stories to tell, but one must choose and then find the way to retell it to generate interest in readers. . . . Perhaps, I'm finally starting to get comfortable on this couch.

The first is specialized prose that appeared in *College English,* a scholarly journal for English professors. The author, Douglas Hesse, assumes his readers will know what "mediated" and "narrativized" reality is and will read on with understanding. The second, by Mimi and Sondra, covers the same territory in language meant for writers of varying ages and abilities. Both definitions offer general guidelines for understanding creative nonfiction, a useful tool when trying to grasp this genre. But if you are about to write creative nonfiction for the first time, it helps to read our student Emari DiGiorgio's definition. Assigned, in class, to define creative nonfiction by writing it, DiGiorgio gives us a highly personalized definition that makes the characteristics of creative nonfiction come alive experientially, by putting readers on that brown couch.

Creative nonfiction fills a niche that will never be filled by either fiction or traditional nonfiction . . . about the things that happen to people in real time and the ways those things change us a day or a decade later.

— GERALD N. CALLAHAN

An Umbrella Term

Creative nonfiction is an umbrella term that covers everything from childhood memoir to literary journalism about the world at large. In between are personal essay, portrait, lyric essay, travel memoir, nature writing, photo essay, opinion essay, investigative memoir, and all nonfiction that values language, voice, memory, research, and imagination to recreate the real world. Some people argue that the more subjective memoir (which relies heavily on memory) and the more fact-based literary journalism (which relies heavily on research) don't fit under the same umbrella. We believe they do. In fact, we'd include all nonfiction that shares the following characteristics:

- An engaging voice that gives personal authority to the writing and pulls the reader in—whether the "I" is at the center of the text or on the sidelines.

- A desire for self-exploration and discovery, whether writing about yourself or others. Often, the writer's mind at work, struggling to understand, is as interesting as the subject matter—or more so.

- An allegiance to veracity, drawing on fact to write truthfully about the *real* world—and drawing on memory and imagination to show us this world in full color. If you are changing or inventing facts to make a better story, you are writing fiction. If you are using existing facts to write the story of your experience, you are writing creative nonfiction.

- A commitment to be interesting, using a full range of storytelling devices—dialogue, description, metaphor, anecdote, character development—to draw your reader into the writing.

- A freedom in form and language to go wherever meaning and imagination take you.

- A fine-tuned sense of the rhythms of language.

❧ An ability, as essayist Cynthia Ozick says, to find "the extraordinary in the ordinary" so that the small things in life illuminate the big ideas that make readers care.

The Subgenres

When people ask, "What do you generally write?" we answer "creative nonfiction." But if they ask, "What are you working on right now?" the answer narrows to "a personal essay" or "a portrait" or "a piece of literary journalism." All share the general characteristics mentioned above, but these subgenres—and others—have their own special concerns. It is useful to know the subgenres before you start, when you are looking for possibilities, and also after you have a solid draft and want to revise. In between, we recommend that you set labels aside and write to see what emerges.

Note: In our anthology of readings in Part II of this book, you'll find examples, with descriptions, of each subgenre.

Memoir

A memoir consists of stories about a slice of life, as opposed to autobiography that tells the whole life story from the day of birth to the present. Memoir relies heavily on memory, a subjective tool but essential for recapturing what's important in your past. To fill in the unremembered spaces, research can help, but the emphasis is on perceptions and feelings. How you, as writers, experience your world is at the heart of memoir; it's *your* story, not history. In memoir, you bring readers into your world, so they can meet the people, live in the landscape, and understand the historic and cultural context as you remember it—even if you have no photos, film, or tape recordings to support that memory. Here, for example, Alice Walker, the adult, is recreating a childhood conversation that happened soon after a terrible injury to her eye. While writing, she becomes, once again, that young girl:

Have volunteer read aloud

I am twelve. When relatives come to visit I hide in my room. My cousin Brenda, just my age, whose father works in the post office and whose mother is a nurse, comes to find me. "Hello," she says. And she asks, looking at my recent school picture, which I did not want taken, and on which the "glob," as I think of it, is clearly visible, "You still can't see out of that eye?"

—*"Beauty: When the Other Dancer Is the Self"* (Chapter 11, Memoir)

Personal Essay

Personal essays—or familiar essays, as they are also called—focus less on the past and more on the present, exploring some aspect of the here-and-now, which can also include connections to the past. Kandi Tayebi's essay, for example, begins as she and her husband are watching the news on TV:

Volunteer read aloud.

"They should take off their rings," my husband stated matter-of-factly as we watched CNN broadcasting more trouble in the Middle East. For two years he had fought in the Iran-Iraq war, but he rarely shared his experiences with me, perhaps feeling that his American-born wife might have difficulty relating to the realities of warfare in one's homeland. . . .

—*"Warring Memories"* (Chapter 12, Personal Essay)

Many consider the short memoir a form of personal essay, and the lines do blur as writers move back and forth between past and present. When the main focus is on the past, when the writer is saying, "This is what happened to me," we call the piece memoir. When the focus is on the present, when, as in "Warring Memories" the past enlightens that present, we call the piece an essay. Often, the difference is a matter of length. Memoirs can be book length. Personal essays are usually under thirty pages. Both, when working well, tell a larger truth about the writer's experience, one that readers can relate to their own lives.

Portrait

A portrait makes a person other than the "I" come alive on the page. Also called a profile or a biographical sketch, a portrait can be about someone you know well or about someone you've just met and/or read about. The first relies on personal experience; the second, on research. Either way, interviewing and gathering background material will enrich your portrait, making readers see, hear, and care about this person by conveying what, to you, is unique. Consider how Alice Steinbach recreates her ninth-grade teacher in "The Miss Dennis School of Writing" (Chapter 13, Portrait), using description and her character's own voice:

Student to read:

> . . . But it was not Miss Dennis' appearance or her unusual teaching method—which had a lot in common with an out-of-control terrier—that made her special. What set her apart was her deep commitment to liberating the individual writer in each student. "What lies at the heart of good writing," she told us over and over again, "is the writer's ability to find his own unique voice. And then to use it to tell an interesting story." Somehow she made it clear that we were interesting people with interesting stories to tell. Most of us, of course, had never known we had a story to tell, much less an interesting one. . . .

Essay of Place

An essay of place captures a setting or a series of scenes by combining factual information, strong sensory detail, a story line, and the writer's point of view. If you are writing about Washington Square in Greenwich Village, New York, with just a series of facts and no point of view, you are writing straight nonfiction, as in this Gault/Millau guidebook description that begins, "Around the park's central water fountain you'll see street musicians, ventriloquists. . . ." It's when you make us feel your experience at Washington Square, as essayist Cynthia Ozick does, that you are writing creative nonfiction:

Student read aloud:

> . . . already late, I begin walking very fast toward the park. The air is smoky with New York winter grit, and on a clogged Broadway a mob of trucks shift squawking gears. But there, just ahead, crisscrossed by paths under high branches, is Washington Square.

Opinion Essay

This form presents a point of view you feel strongly about and is often found on the op-ed page of a newspaper. (Op-ed literally means "opposite the editorial page.") Most opinion essays are straight nonfiction in that they use detached logic rather than personal experience to be persuasive. But when writers use a strong personal voice and storytelling to make their arguments, as Dave Eggers does in his op-ed essay, "Serve and Fail," we consider their work to be creative nonfiction:

Volunteer to read:

> About now, most recent college graduates, a mere week or two beyond their last final, are giving themselves a nice respite. Maybe they're on a beach, maybe they're on a road trip, maybe they're in their rooms, painting their toenails black with a Q-tip and shoe polish. Does it matter? What's important is that they have some time off.
>
> Do they deserve this time off? Well, yes and no. Yes, because finals week is stressful and sleep-deprived and possibly involves trucker-style stimulants. No, because a good deal of the four years of college is spent playing foosball.
>
> I went to a large state school—the University of Illinois—and during my time there, I became one of the best two of three foosball players in the Land of Lincoln. I learned to pass deftly between my rigid players, to play the corners, to strike the ball like a cobra would strike something a cobra would want to strike. . . .

Note: Visit our website at <college.hmco.com/english> for the full text of this opinion essay—and others that use creative nonfiction to present their arguments.

Literary Journalism

This form of journalism combines investigative reporting with personal voice, storytelling, and memorable language. Rather than just convey the journalist's facts (who, what, when, where, and why), the writer wants to recreate the experience of the world being investigated. There's a strong authorial presence even if the "I" is mainly a guide, rather than a key character. Tracy Kidder, for example, spent a year observing Chris Zajac's fifth-grade classroom before writing *Among Schoolchildren*. He doesn't use the pronoun "I," but we feel his presence in the room nonetheless:

Volunteer to read,

> When Chris had first walked into her room—Room 205—back in late August, it felt like an attic. The chalkboards and bulletin

boards were covered up with newspaper, and the bright colors of the plastic chairs seemed calculated to force cheerfulness upon her. On the side of one of the empty children's desks there was a faded sticker that read, OFFICIAL PACE CAR. A child from some other year must have put it there. . . .

Kidder doesn't just report; he recreates experience. Rather than just *tell* what happened, he *shows* characters and scene—and as readers, we begin to understand that deeper levels of meaning lie beneath the facts. This difference distinguishes straight journalism from literary journalism in that the apparent subject (what happened) is not the real subject (what the events mean). This interpretation gives literary journalism its timeless quality, making Chris Zajac's classroom in 1988 still seem relevant today. (See Chapter 15 for more of Kidder's writing on Chris Zajac and her classroom.)

Almost any writing—book reviews, cultural criticism, "how to" pieces, photo essays, even academic essays and literary criticism—can be creative nonfiction if the writing has voice, uses storytelling well, and has a grace of language and sensibility that *shows and tells.*

Ultimately, what is creative in creative nonfiction is, in the words of our friend and colleague, Ed Hack, "discovery in memorable language," writing in which your readers "feel, word by word, a network of associations building, levels of meaning consolidating, a drama of an unfolding situation, whose essence is the insistence on *making each line count.*" If we do this well, readers not only enter our worlds, but they reenter their own worlds in new ways. That is the power of creative nonfiction or, as we like to think of it, of "writing true."

Shows + Tells
each line count
Ways In. . . *writer has a voice*

These exercises offer ways into writing creative nonfiction. Try some or all of them and experience how the objective and the subjective can merge or complement each other. We recommend keeping a notebook where you can experiment with—and revisit—all of the "Ways In. . ." that end each of our ten chapters. For more on notebooks, see the next chapter, The Power of the Notebook.

Read aloud: Students to do in class +
1. Writing Your Name—In Four Parts   *finish for 1st essay due on*   *2 PS typed*

Mon Feb 1st

A. Write only the verifiable facts about your name: What it
means, how you got it, how to spell it, what your nickname
is, who else has your name. Stick with what other people
would agree upon—and leave your point of view out of it.
Don't think first. Start writing—5 minutes max.

Mimi writes the objective, verifiable facts:

My name is made up of 2 m's and 2 i's, short for Miriam, which
comes from the Bible—either Moses' sister or his nursemaid—
depending on what you read. It's thought of as a Jewish name,
a girl's name. Given to me by my parents Arthur and Gerda. Re-
named by sister as Mimi at around age six.

B. Now write about your name "from the inside out" as only
you could write it. Make it highly subjective, exploring how
your name feels to you—and surprise yourself. If you are
writing only what you know, it's nonfiction without a creative leap. Again, don't think before you write—5 minutes
max—and forget about grammar, spelling, or making
sense.

Mimi writes the subjective truths:

I love the perkiness of Mimi, the optimism and energy of those
4 letters bouncing around without the weight of the past, the
Jewish past of Miriam to drag me down. I'm reinvented as Mimi,
set loose to define myself, unshackled, except when others define
me with a shift of vowels: MEME vs. Mimi, the girl of immigrant
German Jews who got out from being MEEERRYAM, as my Aunt
Kaethe said it, bleating it like an old German goat on the Rhine.
Mimi made me American until I got to U of M and became MEME
who had to start saying TEARABLE and WHOORABLE like a true
Midwestern. Oops, there goes the past again.

C. Read Brian Doyle's "Being Brians" to see how he used the
Internet to research his name and how he worked that information into his essay. You can also research your name—
using the Internet, asking your parents, looking through
name books, and/or interviewing others about how they
feel about their names. Questions to ask: How did you get

If did not read for hw- read plenty or won on essay.

your name? What nicknames do you have? What experiences—good or bad—have you had with your name? Do you think of it as masculine or feminine? What other names would you rather have?

D. Start writing again—either adding to what you have or starting anew—and see where it takes you (10-minute timed writing).

2. **Identifying Creative Nonfiction**

   A. Using the guidelines from this chapter, read the Short Shorts in the anthology and find a piece of creative nonfiction that speaks to you. Star a few passages that pull you in as a reader and ask yourself why. Share your choice with others, reading paragraphs out loud and then discussing what makes this piece creative nonfiction and what subgenre you think it is.

   B. Locate a piece of creative nonfiction not reprinted in this book. Make copies of it to share with others and explain why you think it falls in the creative nonfiction category.

3. **Writing About Place—In Four Parts**

   Here's an exercise that shows how memory, here-and-now observation, and research can join forces to capture a special place on the page. It works best if you do all four parts in sequence.

   A. Think of a place that interests you and write about it—first from memory, focusing on what makes this place vivid for you (3–4 minutes max).

   Sondra chose the subway:

   > The faces of humanity—so many stories, so many lives literally rubbing elbows. And the pace—hurtling in darkness, bumping, lurching, traveling at lightning speed. My body alive underground.

   B. Second, go to that place, and record what you see, feel, and hear. Capture as many details as Sondra did:

Kids, backpacks, CD players, fluorescent lights, man asleep, mouth open; girl, chewing on a yellow pencil, reading Tolstoy; man with a cane, *The Wall Street Journal* under his arm; teens, huddled together at the end of the car, their hands all over each other; a kid, tugging at his mom; she rolls her eyes.

C. Now, look up factual information about that place—Sondra found hers on the website of the Metropolitan Transit Authority:

The New York City subway system, which officially opened on Thursday, October 27, 1904 . . . has 468 stations serving 24 routes—more than any other system in the world. Two hundred seventy-seven of the stations are located underground. There are 31,180 turnstiles; 734 token booths; 161 escalators. . . . Each day, more than six million people use New York City Transit—almost 2 billion customers annually.

D. Finally, start again, using at least one thing from A, B, and C. You might begin by reading a few essays of place, such as Alexandra Fuller's depiction of Africa, which relies primarily on smells and sounds, or Gretel Ehrlich's lyrical depiction of an island, or Gretchen Legler's visual depiction of Antarctica. Here is what Sondra wrote:

I never tire of watching, looking, imagining. Where are they all going? Who is in love? Who's upset? The girl reading Tolstoy; the man with the *Wall Street Journal* tucked elegantly under his arm; the mom who wishes her kid would stop whining—who are they? The lovers in the corner can't take their hands off each other. The high school kids with their bulging backpacks and CD players move their hips in time to the music, oblivious, caught in the spell of their own private worlds. So too is the heavyset man across from me, dozing, his mouth ajar. I sit here and marvel that we are a fraction of the 6 million people who use the subways each day, breathing the same air, tucked away in a gray steel compartment, traveling at lightning speed through the bowels of Manhattan.

4. Definition–In Two Parts

Pick an abstract word that is important to you—Justice, Desire, Dating, Work, Faith—and copy out a dictionary definition, adding a few more attributes that you think most people would agree on. Then skip a line and write a highly personalized definition of the word, as DiGiorgio does when she defines creative nonfiction in terms of a brown couch or Kathleen Norris does in "Rain" and Bailey White does in "Buzzard." Tip: Ground your definition in something concrete, as these three writers in our workshops did:

Love

1. Profoundly tender, passionate affection for another person; intense personal attachment or affection; strong enthusiasm or liking.

2. Mixtapes. Pancakes. $3 hide and go seek. Out of print books. Milkshakes. Watching horrible movies b/c it makes her happy. Enormous phone bills. Frequent oil changes. Mid-exam text messages for good luck. Hat stealing. Letting her eat your favorite ice cream. Covering him w/ covers in the middle of the night. Not talking when he brushes his teeth. Marriage proposals with vending machine rings. Being the only one to realize when she quotes corny movies. Smiling when he finds her hair on his pillow. Loving her even though she can out-burp him. Making wishes on eye lashes. . . .

— LAURA CROLL, *Creative Nonfiction Workshop*

Home

1. The place where one lives; the place where one was born or reared; a place thought of as home; a household and its affairs.

2. *Home* is walking out of the airport terminal, knowing how close you are to everything you've missed. It's walking into your living room and taking a breath, even if unconsciously. It's the smell of your father's famous cheese enchiladas, the sound of your dog's nails against the new hardwood floor, the unidentifiable smell from your brother's room. Home is the desire to be there when you're not. It is more than a house; it is that house with that family, on that street, in that neighborhood, in that city.

— KIRSTIN MITCHELL, *Creative Nonfiction Workshop*

Courage

1. The state or quality of mind or spirit that enables one to face danger, fear of the vicissitudes with self-possession and resolution; bravery.

2. Facing my big brothers every night when I was pledging; getting off the ski lift for the first time to go down the bunny slope; telling someone you're in like, not love; sitting in the last seat on a roller coaster; moving out; not moving back in; cutting off my dreadlocks after 13 years; growing them in the first place.

— Kevin McCall, *Creative Nonfiction Workshop*

CHAPTER 2

The Power of the Notebook

It takes an awful lot of time for me to write anything. I have endless drafts, one after another, and I try out 50, 75 or a hundred variations on a single line sometimes. I work on the process of refining low-grade ore. I get maybe a couple of nuggets of gold out of 50 tons of dirt.

— JAMES DICKEY

Some call it a notebook, some a journal or a daybook. Whatever the name, it is a valuable tool for writers intent on finding what, in their everyday lives, is worth writing about. The more we write down, the more there is to work with — or, to use James Dickey's metaphor, if we're to find "a couple of nuggets . . . [in] 50 tons of dirt," we first need dirt. The richest stockpile comes from frequent jottings, by hand or by computer, of whatever seems to be surprising and provocative at the moment. The more vivid the detail, the more likely these nuggets will turn up — maybe right away, maybe a day, a month, or years later.

Not knowing when is what gives the notebook its power, for it invites us to write first and discover why afterwards. Poet Theodore Roethke, who left 277 notebooks when he died, wrote the famous line — "a sidelong pickerel smile" — as a notebook fragment years before it appeared in his poem, "Elegy for Jane." Charles Darwin drew asymmetrical trees in his notebooks long before he formulated his asymmetrical theory of evolution. It was the notebook, for both, that led them to their nuggets, buried — and then found.

Notebook entries can include fragments of conversation, quotations from books, favorite lines, images from memory, travel notes, current struggles, the "what if's" we imagine every day—or just stream-of-consciousness writing, jumping randomly from one topic to another. Notebooks can be catch-alls for whatever comes to mind, or they can be specialized, what Alexandra Johnson in *Leaving a Trace: On Keeping a Journal* calls "single-purpose journals." These include travel journals, nature journals, garden journals, crisis journals, reading journals, family chronicles, or dream books. Whatever you choose, "an observing notebook," she says, "is ideal for anyone numbed by repetition, meetings, schedules. It will reconnect us to the very living we're too busy . . . to notice."

Unlike a captain's log, these entries are *not* meant to record the day's events: "Woke up at 6:00 a.m., light drizzle, lunch at noon as usual." They focus instead on what seems unusual and worth remembering. As Joan Didion points out in "On Keeping a Notebook":

> . . . the point of my keeping a notebook has never been, nor is it now, to have an accurate factual record of what I have been doing or thinking. That would be a different impulse entirely, an instinct for reality which I sometimes envy but do not possess. At no point have I ever been able successfully to keep a diary; my approach to daily life ranges from the grossly negligent to the merely absent, and on those few occasions when I tried dutifully to record a day's events, boredom has so overcome me that the results are mysterious at best. What is this business about "shopping, typing piece, dinner with E, depressed"? Shopping for what? Typing what piece? Was E depressed or was I depressed? Who cares?

The aim, then, in keeping a notebook (or journal or daybook) is to interest our future selves, allowing us to remember not so much what we once did, but who we once were and how that past self connects to who we are today. As writers, it is also a place to experiment with form and language, to record details, and to take the kind of risks that explore what we didn't know we knew—and still don't know. E. M. Forster, the novelist, liked to say, "How do I know what I think until I see what I say?" In the notebook, we can find out—*if* we use it to allow the creative to kick in by keeping the following in mind.

Forgetting about Correctness

Grammar, spelling, punctuation. None of these counts in a notebook as long as the writer can read the entries and remember what happened. If others read the notebook, they have no right to ask for clarity, full sentences, or sense. For works-in-progress headed for a public audience, yes. But in a notebook words are private, for the writer only.

In the notebook, we give ourselves permission to play with language in a kind of stream-of-consciousness prose that Peter Elbow calls "free writing" in a headlong, pell-mell rush into unforeseen meaning.[1] Like the poet Byron, we may find that a shorthand of dashes works well:

> **Sept. 21**
>
> Left Thoun in a boat which carried us the length of the lake in three hours—the lake small—but the banks fine—rocks down to the water's edge—Landed at Neuhause . . . passed Interlachen—entered upon a range of scenes beyond description—or previous conception—Passed a rock—inscription—2 brothers—one murdered the other—just the place fit for it—After a variety of windings came to an enormous rock—Girl with fruit—very pretty—blue eyes—good teeth—very fair—long but good features—reminded me of Fy bought some of her pears—patted her upon the cheek. . . .
>
> *—Byron's notebook*

We don't even have to make sense, as writer Deena Linett shows in an entry called "an experiment in merriment to see what I meant":

> Oh
> Cello cello hello cello violin viola ilivia
> Viola violent violet viola violin
> Violent Viva Vivaldi Viva Vicace

[1] For more about free writing, read Peter Elbow, *Writing without Teachers,* New York: Oxford University Press, 1971, or Peter Elbow & Pat Belanoff, *A Community of Writers,* New York: McGraw-Hill, Inc., 1995.

Viva Vivaldi Vincent Vincent Vincent
Starry starry night the flying Dutchman
The Flying Dutchman. . . .

Fooling around is how Linett, as poet, finds new ways of using rhyme and repetition: "With this kind of word play," she notes, "I give my imagination permission to play."

Recording Plenty of Details

Details, at the heart of all good writing, often fade with memory, so notebook entries need to be filled with specifics that can bring the experience back in all its fullness. Generalities, like these, won't do:

The Galapagos were fascinating—full of exotic animals you won't see in New Jersey. I could have stayed there a week watching them all. Definitely worth the trouble of getting here.

What trouble? What animals? What was worth staying a week for? Three years after writing that, you'll know you had fun (you don't need a notebook to know that), but you will have nothing concrete with which to anchor those pleasures. It's only through details that you can relive that moment—and recreate it for others as Mimi does in her essay, "Under the Sunblock":[2]

. . . We are off to see the blue-footed boobies, Pablo says, and the twelve-year-old from Chicago, daughter of tall, bearded Ben and the quiet, brown-haired librarian, claps her hands. The boobies are famous for their turquoise feet that match the ocean color here, but also, I suspect, because of their name. Everyone likes saying "boobie," which means dummy—that's what the Spanish sailors thought of the silly birds dancing like clowns, *bobos,* on the ship's hull. . . .

---

[2] Mimi Schwartz, *Thoughts from a Queen-sized Bed,* Lincoln, NE: University of Nebraska Press, 2002.

Capturing the Small Moments

The small moments of our lives—the anomalies and the ironies—
are often recast in conversations with friends and then forgotten.
The notebook preserves them for future use. Even an everyday trip
to the supermarket can become a springboard for an essay if you jot
down what happened, as Penelope Scambly Schott did:

Report on the Difference Between Men and Women

After 13 years and 27 days of marriage, my husband turns to
me and asks, "How come we never have lemonade?" He pauses.
"That kind that comes frozen in a can?"

It's not like he's never been to the grocery store, or I haven't
asked him regularly if there's anything he'd like me to pick up,
anything special he's in the mood for.

So on the 28th day of our fourteenth year of marriage, I go
to the store and buy lemonade, that kind that comes frozen in
the can. At the checkout, I push the frozen pale yellow cylinder
onto the conveyor belt and look into the eyes of the middle-aged
woman who is ringing up my groceries. Without preliminary, I
announce, "After all the time we've been married, my husband
just asked me yesterday, out of the blue, 'How come we never
have lemonade?' "

She looks back at me. The edges of her mouth flicker in and
out. First the whole bottom of her face and then her shoulders
begin to tremble. She convulses into giggling.

I go home, defrost the can, mix up his lemonade in a tall jar,
shake it well, and put it in the refrigerator, front and center on
the top shelf where even he can't miss it. When he comes in from
work and starts browsing for something to drink, I say, "I bought
lemonade today. It's right here in front," and I point to it. He
pours an enormous glass.

I wonder what else he secretly wants.

Schott says she came home that day—"still thinking about how the
checkout lady had started to giggle." She went to her computer to jot
down the story, mainly to preserve the joke. For the next few days,
she found herself drawn back to her computer, busying herself with
cutting and deleting, "taking out everything that wasn't hysterical."

Next came a title, something big for a very small moment, and she had an essay, published three months later in *Fourth Genre*.

"Without my jotting down the story . . . it would have been gone," says Schott, who doesn't keep a formal notebook. Aside from quick jottings "usually about something funny," she keeps a file of 3-by-5 cards of quotations from books and conversations, including a collection of children's observations. A favorite is still her daughter's at age six, saying, "Life would be so much easier if only everyone would agree with me!"

Writing to Surprise Yourself

The notebook is the place to practice pushing ourselves into the unexpected. When we find a nugget, we need to write more, dig deeper, and hope to strike the mother lode. This discovery process can be seen in Patricia Hampl's essay, "Memory and Imagination" (see Chapter 16, Stories of Craft). She first wrote a fragment about a piano lesson she had with Sister Olive Marie—and then wondered why, of all her childhood memories, this one stuck.

> When I was 7, my father, who played the violin on Sundays with a nicely tortured flair which we considered artistic, led me by the hand down a long, unlit corridor in St. Luke's basement, a sort of tunnel that ended in a room full of pianos. There many little girls and a single sad boy were playing truly tortured scales and arpeggios in a mash of troubled sound. My father gave me over to Sister Olive Marie, who did look remarkably like an olive. . . .

The answer, it turned out many drafts later, had little to do with the piano or her father or even Sister Olive. What kept interesting Hampl was *why* she had written what may, or may not, be "lies." *Was the nun's name really Olive Marie? Did she really sneeze in the sun?* Exploring these questions led Hampl to more questions—and some answers—about the relationship between memory and imagination in creative nonfiction. She could never have guessed at the start where she would ultimately end. In a notebook, we don't have to.

Exploring "How It *Felt* to Me"

The notebook is the place to record and preserve our emotional truths. "How it felt to me!" is what Joan Didion tells relatives who complain about her version of the past. Didion is more interested in capturing her feelings when she first saw her father after a five-year absence than in accurately reporting what she ate for lunch on the day they finally met. Maybe someone ate cracked crab, maybe not. But the cracked crab with its hard, jagged edges captured the jaggedness of the remembered experience, filling in emotional space that felt true to Didion. The same kind of emotional truth shapes her memory of a cold August day in Vermont.

> . . . The cracked crab that I recall having for lunch the day my father came home from Detroit in 1945 must certainly be embroidery, worked into the day's pattern to lend verisimilitude; I was ten years old and would not now remember the cracked crab. The day's events did not turn on cracked crab. And yet it is precisely that fictitious crab that makes me see the afternoon all over again, a home movie run all too often, the father bearing gifts, the child weeping, an exercise in family love and guilt. Or that is what it was to me.
>
> Similarly, perhaps it never did snow that August in Vermont; perhaps there never were flurries in the night wind, and maybe no one else felt the ground hardening and summer already dead even as we pretended to bask in it, but that was how it felt to me, and it might as well have snowed, could have snowed, did snow. . . .
>
> —*"On Keeping a Notebook"*

"How it felt to me" can also apply to here-and-now entries meant to capture emotional states: anger, sadness, amusement, frustration. Not only is this venting on paper therapeutic, it can lead to an angle, a point of view, an insight that can transform private complaint into something with public possibility. Take this notebook entry written by Julie Mazer, Mimi's daughter, while she was traveling in Greece at age 17. It begins as a gripe and then moves toward cultural awareness:

> I guess now is the perfect opportunity to write since I am trapped, alone, on a ship for six hours. What looks to be a half-crazed

man, escaped from prison with scars on his face, is staring at me.
I think I'll move. . . . I'm on my way to Rhodes to try and find
out what the hell has been wrong with my fingers for the past
month. I'm frustrated because although my fingers are swollen
and infected, it seems like a stupid thing to have to travel six
hours on a ferry just to see a skin doctor. You'd think that something like that would just go away by itself, but it hasn't.
   Well, anyway, I'll get to see Rhodes and experience traveling by
myself. . . . Damn. Someone is blowing smoke in my face. But it is
hard to look up at people because I feel conspicuous, so American.
If I look up and see eyes looking at me, I shy away. One thing this
culture is doing is making me very modest and even petrified. . . .

Here, once again, the strength is in the details that move this piece
beyond a complaint about a boat ride. Had Julie written "I was so
bored on the boat to Rhodes. I am so lonely away from home. I am
so worried about my fingers. . .", she would have little to work with
later on. A few generalized feelings would not lead her back into the
power of the memory.

Gathering New Information

Essayist Kim Stafford keeps a little notebook in his shirt pocket to
record interesting graffiti and overheard conversations while traveling or having a meal. [Read how he does this in "The Writer as Professional Eavesdropper" (Chapter 16, Stories of Craft).] Pulitzer
Prize–winning poet Stephen Dunn keeps a notebook handy while
reading, so he can write down quotations that strike him. He says, "I
like being surrounded by snippets of pithy thoughts or beautifully
balanced sentences. I often imitate or depart from them as a way of
beginning a poem." Dunn's selection of quotes comes from everywhere: from the sports page to chemistry books to erudite essays of
literary criticism. Some recent favorites include:

- Mike Tyson—"Everyone has a plan until you hit them."

- French critic Baudrillard—"Seduction is the world's elementary dynamic."

❧ Photographer Robert Bresson—"Vigor comes from precision. Precision is vigorous. When I am working poorly I am imprecise. Precision is another form of poetry."

❧ Unnamed Zen Master—"Now that you have achieved total perfection and enlightenment, you may expect to be as miserable as ever."

Dunn uses these quotations to challenge, confirm, and deepen his own work. You'll find them as epigraphs or built into his poems and essays, adding other voices to his own.

The notebook can also serve as a place for taking notes while working on a specific project, particularly those involving research. The aim is to record as much as possible, says Barbara Hurd, because you never know what you'll need or where one fact may take you. When writing *Stirring the Mud: On Swamps, Bogs and Human Imagination,* she told us that without her many folders of research notes, her work would lack the literal and metaphorical layers it needed:

> . . . [w]hen I was working on the essay about swamp as refuge, I stumbled on the fact that a typical wetland plant called the pitcher plant appears to act as a safe haven for insects. They crawl or fly down the plant's throat and into its main body where they are protected from marauding birds or bats. But when the predators give up and go away, the insects find they cannot climb back out of the slick throat and end up dying, and the plant, which turns out to be carnivorous, has its meal. [personal communication]

When taking notes, Hurd hadn't realized that the pitcher plant would become important to her. Only later does she conclude, "It was this plant and the fact that it's really a disguised death trap that led to my thinking about the broader issue of the dangers of refuge and how safe havens can sometimes become permanent and stifling."

For Hurd, the pitcher plant becomes a metaphor for danger. It appears in the middle of her essay about the joys of refuge as a counterpoint to the human desire for escape:

> The hapless bug then spends the rest of its life, which isn't long, trying to shinny up the sides of the throat, to take off without a

solid runway, to keep its exhausted head above water. Eventually, the insect drowns and the plant has its dinner. If the bug was anticipating an eventual return to leafy branches, a summer of night skies and porch lights, it missed the point of return, misjudged the way a trap can disguise itself as retreat.

—"Refugium," *Stirring the Mud*

We, as readers, get it. We imagine ourselves as the bug on those leaves, and read on, watching more carefully for the hidden dangers of the refuges we all, at times, seek. (To read Barbara Hurd's full essay, visit our website <college.hmco.com/english>)

Adding Visuals

Pressed flowers, stamps, clippings, photos, and drawings can all help to invoke ideas, memories, and experiences—particularly when coupled with jottings about how we felt at the moment. An old ticket to a Nirvana concert can bring back the event, especially if there is also an entry about the mood of the crowd, the faces of friends, the ripped jeans we were wearing.

Experimenting with High-Tech Approaches

Thanks to the computer, people are finding ways to write a shared notebook, recording impressions then exchanged with others. E-mail has become old-fashioned letter writing with a new twist: you can both send and receive response within minutes. Ed Hack, one November day, observed the weather and sent this e-mail entry to Sondra with whom he's been sharing thoughts for three years through an online teachers' network (they have yet to meet):

Yes, another gray day . . . a day for a fire, a good glass of wine, a good novel. Or work on the leaves or with wood and a saw: it's best to be busy in November, dear S. I'm an expert on November. It's the time that Nature strips herself down; it's a merciless, gorgeous month of going naked to withstand the winter. There are no secrets in November, for it's a month of revelations: what's the

> true shape of this tree; what happens after green goes; what do
> you do with the world stripped to bone, when the sun glares
> off glass and stone, when subtlety is replaced by facts? Leaves,
> leaves, leaves we kick through, that come into the house on our
> soles, that, when it's dry, smell like spent fire. . . .

Entries like these between real or virtual friends take on a rhythm of their own—daily, weekly, monthly, giving writers room to explore thoughts and perceptions with a receptive reader who writes back. The Internet also allows writers to share entries with groups of readers they know or don't know. Weblogs, or blogs for short, invite writers to post jottings on shared areas of interest ranging from professional concerns to hobbies to politics, humor, and health—the list is endless.

Whatever the format—private, public, handwritten, or on the computer—the point is to record fleeting ideas and quick impressions as we live our lives. Having done so, we can, in the future, recover what we were thinking and revisit the person we were at another moment in time. It's at that juncture of past and present, of old and new selves reconnecting (a day, a week, or years later), where we find the nuggets that lure us to write on.

Ways In. . .

You can write in a notebook by hand or on a computer or both. We like how a three-ring binder lets writers move entries around and add afterthoughts easily. But whatever you choose, avoid tight, single-spaced writing with no margins. Lack of empty space cools the urge to add more later, whereas double-spaced entries with wide margins make room for new thoughts. We also suggest giving each entry a heading, a number, and its own first page—for ease in relocating.

Eight Ideas for Getting Started

Pick at least three or four—or more—to loosen up, reflect, notice, and practice self-exploration that is at the heart of creative nonfiction.

1. **Free writing.** Let yourself write freely, without stopping. Don't worry about whether you are staying on topic or writing well—just keep your pen moving. You might want to set a kitchen timer for, say, 15 minutes, and do this regularly for a week. Try different times of day to capture different moods, and don't worry about making sense, correcting your spelling, or writing complete sentences.

2. **Springboard Line.** Pick a line from one of your readings—a novel, textbook, a newspaper headline, an ad—and copy it out. Skip a space and start writing. No need to explain why you picked it. Let the associations come as they may and don't feel a need to stay on topic.

3. **Morning or Dusk Walk.** Writers need to observe the smallest detail. One great way to do this, says writer/teacher Robert Vivian, is to take a candlelight walk at sunrise or sunset, notebook in hand, ready to record the wonders of the ordinary: the way, for example, the morning light hits a cracked sidewalk. Vivian's students go together, sharing their work afterward.

4. **Listening to Others.** Take your notebook on a train or bus or into a lunchroom and record what you hear, the way essayist Kim Stafford does in "The Writer as Professional Eavesdropper" (see Chapter 16, Stories of Craft). Include a conversation with dialogue, making sure to set the scene where you heard it. Also look for interesting graffiti to copy into your notebook.

5. **Snapshot of Memory.** Memories often are held as snapshots in our heads. Think of one before you were ten, as Patricia Hampl and Joan Didion did, and write it two ways: first write the facts everyone would agree on about this moment; second, write "How it felt to me" (5 minutes—listing is fine). Now try a third version, recapturing the whole memory, combining both as you see fit, and going deeper. Tip: Be sure to use enough sensory details—at least one sight, sound, taste, touch, and smell.

6. **Recording Quotations.** Begin keeping a page of quotations that strike you as interesting. Look for them in magazines, newspapers, books, song lyrics, poems—even in what people

say to you that amuses, annoys, or seems wise or foolish. Keep adding to this page, the way Stephen Dunn does, over the months to come.

7. **Small Moments.**   Capture a here-and-now moment in your day. It may be a daily activity or a once-only moment like Penelope Scambly Schott's buying of lemonade at the supermarket. Record something that is funny, or strange, or infuriating, and, if possible, write it while you're still in that same mood. Try writing nonstop for at least 20 minutes.

8. **Private and Public.**   To explore the difference between private and public writing, think of a topic and write it two ways. First, write only for yourself; then, write for others to read. Reread both entries a day later, and ask yourself: Which one would you want to share? Is it the same one you expected not to share? Why or why not?

General Tips for All Entries

Try to make entries at least two pages long. People stop writing just when an entry gets interesting, worrying that they will have too much to write, and it will take too long. Or they begin feeling emotionally uncomfortable, that they are writing what they shouldn't. Push on, remembering writer Ann Lamott's advice to "write to the emotional center of things. Write toward vulnerability. . . . Tell the truth as you understand it."

CHAPTER 3

Ten Ways to a Draft

You are not always conscious of working. . . . And then it happens. It erupts like a volcano . . . your imagination is working all the time in a subterranean way.

— ERICA JONG

Sometimes we know what to write about. We find ourselves on a roll, words inspiring words until a draft writes itself — almost. But sometimes, our topics seem stale, overworked, self-indulgent — or risky. Or they seem too complicated to tackle. Some stop writing, saying they are not inspired — a feeling that can last a day or a lifetime. Others know to keep going, drawing on a reservoir of techniques to loosen a thought or two and summon the Muse.

These techniques, which we call *Idea Generators,* are often the jumpstart needed to launch a topic or to develop one in depth. All require a few of the same basics:

- To block out enough regular time and space to write.

- To put the voice of what poet Robert Bly calls "The Criticizer" to sleep. This voice is usually heard as a censoring, "That's wrong. You can't say it that way!" Tip: One way to silence the voice is to write with your wrong hand for a minute or two. Guaranteed to give The Criticizer a nervous breakdown — at least for one morning.

- To be patient and receptive, waiting at the edge of thought for whatever words come.

The late poet William Stafford reserved every morning to write, waking at 4 A.M. to a quiet house, first making coffee, then reclining on his favorite couch with pen and paper, and letting words "string out," without judgment:

> To get started I will accept anything that occurs to me. Something always occurs, of course, to any of us. We can't keep from thinking. Maybe I have to settle for an immediate impression: it's cold, or hot, or dark or bright, or in between! Or — well, the possibilities are endless. If I put down something, that thing will help the next thing come and I'm off. If I let the process go on, things will come to me that were not at all in my mind when I started. . . . If I let them string out, surprising things will happen.
>
> —*Writing the Australian Crawl*

Many other writers talk of a similar approach. They have learned what nonwriters have not: that the Muse of inspiration can be shy, even petulant, and coaxing may be needed to go from wishing for a draft to creating one.

Rereading the Notebook

Rereading old entries from a notebook leads to topics worth developing for an audience of more than one. Look for a few lines, or a few pages, that grab your attention, making you want to say more. Also look for passages with tension, ones that make you uneasy — Did I write that?—without knowing why. Start writing again to find out.

Freelisting

Freelisting involves picking a subject, big or small, and jotting down phrases, as many as possible, in a few minutes. The trick is not to think too hard while quickly developing a long list. The more concrete your details are, the richer your writing will be. Start each phrase on a new line and aim to jot down at least eight before you start writing. You may end up using everything in your list or only a few items. Either way, you're on your way.

Freelisting works for finding a topic (you can, for example, make a quick list of "Key Moments") and for going deeper with an existing topic. If you have a draft with underdeveloped characters, freelisting can help to flesh them out. Here's one used to develop a portrait of a father. Notice how concrete images (light bulb, light switch) reveal a mercurial personality:

🖖 Bald head that shines like a light bulb

🖖 Eyes that crinkle

🖖 A full-throated laugh

🖖 Pot belly from too much beer

🖖 Bulging veins

🖖 Red face, shouting

🖖 Always yelling, "Where's the mustard?"

🖖 Rage into smiles into rage

🖖 Like a light switch

If the freelisting had been — fat, funny, angry but good-natured — the

Lists I Could Make

The pets that died
The men that dumped me
The men I dumped
The classes I took in college
The degrees I didn't get
The number of days spent crying
The number of days spent happy
The number of days spent sick
The number of times I've changed my mind
The things I didn't do
The apartments I've lived in
The trips I've taken by myself
The pros and cons of my Pilates career
The errands I need to do
The projects yet undone
The people I need to call
The ways I indulge myself
The ways I turn against myself
The pairs of shoes bought and never worn
The ways I am ashamed
The ways I am proud
The wrong men I've known
The times I've fallen in love
The best days of my life
The ways I am angry at my father
The ways in which my mother turned out to be right
The things I wish I'd said

— ROBIN SCARLETT,
Vermont College Workshop

writer would have less to trigger language that moves beyond the predictable.

Line Starters

Line starters can be found anywhere: in a phrase that jumps out from your notebook or in newspaper headlines, poems, magazines, TV ads — whatever provokes, challenges, annoys, saddens, or makes you smile. Copy the line or phrase onto a blank page and start writing. Keep going for at least 10 to 15 minutes. If it's an hour or two, so much the better.

You might also try one of these tried-and-true line starters that work especially well to retrieve memories that lead to memoir. You can focus on one or keep repeating the same line over and over in a series of vignettes:

- I used to _____, but now I _____.

- I remember. . . . I remember. . . . (Or start with —I don't remember. . . . Or switch back and forth.)

- If I had to do it again, I would _____.

- A saying I always heard around the house was _____.

- The first time I heard the song _____, I was (or we were) _____.

- _____ is the sort of person who _____.

- One rule I never live by is _____.[1]

---

[1] Some of these starters are adapted from Anne Bernays and Pamela Painter's book, *What If?* (New York: Harper Perennial, 1990), a great source of writing ideas for fiction writers. Many of their ideas also work for writers of creative nonfiction.

Memory Chain

Developed by James Moffett, the memory chain unearths memories through free association. You can't predict when you start just where you will end up — and that's the fun of it. Here's how it works:

> You look at an object in the room. Say it's a water bottle. You ask yourself what the water bottle reminds you of and wait for a moment for a memory to arise. Maybe it's the time you went to the supermarket and your sons put a case of Poland Spring water bottles on the bottom of the shopping cart and neither you nor the checkout person noticed and you walked out of the store without paying for them. And that reminds you of the time your daughter got caught shoplifting (sexy underwear, no less) and how upset you were with her and how you made her write a letter of apology to the store and how she yelled at you that you just didn't understand. And that reminds you of the time you, at age 13, shoplifted lipstick and how for years you felt guilty and would refuse to wear lipstick and wished you had had the courage to apologize. . . .

The idea, when doing a memory chain, is to write enough details for each memory to have the *beginning* of a story without writing the whole story. You are looking, initially, to generate a chain of memories, not to develop one in depth. Memories may unconsciously center on a theme — as Sondra's did above — or they may jump around without any apparent connection. Both ways are fine as long as you generate at least six to eight links on your chain. If you stall before that, look around the room, choose another object, and start again. Do this exercise for at least 10 to 15 minutes, writing quickly. Tip: Stay as concrete in imagery as possible. If you write: "The water bottle reminds me of water which reminds me of the ocean which reminds me of the moon which reminds me of the space shuttle," you'll have no details linked to specific events of your life, nothing to coax that Muse with.

Clustering

Gabrielle Rico, who has written several books on clustering, says it "unfolds from a center, like ripples generated from a rock thrown into a pond."[2]

In clustering, you choose a word and put it in the middle of a page. Then you draw a circle around it and jot down associations that come to mind, putting circles around every new association. Draw lines between circles to show the connections. For example, if the new image comes from the center word, connect to that. If it comes from an offshoot, connect to that. Write without thinking, letting the associations build and grow for about two minutes. You will begin to experience an "aha" moment — a sense that you want to start writing. Begin writing, then, and continue for eight to ten minutes. You are looking to create what Rico calls "a vignette," a short, self-contained piece of writing that tells a story. To end the vignette, to establish a sense of wholeness or roundness, reread your first line, and see if you can repeat a word or a dominant thought in your last sentence. Here's what emerged from a clustering on "Purple" in which only the images on the left side were used. But notice how the darker images from the right side — "cars, sharks, rocking boat" — set a tone that ends the vignette. A draft emerging from this vignette would have more than a good sailing day to work with:

> I love how the sails catch the wind and the porpoises leap into the air like escorts to paradise. And how the waves splash high enough to delight without drenching and the breeze makes even a bad hair day good. I should relax, seeing only the splash of pink and purple luring the sun to the horizon, but the water shadows make me stiffen with what ifs. What if Rob, the only one who knows how to sail, falls off the boat? What if a freighter looms out of the oncoming night, turning this delightful moment into a disaster — if not by fact then by worry?

[2] If this technique works for you, try one of Rico's books of clustering ideas: *Writing the Natural Way,* Los Angeles, CA: Jeremy Tarcher, 1983; *Pain and Possibility,* Los Angeles, CA: Jeremy Tarcher, 1991; or *Creating Re-Creations,* Spring, TX: Absey & Co., 2002.

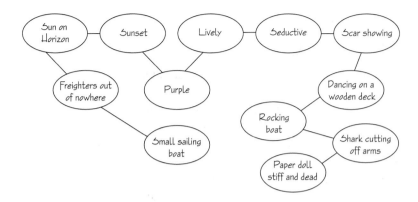

Clustering is also a fine technique for breaking through resistance to a subject that seems overwhelming or too risky. Put the loaded word in the center circle (words like "divorce," "dieting," "murder," "bullying"), stay specific in imagery, and discover what happens.

Tip: Be outrageous in your associations: the less logical, the better. If "empty milk bottle" leads to "leaky pen" leads to "plane crash in Russia," the results will be more interesting than if "milk" leads to "cow" leads to "moo." Also concrete images (no more than a few words) work better than abstractions.

Using Photographs

Pictures provide the concrete details that can trigger fresh writing. Describing the details can recreate a whole family story, as in Louise Gluck's poem "Still Life." Notice how she never *tells* us how people feel about each other but *shows* us the tension with details like "not one of us does not avert his eyes."

Still Life

Father has his arm around Tereze.
She squints. My thumb
is in my mouth: my fifth autumn.

Near the copper beech
the spaniel dozes in shadows.
Not one of us does not avert his eyes.

Across the lawn, in full sun, my mother
stands behind her camera.

In this digital age, photos are increasingly making their way into written texts, but Gluck creates the picture with words alone, as does Norma Elia Cantú in her essay, "Tino & Papi" (see Chapter 17, Short Shorts).

To find your own "Still Life," look through family albums, old wallets, scrapbooks in the attic, framed photos on the walls and the bookshelves of family members, and start writing. You might also try some of these ideas:

- Find a picture of a "former" you, and write in the present tense about what you were thinking and feeling. Do this as an interior monologue — as if you are talking to yourself.

- Create a dialogue between yourself and someone else in the photo.

- Describe the setting, who the people are, what they are like, and what the social dynamics are. Like Gluck, use details that show, more than tell, the mood of that moment. Try including dialogue.

- Imagine what others in the photo are thinking, and write about the moment from their points of view, using their voices.

- Lay out several group photos of family and friends. Look for a dominant impression that strikes you. Who is always smiling? Who is not? Who looks away from the camera? Do a freewrite or a cluster based on what you discover.

- Find a photo of a place you have visited, or want to visit, or would never visit — and start writing.

ESSO GAS STATION

BEAUTY PARLOR HARDWARE DRY CLEANER BAKERY

66th STREET

BERGENLINE AVENUE

VIRGINIA DOMINIC   "CONSIDERING COUSINS"   2/7/05

My three cousins, Phyllis, Arthur, and Joey Becker, lived two doors up from us on Bergenline Avenue in West New York. My family lived over the dry cleaners, and my cousins lived with Aunt Ree above Nellie's Beauty Parlor. She was my mother's sister and a widow after my Uncle Joe died of cancer.

I remember looking up to all of them (they were older), but especially to Phyllis. When I was ten, she was seventeen and knew everything. She had long thick black hair that curled under, smooth complexion that was flawless, and a great figure that gave her a regal look. I had curly red hair, tons of freckles, and was as skinny as Olive Oil in the Popeye comic strip. I rode my bike all over West New York, much to my mother's dismay, for I was her only daughter and a tomboy. Not like Phyllis who looked more like my mother than I did. I looked like Aunt Ree, who was also a readhead. . .

Mapmaking

Drawing your bedroom, neighborhood, school, or community (from your past or your present) can reawaken memories, especially of place. Your drawing can be realistic or impressionistic. It can even be surreal, making your favorite oak tree larger than your house, for example. Devote no more than 10 to 15 minutes to drawing. Your aim is to build up energy for writing, not drain it. Some like to share their drawings with peers before writing; others prefer to move quickly into a draft.

Doing Personal Search

Interviewing a family member, surveying friends, looking up old newspaper articles, reading old letters, fact checking in an encyclopedia — all provide creative jolts for a draft. Depending on the topic and the writer, some do this before they start; others wait until they have something written on the page. Either way, the creative potential of this kind of research is powerful. For more on how and why, see Chapter 9, The Role of Research.

Making a Timeline

Timelines offer a way to explore a subject over time, against the backdrop of history and culture. They work well for reviewing key moments of your life, uncovering ongoing themes, the ones that don't go away from one year to the next. Timelines also connect the personal and the political in surprising ways that move memoir and personal essay into larger social contexts, linking one person's story to a larger cultural one. We recommend making four columns, as follows:

Year/Age   Local/World Events   External/Facts   Internal/Feelings

Under "Local/World Events," list political or cultural events that have had an impact on you and/or your family. These might include events that took place close to home, like the fire at the local skating rink; they might include social or cultural events, like a Red Hot Chili Peppers concert; or they might be major world events like the Iraqi War or the destruction of the World Trade Center. (Note: To jog your memory, make use of the many chronologies that list social, cultural, and political events by year, such as *American Decades* and *The People's Chronicle,* available in libraries or on the Internet.)

Under "External/Facts" list the events in *your* life that shaped
you. Choose ones that others would agree had an impact, like moving to a new neighborhood, getting braces, or losing something important, like weight or car keys — or a friend.
Under "Internal/Feelings" record attitudes and insights that
others may or may not know, describing the way those particular
events "felt to you."
You do not need an entry in every column for each year, and you
need not list every year. From the timeline, you will have a wealth of
material that will suggest forgotten stories, unexplored connections,
and surprising themes to develop into a piece of writing. Tip: Begin
developing one theme or one memory by freewriting soon after
completing the timeline. Use only what seems relevant; save the rest
for another time.[3]
Here's what the beginning of a timeline might look like:

Year	Age	Local/World	External	Internal
1956	infant		I am born. My sister is 10; my brother is 5.	
1959	3		My paternal grandfather dies.	
1961	5	John Kennedy is elected president.	I begin kindergarten, crying.	I like school. I try to be good.
1963	7	Kennedy is assassinated; Johnson is sworn in.	My Nana dies; my father is shot; I am sitting in school wondering why my parents have not come for me.	Sad about Grandma; I see my mother's vulnerability; I am moved by my father's efforts to comfort her.
1965	9	Thomas is killed in an accident.	My teacher cries as she talks about his death.	I realize that children can die.

[3] We thank Marcie Wolfe, director of the Institute for Literacy Studies at Lehman
College, CUNY, for sharing this version of the timeline with us.

A Guide to Felt Sense [4]

Felt sense refers to what we know intuitively, in our bodies, before words come. Too often writers don't slow down to listen carefully enough to their inner voices. Sondra has developed a process called the "Guidelines for Composing," which is designed to help writers relax, contact a felt sense, and write from a centered place.

The Guidelines consist of a series of questions. They work best when someone else reads the questions aloud to you. After each set of questions, the reader pauses to allow you time to jot down your answers, usually two to five minutes per answer. To complete the Guidelines, you need a minimum of 40 minutes. If you have more than 40 minutes, you can take more time to jot down fuller answers.

If you are interested in using this Idea Generator, visit our website at <college.hmco.com/english>. There you can access the complete set of questions and read a more detailed description of felt sense.

What's Next?

These Idea Generators help to begin a draft, but they rarely produce finished writing. For that, time and reflection are needed so you can reread and shape first words into finished work. As Steven Harvey says in "The Art of Self":

> What makes writing — writing of any kind — an art is not inven-
> tion, but shape. Shapeliness. The facts, the events, the invented
> flights of fancy do not make up a work of art. . . .

Our next chapter deals with finding and crafting that shape.

---

[4] From Sondra Perl, *Felt Sense: Writing with the Body*. Portsmouth, NH: Heinemann/ Boynton-Cook, 2004.

Ways In. . .

Some writers like to use clustering; others prefer sentence starters or freelisting or timelines or personal research. To identify the techniques that work best for you, we suggest trying all of the Idea Generators, perhaps one each week. Then regularly use those that work best.

CHAPTER 4

Taking Shape

I work in what I call — accordion-style writing. The approach is write-write-write-expand-expand-expand-expand, and then when it is so expanded that it is bloated, cut it down to as little as I can and start over.

— DOROTHY ALLISON

One of the great strengths of creative nonfiction is its flexible, often experimental form. We can tell a story from beginning to end, or start in the middle, or begin in the present and flash back. We can write in present tense, or past tense, or shuttle back and forth in time — and in voice. We can add bits of poetry, news headlines, interior monologue, or letter excerpts. All fall under the rubric of creative nonfiction, the word "creative" having as much to do with freedom of structure as with language.

The only "rule" we need to keep in mind is that, by the final draft, structure and meaning must complement each other. By that we mean:

> . . .the beginning sets up a promise that intrigues
> . . .the middle develops that promise
> . . .the end satisfies without readers saying. "You already said that!"

How to make that happen changes from piece to piece. A short work may need nothing more than a quick listing or 10-minute freewriting to find its shape. A book-length project may need a drawer full of fragments and a chapter outline before the writer can begin. Here we will focus on short works.

Sometimes, when we are lucky, the right shape appears in draft one, as in Penelope Scambly Schott's short lemonade essay. She came home from the supermarket, started writing, and there it was. A few days of tinkering, cutting, and adding a good title, and voila! her piece was complete. Sometimes only *part* of the shape appears early on, and we must discover the rest by rereading and writing more, as Patricia Hampl did in her essay "Memory and Imagination." She began with a fragment about her first piano lesson, assuming it would be central to a memoir, but in subsequent drafts, the shape evolved into an essay with a much larger focus: the role of memory in creative nonfiction. (See Chapter 16, Stories of Craft.)

Sometimes shape can precede content. We begin with the idea of writing from two perspectives, in two alternating voices, for example — and *then* decide who the characters will be and what they will talk about. Occasionally, as Annie Dillard points out in *The Writing Life,* the structure we think of as solid for several drafts becomes shaky and we worry: Will it hold?

> Some of the walls are bearing walls; they have to stay, or everything will fall down. Other walls can go with impunity; you can hear the difference. Unfortunately, it is often a bearing wall that has to go. It cannot be helped. There is only one solution, which appalls you, but there it is. Knock it out. Duck.

Fortunately the courage for total demolition is not usually needed. Still, Dillard's advice is worth remembering, as a reminder of a key attitude that experienced writers assume and novices often do not: *Early drafts are not carved in stone.* Nothing is sacred. Everything can get renovated — demolished and rebuilt — and the only way to know what shape works best is to consider the full range of possibilities.

But first, you need a full draft to work with. "Full" means rich with ideas and images, shapeless or not, and "full" means a draft that moves from beginning to end, no matter how clumsily. Push yourself to reach an ending, even if it feels unsatisfying. You may have gaps in your narrative and write margin notes to yourself like "Find out" or

"Fill in later"—after there's been time to do research, interview, meditate, read, talk, and dream. But don't stop writing. If you wait until "later"—especially on short pieces—you may get stuck perfecting a beginning you can't use. You may even end up like the would-be writer in Camus' *The Plague* who kept reworking the first line of his novel over and over again, for years. He wanted his imagined editor to be transfixed from the start, to say, "Hat's off!" at every line. This would never happen because Camus' writer hadn't learned what Annie Dillard had: that the part you must jettison is often "the original key passage, the passage on which the rest was to hang, and from which you yourself drew the courage to begin." Like scaffolding, the original opening is needed at first, but it can hide the true shape—until it is removed.

The Power of Rereading

Once you have a full draft, you will want to find its strengths, the parts that are most likely to remain, whatever the ultimate shape. A good way to begin is by rereading your draft to see what shape may be there—or half there. These techniques help the search:

- *Star your favorite parts and look for connections:* Ask yourself, What do these good sections have in common? Why are they so important to me?

- *Look for the narrative arc:* A narrative arc links the beginning of your piece to the end and reveals how thoughts, characters, and events have changed. To find it, ask yourself what the "I" of the piece has learned—and also ask, What have I, as author looking back, learned?

- *Look beyond the first line:* Rarely is your first line the best beginning. Read down the draft to see where there might be a stronger opening. It helps to listen for a rhythm that grabs you. Often, opening lines are warm-up lines, the language flat until suddenly sentences begin to zing with a melody that leads to a voice that leads to what the piece is trying to be about—and its future shape.

Consider this opening:

> Anyone who espouses that kids are always having fun doesn't
> know very much about children's hardships, how many painful
> times they experience in their childhood and how they deal with
> these times. When I was a child, I'd tell my friends that my par-
> ents were imaginary, especially my Dad. . . .

Listen for the difference. The first line might work for a textbook discussion of children's hardships, but it's the next line — about a child
who tells everyone that her parents, especially her father, are imaginary — that is a promising start for creative nonfiction.

- *Try Scissors:* Writer/teacher Pamela Painter has her students write on only one side of a piece of paper. Then she
  asks them to bring scissors and tape to class. They cut up
  their drafts wherever a new thought or scene appears and
  rearrange the pieces. This is a great way to think imaginatively about alternative ways of organizing and also to see
  what needs developing (a skinny but good two-liner) and
  what needs cutting (a skinny and irrelevant two-liner). This
  technique is used, even by the greats. According to Richard
  Howarth in the *John McPhee Reader,* Pulitzer Prize winning
  author John McPhee also cuts his notes into a thousand
  scraps to find order and promising new shapes.

- *Finish the line "I want to tell you that . . ." and then write three
  titles.* After a draft you need to figure out what your piece is
  about. What's at stake here? There may be many possibilities
  but one needs to become dominant while others become
  subordinate — or get saved for another piece. Writing titles
  and finishing the line "I want to tell you that. . ." can help you
  decide. Be specific, especially in your titles. "A Childhood
  Memory" or "Reflections" won't provide much focus, but a
  title like "Lion in the Attic" will keep you (and readers) asking what the beast is doing up there — and what it means.

- *Look for repetitions that can be used as organizing devices:* Alice
  Walker organizes her essay "Beauty: When the Other

Dancer Is the Self" (see Chapter 11, Memoir) by using the
date and her age to capture key moments in her life:

It is a bright summer day in 1947. . . .
It is Easter Sunday, 1950. . . .
I am eight years old and a tomboy. . . .
I am fourteen and baby-sitting for my brother Bill. . . .
I am twenty-seven, and my baby daughter is almost three. . . .

Repeating a key element, an age, a phrase, helps readers
orient themselves and provides a unifying structure that
keeps the piece on track. You can see it again in Susan Allen
Toth's "Going to the Movies" (see Chapter 13, Portrait).
Each of the four sections of her essay begins with a line
about going to the movies — and sets up four kinds of dates:

Aaron takes me only to art films. . . .
Bob takes me only to movies that he thinks have a redeeming
    social conscience. . . .
Sam likes movies that are entertaining. . . .
I go to some movies by myself. . . .

Scene, Summary, and Reflection

Whatever the outer shape, the same three building blocks of creative
nonfiction are used for the inside: scene, summary, and reflection.

Scene makes characters come alive on the page, using dialogue
and description to zoom in, like a camera close-up, on key moments
in the story. It's a great way to dramatize what is crucial and is often
a good way to begin. Notice how Gloria Anzaldúa introduces her essay on language and dialect, "How to Tame a Wild Tongue," by placing herself in the dentist's chair. The humorous scene foreshadows,
through humor and metaphor, the larger theme of silencing to come:

"We're going to have to control your tongue," the dentist says,
pulling out all the metal from my mouth. Silver bits plop and tin-
kle into the basin. My mouth is a mother lode.

> The dentist is cleaning out my roots. I get a whiff of stench
> when I gasp. "I can't cap that tooth yet, you're still draining," he
> says.
>   "We're going to have to do something about your tongue." I
> hear the anger rising in his voice. My tongue keeps pushing out
> the wads of cotton, pushing back the drills, the long thin needles.
> "I've never seen anything as strong or as stubborn," he says. And
> I think, how do you tame a wild tongue, train it to be quiet, how
> do you bridle and saddle it? How do you make it lie down?
>
>   — *Borderlands, La Frontera*

Alice Walker, in "Beauty: When the Other Dancer Is the Self,"
opens with a childhood scene — and uses present tense. Even without dialogue, she makes us feel as if we are there:

> It is a bright summer day in 1947. My father, a fat, funny man with
> beautiful eyes and a subversive wit, is trying to decide which of his
> eight children he will take with him to the county fair. My mother,
> of course, will not go. She is knocked out from getting most of us
> ready: I hold my neck still against the pressure of her knuckles as
> she hastily completes the braiding and beribboning of my hair.

In both passages, readers are put into the experience rather than being told about them secondhand. That is the power of scene.

   Summary fills in the back-story, spelling out what happened
before, after, and in between these close-up moments. We learn the
history of people and events, and we gain insight into cultural and
political contexts through summary. The trick is to do it gracefully,
as Walker does. After the "beribboning of my hair," she gives us back-
story of her Dad's job and its socio-political implications so seamlessly that it all feels part of the narrative:

> My father is the driver for the rich old white lady up the road. Her
> name is Miss Mey. She owns all the land for miles around, as well
> as the house in which we live.

Many beginning writers feel they must put summary up front, giving the facts *before* the narrative begins. But as Walker shows, you

can weave the facts of summary into the storyline, here and there, when appropriate, without overloading the reader with too much information.

Reflection offers the writer's thoughts about what is happening and what it means. Reflections can include thoughts about the moment or thoughts looking back. After introducing Miss Mey (above), Walker reflects as an adult, looking back and remembering Miss Mey's treatment of her overworked mother. She then returns to being the child narrator again:

> All I remember about her is that she once offered to pay my mother thirty-five cents for cleaning her house, raking up piles of her magnolia leaves, and washing her family's clothes, and that my mother — she of no money, eight children, and a chronic earache — refused it. But I do not think of this in 1947. I am two-and-a-half years old. I want to go everywhere my Daddy goes. . . .

Reflection works well when you *ground your writing in the particular,* as Walker does. "Thirty-five cents" conveys Miss Mey's stinginess far better than a generalization like "Miss Mey insulted my mother by paying her very little."

Reflections must also add something new to the story, something not obvious to the reader. Examine these two different endings to a family vignette:

> I couldn't believe I had gotten a drum set. It was amazing, terrific. "Thanks!" I yelled, full of gratitude.
> "Our pleasure!" my parents said, smiling. We were all so happy.

Here the writer is merely repeating what the reader already knows from the dialogue. "We were all so happy" is expected if parents are smiling and saying "Our pleasure." But what if the writer goes deeper, beneath the surface experience, and writes:

> "Our pleasure!" my mother said, scowling. I had not yet learned to read the signs.

In this version, the writer's reflection captures a tension that moves the story onto more complex emotional ground.

These three building blocks — scene, summary, and reflection — are not generally used in equal amounts. Writing about events over time will need more summary than writing about a single moment. A meditation on friendship will be more reflective than a series of scenes about friendship. The first will tell more; the second, show more. Sometimes, it's a matter of style. Writers tend to be partial to showing *or* telling, but good writers use both. And both can work if the voice is confident and moves comfortably from scene to summary to reflection, as needed.

A Word About Riffs

In jazz, riffs allow musicians to take off from the main melody and return. In writing, riffs allow writers to add scenes, summaries, or reflections and then to return to the main story line. Patricia Hampl once said, "You can describe taking a sip of your coffee and riff about who knows what for three paragraphs, or three pages, before returning that coffee cup to its saucer."

Eric Liu, for example, in the middle of discussing his personal struggle with assimilation as a Chinese American, uses a riff to add social history as back-story. Here the riff adds perspective, making the issue more than just Eric's:

> There was a time when assimilation did quite strictly mean whitening . . . You "made it" in society not only by putting on airs of anglitude, but also by assiduously bleaching out the marks of a darker, dirtier past. And this bargain, stifling as it was, was open to European immigrants almost exclusively; to blacks, only on the passing occasion; to Asians, hardly at all. . . .
> —"Notes of a Native Speaker" (Chapter 12, Personal Essay)

Riffs work well to add dialogue, scene, and reflection, as needed. If you have a key moment that goes by too fast, riff with a scene. If you are missing back-story about a character, place, or event, riff with summary. When you are short on reflection, riff with a few interesting reactions to what is happening. Tip: To riff without worry about messing up a text, try using bold font on the computer. It makes the additions feel temporary until later, when you reread and decide what to keep and what to cut so that the new information fits with the old.

A Repertoire of Forms

Finding the best shape for a particular work means having a repertoire of forms to draw on. The one we grow up with is the chronological story that begins at the beginning and moves in a straight line from beginning to end. The "Once upon a time" stories like "Cinderella" and "Snow White" often rely on this structure. But there are many others, not organized chronologically. They may begin in the middle, like *The Odyssey,* and move back and forth in time. They may be organized episodically with segments or vignettes as in the HBO series *The Sopranos* or in afternoon soap operas.

What follows are twelve structures worth knowing. It's worth trying all of them to explore their possibilities. We liken this to playing basketball or tennis: the more shots you've mastered, the better your game.

Chronological

This form, which moves forward from beginning to end in a straight narrative line, usually has a rising action, climax, and resolution. It is good for stories with a surprise, a twist of plot, and an emphasis on suspense; it usually requires solid amounts of scene, summary, and reflection to work well. (See Tony Earley, "Somehow Form a Family" and David Sedaris, "Let It Snow," Chapter 11, Memoir.)

Segmented

This structure uses ways other than time to organize reality: by free association, by theme, by juxtaposing disparate thoughts. It uses white space or asterisks between segments to signal shifts from one segment to another. Sometimes, subheadings and fonts change as well. For a more detailed discussion of segmented essays, see the next section. (See Lisa Chavez, "Independence Day, Manly Hot Springs, Alaska" and Alice Walker, "Beauty: When the Other Dancer Is the Self," Chapter 11, Memoir; and Scott Russell Sanders, "Under the Influence" and Connie Wieneke, "Snakebit," Chapter 12, Personal Essay.)

Framed

This structure starts in the present, flashes back to the past, and returns to the present. It's good for connecting who you are with who you were — and showing how the past lingers in your life.

Compare and Contrast

This form compares events, people, and ideas either by (1) weaving back and forth fluidly or (2) setting up a comparison, discussing one, then the other, and finally summing them up. (See Susan Allen Toth, "Going to the Movies," Chapter 12, Portrait.)

Multiple Perspectives

It depicts one event from many points of view. A car accident, for example, might be described both by those involved and those who observed. It is good for showing how different cultures perceive events in different — and often opposing — ways and also for letting readers decide truths for themselves. The author's reflection is minimal — coming through the characters. Tension and power come through juxtaposition. (See Anne Fadiman, "Do Doctors Eat Brains?" Chapter 15, Literary Journalism.)

Episodic

It gathers together a series of vignettes about the same people or places over time. TV programs like *ER* are episodic, both within one show and from week to week. (See Susan Allen Toth, "Going to the Movies," Chapter 13, Portrait.)

Q & A

The Q & A form relies on a series of questions. It is used primarily in interviews, particularly for profiles. But it can be used when no interviews are involved, as a Q & A with oneself, for example. (See Sondra Perl's interview with Maureen Stanton on our website at <college.hmco.com/english>.)

Epistolary

It uses the letter format to tell a story — either in one letter or in an exchange of letters. They can be addressed to those you know or those you hope to reach. They can summarize a year at holiday time or capture a trip. Our friend, Donna-Rich Kaplowitz, sent twenty-two e-mail letters from the jungles of Costa Rica to her friends.

> . . . The rain beats down with such force that it seems make believe. I have never witnessed water falling from the sky with such determination. Forty-five inches in three weeks. Then suddenly, an image of the perfect cerulean blue of Michigan summer skies, the smell of cut grass, and I am swooning for the want of it. . . .
> — excerpt of *Letter 19: On Missing Home*, June 2, 2004, Costa Rica

Kaplowitz's aim is to make a book of letters or to let the e-mails evolve into another.

Multi-Genre

It uses bits of poems, letters, interior monologue, and other fragments to tell a story. Different fonts are useful to indicate shifts from one form to another, say from poetry to prose, or inner thoughts to spoken dialogue. If the work includes photographs and drawings, it may also be called a collage, especially when the visual also becomes the organizing strategy. (For more on multi-genre, see Chapter 8.)

Inverted Pyramid

It places key facts — who, what, when, where, how — first. A mainstay of newspaper reporting, it begins with a strong lead sentence to draw readers in. The details of the facts come in subsequent paragraphs.

Not conducive to storytelling because it emphasizes exposition over drama, telling over showing. (See the front pages of newspapers for examples.)

Deductive

This form begins with the main idea or thesis statement, followed by support for this idea. A popular form of analytic writing, it works best when you are writing to convey what you know rather than to explore what you don't know. Its short form, the five-paragraph essay, is frequently taught in school, and although its restrictive structure doesn't lend itself to surprises, in the hands of a writer like Bertrand Russell, it too can embody voice and lyricism. Notice his graceful structure, the repeating form of threes, and how transitions link sections with ease.

> Three passions, simple but overwhelmingly strong, have governed my life: the longing for love, the search for knowledge, and the unbearable pity for the suffering of mankind. These passions, like great winds, have blown me hither and thither, in a wayward course, over a deep ocean of anguish, reaching to the very verge of despair.
>
> I have sought love, first, because it brings ecstasy — ecstasy so great that I would often have sacrificed all the rest of my life for a few hours of this joy. I have sought it next, because it relieves loneliness — that terrible loneliness in which one shivering consciousness looks over the rim of the world into the cold unfathomable lifeless abyss. I have sought it, finally, because in the union of love I have seen, in a mystic miniature, the prefiguring vision of the heaven that saints and poets have imagined. This is what I have sought, and though it might seem too good for human life, this is what — at last — I have found.
>
> With equal passion I have sought knowledge. I have wished to understand the hearts of men. I have wished to know why the stars shine. And I have tried to apprehend the Pythagorean power by which number holds sway above the flux. A little of this, but not much, I have achieved.
>
> Love and knowledge, so far as they are possible, led upward toward the heavens. But always pity brought me back to earth. Echoes of cries of pain reverberate in my heart. Children in famine,

victims tortured by oppressors, helpless old people a hated burden to their sons, and the whole world of loneliness, poverty, and pain made a mockery of what human life should be. I long to alleviate the evil, but I cannot, and I too suffer.

This has been my life. I have found it worth living, and would gladly live it again if the chance were offered me.

—*The Autobiography of Bertrand Russell, 1891–1914*

Note: For more examples of how academic writing can incorporate creative nonfiction, visit our website at <college.hmco.com/english> and click on the section called "Crossover Essays."

More on the Segmented Essay

Over dinner one night, a friend of ours was debating how to write about growing up in a family of missionaries. Should she tell her story chronologically, beginning with her great grandfather? Or organize her stories by the countries she lived in? Or by survival techniques? Or by the letters that she and her family wrote, all of which had been saved in shoeboxes by her meticulous mother?

The first is the easiest, organized by time. But others may capture her life in ways she can't predict. "You won't know," we advised, "until you start experimenting with different shapes to see what happens." Maybe chronology will win out, but chances are her memoir is ripe for a segmented essay — one of the most popular forms of creative nonfiction today. It provides nonlinear ways of perceiving reality, not bound by one story told in a straight sequence from beginning to end. In our increasingly multitask world, the segmented form, thanks to computers and television, is all around us, presenting us with simultaneous action. Sport replays coexist with real-time plays. Computers let us work on two files on our monitor at once. A night watching TV dramas involves three or more separate stories told side by side. No wonder writers and readers are comfortable with a literary form that gains power by juxtaposition, one section building on the last without traditional transitions. And so we devote one separate section to this contemporary form that reflects our lives.

Use segmentation to capture a lifetime problem as Nora Ephron does in "A Few Words About Breasts" (Chapter 11, Memoir). Or to highlight an adventure as Gretchen Legler does in "Moments of Being: An Antarctic Quintet" (Chapter 14, Essay of Place). Or to depict changing perspectives as Mary Elizabeth Pope does in "Teacher Training." (Visit our website to read Pope's essay.) She shifts back and forth in time, alternating between being a first-year teacher of writing and being a student in fifth grade. By the end, she's captured how the fifth-grade teacher she disliked so much spurred her on to become a more caring one. She uses space and italics to indicate shifts 14 times throughout the piece. In the excerpt below, she uses regular font to describe her experience as a teacher, italics to describe her experience as a student:

> . . . Holly comes to my office at least once a week. She worries all the time; so much so, that she is terrified to commit anything to paper. She is careful to meet all of the requirements in an assignment, yet she is so careful that it stifles all of the creativity in her expression. She always asks me what I want her to write. . . .

> . . . *Mrs. Crane stood regally before the class, holding a stack of reports in her hand. I could hardly wait to get mine back and read what she had written. I had worked so hard, and had so carefully and creatively constructed the cover, that I was sure she would love it. "Class," she began, "why don't we take a look at some of the reports you handed in to me?" I was even more excited.* . . .

Both vignettes are about creativity and risk-taking. Without telling us, Pope signals by juxtaposition that Holly's terror may have resulted from having had a teacher like Mrs. Crane, who praised Kevin's report, criticized James's "crumpled paper," and when it came to Mary Elizabeth's essay, "made no comment on it at all, quickly replacing it on the bottom of the pile."

Here are some reasons to write a segmented essay:

- ❧ Your plot moves too slowly to tell the story chronologically. As essayist Robert Root writes, "There's a reason no one is proposing to cash in on the natural disaster film genre like 'Twister' or 'Volcano' with a movie called 'Glacier!'"

- ❧ You have too much detail to organize chronologically. A trip is a great example. If you start on day one of a three-week adventure, covering morning to night, chances are you will lose your audience by the lunch on day two — if you are a *good* storyteller. Otherwise, it will be by lunch on day one!

🖋 You want to capture your mind at work. The mind thinks by free association: Something your mother says reminds you of your grandmother's cookie jar, and that makes you think about going on the Atkins Diet, which makes you think of your ripped red dress at the Senior Prom. . . . These free associations, once arranged and shaped, reveal a character struggling to figure out the world independent of a specific time and place.

🖋 You want to explore multiple perspectives, capturing the same experience from different angles so that the reader gets a more differentiated and complex picture.

🖋 You want to put your personal story in a cultural context. In "Under the Influence," Sanders includes segments about alcoholism in the United States to place his personal experience on a larger social canvas (Chapter 12, Personal Essay).

🖋 You want to compare experiences of then and now as Norma Elia Cantú does, looking at two photos of her brothers, taken years apart, in "Tino & Papi" (Chapter 17, Short Shorts).

🖋 You want to examine relationships, not events, as do Scott Russell Sanders and Susan Allen Toth (Chapter 12, Personal Essay, and Chapter 13, Portrait).

Tips for Writing Segmented Essays

Whatever your reason for using a segmented essay, you need to help readers locate where they are in each segment, who is speaking, and when. Here are some tips for avoiding confusion:

🖋 Use white space or asterisks between segments. Or other icons. (Mary Clearman Blew, when writing about rivers, used fishhooks.)

🌢 Use clear markers to let readers know what is going on. For example, Mary Elizabeth Pope uses italics plus spacing to indicate shifts in time and speaker. Toth uses roman numerals to set off her segments — I, II, III — for each trip to the movies. Other markers that signal a shift: the repetition of a line or word; a recurring object, action, or scene; the use of dates; a recurring sound or smell or linguistic rhythm; a shifting of tenses — past, present, or future; a shifting of voices — child/adult or angry/sad.

🌢 Beware of using the segmented form as an excuse for not knowing what your essay is about. It's easy NOT to ask, "Why are all these segments in one essay?" but if you don't, your reader will, followed by "Why should I care about this?" Each segment must move the whole piece forward, adding something new emotionally and dramatically.

Ways In. . .

1. Scene, Summary, and Reflection

1. Study this short vignette from "The Opposite of Saffron" by Mary Paumier Jones, and see if you agree with our analysis of what is scene, summary, and reflection:

Scene = Bold
Summary = Italics
Reflection = Underlined.

Minneapolis, Minnesota

I don't remember this. I was too young. *But my mother and father told of my childhood habit time and again. From their point of view: their first child wakes in the middle of the night, wakes them up too, not with cries but with giggles. She laughs and recites all the words they have taught her, her litany.* I picture Mom getting back in bed after the first time. **"What's the matter?" "Nothing, she's laughing and**

reciting her words." "Now?" "Yes, now." *Night after night I did the same.*

One day Dad taught me to say Minneapolis, Minnesota, <u>a triumph of such magnitude it became my permanent finale, new words inserted before its resonance.</u> When they heard "Minneapolis, Minnesota," my parents knew they could go back to sleep.

2. Examine two or three of your notebook entries to see how much scene, summary, and reflection you use. Label as you read, and then tally the score. Whatever you least use — scene, summary, or reflection — is the one you most need to try out. If you have no scenes, find a place to add one — with a few lines of dialogue. If you have no back-story, find a place to add a few lines of summary about character or place. If your entry is all action and summary, find a place to add a few lines that reflect on what the action means. Be sure to read your addition, plus what comes before and after, *out loud.* Listen for rough edges that need smoothing.

3. Write a new beginning for an existing entry, using a scene with dialogue as Gloria Anzaldúa does. Or try ending an entry with a scene.

4. Take a work-in-progress and duplicate it on one side only, so you can cut it up where each new thought begins. Lay all the sections out on a desk or floor. Reshuffle your original order by asking yourself: Where else might this piece begin? Where might it end? How might the middle change? Also, look at the size of each section, noticing which sections are fat, which are thin, which would benefit from more detail, which seem superfluous. Take away the latter, add onto the former, and when satisfied, tape together your new shape.

5. Choose an activity that has affected you over time (learning to play an instrument or a sport, moving, dieting, dealing with loss or illness). Create a series of vignettes that capture key moments, leaving a space between them. Each vignette should show, more than tell, how this activity has had its impact on you.

6. Compare something in your life now to something in your past by juxtaposition. Write one segment in first-person present and the other in first-person past as Mary Pope does in "Teacher Training." Make at least two shifts. For example, write about learning how to swim and becoming a lifeguard; or dating versus having a steady relationship; or being a redhead, a blond, and a brunette. Make sure your voice matches your age and mood.

7. Explore the same event from different perspectives. Your aim is to let your characters have their say in their respective voices, so that readers learn as much about their personalities — and social dynamics — as about the event.

8. Look at a home video, thumb through a family album, listen to a song, read a poem, etc. In your writing, move back and forth between the stimulus — be it visual (a video or photos) or verbal (poem, letter, song) — and your thoughts, so readers see your connections. Gerald N. Callahan's "Chimera" offers a fascinating example of how the image of a woman is woven through thoughts about how and why the body remembers and forgets. (See Chapter 12, Personal Essay.)

CHAPTER 5

Finding Voice

It is the still small voice that the soul heeds; not the deafening blasts. . . .

—WILLIAM DEAN HOWELLS

Voice conveys personality.

One of the strengths of creative nonfiction is its person-to-person feeling, as if writer and reader were friends. It happens when the writer sounds genuine and trustworthy, thanks to a mix of words, rhythms, and attitude called *voice.* Voice conveys personality—someone to believe in, or not; someone who mysteriously charms, or not. When the voice is strong, there's a sense of a real person behind the words, not the anonymous monotone of, say, medical reports and car manuals. The latter may convey important information, but anyone could have written it. *Who* doesn't matter.

In creative nonfiction, "who" does matter. Voice counts as much as information, because it's the world *through one writer's eyes* that engages us. Voice also helps writers sort out their relationship to the material: Am I sad, happy, angry, or bemused by this subject? And voice makes readers decide: Do I care enough to read on?

Of course, "*All* good writing is about voice," Joyce Carol Oates reminds us. In creative nonfiction, we argue, voice matters even more because the author and the "I" narrating the story are one and the same. Fiction writers can say, "That character is not really *me!*" Journalists and scholars can say, "This writing isn't *about* me!" But creative nonfiction writers take full responsibility for the "I." "That's me on the page all right!"—and readers either lean forward or lean away. *Who* is saying it and *what* is being said rise and fall together as a team.

It's no wonder, then, that if you ask creative nonfiction writers how their work is going, you'll hear a delighted, "I found the right voice!" or a dull, "Not so good. I can't find the voice. . . ." They know that when the voice is off—too whiny, stodgy, pompous, self-indulgent, self-serving, or just annoying—the piece isn't working yet. When the voice is on, whatever the subject, people listen.

Consider these two reflections written by doctors, each writing about their retirements from medicine. Both use colorful language. Both express their feelings. Yet their voices—in tone, pitch, and sensibility—couldn't be more different. The first, louder, is full of certainty; the second, quieter, is full of questioning:

Read aloud

read aloud

I. Being a doctor is a noble profession, a beacon of light for the ill.
    I have felt the power of that light for over fifty years, in dark
    gloomy nights of weather full of torrential rain and snow—and
    in the eerie silence before the sun rises. Many tough times I've
    had, but so gratifying! The memories will continue to fill me with
    fondness and awe—and will fuel the pages of my writing about
    this life commitment. . . .

II. It is twelve years since I walked away from my beloved workbench
    in the operating room. It was not done with a cheery wave of the
    hand. For a long time, there was a sense of dislocation as if I was
    standing on the bank of a stream, and it was the bank that was
    flowing while the stream stood still. Surgery was my native land.
    The writer who cuts himself off from his native land does so at
    great risk. The subject of so much of my writing had been my
    work as a doctor. Would I be punished for sending myself into
    exile? Have nothing left to say? I needn't have worried. There is
    always the sharp and aching tooth of memory.

— The Doctor Stories

The second voice, that of doctor/writer Richard Selzer, is understated. It does not try to impress with a life that's "a beacon of light for the ill," spending countless nights "in dark, gloomy weather full of torrential rain and snow." Instead of self-congratulation, Selzer lets us in on what retirement felt like *for him,* how it produced "a sense of dislocation as if I was standing on the bank of a stream, and it was the bank that was flowing while the stream stood still." As readers, we empathize, even if we are 40 years away from retirement. Why? Because Selzer sounds like a genuine, thoughtful guy. He's someone who doesn't have all the answers figured out, someone we might like to know.

Because voice shifts with each piece, there's no one way to find the right one. It evolves as we write and depends on our relationship to the subject; but these guidelines help in the search:

- *Individualize your voice by drawing on experiences that only you have.* The more general your statements, the more they could be written by anyone ("Being a doctor is a noble profession"). The more specific you are, the more distinctive your voice becomes ("It is twelve years since I walked away from my beloved workbench in the operating room").

- *Stay away from the predictable.* Avoid platitudes (". . . memories will continue to fill me with fondness and awe") and find fresh language that surprises ("There is always the sharp and aching tooth of memory").

- *Avoid straining to sound eloquent.* A convincing voice is one that sounds natural and trusts readers to "get it" without being hit over the head. A phrase like "in dark gloomy nights of weather full of torrential rain and snow" feels like overkill. Readers tend to lean away.

- *Show a mind trying to figure things out.* A voice smug with certainty is less compelling than one trying to sort out complexity. ("Would I be punished for sending myself into exile? Have nothing left to say? I needn't have worried.") Creative nonfiction is less about providing answers and more about struggling with questions. Readers are drawn in.

- *Don't present yourself as the Hero.* Readers like to see the "I" struggle and show some vulnerability. A voice that brags (especially without realizing it) and is convinced that the rest of the world is wrong turns people off—as in real life.

Who Am I in This Story?

We all have many voices. Finding the right one means finding which of our many selves works best to tell a particular story. All can be authentic in that they reveal honest responses to experience, but over time one wears better than the others, feels more comfortable, truer. When that happens we have to switch, as Mimi did when writing about a trip to her father's German village when she was 13. She began the essay by using the bratty voice of a teenager that initially felt right to her. But eventually, with much reluctance, she let another voice take over, one that allowed her to reflect on her teenage self and the forces that shaped her: *Read aloud.*

I.   I am being dragged through Europe by a father who's intent on convincing me that Forest Hills, Queens, is not the world. He hates that his Yankee-born daughter—ME!—wants to be exactly like my best friend Arlene, whose mother has bleached blond hair and serves Campbell Soup for dinner. "In Rindheim, you didn't do such things!" he'll say, 100 times a day—especially when I want to hang out at Penn Drug on Friday night after the basketball games. Or when I want to go to a party where he "doesn't know the family."

Bratty

II.   For years I heard the same line: "In Rindheim, you didn't do such things!" It was repeated whenever the American world of his daughters took my father by surprise. Sometimes it came out softly, in amusement, as when I was a Pilgrim turkey in the P.S. 3 Thanksgiving play. But usually, it was a red-faced, high-blood-pressure shout, especially when my sister, Ruth, became pinned to Mel from Brooklyn or I wanted to go with friends whose families he didn't know. . . .

Voice of reflection

Soon after the adult voice appeared, her essay, "My Father Always Said," which she'd struggled with for years, was finished.[1] Why? Because the new voice offered her a perspective that, unconsciously, she'd been missing: *Read aloud*

her opinion on the shift in voice

I loved the first voice, still do. I loved being thirteen again. But by page six of the essay, when I began talking about my family's loss

[1] It appears in *The Fourth Genre: Contemporary Writers of/on Creative Nonfiction,* New York: Longman, 2001.

and dislocation from fleeing Hitler's Germany, that voice seemed shallow and flip—and I felt trapped in it. I needed one that could make connections between that 1950's trip, my father's Holocaust experience, and me today. My bratty 13-year-old couldn't do that, even though I kept trying until many drafts later, my friend Penny Dugan finally said, 'Dump the kid!' Reluctantly I did.

The Voice of Innocence Versus the Voice of Experience

on board

Memoirist Sue Silverman talks of two writing voices: the voice of innocence that, like Mimi's 13-year-old, responds to the moment; and the voice of experience that looks back and reflects on the past. One voice usually dominates, but both, especially in longer works, can be heard side by side. In fact, it's the tension between the two voices, Silverman says, that makes first-person nonfiction come alive.

You can see that tension at work in essayist Scott Russell Sanders's "Under the Influence" (see Chapter 12, Personal Essay), which explores the legacy of his father's drinking. The voice of his opening paragraph is the adult looking back in anger and sadness:

Read aloud

> My father drank. He drank as a gut-punched boxer gasps for breath, as a starving dog gobbles food—compulsively, secretly, in pain and trembling. I use the past tense not because he ever quit drinking but because he quit living. That is how the story ends for my father, age sixty-four, heart bursting, body cooling and forsaken on the linoleum of my brother's trailer. The story continues for my brother, my sister, my mother, and me, and will continue so long as memory holds.

But in paragraph two, he becomes the child again. Using the phrase, "In the perennial present of memory" he shows us what it was like to live with an alcoholic father. Writing in present tense, he puts us back in time: "I slip into the garage or barn to see my father tipping back the flat green bottles of wine, the brown cylinders of whiskey. . . ." We listen as father and son talk, pretending that everything is normal:

> "What's up, buddy?" he says, thick-tongued and edgy.
> "Sky's up," I answer, playing along.

"And don't forget prices," he grumbles. "Prices are always up. And taxes."

The two voices—one of innocence, one of experience—work in tandem, so that readers experience, with immediacy, what Sanders experienced and also understand its effects over time. The two voices continue throughout the essay, back and forth, insisting on the truth of their duet.

In my nonfiction, the voice is as close as I can come to my own deliberate speech. I realize, of course, that the persona on the page is made out of words; I realize that it's constructed. But the construct bears a close and steady relationship to the person I am outside the page.

— SCOTT RUSSELL SANDERS

Other Duets of Self

As writers, we often hear conflicting voices within ourselves. There's the super rational "I" versus the irrational "I"—the first speaking calmly, while the second rages. There's the twosome who loves to debate issues: "On the one hand *this,* on the other hand, *that.*" There's the optimist, seeing the glass half full, and the pessimist, seeing it half empty. There's the timid, content-to-be-couch-potato side, pushing its fearless-to-go-bungee-jumping opposite. Let them all be heard, we say.

The chorus of conflict they produce makes for truer writing, as Linda Williamson Nelson points out in her essay, "On Writing My Way Home." Nelson grew up hearing two opposing dialects in her home: Her mother's:

> starched Jamaican English, a tribute to the success of *her* mother's warnings against the use of the Creole of the lower class.

Her father's, in the voice of

> . . . a Mississippi share-cropper, who spoke to us sparingly in meandering folktales of talkin' alligators in swamps, of cullud boys making they way through graveyards at dusk, and my great grandfather, a runaway slave who "nare one heard tell of sence."

Whenever she wrote, from fifth grade on, Nelson ignored her father's voice and all it represented, as well as the many other voices she heard on West 177th Street in the Bronx, where she grew up. Instead, she used a "book jacket" voice about a life that wasn't really hers. For school success, she "laundered" not only her voice but also the account of her life.

> What I knew best in those early years was Dad's daily departure from our cold-water flat to look for work, but what I wrote was that he was self-employed as a house-painting contractor. When I should have been describing the long afternoons I spent exploring vacant lots, I wrote about trips to the zoo or the circus and family picnic feasts in Central Park. Our actual feasts were five of us kids sitting Indian-style on the living room linoleum eating rice and beans and neck bones while my father gave us guitar concerts of his down-home improvisations called "Spanish Fling Dig" and "Mississippi Back Road Boogie Woogie."

It was years later, while writing her doctoral dissertation on the oral and written narratives of African-American women that Nelson's own legacy of voices—and the truth they spoke—said, "Enough!" In a personal essay exploring her experience writing the sanitized language that led to what she calls "laundered news," Nelson heard them and let them speak. They speak still, not only in creative nonfiction which she continues to write but also in her academic work as an anthropologist: "I just get bodacious and let the truth be told, even if it challenges the way some think it ought to be." (To read Nelson's full essay, visit our website at <college.hmco.com/english>.)

Where Does "I" Stand?

If you draw a circular stage that represents one piece of writing and mark where the "I" stands, it could be in the center, telling personal stories like the doctors. It could share the spotlight with others, as Brian Doyle does in "Being Brians" (see Chapter 12, Personal Essay). It could be near the edge, playing a small role as guide or emcee, as Susan Orlean does in "Meet the Shaggs" (see Chapter 15, Literary Journalism). Or it could be off-stage: the observer who is never seen, but heard (see Tracy Kidder, Chapter 15, Literary Journalism; and Colson Whitehead, Chapter 14, Essay of Place).

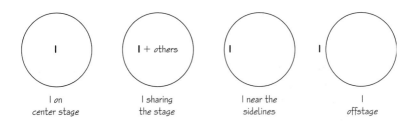

| I on center stage | I sharing the stage | I near the sidelines | I offstage |

Wherever the "I" stands, its voice must be right for the part. If readers think it's too loud and self-centered, they get edgy. Consider this opening paragraph for a profile of a college president:

> I have to admit I've always been a little afraid of Alice Chandler. Part of my fear came from her title—president of the State University of New York at New Paltz. . . . I've always found it hard not to be intimated by the president of anything. . . .

A pleasant voice, friendly. Appropriate *if* the essay is going to be about the writer. But if this is a profile of a college president, the "I" should relinquish center stage.

Sometimes the opposite is true. The voice of "I" disappears when it shouldn't. The reader is handed information without interpretation. In travel essays, for example, readers need description, but also someone reacting to the landscape, highlighting what's special.

Gretchen Legler shows how to strike the right balance between voice and description in "Moments of Being: An Antarctic Quintet" (Chapter 14, Essay of Place). She lets readers experience the brightness of this new world for themselves, through her eyes:

> At the peak of the Antarctic summer season it is light twenty-four hours a day. The light is bright, sterile, technical, like the light in a hospital operating room. It is unavoidable light that actively seeks and annihilates corners of darkness and mystery. It was a shock to be out with friends, leaving McMurdo's coffeehouse near midnight, and have to blink into the brightness, shading my eyes with my hand. . . .

It is also possible to have a strong voice with no overt "I." Literary journalists like Tracy Kidder often stand at the edge of the circle, observing events and interpreting them with little reference to themselves. In chapter one of *Among Schoolchildren* (Chapter 15, Literary Journalism), for example, he describes teacher Chris Zajac with a strong authorial presence even though he's not overtly in the scene:

> She was thirty-four. She wore a white skirt and yellow sweater and a thin gold necklace, which she held in her fingers, as if holding her own reins, while waiting for children to answer. Her hair was black with a hint of Irish red. It was cut short to the tops of her ears and . . . she was short—the children's chairs would have fit her. Although her voice sounded conversational, it had projection. She had never acted. She had found this voice in classrooms. . . .

Colson Whitehead, too, is a master at creating scenes while keeping the "I" offstage (Chapter 14, Essay of Place). Even his description of the way luggage shifts on a long bus ride makes us feel as if he is there, on the spot:

> Something happens to the bags up there in the luggage racks. When you go to get something out of them they are inexplicably heavier, as if they repacked themselves when you weren't looking. Zippers won't close, hang open in half smiles. Innocuous imperfec-

tions in the highway have consequences. Shampoo oozes onto garments, a drop a mile.

The Need for Outside Voices

"Any voice—no matter how adorable, witty, brilliant, or miraculous—becomes dull over time," writes essayist Steven Harvey in "The Art of Interruption" (see Chapter 16, Stories of Craft). Other voices are needed to affirm, support, challenge, judge; it doesn't matter what so long as they interrupt the monotony of the same voice, page after page. *How to interrupt the monotony of one voice?*

1 **An effective way to do this is to add dialogue.** Hearing conversations as if we are in the scene is always more compelling than hearing about what was said. Had Sanders summarized the silence about his dad's drinking—without dialogue—his essay would not put us in the garage of long ago, listening firsthand.

Some might object, arguing that Sanders cannot include dialogues from the past if he has no record—no audiotape or transcript—of the conversation. We respond that in creative nonfiction, especially memoir, tape recorders or transcripts are not essential. Why? Because the aim is to capture *the spirit* of a relationship. Even in literary journalism, the more fact-based end of creative nonfiction, when writers often tape conversations, they still select and shape recorded conversation to highlight what's important. Verbatim transcriptions, the kind made by courtroom stenographers, for example, may preserve fact for a court of law, but the truth of experience can easily get lost in endless, unedited detail. As writers of creative nonfiction our aim is to capture the essence of what transpired, the *felt truth* of what was said and heard.

Gay Talese, one of the journalists who spearheaded the New Journalism movement that is a forerunner of today's creative nonfiction, says this about using exact quotations: "Since my earliest days of journalism, I was far less interested in the exact words that came out of people's mouths than in the essence of their meaning. More important than what people say is what they think. . . ."

For memoirists depicting their childhoods, this attitude is essential, for how else can they let the people they once knew speak for themselves? Writers can't claim, with credibility, to recall the exact words spoken 15 or 50 years ago. What they can claim is to offer the truthfulness of the relationships *as they remember them*. (For a fuller discussion of this issue, see chapter 10, The Ethics of Creative Nonfiction.)

(2) **Quotations add voices of authority.** We quote famous writers throughout this book, hoping to signal, "You see, we are not the only ones who think this is so! Gay Talese, Joan Didion, Joyce Carol Oates, Patricia Hampl, all these writers are on our side." And it's not just the famous who enrich a text, as Brian Doyle shows in his essay, quoting random Brian Doyles whom he found on the Internet.

Quoting others, however, does not mean abdicating your own authority. The writer stays in charge, as essayist Steven Harvey makes clear: "I get to play with the words of those who have, for the moment, usurped my own. I make them my own." He shows us how he keeps control, simply by deciding where to interrupt his speaker (Chapter 16, Stories of Craft). In this case, his power comes from deciding where to put the phrase "Orsino says" in Shakespeare's quotation: "If music be the food of love, play on."

> If I put the "he [Orsino] says" there, at the comma, I share Shakespeare's notion that his sentence is about love, the word just before the interruption. If I want to shift our attention away from love to music, I change the syntax. "If *music,*" Orsino says, "be the food of love, play on." On days that I'm particularly fussy I might try an earlier interruption, "*If,*" Orsino says, "music be the food of love, play on." And when I'm feeling downright athletic I would write the sentence this way: "If music be the food of love, *play,*" Orsino says, "on."

(3) **Opposing points of view (OPV) add credibility.** When he teaches a class on "Argument and Persuasion," our friend and colleague Jack Connor always talks about the need for OPV. Without it, the writer sounds one-sided, unreasonable, on a soapbox or a high horse. With it, the writer becomes someone who sees the world in more than one

dimension. Credibility goes up; so does complexity and dramatic tension.

You can add OPV by challenging your own opinion. If you write, "My stepmother never said one nice word to me" and prove it in four pages of details, you must think of one time when she was nice, if not to you, then to someone else. Add it, and see how it deepens your argument, as Lee Martin shows in his essay, "Telling Our Private Truths." Martin talks about how his childhood with his father was both tender and violent. Both sides were needed to depict the truth. (Visit our website at <hmco.college/english> to read Martin's essay.) You might also let another character add OPV, the way Connie Weineke lets her mother speak for herself in "Snakebit" (see Chapter 12, Personal Essay). The tension of two voices remembering one event is what makes her essay work.

How to Find the "Right" Voice

Sometimes the "right" voice appears early on. Sometimes it appears only late in the process—*after* we have grappled with our subject for a while. The more emotionally loaded the subject, the more that early voice can mislead us. It may be too angry or too mild, too full of self-pity or too flip, too earnest or too know-it-all. Often, it takes time and many drafts to write our way into a truer voice that one day magically appears. When it does, we smile, gratefully, and write on, still listening.

You never know when the "right" voice will appear, but these strategies may quicken its arrival:

- ❧ Write a first draft quickly without thinking about voice. Remember, you can't consciously choose a voice; it chooses you. Trying too hard for voice will lead to a stilted self-consciousness.

- ❧ Let the draft sit for a few hours, a day, a week—long enough for you to switch hats from writer to reader and so gain the detachment needed to hear yourself as others will.

> ❧ Read your draft aloud. When your reading voice drops or flattens out, you know your written voice is off.

> ❧ Listen for rhythms that are often buried in an early draft. In an article describing the move from gathering research to drafting, Pulitzer Prize–winning journalist Donald Murray first created a dull opening. Reading it over, he heard a rhythm he liked which led him to a voice he liked—which led him to delete the first twenty-two words and then add eight more:

Original:

~~Unless I am completely controlled by a deadline and forced to~~

~~write before I have completed my research, I am aware that~~ it is

time to ~~think about~~ writ~~i~~ng when I know the answers ~~I will~~
to my questions
~~receive to my questions~~ before I ask them~~e~~, when I know

what my sources reveal before I read them.

Revised:

["It is time to write when I know the answers to my questions before I ask them, when I know what my sources reveal before I read them."]

—*A Writer Teaches Writing*

> ❧ If you don't trust your voice, try a new beginning, or two, using a new tone. If you were earnest the first time, try lightening up. If you wrote with great anger, try for more compassion. Don't be false. Just try to get in touch with other dimensions of feeling that may have been buried or silenced but are valid.

A Question of Authenticity

In academic circles, the term "voice" raises questions about identity. Can one ever really write in an authentic voice? Isn't the notion of a genuine voice naïve because the language we speak is always based on class, culture, race, and gender? We say, yes, of course. Voice is constructed—but constructed doesn't mean false. Authenticity, for writers, means finding the language to convey the complexity, irony, and ambivalence of what we—as individuals—experience in our lives. In creative nonfiction, in particular, we are not making universal claims of Truth, but rather presenting one person's truths about the nonfiction world. For that we need a voice that speaks the words that, as Adrienne Rich says, have "the heft of our living behind them."

For us, then, writing true is an invitation to plumb the depths within ourselves, to find the right voice(s) for the occasion, one(s) able to capture what matters in the worlds we inhabit. Our capacity to do so is what empowers us. This is particularly true for those who are least heard, who often feel little if any entitlement to speak— or write. Creative nonfiction, we suggest, is the most democratic of genres, for it legitimizes the right of all of us to tell our real stories, in real voices—not made-up ones. If done well enough, whatever the subject, however controversial, others who may not agree may still listen.

★ Read aloud, pp 210-211 as class
Then

Ways In...   *★ pg 183-184 aloud as class*

Assign in class

1. Writing in the Voice of Innocence and Experience

A. Think of a first in your life: first kiss, first communion, first night away from home, first secret, first Big Mac, first betrayal, first whatever. . . . Choose something that happened before you were 16. Write, as Mimi did, in first-person present tense—as if you were again 8 or 10 or 12 years old. ["I *sit* in Mrs. Tan's class, sure that Jimmy *sees* me. . . ."] Try to capture the voice of who you once were, choosing the words, rhythms, and attitudes you had at the time. Aim for the immediacy of the moment by using lots of sensory data—sights, sounds, smells, touches, tastes, objects, other voices. Tip: Before writing, read Alice Walker and Lisa Chavez (see Chapter 11, Memoir) to see the power of present tense.

Then Do B — In class

B. Now write about the same experience as an adult looking back. ["How cocky I *was* in Mrs. Tan's class, like I was Madonna and Superman all in one."] Reflect on why you felt that way and why this memory still sticks with you today. What was at stake then, and do you still feel that way today?

C. Read both out loud and decide which voice you like best for writing more. If both seem equally appealing, you might want to continue with both. Shift back and forth, the way Sanders does in "Under the Influence" (see Chapter 12, Personal Essay).

2. Adding Other Voices

Pick an entry from your notebook on a topic you care about. Interview at least two people about their ideas and experiences on this topic. Work in a quote or dialogue based on your findings, as Brian Doyle does in "Being Brians" and Connie Weineke does in "Snakebit."

3. Adding OPV

Find a line or two in your writing that expresses a strong opinion. Write against that opinion. For example, if you wrote "My sister Jenny always drove me crazy, especially in high school," think of a time she didn't. Or think of what she might say about you, her OPV. Add it to your text: "Of course, I drove Jenny crazy, too. . . ."

4. Adding Dialogue

If you are a writer who doesn't use much dialogue, discover its possibilities. Find a place in a draft that seems ripe for a scene with conversation and add three or four lines of dialogue, the way Sanders does:

"What's up, buddy?" he says, thick-tongued and edgy.
"Sky's up," I answer, playing along.
"And don't forget prices," he grumbles. "Prices are always up. And taxes."

Tips for writing dialogue: Start each speaker with his or her own paragraph, as Sanders does. Use gestures to enrich what is being said, as Sanders does ("he says, thick-tongued and edgy"). Try to set up a tension between what is said and what is thought. Dialogue should do more than tell the readers what they already know.

5. Analyzing Where "I" Stands

Choose several readings and/or several of your notebook entries. Analyze where the "I" stands in each.

[handwritten notes:]

☀ tell students you will call them up to discuss research topic while they are writing

Ask Students to read a few aloud in class — if time permits. If not have them rework + be ready to share next class.

→ go over a few A's.
☀ Visitors writing
library wed.

Twenty Ways to Talk About Creative Nonfiction

Listen to seasoned writers talk about work-in-progress and you will often hear terms like "back-story," "foreshadowing," and "pacing" to point out strengths and weaknesses. Terms like these lead to deeper discussions than is possible with a vocabulary built on "It flows!" or "It needs more!" The glossary below is a compilation of some of the most frequently used terms for talking effectively about writing. Use them to think about your own work-in-progress, to comment on the work of others, and to analyze the readings in the anthology.

1   **Back-Story:** A story never occurs only in the moment; it has a context. The characters had lives before the readers met them; the events discussed had forces that shaped them. The back-story provides the social, political, cultural, and personal context that is relevant information for the reader to know, information that the writer often takes for granted. If you hear, "But what's the back-story?" you need to add more history about the characters (who they were) and the events (what happened) before your story begins. Research often helps.

2   **Challenging Your Own Assumptions:** One way to avoid predictability is to challenge your own assumptions. If your brother means everything to you, think of something that isn't dear and sweet about him and show why you love him anyway. Using what we call opposing points of view (OPV) is a fine way to present—through dialogue and reflection—perspectives other than your own.

3   **Cliché:** Good writing means avoiding the obvious in your observations and in your use of language. If you hear, "It's clichéd," you are offering the reader no surprises. At a language level, "clichéd" refers to stock phrases like "the sparkling blue water" and "the crystal clear air." At a subject level, it refers to obvious sentiments such as "Falling in love was the best part of growing up." Without words like "but . . ." or "until . . ." that demand complication, there is no dramatic tension. Readers may be pleased that you fell in love, but they'll find nothing compelling about that.

Delivering on a Promise: Every piece of writing sets up a promise in the first paragraph that it must deliver on by the last paragraph so that readers feel satisfied. If you hear, "It set up a promise it didn't deliver," you better take a look at your beginning and then examine your ending.

Facing the Dragon: This term refers to the need to write toward the tensions of the subject, not away from them. The more emotionally loaded the subject, the greater the difficulty in facing the dragons. But even less personal forms, like literary journalism, have dragons lurking in them — sensitive topics that make writers back away from the fire, fearing self-revelation or reader disapproval, or both.

Factual versus Emotional Truth: These terms refer to the different ways we can depict what "true" is. Factual truth is the "who, what, when, and where" that most people agree upon: the time, date, location, hair color, number of people — whatever is verifiable. Emotional truth refers to how one person responds to an experience. It is subjective, the experience seen through the writer's eyes. If you hear, "Where are you in all this, what is your point of view?" you need to move beyond the facts. If you hear, "This is too much in your head, too abstract for me to feel grounded," you need to add more external details.

Flatness of Dialogue: This phrase is used when the language doesn't sound as if real people are talking. The usual problem: either every voice sounds the same or the dialogue is being used as exposition (to provide information) rather than to recreate a scene.

Foreshadowing: Even with surprise endings, readers like to feel as if they could have guessed what was coming. Then the surprise is accompanied by a satisfying, "Of course." If there are no clues, there is no foreshadowing—i.e., the hints that make what happens next seem inevitable, at least in retrospect. For example, if you open with humor and end with tragedy, you need to fore-shadow that something tragic might happen. Movies use music to alert us. Writers use words.

9 **Narrative Arc:** Where did the writing end up *vis-à-vis* its begin-ning? How have characters changed? What's been learned by writer and reader? The narrative arc spans the entire writing from beginning to end. To see it, writers must stand back and look for the big picture of dramatic movement needed in their work.

10 **Narrative Tension:** Every piece of writing has tension points that draw the writer toward the subject and, if well developed, keep the reader engaged. Too often the tensions are avoided, leaving readers asking, "Why, of all the stories you can tell, did you choose this one?" or "What's at stake here?"

11 **Pacing:** This term refers to how quickly or slowly the writing moves along. If someone says, "It takes too long to get there!" the pacing is too slow. If someone says, "It goes by too quickly!" the pacing is too fast. Tip: The latter often happens at key mo-ments, full of tension that needs exploring.

12 **Riffs:** Borrowed from jazz, the word in writing refers to digres-sions that give back-story about characters and events—and/or offer scenes and reflections by the writer. A riff can move away from the main story for a paragraph or several pages before return-ing back to it. If you hear, "I'd like a scene here," or "I'd like to know more about. . .", then consider a riff.

13 **Serving the Story:** This phrase refers to the need for every part of the writing, be it a short essay or a full-length book, to add something to the whole. When someone says, "This doesn't serve the story," you need to consider cutting. When writing episodically, ask yourself, "In what way does each episode serve the whole?"

Showing and Telling: This pair refers to the need to recreate scenes (showing) and to reflect on them (telling). They must be in balance for the writing to work. If someone says, "Show more, tell less!" that means you are summarizing events without letting readers experience them. If someone says, "But what do *you* think? Where do *you* stand?" he or she is asking for reflection that reveals your point of view.

Split Focus: Often a piece seems to be about two or more things, which is fine as long as connections emerge through the writing. If that doesn't happen, the problem is called a split focus. The writer must ask: "What, if any, are the connections here?" "Why is this all one story?" Then rewrites are needed to make the connections clear. Sometimes that involves subordinating one idea to another or omitting one focus, saving it for another time.

The Extraordinary in the Ordinary: Often the big stories are in the small ones. A writer's job is to find them in the world and make them shine. We must also look for them in our own writing, finding "the nuggets in 50 tons of dirt," as James Dickey reminds us.

The Story: What's the story here? That is a central question for writer and reader alike. "Story," in this context, does not refer to the plot, but to the meaning of the piece: *why* the writer wrote it, *why* the reader should care. If you hear, "I understand what is happening here, but I don't really know why it matters," you need to figure out what your piece is about and convey that.

Trusting your Readers: Writers need to have faith in their readers' abilities to "get it." If you hear, "No need to beat me over the head!" you may need to be subtler in your word choice and refrain from repeating the same thing over and over again. (Hint: It often involves cutting adjectives and adverbs that clutter as in

"The cute, cuddly, sweet Panda sat quietly and patiently on the soft, white, pristine bedspread. . . .")

Verisimilitude: Fact is stranger than fiction, people like to say. All the more reason for verisimilitude, which literally means "the appearance of being true." An event may have happened exactly as you said, you may have won the lottery on the day the credit card company dropped you, but that is not good enough. What *is* true must also *seem* true, for readers to believe you are credible and not making life up to be interesting.

Voice: If a piece of writing does not have a strong authorial presence, a sense that an individual has written the words, it lacks "voice." Voice is at the heart of creative nonfiction, whether "I" is used or not. If the voice is "off," the writer must adjust it. If the prose sounds anonymous, like an automaton, the writer best start again.

CHAPTER 6

Workshopping a Draft

Writing is a communal act.

— NATALIE GOLDBERG

For most of us, the first stage of writing is a solitary struggle to produce a decent draft, something that interests us, something with potential. But what happens next, when we want to improve the draft? The struggle can remain a solitary one, or we can try to bring other views and voices into our writing by doing what is often called *workshopping a draft.*

Workshopping invites a group of "live" readers to tell us what they hear in our work-in-progress. Some groups are large, some are small; either way their purpose is to let the writer know what's coming across in the writing, what they see as strong, and what they sense might be missing. More and more writers, in classrooms, in libraries, or in living rooms, are discovering that this sort of response can mean the difference between producing a mediocre work and a strong one. Workshopping—if done well and with good spirit—can also turn writing into a social act that is surprisingly pleasurable, one that reinforces the writer's energy, confidence, and insight. This chapter provides strategies to show you how.

Starting Out in a Writing Group

You are in a group with three other writers.[1] Everyone is working on a piece. Everyone has brought copies for each member of the group. You have 75 minutes. You divide up the time so that everyone gets an equal share.

You volunteer to go first and pass out copies of your draft. You are tempted to say, "This isn't very good. I'm not happy with it," but you suppress the urge, knowing that such disclaimers arise because you are trying to mask your nervousness. You tell yourself this is how everyone feels.

You read your piece out loud. It's a slice of life about going to see the film *Dogville*. You're not sure about the tone or the balance. Is the piece really about you or the movie? But you don't say any of this yet. You just start reading.

You read slowly, tasting the words in your mouth, and by the second page, your voice is stronger. You are feeling a bit more sure. This isn't so bad. When you finish reading, you look up. You want to hear the group's reactions immediately, but you know it takes a minute or more for readers to figure out what to say. You wait quietly, expectantly.

You are in a new group, using a technique called *active listening*. The task of your readers is to tell you what they have heard in the piece. Not what they like or dislike, not what the piece makes them think of, not their good ideas for what you might do next, certainly not which words you misspelled: *No*. Their initial task is to listen carefully to the piece and then *to say back to you what they have heard*.

A guy, let's call him Tom, sitting to your right, begins. "You are writing about seeing *Dogville,* and how odd you found it, how beautiful Nicole Kidman is, and how she reminded you of an angel. I feel as if the piece is about your own desire to find something . . . I don't know, maybe redeeming in it? Or in yourself?"

---

[1] We use a group of four here for illustration. But these practices can be readily used in any large or small group format, with partners, in trios, in class—or out.

You are excited. Tom has captured precisely what you were trying to convey—and he's done so in a questioning tone, one that invites you to think more about your intentions. "You're right," you say. "I was captivated by Kidman and, yet, in the end I left feeling cheated." But you don't want to say too much until you hear from the other readers. You make a note to return to this idea.

Another reader, Susan, responds: "What I hear in this piece is your anger. I see you wanting to defend the townspeople, and yet they all do such horrible things that you can't like them. I hear you struggling for compassion."

"Hmmm," you say. "I *am* angry, but not at the people. At the conditions. Maybe that's not clear enough yet."

"What I hear," says Alex, your third reader, "is you, the viewer, watching the film in your seat, fantasizing about Nicole Kidman, and you the activist, wanting to change the world. Aren't both present?"

"Maybe," you respond. "I was unsettled by the film so I guess I am also trying to use it to make a social commentary. . . . But I want to go back to the idea of being cheated. It's like everyone in the movie was cheated. Even the dog. It's about a morality that has failed. . . . hey, it just hit me, *that's* what's important to me . . . this idea of failed morality. . . ." Smiling, you jot down some notes so you know where to pick up when you begin writing again.

Active Listening

Active listening is, in our view, the best way to begin response, for novice and veteran writer alike. It sets a thoughtful tone in which people listen carefully to each other's words. Most of us have heard about or experienced writing groups that don't work: when writers leave a group session demoralized by negative comments and/or by advice that feels wrong for the piece. The experience can be so deflating that writers vow never to show their early work to anyone again. We offer a different approach: It begins with active listening. Here's why.

At the early draft stage, what we want to say is, more often than not, still unformed, often fragile. Key ideas and experiences may not be down on paper, but only hinted at, lurking somewhere below the surface. To coax them into the open, we need people who know how to listen generously and respond by giving back to us what they hear, sticking close to our texts. These responses, delivered in kind and thoughtful ways, are what often encourage us to keep going, to keep digging, to keep shaping.

The first step of active listening, then, is for readers to reflect back to the writer what they each hear in the piece. It sounds easy, but it can be quite hard because of the strong urge to judge and offer "good ideas." So if you are an active listener, simply say back to the writer what you hear—without adding anything extra. Keep in mind, though, that you are not a tape recorder. You don't have to memorize the text, just listen for the heart or the gist of the piece and give the writer your sense of what he or she is trying to say.

Your tone is crucial. If you respond to the writing in a series of flat, declarative sentences—"First you said this, then you said that . . ." the writer will merely nod and say, "Yeah, that's right,"— leaving little room for insights in the making. But if you use a questioning tone, even raising your voice slightly at the end of your sentence— "So what I hear you saying is x . . . ?"—you will be helping the writer reach new ground where thoughts and experiences may be reconsidered, modified, and extended. A questioning tone—not a direct question—invites the writer to pause, to take another look, and to say more. He or she might say, "Yes, that's right . . . *and* . . ." or "Well, no, that's not quite it . . . . What I *really* mean is . . . ." Either way, the writer will be off exploring explicitly what was, just a few moments ago, implicit but not expressed in the draft.

Helping the writer explore new ground is, in many ways, the point of this practice. Through active listening, writers confirm what is on the page *and* see the possibilities that lie beyond it. It's as if once we, as writers, have been heard, we are able to move on: able to see what is there and what needs to be there. We also discover what isn't there: where we didn't express what we intended and where we might need to take a new tack. The decision of what to do next is always ours. But now we have other readers' voices in our heads to accompany us as we revisit our drafts.

Beyond Active Listening

For some writers, having others pay close attention to their words is all they need to return to the piece and keep writing productively. Even seasoned writers are often surprised by how gratifying active listening can be. As a veteran of many writing workshops recently told us, "I've been in tons of groups where people told me what to change or what they didn't like, but never before have people just told me, plain and simple, what they heard. I feel as if I've just received a gift." Some groups use all of their time for active listening. But most writers, once they feel comfortable, value direct feedback about what works and what might need more work. This kind of feedback, called *critiquing*, is used when writers have the time, energy, and desire to revise. To include both kinds of responses in a group session, we suggest using about one third of your time for active listening and two thirds for critiquing—and to work in rounds:

Round 1: *Active Listening:* Readers "sayback" the gist of one particular idea they hear in the piece. The writer responds briefly to each reader, using each comment to confirm where the piece is going and/or to extend it by elaborating on a new idea.

Round 2: *What Works Well:* Readers each identify something that works well for them in the piece. It may be a line, a series of images, an insight, a character, a point of view, to name just a few. The writer listens and takes notes but does not necessarily respond.

Round 3: *What Still Needs More Work:* Readers each point out one place in the text where they want to know more, or are confused, or lose interest, or find something that strikes them as off. Because the tendency is to jump to this place first, we recommend that you curb this impulse until this round. The writer mostly takes notes and talks minimally, if at all.

Round 4: *Checking In:* The writer is asked if he or she needs anything else to move the piece forward before the group moves on.

In the beginning, most groups set up a structure that moves from one round to the next, keeping an eye on the clock to make sure there is enough time for each. Later on, as people come to know one another and to understand one another's work, some groups opt for a less formal structure with one round casually merging into the next. And, of course, depending on how developed a draft is, writers should be able to request the kind of response they think would be most useful.

A Writing Group at Work

What happens when writing groups move from active listening to critiquing? Let's listen as three college writers, Nina, Alison, and Michael, enrolled in their first class on creative nonfiction, work together. They have known one another for a month and are beginning to understand each other's strengths and weaknesses.

Nina, a committed but inexperienced writer, passes out copies of her draft. It's the beginning of a personal essay about her cousin, written in segments that move back and forth in time. She has worked on it for days; there are parts she feels pretty good about—and others that just haven't jelled yet. As she reads aloud, Alison and Michael follow along with pens in their hands, marking places to talk about once Nina finishes reading:[2]

> The Channel Four meteorologist proclaims it "a perfect day." The early July temperature is sixty-five at eight this morning. The sky is a blank blue slate, and the occasional breeze washes over my face with a cool flutter as I wait for my cousin Kate on the back porch of her newly renovated house. The honey-stained railing steadily props my feet, and the tilted mug of Mocha Java rests precariously on my knee. The trees have grown huge since my last visit. The gardens that were once pristine are now somewhat wild. The suburb hides behind the walls of feathery Japanese maple, thick oak, and tall, tall prickly holly. A perfect day, the meteorologist claims, is what we've all been waiting for.

---

[2] Nina's draft originally ran to six pages. Due to the limits of space, we present here only the first two.

"Nini, hurry," Kate always called to me when we hiked up the tree-lined hill underneath the canopy of branches that led to Nana's house. Kate grabbed my arm as we dashed through the front door and into the kitchen where the thick aroma of boiling chickens mixed with the faint sweet smell of cinnamon-sugar, poppy seeds, and prunes filled the air. (It seems like a dream, gnawing on the soft succulent capon feet that Nana gave to us for a snack. Now the thought leaves me with a queasy lump in my throat). *The weekend preparations were always completed by sundown on Friday. The cookies were carefully packed in blue tins lined with waxed paper. The chicken wings, legs, and thighs were torn apart and added to the dilled soup broth, and the tender breasts, sprinkled with Hungarian paprika, were set out to cool in the screened back porch. Our grandmother was our only tie to the Sabbath—a tradition that our mothers let slip away.*

"Morning, Nina," Kate half whispers. She looks forward to the weekends, hoping to sleep longer at least one day out of the two she has off from her job at the hospital's cancer clinic. She's been up since six. The routine of the last fourteen years is rhythmically engrained in her body.

"M-m-m-m, good morning." I watch my cousin float across the deck with a platter of fruits and homemade banana-blueberry breakfast bread. Kate always has something delectable waiting for me whenever I come to visit. The freshly made braided mozzarella from Delarosa's farm is the family favorite. I could devour an entire loaf if left alone with the salty cheese and a crusty baguette. "How'd you sleep?" I ask as she passes the platter while nibbling on a tender sweet strawberry that dribbles a deep-pink teardrop on the breast of her nightshirt. "I guess okay. A little restless," Kate answers coolly. My mind is flooded with memories, memories that I can't tell apart from my dreams. . . .

After a pause, Alison begins, providing a response that combines active listening with what works: "I'm really impressed with the rich detail you have, especially the food descriptions and the relationships— you and your cousin, your mothers, your grandmother, the sense that the old ways are not carried on any longer but something has certainly been passed down."

Nina nods. At this point she knows she just wants to listen and take notes, gathering as many responses as she can.

"I agree," responds Michael. "From the Mocha Java to the boiling chickens with all those spices, the cinnamon and the paprika, and then mozzarella cheese and that strawberry, well, you are making my mouth water. But, you know, underneath the pretty picture, the 'perfect day' announced by the meteorologist, I sense some foreboding. As if something is about to go wrong or is already wrong."

"I had a similar thought," says Alison. "It's as if you are hoping for a perfect day for some reason. And when you ask Kate how she slept and she says 'a little restless,' I sense something is wrong with her, especially when the strawberry juice makes a pink stain on her nightshirt. I can see it spreading out across her breast."

Nina looks delighted. "It's not too forced?" she asks. "Too obvious?"

"Not for me," says Alison. "But I do get lost sometimes in all of your long sentences. I'm not sure a breeze can wash your face with a flutter or even if the railing can actually prop your feet up. I can feel that it's one of those wonderful, warm, breezy days at the beginning of summer, but for me there is too much clutter in the sentences. Sometimes I get sensory overload, maybe even in the strawberry image."

"Yeah," says Michael. "A sweet strawberry dripping onto a nightshirt without the teardrop would be enough for me."

Nina puts a check mark on that line.

"I'm also not sure of the time sequence," Michael says. "I'm pretty sure you are starting in the present and then the italics are signaling the past when you and Kate were girls, but when you say in the middle of that passage that sucking on chicken feet makes you queasy today, I am jarred. The adult commentary takes me out of the past."

"I'm also puzzled by one other thing," says Alison. "I can't tell how often you see Kate. You say the trees have grown huge since your last visit, which would mean, to me, it's been years, but then you say that she always has something delicious waiting for you when you visit."

Nina takes notes and then tells Michael and Alison that she and Kate are close, they talk on the phone all the time, but, no, they don't see each other all that often. Kate is ill. Nina does want the reader to sense the fear growing in both of them against the backdrop of their large family. And yes, food figures heavily in their lives, in the past and today.

In the memoir, Nina explains, the two women will soon get dressed and head into the city to see the doctor. Kate has asked Nina to accompany her. The piece will also address Nina's anxiety that she won't be strong enough to help her cousin.

"What's this last line about memories and dreams?" asks Michael.

"Oh, yeah—that—I'm not sure what I was trying to do there," Nina muses. "My memories of our childhood are so vivid and yet they also seem like dreams to me—from another world. I don't know if I should weave in another flashback here or if I should stay in the present, move into the day."

"I think you've made a great start," says Alison, "but soon I'll want to know what's wrong with Kate. You might want to give more of a hint when you talk about the lump in your throat. I'd stay in the present more."

Michael adds, "I don't think you need to decide yet. If it's a long story, you can afford to linger in the past, but if this is going to be short, you may need to stay in the present. Mainly, I think you should just keep writing."

"Thanks," says Nina, smiling. "This has been really helpful."

Principles for Responding

There is no formula or sure-fire way to respond to writing. So much depends on the author's intentions and needs, the dynamics of the writing group, the amount of time available, and the experience of participants. It takes time to learn how to read a draft, to listen sensitively, to figure out what's strong, and to see what isn't there yet. It also takes time to develop a language for talking about writing. Specialized vocabulary—terms like pacing, foreshadowing, narrative arc, and back-story[3]—will ultimately enrich group discussions, but to begin, we offer basic principles and guiding questions that make workshopping interesting, productive, and fun for writers at all levels.

---

[3] See "Twenty Ways to Talk about Writing" at the end of Chapter 5 for terms worth using in writing groups.

Work from Strength

Ask yourself, "What are the strengths of this piece?" Then tell the writer what you like best or what, in your eyes, is most effective, giving specific examples. Focus on what strikes you as particularly strong and interesting, using specific lines and images to make your case. Most important, explain why. Comments like "That's good!" tell the writer little. But if you say, "I can really picture that guy chugging his beer . . ." or "I like the tension in the dialogue on page two . . .", the writer learns a lot.

Be an Active Reader

Let the writer know how the draft affects you: What are you feeling, thinking, experiencing at various points in the text? Writing teacher Peter Elbow calls this providing "movies of your mind." It gives an ongoing account of your reactions as you move through the work. This technique is similar to active listening, only now you are focusing more on conveying your response and less on what you think the writer is trying to say, as in the following example:

> Reader: "I am really with you here as you are sitting on the plane and wondering what awaits you when you get to California. I can feel your annoyance with all the announcements and the small TV screen in front of you that has boring shows on cooking. But then when you deplane, I don't quite see the scene. I know you are looking for your friends and you are worried that they won't show up—when you wipe the sweat from your neck, I can feel your anxiety—but I can't tell exactly where you are as you say this. I feel lost. Are you walking through the terminal? Are you at the luggage area? . . . ."

Help the Writer Delve Deeper

We've found the best way to do this is to ask yourself questions as you are reading. Your answers will help you figure out what to ask the writer so that he or she can flesh out what needs more developing.

Below is a long list to choose from, depending on the draft being workshopped. Tip: These questions are also worth asking when rereading your own drafts before revising.

Basic Questions:

🔥 What are the strengths of this piece? What pulls me in and makes me want to know more? What isn't there yet? What needs connecting? What seems irrelevant right now? What, beside the plot, is this piece trying to be about? What is at stake here? Why did the writer want to write about this?

Detailed Questions for More In-Depth Response:

🔥 *Listening for Voice:* What is the dominant voice of the piece? Is it angry, sad, ironic, humorous, scholarly? Does it pull me in? Why or why not? Is the voice consistent? Are there places where it becomes too formal or informal? If there is more than one voice, is each one distinct? How well do they work together?

🔥 *Studying Scenes and Dialogue:* Where does a scene work— with or without dialogue? Where might dialogue be added? Where does the dialogue sound flat, not like real people talking?

🔥 *Focusing on Setting:* Can I picture the setting? Is more description of place needed to make me feel as if I am there? Where does the description go on too long?

🔥 *Developing Characters:* Where are the characters well drawn? Where do I need to see and hear people more fully?

🔥 *Developing an Argument:* Is an argument being made? What evidence is most convincing? What else might be added? Does the writer include the opposing point of view so that I know what others who may not agree think about this?

🔥 *Looking for Tension:* What are the tension points in the piece? What tensions might be developed further?

❧ *Looking for Growth or Change:* What is the movement of the piece? How have characters changed from the beginning to the end? How has the author's understanding changed? How has my understanding changed?

Be Straightforward—and Sensitive

Let the writer know where you are confused or lost or bored or annoyed by pinpointing the areas that give you trouble. But be sure to use what we call *I-based comments* that tell the writer that this is how you—one reader—see the piece:

> I am lost here. . . .
> I am not sure where you are going with this. . . .
> I can't picture the scene. . . .
> I want to know earlier that. . . .
> It would help me to see. . . .

These comments are much more palatable than comments like, "That's confusing." "You ramble on." "Your characters are weak." Such pronouncements imply that "Any idiot in the world knows that!" and can be insulting, especially to the novice and the thin-skinned. (Aren't most of us?) Our experience is that the main thing writers learn from such comments is to risk little in this group.

When you make suggestions for change, also be aware of tone. Saying "You should do this . . ." or "You should move that there . . ." makes it sound as if you have suddenly taken charge of the piece. It is much more effective to offer suggestions in a tentative way:

> If I were writing this, I'd try. . . .
> What if you tried . . .?
> Have you considered . . .?

Such phrases signal your recognition that the writer, not you, decides what to do next—that your job is to raise possibilities, not take over.

Avoid Using Group Time for Editing

It's easier to talk about commas and spelling than to figure out what works or doesn't work in a piece. So beware. If editing is needed, allot special group time for that, but first, focus on discovering, developing, and extending the writer's meaning using the methods and questions we have described above.

Check in with the Writer

Before moving on, make sure the writer getting feedback feels satisfied. Is there anything not yet addressed? What concerns, if any, does the writer still have about the piece? What still worries him or her? Does the writer have a sense of what to do next? If yes, you've done well. Tip: Watch the clock here and move on after a few minutes.

The Rhythm of a Writing Group

All groups find their own rhythms. Some move quickly; others slowly. Some laugh a lot; others remain serious. Some stay on task and finish promptly; others love getting sidetracked and extending their time. Three men in a writing group in one of Sondra's evening classes became so engrossed in each other's work that their animated discussion accompanied them down three flights of stairs and into the college parking lot, where they would continue talking for another hour or so, even on wintry nights. This group eventually dubbed themselves, "The Parking Lot Guys." Five years after the workshop, they are still writing and still meeting—generally indoors.

The size of a group also affects its rhythm. If your group of three or four meets regularly, responding to work on the spot, your pace will differ from that of a class of twenty, where the entire class responds to pieces they've read in advance. But regardless of the setup—partners, small groups, or whole classes—there are standard moves that help all groups workshop effectively:

Setting Up the Group—Format and Agreements

🔥 Whenever possible, group members should hand out copies of work. It is possible to provide good gut responses without having a copy of a draft in front of you, but for thoughtful, in-depth responses, copies are important. If the group is set up so people get a chance to read and comment beforehand, so much the better.

🔥 Writers should prepare to read their work aloud to the group. Jotting down questions you'd like the group to address also helps. When you go home, you should have some answers.

🔥 See how many people have brought work and how much overall time there is. Then divide up the time so that everyone gets an equal amount.

🔥 Choose someone to serve as timekeeper and stick to the time limits.

🔥 Agree that whatever is discussed in the group, including the content of the work and the responses to it, will remain in the group. No one wants personal stories or sensitive information revealed to those who weren't there.

🔥 Decide on whether to formalize rounds—moving from active listening to what works to suggestions for revision to checking in with the writer—or whether you want to work more informally.

🔥 Make sure all group members respond. Writers should feel free to ask questions of members who are quiet.

🔥 Remember to keep the confidentiality agreement.

🔥 Be kind.

When You are the Writer

🔥 Read your piece aloud, reminding yourself not to rush. No matter how slowly you think you are reading, you are probably going too fast. Slow down. Tip: If the group

doesn't have copies, the piece is short, and there is
sufficient time, read it aloud twice: first, to orient your
listeners; second, to allow them to collect and note their
responses.

❧ After the reading, listen to your peers and take in what
they have to say. During the active listening go-round, respond briefly to each reader, acknowledging if each one
has managed to say back what you were intending to do.
Feel free to say more, to rephrase, rethink, or extend your
ideas. In the later go-rounds of critiquing, talk less and listen more. You already know what you think; you want to
know what others think.

❧ Take notes as others speak. You think you'll remember, but
you won't. You never know what will turn up as relevant or
trigger a new thought when you are revising.

❧ Encourage group members—especially quiet ones—to
elaborate on their responses by stating directly: "I'd love to
know what you think about X," or asking directly, "Can you
tell me more about . . . ?"

❧ Do not feel as if you have to agree with group members or
take their advice. But don't waste time quarrelling with
them. We like Peter Elbow's cardinal rule: "Listen; don't
defend." You will go home and do what you think is best.
Tip: If one person offers a suggestion, it may or may not be
important. If many offer the same suggestion, you may
want to take it more seriously.

❧ Realize that the best response may be the one you have secretly been worried about hearing. That's where you will
likely hit pay dirt.

When You Are a Responder

❧ Set aside the daily distractions and ready yourself to listen carefully, knowing you will be asked to say back what
you hear.

- Jot down or underline words or phrases that catch your attention as the writer is reading. If you have the piece beforehand, you can do that at home. Tip: Ask questions in the margin, put checkmarks next to favorite spots, squiggly lines under what needs work. This kind of preparation makes it easier to be text-specific—and to work quickly. The group can say more in less time. If you are giving the writer your written comments after the group session ends, be sure you include a key to your marks.

- In the first go-round, reflect back what you hear as the main point of the piece, its center of gravity, its tone, its tensions or whatever strikes you as what the author is trying to say.

- Give the author time to respond to your comments, even engaging in a short dialogue.

- Pay attention to group dynamics, making sure that no one reader dominates and that everyone gets a turn to respond with each new round.

- If it is relevant, make a brief connection to your own life ("I had the same thing happen to me on a bus to Chicago, same fear, same thoughts"), but suppress the urge to tell your story. Remember group time is dedicated to the writing, not to you.

- Do your best to be supportive, thinking of yourself more as a coach than a judge. Your aim is to help the writer with his or her work, not to grade it.

- In rounds two and three, beware of a tendency to take over the piece. If you see a problem in the piece, say so, but realize that it is not your job to figure out the solution.

- Be sure to speak your mind, especially if you disagree with comments made by the group. You may be onto something that others are overlooking.

❦ Ultimately, look to answer this question: What do I, as a reader, still need in order to feel satisfied reading this piece?

After Three or Four Meetings

Over time, your role in a group—both as writer and as responder—will become more familiar. If you workshop your drafts with the same people, you come to know whom to count on for what. Some readers are great at finding themes; others, at developing characters; still others, at focusing on language. As a responder, you begin to recognize strengths and weaknesses of drafts more quickly. If you work with the same people, you'll learn who usually needs to add detail, who gets lost in too much detail, whose voice lapses into stiffness, who needs help with endings.

Aside from the help we get and give, workshopping has one final perk: it helps us read our own drafts more effectively. What we admire in others' work—a great image, a lively voice, an innovative form—we look for in our own writing. And what we suggest that others consider—"How about more detail here?" "How about cutting this? It doesn't serve the story." "Why not try some dialogue?"—rings in our own ears as we read our own drafts with the aim to make them better.

Editing Groups

Some writing courses include editing sessions that focus specifically on grammar and punctuation. For those doing this, consider these two strategies which, we have found, go a long way in helping writers clean up their drafts.

❦ *Read your work aloud.* If you are working with a partner or a small group, pass out copies of your draft and then read it out loud as others listen. Ask your peers to notice when there is a mismatch between what you read aloud and what is on the page. Often we "read in" the word we want and don't notice that we have written something else. Slowing down, paying attention to the words and word endings, helps to clean up a draft.

❧ *Look for patterns of errors.* Errors tend to fall into patterns. An analysis of a paper with 50 marked errors will likely reveal 5 different errors each repeated 10 times. If you are often told to "Proofread your work," see if you can determine which types of errors you make. What category do they fall under: verb tenses, subject-verb agreement, homonyms, fragments, run-ons? If you can identify the kinds of errors you make, you can proofread looking specifically for—and then correcting—one type at a time.

If editing and proofreading give you trouble as a writer, we recommend working with a friend or a colleague whose ear for language you trust. If you have access to a college writing center, work with a tutor there on grammar and punctuation. Most important, invest in one of the excellent handbooks currently on the market.[4] They have easy-to-use indices for quick answers to questions like: Should I use "lay" or "lie" here? How do I punctuate dialogue? Am I overusing the dash or underusing the semi-colon? Once you have a draft you care about, finding the correct form matters if you want others to care. We liken it to wearing a knock-out shirt or dress with a stain on it. Leave it there, and the only thing people will notice is the stain.

Variations on Group Work

❧ If your group will be meeting weekly, you can set up a writing and response schedule that works for each member, deciding ahead of time who will bring work on which dates.

---

[4] We recommend Ann Raimes, *Keys for Writers: A Brief Handbook,* 4th ed., Boston: Houghton-Mifflin, 2005, or Diane Hacker, *A Writer's Reference,* 4th ed., Boston: Bedford/St. Martin's, 1999.

❧ When you are working on pieces that extend beyond four or five pages, consider giving drafts to group members a day or two before the group meeting, via e-mail if possible. Then when the group meets, you can choose just a few pages to read aloud, knowing that your group has already had a chance to read the entire draft.

❧ If you are well into your work and you have specific questions about it, you can begin by describing your concerns and telling the group what kind of response you would like.

❧ If you have time to respond in writing before the group meets, here are two ways to write comments that the writer will find helpful to read:

> *Margin Notes:* These let you ask questions, point out what works, suggest where to cut or add, etc. right where the suggestion occurs to you. You can use a highlighter to indicate what you like best. Or you can use a series of codes: a smiley face or a straight line in the margin to indicate something you like; a wavy line to indicate an area that leaves you confused or feels awkward. Be sure to let the writer know your code.

> *End Note:* This lets you give an overview that margin notes cannot. We suggest writing a letter, starting with "Dear _____," and ending with your signature. Begin with what you think the piece is about, move on to what touches you about the piece, what you see as its strengths, and what you think the writer should keep in mind when rewriting. Remember to use "I-based comments": "I suggest. . . ." not "You should. . . ."

Responding as a Social Act

Writing groups bring others into our work. They end the isolation of writing and embed it within a lively, social context, full of engaging talk and collaboration. When groups work, they enliven us—bringing others into our lives and bringing us into theirs—all through the language we use. Eventually, as drafts turn into finished pieces, it's fun and rewarding to share them again with the group. After all, these fellow writers, like midwives, assisted in the birth of a new work—and are often understandably proud to see what has grown from their efforts.

Even the best writing group won't solve all the problems in our drafts. But when groups work well, when the members workshop the drafts so that writers see them freshly, everyone goes home with new energy and creativity for revision – the subject of the next chapter.

Ways In. . .

1. To practice active listening, try it with one partner. Take turns saying back what you hear on a draft and then discuss what was helpful and what wasn't. Be sure to use a questioning tone, as in, "So what you are writing about is . . . ?"

2. After working in a writing group for several sessions, discuss how the group is working—orally or in writing. Consider: What has worked? What hasn't? What do you wish could happen? This is a useful way to make adjustments to improve the group.

3. Find a piece of published writing, and ask yourself, "If this writer were in my writing group, what would I say about what I like, where I'd like more information, where I am confused, an- noyed, overwhelmed." Write a letter to that writer and send it— or not. Either way, this is a great way to practice becoming a bet- ter, more articulate reader.

4. Go over "Twenty Ways to Talk about Writing" (pp. 80–84). By yourself or as a group, see how many examples of these terms you can find in one reading in the anthology. Or go through your own work—in a notebook or an essay—and see how many of these terms apply. Share your observations with another writer.

5. For teachers or large group facilitators: Early in the semester set up a "fishbowl of four" to demonstrate, and then discuss, the dynamics of workshopping. Ask one writer to bring copies for the entire class and three others to serve as the writing group. The four move their chairs into the middle of the room (they are in the fishbowl) and workshop one piece using the rounds we discussed early in the chapter. After the group has finished, the onlookers discuss what they noticed, what responses seemed to work well, and what suggestions for improvement they had. Be sure to invite "the fish" to comment on what this experience was like for them.

CHAPTER 7

The Craft of Revision

I have never thought of myself as a good writer. Anyone who wants reassurance of that should read one of my first drafts. But I'm one of the world's great rewriters.

— JAMES MICHENER

Beginning writers often assume that talent and luck determine writing success, but experienced writers know to credit one more key factor: revision — and its power to transform early drafts into worthwhile work. Pulitzer Prize–winning author James Michener, who has written a dozen best-sellers, expects that good writing *is* rewriting, a given, a fact of the daily writing life. You do it until you've solved most problems, even if you are Ernest Hemingway.

> HEMINGWAY: I rewrote the ending to *Farewell to Arms,* the last page of it, 39 times before I was satisfied.
>
> INTERVIEWER: Was there some technical problem there? What was it that had you stumped?
>
> HEMINGWAY: Getting the words right.

It's that simple and that hard: to get the words right. Even when we don't need 39 drafts, we should expect revision to be an integral part of our writing process, involving as much, or more, energy than the first draft did. It's easy to read published authors and assume their words appeared effortlessly on the page; but some renowned veterans like John Kenneth Galbraith admit the truth: "There are days when the result is so bad that no fewer than five revisions are required. In contrast, when I'm greatly inspired, only four revisions are needed."

In Chapter 4, Taking Shape, we talked about the kind of intuitive revision that happens as the first rush of language moves us toward a solid draft. In this chapter we focus on what happens *after* writers have a draft with a promising topic, voice, and shape. This kind of revision works best when writers are able to let the draft sit for a while — a day, a week, a month, sometimes longer. Time provides the much-needed distancing to approach the text with a fresh eye and ear. So does useful feedback from readers. (For more on responding, see Chapter 6, Workshopping a Draft.) Armed with both, the time is right for the craft of revision. It's still an intuitive act, sparked by reentering the text after a writing break; but it's also sparked by a more conscious and critical assessment of a draft's language and meaning.

The Situation and the Story

Vivian Gornick, in a wonderful little book on creative nonfiction called *The Situation and the Story,* makes the distinction between "the situation"— the events we depict — and "the story" that makes that situation worth writing about. The first, "the situation," is easy to write down; it's the plot line, the facts of what happened, the "who, what, when, where, and how." The second, "the story," is more elusive and much more important for success. Gornick explains the difference this way:

> The situation is the context or circumstance, sometimes the plot; the story is the *emotional experience* that preoccupies the writer; the insight, the wisdom, the thing one has come to say.

One way to look at revision is as the act of discovering *why* "the situation" matters and then conveying that *why* in a way that will make readers care. This means finding "the story" that drives the telling and sharpening its focus so that whether or not readers know the writer, they are engaged. "The situation" alone won't do that, because most of us are ordinary people reacting to real life experiences. We are neither famous nor renowned experts in our fields, so our "situations" are rarely of inherent interest. It's "the story"—*our* take on "the situation," *our* struggle to understand it — that makes our words, if we find the right ones, of interest. As Gornick puts it, "What happened

The Bull (December 18, 1945)

The Bull (December 24, 1945)

The Bull (January 2, 1946)

to the writer is not what matters; what matters is the larger sense that the writer is able to make of what happened."

To find where "the story" lies, Gornick says that "the power of imagination is needed." By "imagination," she is not referring to the imaginary or to make-believe. Rather, she means a power to go beyond the obvious and make leaps through language into new understandings and new expressions of what is true. That power resides, as we've said often in this book, in a willingness to explore, to take risks, to experiment, to be receptive to new insights. It also resides in the craft of revision, which literally means re-seeing what "the story" really is—first for ourselves and then for others.

Picasso's Bulls

To understand how imagination and the craft of revision go hand and hand, look at four of Pablo Picasso's drawings of a bull (pages 108–110). What changes occur from his early rendering of the bull to his last one? How do they affect you as viewer?

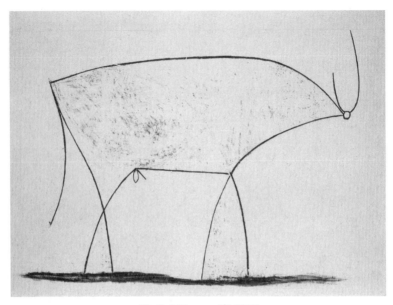

The Bull (January 17, 1946)

In this series, we can see how Picasso's imagination worked to find "the story" of the bull. Others, through revision, might tell a different "story." But this series belongs to Picasso; it depicts his vision of what constitutes "true."

Knowing Your Writing and Rewriting Style

Some writers think a lot before they start, revising before they've written one word. They try out lines and paragraphs in their heads, they talk to friends, they read magazines and books, they may even lift weights or clean closets, waiting for good ideas and a structure to announce themselves before they begin. Others write first, knowing they will discover what is good later on. Like James Michener, they count on revision to create something worthwhile out of the messiness of an early draft.

Those who write first rarely have writer's block because they set the initial bar of expectations low: just write. Those who raise the bar at the outset may have less uncertainty in revision, but more *angst* getting started. Both approaches can produce fine finished work if writers know their styles and how to raise or lower the bar as needed.

This morning I took the hyphen out of Hell-bound and this afternoon I put it back.

— EDWIN ARLINGTON ROBINSON

Once the first words appear, styles again differ. Some writers put down everything that comes to mind; the more language that flows out, the better. For them, revision will mean deciding what's best of what's there. Others hold back, looking for structure and shape. Revision, for them, will mean filling in what has only been sketched.

Sondra is the first kind of writer, what we call an *overwriter.* Her first drafts tend to be too full, ideas going off in many directions. Revision is where she cuts back and finds more focus, as you can see in what happened to the first paragraph of her memoir about teaching in Austria:

Early draft — opening paragraph:

> When the phone rings one January morning in 1996, I have no inkling that the invitation I am about to accept will change my life. I have not even the faintest idea that agreeing to teach a group of Austrian teachers will be the beginning of an odyssey, one that beckons me toward an uncertain future and pulls me back into a painful past. On that Monday morning, I hear only a voice at the other end of the line proposing a fascinating piece of work. Nothing more. Initially I am elated and even flattered.

Final draft:

> When the phone rings one January morning in 1996, I have no inkling that the invitation I am about to accept will be the beginning of an odyssey. I hear only a voice at the other end of the line proposing a compelling piece of work.
> — *On Austrian Soil: Teaching Those I Was Taught to Hate*

Sondra says she made these changes because the phrase "will change my life" seemed too dramatic for an opening. So did "beckons me toward an uncertain future and pulls me back to an uncertain past." It's not that these sentiments weren't true. They were. But Sondra felt, "The entire paragraph told too much too soon. Why should anyone care if I'm elated or flattered? The reader doesn't even know me yet."

Mimi, on the other hand, is the second kind of writer, the *under-writer*. Her first drafts tend to be skimpy, but once down on paper, she fleshes them out. See how she turned a skeletal opening into a full one for her essay, "Sultan and the Red Honda":

Early draft of paragraph one:

> When I was a child I rode black stallions to be brave. Each Saturday I took the Metropolitan Avenue bus over to Forest Park in my jodhpurs and boots to gallop through the trails, hoping the picnickers and old men and women on their daily walk would look up and say, "Look at her go!" I didn't like it as much when the horse reared once at the stable door and threw me on my face scratching it and skinning my knees so badly that the blood when it dried caked around the rip in my jodhpurs. When I limped onto the bus to go home that day, those old men and ladies looked at me and probably said, "Poor Girl." I didn't like that at all.

Final draft:

> Once upon a time I rented horses to be free. I'd climb on the Queens Metropolitan Avenue bus every Monday, Wednesday and Saturday and head for Stanley's Stables twenty minutes away. There Stanley or his brother Jake would give me Sultan or Rajah or Calamity Max to ride — not around the ring like the other kids, but into Forest Park, alone.
>
> They knew I could sit a horse, they said. So I'd prance across Union Turnpike (even if the light were red) and gallop down trails, where I'd hope picnickers and old men and women on walks would look up and say, "Look at her go!" Up in that saddle, racing through the woods, I wasn't the shy, slouch-shouldered kid who everyone was always telling to stand up straight and smile. I was Roy Rogers,

Elizabeth Taylor and the Lone Ranger all in one: a hero, a winner, a star.

Of course there were off days, like the time when Sultan, whom I loved best because he was wild and liked my carrots, bucked at the stable door and threw me face down into the gravelly dirt. As I limped onto the bus to go home that day, blood caked at the knees of my ripped jodhpurs, everyone stared and shook their heads as if to say, "Poor girl!"

I didn't like that at all. . . .

The small word changes in the first line — "rode" to "rented" and "brave" to "free" — were a creative trigger, says Mimi. "They led me to wonder what riding that rented stallion had to do with buying a red Honda thirty years later. I wrote the essay to find out." Visit our website at <college.hmco.com/English> to read the full essay.

Overwriters and underwriters can both produce great writing — if the writer knows what to do next. The first revises by asking: What's the story here? What, of all I've written, is essential? What can I get rid of? The second must ask: Where can I say more? Where do I need detail or dialogue to make the story come alive? Of course, these questions are asked by all revisers, but depending on style, successful writers know which ones they need to ask more often.

Revision for Better — or Worse

Whatever our writing style, there's one revision tendency all writers must be wary of: rewriting the life out of a piece. Sometimes it happens when an overactive censor inhibits naturalness and the voice stiffens, becoming guarded, distant, false. Sometimes it comes from the impulse to over-refine language, which makes the piece pretentious. Notebook entries, we find, are often livelier, with a more compelling voice than the works-in-progress they spawn. When this happens, writers are usually trying too hard to be poetic or profound — or trying to camouflage thoughts that seem embarrassing or controversial. So we overwrite, cluttering our initial text, or we cut back too much, as the poet Charles Bukowski captures in "It Doesn't Always Work."

"It Doesn't Always Work"

I knew a writer once
who always tried to tighten his lines

like he'd write
an old man in a green felt hat walked down the street.

change to:
old green man walked down street.

change to:
green man walked.

change to:
green walked.

finally this writer said,
shit, I can't fart,

and he blew his brains
out.

blew brains out.

blew brains.

blew.

To counter the more negative impulses of revision, we save all our drafts, dating them so we know which came first, second, third. Then we compare old and new versions to assess which has more energy, something hard to do in the middle of rewriting. We also show old and new versions to friends or to a writing group. Tip: If you put revisions in bold font, the next day you can go right to what is new and see how well the changes work. Once you like it, switch back to normal font. Another perk of bold: the changes don't "count" yet, so you revise more freely.

Three Versions of One Opening

Writer Kay Boyle wrote this paragraph three times until she found the words she wanted for a scene in "The Ballet of Central Park." We present them out of order. Identify which one she chose as her final version and check the end of this chapter for the answer. It may surprise you.

Draft A:

She wore a short blue dress over the black legs of her leotard, and her pink satin toe shoes were slung over her shoulder by their knotted strings. Her light hair was wrenched away from her scalp into a glossy ponytail, and her eyebrows were jet black and seemingly as perishable as the markings on a night-flying moth.

Draft B:

Over her leotard, she wore a short blue dress, and her ballet slippers, their pink cotton laces knotted together, were carried across her shoulder. Her hair was wrenched back into a glossy ponytail, and her brow was round and smooth as a doll's. But it was her eyebrows that startled one in disbelief. They were as delicate and jet black as the markings on a butterfly's wing, and seemingly as perishable. But they were an ancient and indestructible hieroglyphic, saying: "Generations of wisdom, poetry, and perception have inscribed us on this brow."

Draft C:

Over her black leotard, she wore a short dress of gentian blue, and her ballet slippers were slung across her shoulders by their knotted strings. Her hair, as light as cornsilk, was wrenched back in contrast, and seemingly as perishable as the markings on the wing of a butterfly. But this was deceptive, for they were not to be effaced. They were actually an ancient hieroglyphic which, deciphered, read: "Generations of wisdom, of perception, of finesse and tact have inscribed us on this forehead." Her eyebrows were a grave and enduring statement made to the world.

The Rewriter's Concerns

We may wish for a formula for revision, but there can never be one. Revision will always depend on what is on the page and what we are striving for, unnamed until we see it before us.

Some problems, of course, are recurrent: underwriters need to add material; overwriters need to cut. Other problems may be subject-dependent. An emotionally loaded topic can produce a shaky voice. A memory piece may have gaps that require filling in of missing details through imagination and/or research. A story of first love may have to battle sentimentality and cliché. A piece based on extensive research may lack a compelling voice and narrative flow.

In reading drafts over the years, our own and countless others, we have identified some common needs that writers face while working to make their drafts better. Here are ten to consider.

Adjusting a Shaky Voice

Even in a solid draft, we can lose the voice we needed to maintain our rapport with the reader. We may sound stiff in parts, moving from informal to overly formal, usually when attempting to offer information or opinion. Or we can get too chatty for our purpose or audience. Or we may shift from child to adult without justification. (Tip: This problem often reveals itself in a random shift between present tense and past tense within a sentence or paragraph.) Reading aloud is the best way to find a problematic voice. Your ear will hear where you need to rewrite a passage in a more convincing voice. And if the whole draft sounds flat, don't bother to revise. Instead, start again.

Facing the Dragon

There are tensions in every piece; it's often these tensions that draw us, usually unconsciously, to our subject. Revision makes these tensions conscious — for writer and reader — if we are willing to write toward them. Writer Sue Miller calls the process "facing your dragon." In a talk on revision (see Chapter 16, Stories of Craft), she describes the difficulties she faced when writing a memoir about her father's

Alzheimer's disease. It took years because she was struggling with underlying tensions that involved her lifelong relationship with her father. Until she confronted what she had avoided and faced this "dragon," the book remained stalled. That is what writers must do, she says, "whether they triumph (slay the dragon), or whether they're defeated (are slain, devoured)." Happy to say, her memoir, *The Story of My Father,* is now in print. Here's an excerpt:

> My first memory of my father, for instance, is not truly of him but of his absence. Actually, it's one of my first clear memories of any kind. My earlier recollections are fragmentary, odd home movies that show only an out-of-context scene or two before breaking off and flickering dark. This memory, though, is sharp and clear — it has meaning for me as well as detail. And the meaning is that my father has left us: he's gone away.
>
> This was the scene: I was five. My father was in Germany for a long stay, a half-year stay. On a warm early summer's day, a friend of my parents came to take pictures of us — of my mother and my younger sister and baby brother and me — to send to

him. Peculiarly, I can remember clearly the chair we sat in to be
photographed. It was painted a bright blue. It had been set out
in the backyard for this session. The backyard was a communal
one, behind several apartment buildings on the south side of
Chicago in the university neighborhood — Hyde Park. The yard
was hard-packed dirt for the most part, worn barren by the
play of all the children who used it daily. The chair looked strange
to me, out of place and wrong, plopped down out there.

What I remember most of the picture taking was the sense
of yearning connection I felt, thinking of my father as I looked
straight into the camera.

Thinking of my picture, but not me, going to him, far across
the ocean. He had been away at that point for three or four
months — he left soon after my baby brother was born — and
would be gone about three months more.

My memory, then, is not really of him but of the effort of
trying to construct him in my mind, of struggling to imagine
him, of missing him. My memory is of memory, working to find
its object.

—*The Story of My Father*

Notice how Miller's ease with language in this final version does not
reveal the years of struggle, and countless revisions, from which that
ease emerged.

Sharpening the Focus

Often a piece seems to be about two things that may or may not be
connected. We call this a *split focus*. The writer, in revision, must ask:
Which of these is most important? What's the piece really about? And
how are the parts connected? Is there a form that can contain both?
The answer will involve strengthening those connections, subordinating one to the other or, maybe, dropping one for another time.
But think hard before dropping completely. There's a temptation to
"keep it simple"— too simple, so that what remains is clearer, but
duller, and tension-free. The aim in revision is to cut what doesn't
serve "the story" and keep what complicates or contradicts. That's
where the tensions lie.

Transforming Shopping List Narratives

What we call a *shopping list* narrative is prose that lists fact after fact and event after event without selection or point of view. *This happened and then this happened, and then this, and this.* . . . Such narratives reflect what Vivian Gornick means by "the situation" without "the story." To avoid such lists, choose key points to develop, the ones that matter most. Quickly summarize the others or drop them as irrelevant to serving this particular story. The principle is the same whether you are writing a research paper, easily prone to become a shopping list of facts and quotations with minimum interpretation, or a travel memoir, easily prone to become a catalogue of everything that happened day by day.

The same problem can occur when writing autobiographically:

> I was born in Westwood, New Jersey, and lived with my parents, younger brother, and maternal grandmother until I was 7. Then my father requested a job transfer, and we moved to Bridgewater, where I spent the next 17 years of my life, going to a public elementary school, a Catholic high school, and then finally springing to a college near Atlantic City, where I started going to frat parties. I majored in literature and discovered poetry. . . .

Readers won't care much about our student Nicole Ross's list of life events until she finds a focus for an assignment that asked her to write her life story in four pages. Organized around "the stories we tell," Nicole produces a draft that has promise:

> We all have stories, I think, and the stories we tell are carefully chosen. There's the story in which I dance on the table, am witty beyond belief, and everyone wants me. I'm also wearing a slinky black dress and fishnets. That's the one I tell to attractive guys who look at me a certain way. Then there's the story I tell to my conservative grandparents about the latest fraternity party I went to — minus the alcohol, the cops in the bushes, and the guy looped in chains and reeking of Coolwater. . . .

No one cares except your Mama. Unless you make them care.

— NATALIE KUSZ

Adding the Opposing Point of View

Opposing points of view (OPV) add layers of complexity and build in more tension. Rather than eliminate those who don't agree with us, don't like us, or don't support our point of view, let them make their cases. They will help us do what Bret Lott calls, "challenging [our] own assumptions"— a necessary act if meanings are to deepen, moving us closer to the dragon's fire. Events that contradict the main story also count as OPV. If, for example, you are writing about a miserable year, add a good moment — and deal with it — rather than omit everything good.

Developing Back-Story

Early drafts tend to lack contexts. They tell one story without filling the reader in about the background of characters and places that add dimension to the events. Revision, using riffs that can be a line, a paragraph, or a page or more, lets us add descriptions or events that occurred before the story began or reflections that happened after the events ended. It lets us tell more about main characters. It lets us insert research about place, or history, or culture — all of which enrich the storyline.

Adjusting Pacing

Revision means tightening parts that move too slowly and lingering in places where the story moves too fast. That's called *pacing*, and it determines how well the narrative flows, dramatically and thematically. We decide where to speed up and slow down by looking at what we want the overall piece to accomplish. Take our opening to

Chapter 6 on workshopping. We began with this initial draft, which goes on and on:

> When we imagine a writer at work, how often do we see a person, alone, staring at the blank page or the computer screen, struggling for words? How frequently is our image a pain-filled one, the writer, exhausted, the floor strewn with crumpled paper, the story or essay finally finished, each word arrived at through an agonizing search? And once the writer has produced a draft, how eagerly does he or she seek an audience, a friend or a colleague, to share the words wrung so painstakingly from inside? Our answer? Hardly ever.
>
> For most of us, writing is, admittedly, a struggle. And once we have written what we consider to be a decent draft — or sometimes any draft at all — the last thing we want to do is show it to someone else. So much simpler to hand it in and let it go at that. The assignment is finished; the task is complete; it's time to move on to other, more pressing or pleasurable tasks.
>
> This is the scenario as we have come to know it and live it in most colleges and universities. . . .

Several revisions later, 237 words are now the 65 words that ended up in print:

> For most of us, the first stage of writing is a solitary struggle to produce a decent draft, something that interests us, something with potential. But what happens next, when we want to improve the draft? The struggle can remain a solitary one, or we can try to bring other views and voices into our writing by doing what is often called "workshopping a draft."

Why did we cut the rest? Because we decided that not everyone hates to start writing. Because this is a chapter about workshopping, not writer's block. And because it was taking us too long to make our case. If we wanted readers to get excited about workshopping, we needed to pick up the pace. Notice, however, that we also added several phrases to line one, lingering on the word "decent."

At that point we felt we needed to slow down and not rush by the idea too quickly. Tip: To decide on pacing, look for one section overpowering others, and then either cut back, flesh out the others, or both.

Remembering that the Hotter the Subject, the Cooler the Language — and Vice Versa

Highly emotional subjects need understated language while small, silly topics often benefit from exaggerated language. So if you write, "My first love was the most wonderfully exciting thing in my life!" the reader yawns. But if you write, "My front stoop was the most wonderfully exciting thing in my life!" the reader gets interested.

Imagining Your Toughest Reader

Pulitzer Prize–winner Stephen Dunn says that once he has a promising draft, he imagines what his creative writing teacher, Donald Justice, would say to him, and he keeps that in mind while deciding if he's finished or not. We find that thinking of a tough but fair critic helps us find the weak spots before our readers do.

Attending to Copyediting

Lining up subject/verb agreement, adjusting tenses, deciding whether to use two dashes or two commas in a parenthetical phrase: these all make the text better, as does the more obvious editing of spelling and punctuation. But don't substitute these editing concerns for more substantive revision. Line-by-line editing should come last after substantive revisions are more or less complete.

The Rewriter's Toolbox

Here are the basic tools that make all of the above happen. Depending on writing style and what's on the page, some get used more than others, but skilled writers have mastered them all.

Adding

All writers, not only underwriters, need to flesh out early drafts. This can involve adding more sensory detail to make characters and scenes come alive; adding dialogue; adding back-story so readers know more about the context for the story; adding the opposing point of view to provide tension and perspective; adding other voices; adding reflection to show the writer's mind at work; and adding information gleaned from research. The challenge, in revision, is to work in this new information so that the seams don't show. (For more on weaving in, see Chapter 9, The Role of Research.)

Cutting and Tightening

Less is often more, as Picasso's bulls show; cutting can crystallize meaning and turn a dull voice into a lively one. Writers with a draft rich in detail often cut all but the best away. That can mean a phrase, a paragraph, or even pages — either because they digress ineffectually or go on too long. Cutting on the sentence level eliminates words that don't carry their weight. "To be" verbs are likely targets, and so are adjectives and adverbs. Keep those that surprise most and get rid of the others. Also look closely at repetitions. Some add, as in this lyrical opening to Robert Vivian's essay, "Driving to the River":

> Driving to the river is listening to the highway moan in cold asphalt, syllables that rasp a clean wave from Omaha to Lincoln. Driving to the river is looking ahead, past the curve of I-80 where the horizon glows in soft ambers at sunrise, and the sudden, gleaming promise of the Platte near Ashland. Driving to the river is finding that delicate bird-bone in the schoolyard you could almost put in your mouth, which has waited months and years for your small hand to bring it back to the land of the living and the dying.

But other repetitions slow down the text, making the reader say, "I know that already!" Overusing transitional phrases are particularly deadly:

> We entered the living room. Once we entered the living room, we saw the portrait of Jefferson. This portrait was propped against the living room wall. . . .

Tip: Some writers are so convinced about the efficacy of cutting that once they think their drafts are finished, they make themselves cut 100 words or more from, say, a ten-page draft. Their work almost always improves.

Rearranging

While rereading, an idea on page 2 might seem to fit better with what's said on page 5. Using computers makes rearranging easy: you can try different versions and decide later. Some writers when looking for more focus write an outline of their drafts. Every time a new topic is introduced they add it to the outline; then they look for patterns, asking themselves what seems to go together, what might need to be moved, and what might work in juxtaposition.

Substituting

Early drafts provide us with the gist of what we want to say, but our strongest language often comes from time spent examining the words on the page and imagining other choices. Often moving from general to specific makes all the difference, the specifics leading us into new meanings — even at the sentence level:

> We ate in our favorite restaurant in New York. We loved going there. It brought back so many memories.

> We ate in Jubilee, a favorite little bistro on East 54th Street and felt, at least that one night, that we were in love again.

Layering and Weaving

Once we are well into our work, we often discover an image or a refrain that feels as if it is the heart of what we are saying. It may appear early on and disappear, or it may come once, late in the draft. Revision is the time to strengthen its potential by layering and weaving. Layering deepens work, allowing us to complicate without sacrificing cohesion. Weaving pulls the layers through the work, so that the new depth is not just on one page but on every page. We did this, for example, by layering Gornick's notion of "the situation and the story" throughout this chapter, hopefully making the concept of revision clearer. Gerald N. Callahan in "Chimera" also shows how to weave and layer an image — his is of a woman — so that each reappearance deepens the essay's meaning (see Chapter 12, Personal Essay).

Copyediting

The final stage of revision is attending to the grammar, spelling, and punctuation. No piece, no matter how powerful, will be treated seriously without the writer's attention to form.

Revision in Action

I. Kim Stafford, whose essay, "The Writer as Professional Eavesdropper," is in this anthology, has shared his revision process with us. We pass it on to you so you can see how this essay evolved. The genesis was a series of teaching notes that Kim wrote to himself in 1986:

- Writing is easy or satisfying or both when individual episodes of writing erupt from the rich, on-going conversations of my life.

- I overhear and read gifts of knowing; I send and receive letters engaged in the weaving of life and story.

- I try to live joyfully in the presence of opportunities, hospitable texts the world constantly offers me. I don't write; I write back.

- Writing is the crystal that forms by certain faceted shapes and technical details within a solution too richly saturated to remain fluid.

Two years later, these ideas became the first paragraph in an essay Kim wrote about his professional life. That paragraph then became the second paragraph of the recent revision included here. (To see the original essay, visit our website at <college. hmco/english>; to see the revision, go to Chapter 16, Stories of Craft.)

II. In his address to the nation after the bombing of Pearl Harbor, President Franklin Delano Roosevelt substitutes the word "infamy" for the words "world history," turning an informative sentence into a memorable one. Line editing this speech, Roosevelt pays attention to words, word order, and punctuation, but he leaves the basics alone. The structure, or what Annie Dillard calls "the bearing walls," are holding up.

DRAFT No. 1   December 7, 1941.

PROPOSED MESSAGE TO THE CONGRESS

Yesterday, December 7, 1941, a date which will live in ~~world history~~ *infamy* ——

the United States of America was ~~simultaneously~~ *suddenly* and deliberately attacked

by naval and air forces of the Empire of Japan.

The United States was at the moment at peace with that nation and was *still in* ~~continuing the~~ conversation with its Government and its Emperor looking

toward the maintenance of peace in the Pacific. Indeed, one hour after

Japanese air squadrons had commenced bombing in ~~Hawaii and the Philippines~~ *Oahu*

the Japanese Ambassador to the United States and his colleague delivered

to the Secretary of State a formal reply to a ~~former~~ *recent American* message. ~~from the~~

~~Secretary.~~ *While* This reply ~~contained a statement~~ *stated* *it seemed useless to* that diplomatic negotiations

~~must be considered at an end, but~~ *it* contained no threat ~~and no~~ *or* hint of ~~an~~ *war or*

armed attack.

It will be recorded that the distance ~~of Manila, and especially~~ of

Hawaii, from Japan make it obvious that the attack ~~was~~ *was* deliberately *or even weeks* planned many days ago. During the intervening time the Japanese Government has deliberately sought to deceive the United States by false

statements and expressions of hope for continued peace.

III. On this opening page from Stephen Crane's book *George's Mother,* the author finds nothing is salvageable.

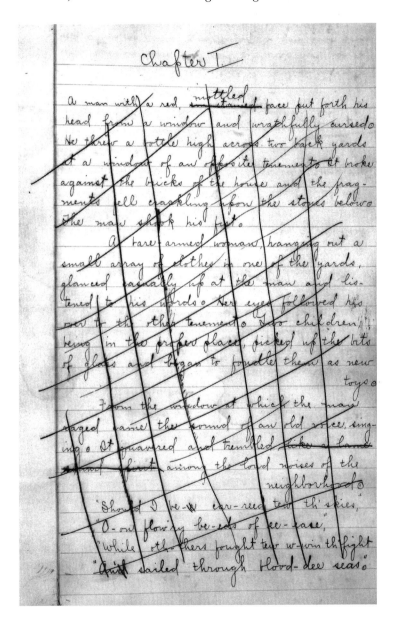

It's worth hoping that revisions can build on what is there, as President Roosevelt does, but also to expect that, like Crane, you may need to start again. Most important, save all drafts because the next day, upon rereading, you never know what may be embedded in old drafts — ready to be revised for "the story."

Ways In. . .

1. Take an early draft that you plan to do more with. Make a diagnosis of what you think it needs, using the list of revision strategies from earlier in the chapter as your guide. Try them.

2. Compare one of your early drafts with a later draft. List the kinds of changes you have made. Which tools — adding, cutting, rearranging, layering, copyediting — did you use the most? Which, the least? Now choose a different piece and try using the strategies you rarely use.

3. Take a draft you feel is almost finished. Cut 5 percent to 10 percent of the words. Do you miss anything you eliminated? Tip: Study each line for unnecessary adjectives or phrases.

4. Revisit Robin Scarlett's freelisting of "Lists I Could Make" in Chapter 3. Her list was written quickly as part of an exercise. If she were going to do more with it, what lines might she cut or rearrange? Compare your suggestions for revision with others, discussing your reasons.

Note: The answer to Kay Boyle query: B is the first draft, C is second, and A is her final version. Would you say she is an underwriter or an overwriter?

CHAPTER 8

A Lighter Touch — or Other Ways to Tell a Story

"I saw heroism in being able to live in the present [with] a lightness of touch."

— ART SPIEGELMAN

Creative nonfiction writers tend to write seriously about the oddities and difficulties of living, particularly in memoir. We try to make sense of our struggles with loss, illness, grief, and despair, topics that can weigh us down as readers and writers. But "serious" is only one approach, and often other approaches, using what Spiegelman calls "a lightness of touch," can capture the truth of our experiences in surprising ways.

Consider these two versions of living as a female in the Islamic Republic of Iran. Both writers mourn the loss of their freedom under a fundamentalist regime that has robbed them of their civil rights. One, Azar Nafisi, recreates that world in prose; the other, Marjane Satrapi, captures it by mixing print text with graphics.

Nafisi, who quit her teaching job at the university rather than wear the obligatory veil, chose to hold private seminars on literature for a small group of female students. At her home, behind closed doors, she and her students found solace in reading great writers from the West, including F. Scott Fitzgerald and Vladimir Nabokov. In her memoir, *Reading Lolita in Tehran,* she explains why:

> What Nabokov creates for us . . . is not the actual physical pain and torture of a totalitarian regime but the nightmarish quality

THE VEIL

THIS IS ME WHEN I WAS 10 YEARS OLD. THIS WAS IN 1980.

AND THIS IS A CLASS PHOTO. I'M SITTING ON THE FAR LEFT SO YOU DON'T SEE ME. FROM LEFT TO RIGHT: GOLNAZ, MAHSHID, NARINE, MINNA.

IN 1979 A REVOLUTION TOOK PLACE. IT WAS LATER CALLED "THE ISLAMIC REVOLUTION".

THEN CAME 1980: THE YEAR IT BECAME OBLIGATORY TO WEAR THE VEIL AT SCHOOL.

WEAR THIS!

WE DIDN'T REALLY LIKE TO WEAR THE VEIL, ESPECIALLY SINCE WE DIDN'T UNDERSTAND WHY WE HAD TO.

IT'S TOO HOT OUT!

EXECUTION IN THE NAME OF FREEDOM.

GIVE ME MY VEIL BACK!

YOU'LL HAVE TO LICK MY FEET!

OOH! I'M THE MONSTER OF DARKNESS.

GIDDYAP!

of living in an atmosphere of perpetual dread. . . . This is one
reason that art and literature became so essential to our lives:
they were not a luxury but a necessity.

Satrapi, younger than Nafisi when the Republic of Islam came
into being, also writes about totalitarianism. She begins her memoir,
Persepolis: The Story of a Childhood, using images as well as words to show
how she and her classmates first respond to the edict to wear a veil
(see facing page).

Both writers feel anger and loss, but each channels those feelings into an approach best suited to her sensibility: Nafisi into an all-
prose memoir that allows her to exploit her gifts as a literary critic,
Satrapi into a graphic memoir that integrates her talent for drawing with her talent for writing. Both are thoughtful and engaging:
the former written in a serious, reflective tone; the latter, in a lighter,
ironic one.

This chapter explores alternative ways to tell stories, using humor,
visuals, comic books, collage, and multi-genre forms to write about
the real world. With the ever-expanding technology of computers,
the Internet, and the emergence of digital and interactive media, we
can expect that creative nonfiction writers will find increasingly creative ways to explore the possibilities now available to them.

The Role of Humor

Sometimes it is fruitful to poke fun at a serious subject rather than
deal with its implications head on. Nora Ephron does this to great effect in "A Few Words About Breasts" (see Chapter 11, Memoir). She
wanted to capture the self-consciousness she felt (and we all feel about
bodies when growing up) but rather than lament the many ways Western culture fetishizes the female body, Ephron uses humor to show
the absurdities—and the pain. Had she written in a serious tone ("I
hated my body. I hated wearing a bathing suit. I wished I had developed earlier. . . . Why must we live in a culture that puts so much emphasis on shapes and sizes . . .?"), she would have sounded whiny. And

predictable. We, as readers, would understand her point but not be as engaged as we are by this account of buying her first bra:

> . . . I went there alone, shaking, positive they would look me over and smile and tell me to come back next year. An actual fitter took me into the dressing room and stood over me while I took off my blouse and tried the first one on. The little puffs stood out on my chest. "Lean over," said the fitter. (To this day, I am not sure what fitters in bra departments do except to tell you to lean over.) I leaned over, with the fleeting hope that my breasts would miraculously fall out of my body and into the puffs. Nothing.

This humor pulls us in. We laugh at Ephron, with Ephron, and at ourselves. We remember our own feelings—whatever our bodies had or lacked—as if it were yesterday. We squirm, even as we smile, at the old inadequacies that still linger. Humor can do that.

Max Apple in "Roommates" also uses humor: to celebrate his beloved grandfather who showed him how to survive a great personal crisis (see Chapter 17, Short Shorts). Readers expect grandfathers to be remembered fondly. Apple engages us with what we don't expect:

> [E]ven in sleep there was nothing gentle about this man. He specialized in hating his enemies, even those long dead. As he talked in his sleep, he exploded in anger. From his dreams I learned the curse words of English and Yiddish. Cushioned by his puffs of breath, visions of destruction crowded our room. Boils sprouted on the intestines of his enemies. Cholera depopulated their villages. The deep background of his life as it escaped through his lips became the chorus of my nights.

Apple shows us a man full of odd quirks, and as we read on, amused, we come to admire the wisdom of this 104-year-old curmudgeon, even as we laugh at his snoring and irascibility. Ultimately, we understand a grandson's love.

A few lines of comic relief are often welcome even in serious works. Scott Russell Sanders, for example, when writing about his father's alcoholism, interrupts his mostly solemn tone to describe the plan he concocted as a young boy: to travel to California, find Ernest and Julio Gallo, inform them of the damage they were doing to his father, and then, if they did not reply appropriately, kill them. Such comic relief helps both writer and reader work through the pain — and affirms that life, no matter how difficult, has its light side that we must look for and embrace.

Poet and essayist Alicia Ostriker, in an interview in *The Writer's Chronicle,* explains why humor matters and why it is effective: "Laughter," she says, "is a strategy. You don't want your readers to feel lectured at so you need some levity. Levity sweetens any message you hope to transmit."

"Cheekiness is a way of keeping readers alert. It cuts through the pious and commonplace."

— PHILIP LOPATE

Visual Attractions

Visuals, whether photographs or drawings, are increasingly integrated into written texts, including creative nonfiction. Some writers use them to enhance descriptions; others use them interactively; still others use writing to enhance the visuals. What follows are examples of how visuals can provide new dimensions of experience for both writers and readers.

Photographs

Writer Sue Miller uses a photo of herself and her younger brother to show how photographs impact on memory (see photo in Chapter 7). As an adult looking at her own image as a child, Miller is transported back in time and place: to the yard's "hardpacked dirt . . . worn barren by the play of . . . children . . . [to] the sense of yearning" she felt as she imagined her father far away, across an ocean. For Miller, the photograph serves as an imaginative trigger, offering her and her readers a way into the past through the lens of the present.

Photos with written vignettes, also called photo essays, also provide ways to remember. Look at one page from a travel album of our student, Julia Orente, who joined photographs and text to capture her trip to Spain. Rather than just record the facts, she recreates experience, so that reading it 10 years later, the events she witnessed and her feelings about them come alive in words and photo:

"Barcelona after the Bombing"

Four days before we arrived here, Basque terrorists blew up an underground parking garage killing 17 Catalonians, mostly working-class people who knew nothing of politics. Yet as we

drove from the airport past the neighborhood where it happened, we passed miles of apartments hanging the yellow and red striped Catalonian flag in protest. By its side hung white sheets marked with black (probably a man's sock) to honor their dead.

When we passed the main cathedral of Barcelona, police block-ades were all around, so that the ceremony for the dead could proceed without further mishap. The machine gun men in uni-form, Sergio said, were reminiscent of Fascist days when Franco's men kept the lid on any Republican intentions in the city. They were familiar sights for our whole stay, patrolling the streets (I nearly walked into a muzzle coming out of our hotel), set-ting up random roadblocks to catch the culprits (even though a week had passed), and stopping Basque-looking young men for ID's.

Later, at a Basque restaurant, I found myself eyeing the garbage bags suspiciously and jumping more than a little when fireworks began, marking the summer solstice. I was not the only one to be edgy. In the underground garage where we parked the car, the elevator was closed for security purposes, so we had three flights of stairs to climb—which wasn't bad after a big meal.

Drawings

In her essay, "Moments of Being: An Antarctic Quintet," Gretchen Legler describes her visceral reaction to the blue of the ice caves of Antarctica:

> . . . I cupped my hands around my eyes, so that all I saw was the blue, and as I stared, my heart began to beat faster and my breath started to come faster and tears started to come to my eyes. It was that blue that made me cry. That blue. . . . (See Chapter 14, Essay of Place, for the full essay.)

At times, Legler draws before she writes. In "The Blue—Inside the Ice Caves," posted on her website along with a short description of the ice caves, she explains that she was "trying to draw the crystals that hung like blooms of flowers. . . trying to figure out where the blue began and where it ended."

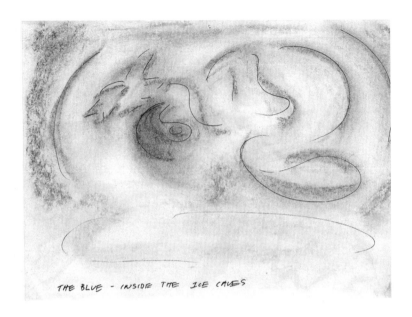

THE BLUE - INSIDE THE ICE CAVES

Legler calls herself "a word person," not a visual artist, but she explains, "I use drawing to help me see what I wouldn't normally look at: shape, color, texture. . . . Drawing is my entry into the landscape." (personal communication)

Graphics

In graphic books, or what are currently referred to as comix, the visuals carry the story line as much as the words do. Like standard comics, they rely on drawings in boxes and balloons for spoken dialogue, but unlike standard comics, the subject matter is often personal and political.

Take, for example, the "graphic memoir," *Persepolis: The Story of a Childhood*, written by Marjane Satrapi with which we opened this chapter. Wishing to reclaim Iran from its predominant image as a country of "fundamentalism, fanaticism and terrorism," Satrapi writes movingly of her early childhood and the changes in Iran that led both to the execution of members of her family and her eventual schooling in Vienna, an attempt on her parents' part to save her from a life of oppression.

Sometimes a lighter touch is the only way to express the inexpressible. It provides the emotional distance without which some writers can't tackle their most compelling subjects. Pulitzer Prize–winner Art Spiegelman, for example, uses the comic book format to address the greatest human traumas: the Holocaust, in his books, *Maus I* and *Maus II,* and more recently, the events of September 11 in his new work, *In the Shadow of No Towers.* In an interview in the *New York Times,* Spiegelman expains why he chooses this format: "After September 11, while I was living in a present that didn't seem to have a future, comics seemed central to me. . . . So far it has been the painful realities that I can barely grasp that force me to the drawing table."

It all happened, Spiegelman and Satrapi are telling us; the events we recount are as we lived them. Their narratives grip us the way powerful novels often do, offering yet another example of the way *creative* and *nonfiction* can work in tandem.

Research, too, is often an important part of graphic nonfiction, as Ho Che Anderson points out. Writing *King,* a graphic book about the life of the Reverend Martin Luther King, Jr., he says:

> In doing the research for this comic book, I read two biographies, and various books on and about the times, watched nearly 35 hours of documentary footage, and studied newspaper articles and photos of the period. Had the option to interview the real-life players in the saga been open to me, I would have surely availed myself.

Collage

A collage uses words, lines, images, and graphics to allow the writer and the reader to explore connections in associative, nonlinear ways. The word *collage* comes from the French *coller* which means "to paste," the first collages produced by Cubists in the early part of the twentieth century who literally pasted disparate objects on canvases to create startling effects.

The collage continued to be an important and quirky art form, eventually making its way into written prose. In 1977, Susan Griffin's

In December the Supreme Court mandate finally took effect in Montgomery, which meant we could all stampede on to the buses like a pack o' wild buffalo and not have to move to the back of the bus.

Course, sometimes you'd see someone who couldn't break the habit. Other folks made a *point* of sitting in the peckerwood section. It was a step forward, and I knew it at the time. Though, part of me had to ask what made them so special we thought we needed to sit beside them.

Martin and Abernathy and Nixon and the rest stepped on the bus that morning. They all got on with a White preacher if memory serves, Glenn Smiley.

The first integrated bus in Montgomery.

It was a new order. For the most part...people just found a way to accept what had happened and moved on....

Jesus Christ

138

Woman and Nature: The Roaring Inside Her was written entirely as collage, combining materials from medical journals, women's diaries, poetry books, interviews, how-to manuals, and people's dreams. By weaving disparate elements into and through each other, Griffin gave herself permission to play, allowing her to orchestrate voices that had never before spoken with one another. Griffin explains her writing process:

> I found that I could best discover my insights about the logic of civilized man by going underneath logic, that is by writing associatively, and thus enlisting my intuition, or uncivilized self. . . . The other voice in the book began as my voice but was quickly joined by the voices of other women, and voices from nature, with which I felt more and more strongly identified. . . .

More recently, Kathy Eldon edited *The Journey Is the Destination: The Journals of Dan Eldon,* each page a collage depicting the art, work, words, and life of her son, Dan, a photojournalist who was stoned to death in Somalia in 1993 at the age of 22. Considered a landmark in the world of art books, *The Journey* is a biography that blends Dan's words with images from his photographs, all excerpted from the seventeen volumes of black-bound journals he kept throughout his short life. "Layered like an archeological dig," his mother explains, "the pages are bizarre and colorful relics of a multi-faceted civilization, intensely personal though inhabited by many different people." His journals enabled Dan to capture the truth of his art and his life, and the collage form allowed his mother to pay homage to it.

Options in Multi-Media

As sophistication with interactive media increases, so do opportunities to add sounds and visuals to words and to publish the results on websites and blogs. The more high-tech creative nonfiction writers are also creating CDs and DVDs, using digital storytelling to present the stories of their lives with sound, image, and voice. Introduced and developed in the early '90s by Dana Atchley III, digital storytelling invites us to write about important autobiographical moments by combining images of artifacts with our own voices—the "I" as present in the story as the voice on the CD or DVD. These multi-media presentations combine print text, video, voice-overs, music, photographs, and graphics usually in three- to five-minute presentations. Topics may be lighthearted or serious—a history of one's village or reflections on the life of a parent or the loss of a friend—and, if done well, can convey the truth of experience with a new kind of richness and playfulness. (For links to websites with digital stories, visit our website at <college.hmco.com/english>.)

Multi-Genre Pieces

Multi-genre pieces make use of a range of print and nonprint forms: straight narratives, diary entries, interior monologues, dialogues, poems, letters, drawings, photographs. The effect is cumulative, drawing on the power of juxtaposition to invoke different perspectives, moods, and voices—all in the service of writing true. Alice Walker, for example, in her memoir, "Beauty: When the Other Dancer Is the Self" combines two genres, integrating poetry with prose (see Chapter 11, Memoir).

Writing teacher Tom Romano invites his students to create multi-genre pieces when they are writing research papers, asking them to include narratives, drawings, poems, monologues, dialogues, songs, and even cartoons. He cautions, however, that the term "multi-genre" is not an excuse for producing unfocused writing. The central premise of the piece not only has to be clear to the writer; it also has to be clear to the reader. Romano, in fact, asks his students to supply forewords or prefaces to accompany their work which will help readers understand what they are about to read—and experience.

"Each genre is a color slide, complete in itself, possessing its own satisfying composition, but also working in concert with the others to create a single literary experience."

— TOM ROMANO

Sondra's memoir, *On Austrian Soil: Teaching Those I Was Taught to Hate,* also uses multiple genres to tell of her experience as a Jewish teacher in Austria. She narrates her story in prose but also includes journal entries and poems, photographs of the town she lived in and the people she came to know there, and letters and e-mails from the Austrians she is writing about. She didn't set out to write a multi-genre piece, but, she explains, "There wasn't one truth to capture in this story; there were many. I couldn't imagine showing the development of my relationships with the teachers if they, too, didn't speak in their own voices."

A Word of Caution

Images, graphics, and sound, as exciting as they are, are not in the end a substitute for the craft of writing, attention to language, telling details—and the right voice(s). A good essay is not made by fancy fonts, humor, artwork, or imagistic flourishes unless they enhance the story. When they do, adding depth, moving readers beyond the superficial, adding a new perspective, or creating an interesting tension between the visual and the words, they can lead to new dimensions of understanding.

Ways In. . .

1. Lightness of touch is about being willing to play—being willing to try something different or even outrageous in approach. You might begin with a bizarre comparison: "My roommate is a rabbit. . . Writing is a bubble bath. . . First grade was like Mission Impossible." Or take a minor event or idea and exaggerate, exaggerate, exaggerate: "The brownies she bakes could break your foot. . ." "The pizza man was the Terminator every Wednesday night. . ." Or juxtapose objects that connect in unexpected ways: photos of you and your best friend both wearing silly hats; a crib blanket and a dishtowel. The aim is to find fresh ways into familiar material and familiar responses—and then to write.

2. Look for visuals to add to a piece or create your own. Experiment. See where this leads. Write in different voices or from different points of view. You may find that you have the workings of a segmented essay, a collage, or a full-fledged multigenre piece on your hands.

3. Imagine recasting a story you have written in comic book format. What would change? Would these changes strengthen or weaken the piece?

CHAPTER 9

The Role of Research

[T]he genre of creative nonfiction, although anchored in factual information, is open to anyone with a curious mind and a sense of self. The research phase actually launches and anchors the creative effort.

—LEE GUTKIND

Research is central to creative nonfiction. It can jog the memory, trigger the imagination, provide new insights and perspectives, add verisimilitude, deepen cultural and historic contexts—and just make a good story better. So why don't creative nonfiction writers dwell on how much energy they spend, for example, looking up facts, interviewing people, or making fieldtrips? Because unlike academic writing, the aim is to make research blend in with the story. The reader isn't supposed to notice it, just experience it.

Take a look at how Laura Hillenbrand pulls her readers into her best-selling nonfiction book, *Seabiscuit*. The narrative energy of the preface comes from the facts gleaned from research.

> In 1938, near the end of a decade of monumental turmoil, the year's number-one newsmaker was not Franklin Delano Roosevelt, Hitler, or Mussolini. It wasn't Pope Pius XI, nor was it Lou Gehrig, Howard Hughes, or Clark Gable. The subject of the most newspaper column inches in 1938 wasn't even a person. It was an undersized, crooked-legged racehorse named Seabiscuit.

Hillenbrand writes as if she were there (no matter that she wasn't even born yet), piling on facts and statistics as if they are on the tip of her tongue. Yet she always manages to sound like a storyteller, not a scholar:

> When he raced, his fans choked local roads, poured out of special cross-country "Seabiscuit Limited" trains, packed the hotels, and cleaned out the restaurants. They tucked their Roosevelt dollars into Seabiscuit wallets, bought Seabiscuit hats on Fifth Ave., played at least nine parlor games bearing his image. Tuning in to radio broadcasts of his races was a weekend ritual across the country, drawing as many as forty million listeners. His appearances smashed attendance records at nearly every major track and drew two of the three largest throngs ever to see a horse race in the United States. In an era when the United States' population was less than half its current size, seventy-eight thousand people witnessed his last race, a crowd comparable to those at today's Super Bowls. . . .

That narrative skill comes from reading old newspapers and magazines, interviewing the people who were there, reading books on horseracing, even going to the racetracks where Sea Biscuit once raced.

Collectively the facts Hillenbrand uncovered add authority and a depth of experience that would be lacking had she written before amassing and digesting a sizable amount of research. Yet her style never seems heavy-handed, calling attention to itself. Citations, including footnotes, are included, but most are placed outside the narrative. We find them in thirty-five pages of "Notes" at the end, including seven for the preface with listings like:

> xi   the year's number one newsmaker: "Looking 'Em Over," *San Francisco News*, SB, January, 1939. . . .

> xi   seventy-eight thousand people witnessed his last race: *There They Go: Racing Calls by Joe Hernandez*, album released by Los Angeles Turf Club, n.d.

> xi   population was less than half its current size: Irvine, E. East-
> man, ed., World Almanac 1938 (New York: New York World-
> Telegram, 1938) p. 241. . . .

These entries lend credence without interfering with the story of
three men and a horse with heart, a story that inspired millions during the Depression years. Hillenbrand's narrative keeps readers turning pages by offering more than a well-documented book about a
racehorse. What she includes as research serves her narrative thrust,
moving interest along rather than just providing information.

How to do this? How to gather, select, and process new information so that readers feel as if the writer just happens to know it? That's
one of the great challenges to nonfiction writers who want to tell stories, not just recount facts. The answers lie in voice, timing, and making the best use of sources — and that's what we'll address in this
chapter.

Become a Researcher, Whatever the Subject

Research makes a difference — no matter how well we know our material. Whether writing literary journalism, like Hillenbrand, or about
home and family, seasoned writers rely on research to enrich their
work. Memoirist Joe Mackall, for example, combines memory and
research to recreate his uncle's murder, weaving his sources together
so gracefully that readers can't separate what he just learned from
what he always knew. He does not cite his sources because he is writing personal history, not a trial report. His source for knowing that
the gun was a ".38 blue-steel revolver" is unimportant to his story. But
for the purposes of this chapter, Mackall shares it with us. (Everything
underlined comes from research.)

> In the middle of the front seat, strewn cold, were car keys, and
> next to the keys, hot and spent, rested the .38 blue-steel re-
> volver, an Arminius Titan Tiger, serial number 023805. [*police*
> *report*] Because Gump had reported his gun stolen, the trail led
> easily to Barnes. He and his minor accomplice were arrested while
> sitting on a couch the day after the murder. Barnes confessed
> immediately. [*interview*]

> Uncle Don was taken to <u>St. John's Hospital</u> where he was pro-
> nounced dead at 10:05 p.m. on Friday, Dec. 13, 1974. [*coroner's
> report*]
> My aunt asked if we would mind keeping the Lincoln at our
> house for a time. Perhaps she asked because my father was not
> only my uncle's friend, but an ex-homicide detective. At first it
> simply took up space in our driveway and in my imagination.
> Soon we investigated it, my father piecing together clues, explain-
> ing to his young sons the likelihood and probabilities: the shards
> of glass told one part of the story, the blood another part, the
> smell — in its utter indescribability — yet another. . . .

Research can also invigorate what Poet Laureate Ted Kooser calls
"local wonders," the subjects we know well from everyday life.
Kooser, in his essay/memoir, *Local Wonders,* includes research on the
locust tree when describing its autumn-gold color on his farm in Nebraska. Two out of four paragraphs are drawn from his old encyclopedia, but his "I-happened-to-be-reading-this-today-kind-of-voice"
makes everything work. Kooser cites the *Encyclopedia Britannica* in the
text: "published in 1917 and my favorite reference" and proceeds to
mix research, metaphor, observation, and personal feelings into one
seamless experience:

> No fabulous treasure chest, hauled dripping in chains onto the
> deck of a ship, has ever spilled more pieces of gold than one lo-
> cust tree in mid-October. My wife and I are just now overcome
> with riches, our front yard completely paved with tiny coins, that,
> clinging to our feet, insinuate themselves into the house, the car,
> and even the secret, warm, grassy-smelling clefts in the paws of
> our dogs. Under the eaves, cobwebs strung by miserly spiders
> flutter with gold. Gold in the grass, gold falling from above, even
> little flurries of gold that lift from the grass and rise back into the
> air as if they weighed nothing, and in fact, nothing they weigh.
> And all for free.
> We have one fifty-foot locust in the front yard, accompanied
> by a half dozen offshoots, to use that word at its best. The locust

has a bad reputation among landscapers, professional and amateur alike, because of its shoots, which disrupt those dreamed-of reaches of electric green, chemically enlightened grass. But I like to see the locust's offspring, a foot tall, defiantly waving their frondy little leaves. And I like the fierce look of the sharp black thorns and the ripply brown pods that dangle like strips of beef jerky from the full-grown trees.

The eleventh edition of the Encyclopedia Britannica, published in 1917 and my favorite reference, says that the pods may be eaten by men and animals and that in Sicily a spirit is made from them. I know the effects of that spirit, a mild giddiness that comes while stumbling through a carpet of locust leaves on the way to the dark, tavern-like atmosphere of the outdoor toilet.

The Britannica says the husks are also called St John's bread from a misunderstanding of Matt 3:4, the passage in which John the Baptist is said to have lived on locusts and honey. But the locusts that John the Baptist ate to sustain himself in the desert were the kind with real wings, the kind that buzz going under the teeth, acceptable food in hard biblical times. Our locust leaves have a lust for riding the wind but never descend upon a field of wheat and eat it to the ground. A plague of falling locust leaves might ruin the looks of a golf course green, might annoy the president of a bank by blowing in under the door, but do nothing else but make us rich with pleasure. . . .

No encyclopedic voice here! Kooser has taken the facts and made them his own. Imagine if, instead, he would have inserted the encyclopedic information into his narrative, as is, something like:

> The locust is one of about 20 plants found in North America. Four of these trees have scented flowers; the others are shrubs. They can grow up to 80 feet tall.

Kooser's voice, his tone, his point of view — all would have been compromised.

Writing So the Seams Don't Show

Using research seamlessly in creative nonfiction depends largely on the writer's voice. If the voice sounds natural, not pedantic, if it conveys a genuine enthusiasm for what's learned (rather than a need to sound smart), then new and old facts can be woven together so no seams show. If the newly learned overpowers the rest, the voice flattens, the energy flags, and the writing sounds more like a textbook.

To assure a strong, original voice — one that doesn't sound imitative of others — many writers prefer to write impressionistically from memory and observation *before* doing research. Doing so helps to identify a point of view (no matter if it changes) and the right language to express it. As Mike Steinberg says of his coming-of-age memoir, *Still Pitching:*

> I needed to know what the book was about first, what the narrative arc was. Once I knew that a chapter was sound, then I'd go back to my stack of baseball books and films and fill in details about Ebbets Field, batting statistics, and player quirks like Jackie Robinson being pigeon-toed.

Without this one-two punch — writing first, researching second — Steinberg says he would have lost his narrative way, his storytelling voice stiffening from information overload.

For other writers, on different projects, research must come first. Joe Mackall explains that he did research before writing about his uncle's murder because he needed to challenge the existing stories that he'd heard growing up. Out of that challenge came the story Mackall needed to tell:

> I had to do a lot of research before I started writing. Our family had its story of what happened, but it wasn't true. There were too many convenient prejudices and useful fictions designed to hide the factual circumstances surrounding the murder.

Whether research comes early or late in the process, most writers agree on the following to hide its seams:

🌢 *You need to internalize the material before you can write with ease.* Like new shoes, new information needs breaking in. You need to walk around with it for a while, thinking, writing, and talking about it. As the material becomes familiar, the right words for morphing old and new information appear. The textbook voice relaxes, and old and new seem like one.

🌢 *You need to gather more information than you'll use — or think you'll need.* You never know, when gathering material, what facts will spark your imagination. Small facts connect in surprising ways, often becoming metaphors for larger connections. Ted Kooser, for example, reads about Biblical locusts and honey, which make him think of a golf course, and then a bank president, and then back to his metaphor of nature's gifts of gold, which ends the piece. That old *Britannica* handed him that ending, but how could he have guessed that until it was there on the page?

🌢 *You need to let what's important rise to the surface.* Too much information often sinks your voice and with it the narrative energy of your piece. The impulse is to show all you've learned (not to mention all the time it took to find it), but resist. Keep only what serves the story. Drop the rest, or condense it so that it fits well with what comes before and after. Tip: Reread your notes, and then — without looking at them — jot down a few things that really stick with you. Work with that.

🌢 *You need, usually, more than one source.* Sometimes one source is enough: to look up the history of the locust tree, for example. But several sources offer a broader perspective. Joe Mackall, for example, in addition to looking in police files, asked his relatives about his uncle, gathering insights not possible if he used only records and one or two interviews.

How Much Is Enough?

When we write about what we don't know, like the career of a horse who lived and died 60 years ago, we obviously must do a lot of research to learn enough, well enough, to write with authority. But how much is needed to write what we know from firsthand experience? That is less clear. For some, there's the danger of becoming inefficient, of using research as an excuse not to write. Essayist Rebecca McClanahan points out: "Once I spent five days reading about roosters to get one fact for my essay, 'The Riddle Song.'"

More common is the danger of doing no research. "Why bother? I know my own life!" we hear often at the start of creative nonfiction classes. Our answer: Don't sell the powers of more information short for adding depth and texture to what you think you know. Research can also:

- *Trigger the Imagination:* We saw that at work in Ted Kooser's piece, how small facts about locusts from his 1917 encyclopedia led to a fine ending.

- *Jog Memory:* What memory forgets, research can fill in, making writing richer and more believable. One student trying to recapture a nursery school experience, for example, wrote in an early draft: "We ate candy bars and played with toys." After looking up the year 1978 online, her memory was jogged by finding a list of candy bars, and she wrote, "My mom packed me Almond Joys, but I'd only eat the nut. The coconut I'd swap with Melissa for a few Jujyfruits."

- *Add Verisimilitude:* The realism in the draft mentioned above brought praise from writing group members: "What a good memory you have! We forgot all that!" followed by a lively discussion about the pros and cons of Almond Joys versus Jujyfruits . . . candy no one had eaten for years.

- *Broaden Perspective:* We tend to see firsthand experience from one perspective: our own. That's important but can

be limiting. New sources, as Joe Mackall discovered, let
writers challenge what they know — and see life in ways
they hadn't considered. Say you are writing about your parents' divorce. You certainly want to capture how it was for
you at that time — and what impact it had. But for a fuller
understanding, it helps to ask parents and siblings what
they remember. It helps to ask friends how, and if, divorce
affected them. And it helps to look up what sociologists say
about divorce at that time and now. None of this may enter
your piece officially as quotes, but it can inform how you
see and reflect on what happened to you.

🌢 *Provide Cultural and Historic Context:* Readers want to know
about us, but they also want to know about the world we
come from. A little bit of research can weave the personal
and political/cultural/social in satisfying ways. Scott Russell
Sanders's essay about his father's alcoholism, for example,
though highly personal, sets alcoholism in a larger social
context. Take the list he catalogued of all the words for being drunk.

Consider a few of our synonyms for drunk: tipsy, tight, pickled,
soused and plowed; stoned and stewed, lubricated and inebriated,
juiced and sluiced; three sheets to the wind, in your cups, out of
your mind, under the table, lit up, tanked up, wiped out; besotted,
blotto, bombed, and buzzed; plastered, polluted, putrefied; loaded
or looped, boozy, woozy, fuddled, or smashed; crocked and shit-
faced, corked and pissed, snockered and sloshed. . . .

Did Sanders use a dictionary and thesaurus? Did he survey all his
friends for names? Did he collect words for *drunk* in his notebook
over the years? Did he find an article with many of these words? Hard
to say, but the list works, making his father's problem a larger social
problem — and, for the reader, that's what matters.

🌢 *Flesh Out Characters:* Whether you are writing about someone you know well, like a parent, or someone you barely
know, it helps to understand who the person was before

your story begins. And to understand the world he or she came from. If you're writing about a grandfather who fought in Vietnam, look up facts about the war. If your family came from Greece in 1917, research the history of those days. Novelist Russell Banks gives advice like this to fiction writers:

> You have to know everything about your character: what she ate in the morning, what she wore to the senior prom, what time she takes a coffee break at work, even though it may never appear in your story.

We say the same to creative nonfiction writers.

> ❧ *Flesh Out Place:* The more details of place that you have, the better. Gather them on field trips, taking lots of notes and pictures, and fill in what you missed or forgot — especially for travel memoir — from guidebooks, encyclopedias, etc.

Another question related to "How much is enough?" comes up in regard to the citing of sources. When must we include footnotes like Hillenbrand — and when not? When should we quote a source directly, like Kooser — and when not? When should a writer make a survey part of the essay, as Brian Doyle does in "Being Brians" — and when not? In creative nonfiction, far more than in informational nonfiction, the answer is, "It depends." If citing the source in the text adds authority, and your voice can make it sound engaging, use it. If not, consider these options:

> ❧ List your sources at the end on a "Notes" or "Works Cited" page.

> ❧ Write a descriptive page of acknowledgments at the end: talking about the books you read, the people who helped you, etc.

> ❧ Use it without citation. The latter only works if the facts are ones you might once have known, should have known, or could know.

A quick look in six literary journals shows that readers (and creative nonfiction editors) don't expect formal attributions, such as footnotes, in memoir and personal essay. Informal attributions are more prevalent, but the tendency is to shy away from notes that undercut story or voice.

Even in textbooks like this, we cite sources sparingly for the same reasons. When we quoted Russell Banks —*You should know everything about your character including what she had for breakfast. . . .*—we didn't say where it came from. We could have written, "In a workshop at Princeton University in the early 1990s, Banks said. . . ." Or we could have added a footnote, "From a class at Princeton University, 1986." But the extra information only seemed relevant if we were writing a biography of Banks or if this quote was something Russell Banks would never say, something outrageous. But Banks probably said these words every semester, said them more than once, in fact, during the semester we wrote them down. We liked the quote enough to start using it in class and have continued to use it for the past 18 years. If asked, maybe we could find our original notes in a file called "Banks." Or maybe not.

A Word About Plagiarism

Plagiarism is copying the written words of others and passing them off as your own. A good rule of thumb is not to use more than five words from someone else's text. Sometimes the borrowing is inadvertent (after awhile Banks's advice can morph into our own); but most plagiarism is easy to avoid if (1) you don't use chunks of material without acknowledgment; and (2) you don't omit quotation marks when using someone's exact words.

Neither should be a temptation in creative nonfiction because the writer's voice and point of view are at the heart of success. Use someone else's words without attribution and you forfeit your own words. Use someone else's experience or opinion, and you forfeit your own. Why do that in a genre that celebrates what an individual, who need not be famous or an expert, has to say? To students who say the temptation comes from being too tired, too busy, or not feeling interesting enough, we offer this caveat: a tired, busy, doctoral student at an Ivy League university in the mid-1980s submitted a borrowed paper that included a footnote he never noticed. It read something like: "I learned this while imprisoned in India in 1910." This young man (who would have had to be an old man to write this footnote) was asked to leave the university.

Seven Ways to Gather Information

Every writer has a few favorite references like Kooser's *Encyclopedia Britannica* from 1917. Others can be found on bookshelves at home or in libraries: dictionaries, almanacs, books of quotations, books on birds and plants, books of Greek myths, the Bible, name books, travel guides, family albums, diaries, journals, letters, quick histories of, phone books, videos, maps, and cookbooks, to name a few. And then there's the Internet and the telephone, both great ways for gathering information without leaving home. We include seven key sources you should definitely try using — and often.

Family Sources

Diaries, journals, private letters, family albums, and family videos offer great opportunities for research, especially for family stories. (We define research as adding information and insight to what we already know.) To keep family peace and protect privacy rights, you may want to change names and/or get written permission (see the next chapter for more on writing about family members), but these primary sources are well worth mining. Tip: Interview older family members, preferably with a tape recorder (and video camera if you have one) so that you have their stories intact for future use. Too often we discover, too late, that a world we want to write about is lost. It helps to use photos, albums, objects, letters, etc., as springboards for questions and answers.

Notebook or Journal

When asked about her sources for writing *Pilgrim at Tinker Creek*, Annie Dillard said, "I knew I had a gold mine in my journals." She drew on years of notes about nature books she had read, observations in the woods, interesting facts she had gathered, "quotations from the Bible and theology, a lot of ideas I had had about art, about poetry." As pre-writing, she took out all the information from her spiral notebooks that she thought pertinent to her subject and copied it on four-by-six index cards.

> It took me a month or so. At the end of that time, I had 1,003 four-by-six index cards. Then I put them into piles — which anyone can do. You know, if you think about writing a book, you think it is overwhelming. But actually, you break it down into tiny little tasks that any moron could do. A pile of index cards divides itself into categories; it is very easy to divide things into categories. Oranges here. Apples and peaches there. . . .
> — *"Annie Dillard Talks about Writing"*

Whatever your project — a book or a short essay — your notebook is a great resource of forgotten experience, quotes, observations that are waiting for the right moment, like maybe today, to be delivered from obscurity. For bigger projects, Dillard's technique for organizing source material is also worth a try, especially when trying to find a shape for what you want to say.

Interviewing

Asking people for their stories and opinions is a key tool of creative nonfiction writers. Strangers let us into new worlds; family and friends let us into familiar worlds through new doorways. Both provide perspectives that energize our writing, whether through a quick phone call to Mom about what was in the attic or through a formal interview with the oldest person in town.

The techniques for interviewing vary depending on how well you know your subject, but several tips stay the same:

- Listen well and enthusiastically. You want your subject to feel as if what he or she says is really important to you.

- Talk as little as you can. Remember when you are talking, you are not learning anything you don't already know.

🔥 Begin with warm-up questions, easy to answer. Straight-forward facts about one's life are good, as in: Where were you born? How old were you when. . .?

🔥 Follow with open-ended questions that can't be answered with "yes" or "no," as in: How did you feel about . . . ? Tell me about. . . .

🔥 Go with the flow. It's good to have prepared questions, but don't be rigid about following them. When your inter-viewee says something interesting, follow up with another question. Use techniques of active listening, rephrasing something that strikes you in a questioning tone, inviting the interviewee to "say more."

🔥 Ask hard questions more than once — in different ways. You may ask a great question and get no answer right then. Try again later, using different wording. If again you get no answer, don't give up. Often the interviewee will work a bit of that answer in later, when you don't expect it. Then fol-low up.

🔥 Before you leave, ask if there is anything else your inter-viewee would like to say.

🔥 Tape record if possible. Also, take extensive notes as ma-chines have a way of conking out at bad times. If you hear a quote you may use as is, put quotation marks around it, so that later you can separate paraphrasing from exact words.

🔥 Write up your interview impressionistically as soon after-wards as possible *even if you use a tape recorder.* You will be amazed at how different your impressions will be from the transcript. Each records different things, and together they will blend fact, quotations, and point of view into something good. Tip: In your impressionistic writing, include details of what was worn, what the room looked like, the neighbor-hood, sounds, the way the light hit objects, gestures — the more the better. As Annie Dillard says, "When you gather enough facts, you will start to have ideas about those facts."

❧ Do your pre-interview homework. If you don't know your interviewee well, try to find out something beforehand. If the person has written anything, read it. If you know something was important to them, find out enough about it to individualize your questions, so they are pitched to this one person, not just to anyone.

Surveys

Surveys help us find out quickly what many people think about a subject. They may be informal, asking questions on the fly of people you know. Or they may be formal written questions asked of those you don't know, the way Brian Doyle surveyed other Brians in his essay "Being Brians" (Chapter 12, Personal Essays). Either way, you are looking for insights and interesting quotations that inform you — whether you use them or not. Tip: For a written survey, follow the same principles as for interviewing: Start easy, avoid questions that can be answered with a yes or a no, allow for open-ended response. Remember your role here is as writer, not sociologist. What you most want are answers that add to or challenge what you know — and that make you think.

Printed Media

Books, magazines, charts, maps, and similar materials are enormously useful to research your subject. To find the best sources for you, get familiar with your library — and make friends with your reference librarian. He or she can be a savior by helping you find what you need without getting lost in information overload. Reference books that condense information are best to begin with, especially encyclopedias, dictionaries, and indices. Here's a sampling of what you can find in the reference section:

❧ Articles in hundreds of popular magazines arranged by date, subject, and author. *Readers' Guide to Periodical Literature* is a popular print index of what is available. More popular now are online databases such as EBSCO that include not only what's in popular magazines but also what is in business, health, and academic articles, plus abstracts for thousands more.

❧ Books, called chronologies, that tell you what happened in history, politics, and pop culture (i.e., popular songs, TV shows, movies, ads, famous quotes) in any given year. Some favorites: *People's Chronicle, American Decades, This Fabulous Century, Annals of America* (this one begins with 1493).

❧ Books that give you biographies of famous people. *Dictionary of American Biography, Who's Who in America, International Who's Who, Contemporary Authors,* to name a few.

❧ Indices of newspaper articles, such as the *New York Times Index.* They give easy access to local, national, and international events — past and present. Also available online.

❧ General encyclopedias giving good information on a wide range of subjects. Some favorites: *Encyclopedia Britannica, World Book, Americana.* Also available online.

❧ Specialized encyclopedias on a wealth of subjects. A sampling: *Encyclopedia of World Sport, Encyclopedia of Fantasy, The Book of Costume, The Folklore of American Holidays, Fieldbook of Natural History, The Great Songbook Thesaurus,* and *A Dictionary of Battles.* Spend a random half-hour on the floor of the reference section of your library to find your favorites.

❧ Balay's *Guide to Reference Books,* an index of all reference books, 16,000 of them, arranged by subject.

❧ *Webster's New Universal International Dictionary,* a listing of every English word, plus its history. Also includes 19 supplements that contain documents like the Constitution and the Declaration of Independence as well as specialized dictionaries on topics from mythology to the latest list of commercial and financial terms.

❧ Quicky histories offering easy-to-find facts, such as *A Lincoln History of Essential Information* and *Facts about the States.*

Whatever you use, record your source carefully, including page numbers, so that if you need to cite it, you don't have to spend hours trying to find it again.

The Internet

Much research can be done online, at home, or in the library. Most libraries, in fact, subscribe to major databases that most of us can't afford. Wonderful, oddball answers can come within minutes. Mimi, for example, wanted a Biblical quote about good neighbors. She went to a search engine, *Google*, typed in "good neighbors – Bible" and two minutes later, for no charge, she had a print-out of twenty biblical quotes using "good neighbor." Sondra had similar two-minute luck when she needed to know what kind of wildflowers would take root in her East Coast backyard.

The danger of relying on the Internet as a research tool is the difficulty in assessing how reliable information is. Government sites (.gov) are probably safer than business sites (.com), for example, when trying, say, to find out about basement mold because the government is not selling a product. With controversial topics — racism, capital punishment, abortion — it takes skill to determine bias. It's hard to know the credentials of the writers: What is their authority? Are we reading an expert in the field, someone posing as an expert, or someone whose agenda is to influence us with misinformation? Sampling opinions is informative to see how many views are out there. But taking opinion as fact is dangerous, so proceed with care.

On Location

Immersing oneself, firsthand, in life experience is still the best research tool for creative nonfiction writers. Some writers spend days, months, or years researching a subject by living it, like Barbara Ehrenreich, who lived on minimum wage for months in order to write *Nickled and Dimed: On (Not) Getting By in America.* But shorter immersions are also valuable, like revisiting an old neighborhood, taking an exotic trip, walking in the woods, interviewing someone at his home. Field trips stimulate your Muse, especially if you take careful notes, jotting down as much sensory data (and the impressions they set off) as possible. If you can't go physically, go vicariously. See a movie or TV show that puts you there, again noting details you can use. Photographs also offer vicarious experiences. Be sure to use the "Image" toolbar on search engines like *Google*. If you are writing about a lion, you can see one in seconds with a few taps on a keyboard.

Some Final Words

In our high-tech age, writers are bombarded by information. In earlier times, writers primarily enlarged their experiences by lots of reading; other options were limited by budget and geography. But today with tape recorders, telephones, TVs, airplanes, cameras, movie theaters, and computers, many more people can travel easily, conduct interviews and surveys, relive history, and retrieve facts. Perhaps the increasing popularity of creative nonfiction comes, in part, from these benefits. We have powerful tools — if used reliably and well — to make the real world, as we see it, more vivid, more authentic, more dramatic. No need to make it up; it's all there — with a little research.

Ways In. . .

1. **Short Interview Exercise**

   Get a partner and decide who is **A** and who is **B.** Each of you jots down three things you are willing to be interviewed about. **A** interviews **B** first, choosing one of the three items that **B** has listed. Using the guidelines for interviewing, ask questions and take detailed notes on the answers. Listen for good quotations to include (you must have at least one direct quote). After 5–7 minutes, switch roles. Now **B** interviews **A,** following the same format. After 5–7 minutes, both start writing up mini-profiles, including at least one direct quote that makes the person come alive (10 minutes). Now share your profiles, making corrections and additions, as needed. Here is an example:

Ian McCoy is a clubber at heart. The twenty-one-year-old chemistry major has been sneaking into clubs since the tender age of sixteen. His favorite is Webster Hall in New York City. It's a two-hour trip there, but he loves the vocals, especially trance-like melodies with romantic grooves and arpeggios to get him going through the night.

Next week, he'll be flying down to Florida for the nightlife in Fort Lauderdale. So ladies, watch out. "I can't wait for my last class on Thursday," says Ian, looking like he can almost taste the drinks and hear the music.

—PAUL WONG, *Creative Nonfiction Workshop*

2. In-Depth Portrait—in Four to Six Parts

Choose a person you want to know more about, someone available to be interviewed.

❧ Do a 10-minute freewriting on this person about whatever comes to mind, including what intrigues you. End with five or six questions you'd like to ask this person.

❧ If possible, do some background work before the interview that includes asking people about your interviewee, looking up relevant history or geography, reading letters, looking at photos, etc.

❧ Interview your subject, using a tape recorder if feasible (if interviewee objects or tenses, it's not feasible). Either way, take notes.

❧ After the interview, do another freewriting, using your notes to jog memory and to establish your point of view. Remember you want to interact with the facts, not just tell them.

❧ If you recorded the interview on tape, transcribe the tape.

❧ When it comes time to write, reread both freewritings and your transcription and then start writing. Good things should happen, if you let facts, quotations, and point of view inform and challenge each other. Tip: Ask yourself what struck you most about this person and use that to shape your portrait. (See Connie Wieneke's "Snakebit," Chapter 12, Personal Essay, for an interesting example of interviewing and shaping of a character.)

3. Researching the Personal

Take an entry from your notebook about a personal topic that is important to you. Try using three of the research tools, including interviewing others about the topic. Write a new draft working in some of what you found out. Cite your sources informally in the text — or in a Works Cited page at the end of your draft.

CHAPTER 10

The Ethics of
Creative Nonfiction

The truth is rarely pure and never simple.

— OSCAR WILDE

Creative nonfiction writers, intent on being creative *and* truthful, walk a thin line that other writers do not. Journalists and scholars, with their allegiance to fact, tend to avoid the ambiguities of memory and imagination. Fiction writers with their allegiance to story have no qualms about inventing interesting worlds. But creative nonfiction writers, with the intent to write good stories *that are true,* must grapple with the boundary between ethical and artistic clarity. Too much reportage and we cross into scholarship or journalism. Too much imagination and we cross into fiction.

In addition, creative nonfiction writers face other ethical concerns: our obligations to the people we are writing about, *real* people, often people we know well, people who didn't ask to be in our stories. Do we use

I remember least of all — that I am sure. I specifically remember that it was way back when and it involved So-and-So who I knew so well.

Yes, I remember the amount also — It was $6, $7, perhaps $20. And I remember that certain group went by the name that was popular back then.

I remember they came in the door like clockwork on the hour give or take ¼ hour.

I remember, and it's all so clear: February, April maybe August, close to the 3rd or just after the 29th.

Yes, definitely without a doubt, it was sometime between Sunday and Saturday.

Take it from me. I have the facts. . . .

— PAT VAN WYK,
Cape May Workshop, 2004

their real names? Do we tell their secrets? The answers involve both ethical and legal questions that we must deal with before we share our work publicly.

Obligations to others also include our readers. We make a pact with them that we are writing truthfully. But memory, one of our key tools, is unreliable, so how much leeway do we have to use our imagination to fill in what is half-remembered — and still call our work nonfiction?

Finally, there are obligations to our subject: to capture what we see as true, *as powerfully as we can.* If, for accuracy, we clutter our descriptions with detail, our truth will be lost on the page. So we select and dramatize for clarity and suspense. We don't change the basic plot or invent characters; but we might condense time, make omissions, recreate once-heard dialogue, and make composite characters — all to allow readers better access to our experiences. To what extent can a nonfiction writer do this? This chapter will explore these questions and offer some guidelines based on what seasoned writers do.

The Intent to Write True

Intent matters. If our *intent* is to capture the messy, real world we live in, we fulfill the first obligation of creative nonfiction. Intent helps us resist the urge to change facts, just to make a better story. It stops us from telling deliberate lies, even as we let our imagination fill in details we only vaguely remember. And it prevents us from using facts to mislead, the way news headlines sometimes do.

Some writers choose to write fiction because the obligation to write true inhibits creativity. Novelist Pam Houston says, "I write fiction to tell the truth." She is more honest, she feels, with the freedom to invent her characters and events. Other writers, like journalist Anna Quindlen, write fiction to avoid the pressure for factual accuracy. When writing a memoir, Quindlen recalls that she checked the weather charts before she could publish the line, "It was very cold the night my mother died." (To read her full essay, "How Dark? How

Stormy? I Can't Recall," visit our website at <college.hmco.com/ english>.) Her impulse as a journalist, she explains, was to fact-check: "Was it very cold or was that just the trick memory played on a girl who was sick and shivering, at least metaphorically?" To avoid such concerns, she writes fiction where she can create new worlds with "the imagined minutiae of the lives of characters I invent."

"But what about your *true* stories?" we ask. Don't we tell our friends, family, especially our children, about who we were and who our family was? And don't we want to preserve those stories? If we stick only to hard, verifiable facts, our past is as skeletal as line drawings in a coloring book. We must color them in. Writers like Joan Didion relish that, believing that the emotional truth of memory is what the writer must capture. We imagine her saying to Quindlen: If it *felt* cold to you, it *was* cold — whether it was 40 degrees or 2 degrees. No need to fact-check that.

But what happens if others remember differently, if their facts contradict the writer's version of memory? That happened to Connie Wieneke, whose mother remembered no snake biting Connie. (See her essay "Snakebit," Chapter 12, Personal Essay.) And it happened to Mimi, whose mother read her essay about riding a black stallion, being thrown, and taking the bus home in humiliation:

> "I picked you up by car!" she said.
> "You didn't. I took the bus and everyone was staring at my bloody jodphurs."
> "You were crying in the Pontiac."
> "I was not."

One memory versus another. Mimi debated changing her story but decided not to. She reasoned that her mother may be remembering another time; her mother may feel guilty for not picking her up that day; no bus driver was available to ask nor was Stanley who ran the stables (assuming he'd remember one small event 50 years ago); and there was certainly no newspaper account. So "the facts," as Mimi recalled them, stayed. In other writings, she might have mentioned the disagreement (as she is doing here). She might have said, "I can still imagine. . ." to signal ambiguity. But in this short memoir there was no ambiguity: only the young girl, no longer a cowgirl, riding a bus in Queens.

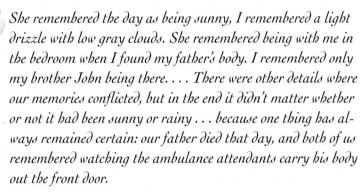

She remembered the day as being sunny, I remembered a light drizzle with low gray clouds. She remembered being with me in the bedroom when I found my father's body. I remembered only my brother John being there. . . . There were other details where our memories conflicted, but in the end it didn't matter whether or not it had been sunny or rainy . . . because one thing has always remained certain: our father died that day, and both of us remembered watching the ambulance attendants carry his body out the front door.

— PETER IVES

Emotional Truth Versus Factual Truth

Go to a writers' conference on creative nonfiction, and two terms — *emotional truth* and *factual truth* — create a storm of controversy. The Anna Quindlens in the room insist on journalistic adherence to factual truth, rejecting even small inaccuracies of memory. The Joan Didions, standing beside them, argue that crafting one's *sense* of truth is what matters.

Partly, one's stance depends on a personal definition of what "true" is. Partly, it depends on what is being written. In stories of childhood, rooted in memory, emotional truth holds sway; in investigative journalism factual truth is expected. And partly, it depends on how famous you are. If you are a national figure writing your memoirs, readers become uneasy with even small discrepancies. But most of us are outside history's limelight. Our small moments remain small. We tell *our* stories, from *our* memories, based on living *our* ordinary lives, and readers accept subjectivity, and some memory glitches, as long as our intent is truthful.

For literary journalism rooted in the here-and-now, we don't have to rely on memory to write true. Aside from observation, we can take notes, record conversations, and take photos to inform our point of view. Anne Fadiman, for example, in "Do Doctors Eat Brains?" relies on fieldwork, medical records, reports, and interviews to understand the East/West clash of medical cultures. In describing an ethnographer's attempts to persuade the Hmong people at the Ban Vinai refuge camp in Thailand to give their dogs rabies shots, Fadiman writes:

> . . . He decided on a Rabies Parade, a procession led by three important characters from Hmong folktales — a tiger, a chicken, and a *dab*. . . . As the parade snaked through the camp, the tiger danced and played the *qeej*, the *dab* sang and banged a drum, and the chicken (chosen for this crucial role because of its traditional powers of augury) explained the etiology of rabies through a bullhorn. . . .

Fadiman's source was not memory but the ethnographer's description. Discrepancies could be resolved by checking other sources (she drew on six people to write these three pages), and those left unresolved were used to heighten what is at the heart of the narrative: the misunderstanding between two views of medicine. (See Chapter 15, Literary Journalism, for a fuller excerpt.)

Selection and Omission

All good writing selects and omits material to shape point of view. The terms may change for academics or journalists, but creative nonfiction writers, too, present their best "evidence," back it up with "support," and provide "outside authority" by *choosing* some quotations over others. Choice always shapes a text, whatever the genre. Writers decide what's important to the subject and leave the rest out.

[E]very structure — be it literary, psychological, social, economic, political or religious — that organizes our experience is constituted and maintained through acts of exclusion. In the process of creating something, something else inevitably gets left out.

— Mark C. Taylor

That explains why Scott Russell Sanders, who wrote about his father's alcoholism in "Under the Influence," barely mentions it in another father/son essay called "Reasons of the Body." Only one line:

> In his sober years, which are the hours and years I measure him by, he would have laughed and then challenged me to a round of golf or a bout of arm wrestling, contests he could still easily have won. . . .

"Isn't that misleading?" students ask, because drinking, after all, was a major issue in their shared life. Or did Sanders's decision to focus on other aspects of the relationship make the second essay truer to itself? We would argue the second. Sanders didn't lie about his father. He didn't make him into a teetotaler. That would have been fiction. But to explore another powerful part of their relationship, he selected what he felt captured a bond built on more than drink:

> For me, the arena was a concrete driveway, where I played basketball against my father, shooting at a rusty hoop that was mounted over the garage. He had taught me to dribble, how to time my jump, how to follow through on my shots. To begin with, I could barely heave the ball to the basket, and he would applaud if I so much as banged the rim. I banged away, year by year, my

> bones lengthening, muscles thickening. . . . Many of those hours
> my father was tinkering in the garage, which reverberated with
> the slap of my feet and the slam of the ball. . . .

It is the same garage as in "Under the Influence" and the same emotional tension exists, but with different facts. All true *and* appropriate. For our lives are never a one-note experience; we must find all the other notes through selection and omission, as Sanders does, to capture the full music of our lives. (To read the full essay, visit our website at <college.hmco.com/english>.)

Where's the Line on Storytelling Techniques?

Omission and selection are part of every genre. So are storytelling techniques such as anecdote and description. But some storytelling techniques — exaggeration, elaboration, collapsing time, and composite characters — make creative nonfiction writers ask: How far can I go and still call my work nonfiction? Worth asking, but only *after* a draft, as every seasoned writer will tell you. To keep "creative" in nonfiction you need to write first and then decide what genre to call it. Many a personal essay or memoir (nonfiction) has become a short story or novel (fiction) — and vice versa — to allow the writer to express what was needed while keeping integrity intact.

Exaggeration

We all exaggerate for effect, but how much is too much when calling work creative nonfiction? Let's take on Anna Quindlen's dilemma: suppose on the night of a funeral it was actually 80 degrees, we remember sweating *and* shivering, and we write: "It was very cold the night my mother died." Is this a lie? We would argue no, not if the writer felt that chill, but we would suggest including the temperature to make the "chill" that much more powerful. Some might argue for a rewrite: "I *felt* very cold the night my mother died." But by changing the pronouns from *it* to I, the distance and some interiority of feeling may be lost. The writer must ask: Is it worth the loss?

Seasoned writers know how to signal exaggeration, as Russell Baker does in his memoir, *Growing Up*. He depicts his first boss, who was interviewing him for a paper route, as a major "executive of the Curtis Publishing Company," creating the humor that makes the scene work:

> He bent low from the waist and shook my hand. Was it true, as my mother had told him, he asked, that I longed for the opportunity to conquer the world of business? My mother replied that I was blessed with a rare determination to make something of myself.
>   "That's right," I whispered.
>   "But have you got the grit, the character, the never-say-quit spirit it takes to succeed in business?"
>   My mother said I certainly did.
>   "That's right," I said.
>   He eyed me silently for a long pause, as though weighing whether I could be trusted to keep his confidence, then spoke man-to-man. Before taking a crucial step, he said, he wanted to advise me that working for the Curtis Publishing Company placed enormous responsibility on a young man. It was one of the great companies of America. Perhaps the greatest publishing house in the world. . . .

For Baker, at eight years old, his potential boss looms like a CEO, and he signals his use of exaggeration by his mother's ongoing insertions. Readers know what the author is up to and laugh.

Problems arise if readers do not know — and feel tricked. Then exaggeration becomes deception. The daughter who writes that her father disowned her when he only threw her out for one night or the soldier who writes he fought in the Gulf War when he never left his base in New Jersey must signal where factual truth and emotional truth part company. Otherwise, they violate a main tenet of creative nonfiction that, as Bret Lott puts it, is simply this: Don't lie.

Elaboration

Memoirists and personal essayists often recreate the past with half-remembered detail. A second-grade teacher needs a name, a face, and something to wear — a pair of jeans and a T-shirt? a plaid dress? — and most creative nonfiction writers trust the subconscious to remember what the conscious self does not. If we have a photo, we use it, but otherwise we assume that readers understand that any true story about second grade is based on a mix of memory and imagination. We, in creative nonfiction, make some of those assumptions even with here-and-now events. Mimi's conversation with her mother about the bus memory, for example, was recreated without notes or a tape recorder. She assumes readers of this genre don't need, "I didn't have a tape recorder, but I think my mother said. . ." in order to make the moment credible. That's what telling a story is all about.

Collapsing Time

When our friend Jack Connor wrote a short essay about taking students to watch eagles in 'Owl Creek, he not only omitted two of four students but also collapsed time — three days into one morning — to move the story along. "Isn't that fiction?" students ask. We would argue no because his intent was true: to capture what students taught him as they watched eagles together on a winter day. If he combined details from day two and day three — even the dialogue — and put them all in one day, we are glad he did as long as he did not make up events that never happened. If, for example, he said they saw baby eagles when they didn't, he'd better call his work fiction. (To read the full essay, visit our website at <college.hmco.com/english>.)

Composite Characters

The most controversial storytelling technique for creative nonfiction writers involves the creation of *composite characters*. Using this technique, writers combine several people into one, often to protect the privacy of friends and family. For example, if you want to write about two friends who suffer from anorexia, you might invent a name, physical traits, and background, and then create a character based on both of their experiences. Your two friends may feel relieved, but will readers appreciate your tact? Absolutely not, some will say, outraged at the deception. Others won't mind, glad that you have *not* invaded the privacy of the nonfamous.

One solution that most creative nonfiction writers agree on: let your readers know what you are doing — and why. Your credibility is at stake. Nobel laureate Rigoberta Menchu wrote about the death of her brother, Nicolas, in her memoir about Guatemala. Only later on did reporters discover that Nicolas was alive. Menchu's explanation: he was a composite figure for all those young men, including other brothers, who were murdered or starved to death. But she never mentions "composite" in her book, and readers felt betrayed, a pact of truth violated. (For more information, including Menchu's defense in her own words, visit our website at <college.hmco.com/english>.)

On the other hand, Cathy N. Davidson in *36 Views of Mount Fuji* freely admits in her Acknowledgments that she used composite characters when writing her memoir about teaching English in Japan. Judging from the book's ongoing popularity, the admission had no ill effects on readers:

> "Composite" characters . . . allow[ed] me to report actual events but to blur details in order to preserve the anonymity of the people involved.

Her concern for the privacy of her friends was so great that until she thought to make composites she found herself blocked as a writer, fearing "a personal account might be embarrassing to the individual Japanese who inspired it." Composites enabled her to tell her story and informing her readers preserved her integrity.

What We Owe Our Readers

Most readers, as Davidson found, don't mind some invention, as long as they are not being duped. To avoid misunderstanding, especially about faulty memory, writers have developed a range of disclaimers. John Irving writes "Please remember that all memoir is fiction" to open his essay, "Trying to Save Piggy Sneed." Mary Carr does the same with the title of her memoir, *The Liar's Club,* and Lauren Slater signals with title and disclaimer, by starting her memoir, *Lying,* with the words "I exaggerate."

When speculating about the past, writers use phrases such as "I imagine her" or "Perhaps he said" to signal imagined scenes. Bret Lott's disclaimer in his essay "First Names" is a lament about not remembering:

> The sad thing, though, is that I can't recall the first day he called me Daddy when I went into his room. I could make up a story about it, here and now; I could tell you how it was on a Tuesday — Melanie's morning — and how there seemed something different in his voice as I came up from sleep, the sheets on Melanie's side of the bed already thrown back, my wife slowly rounding the footboard on her way out of the room. . . .
>
> *—Fathers, Sons, and Brothers*

Finally, writers who change names to disguise identities use a variety of markers — before, after, or in the middle of their work — to let readers know what they are doing. Here are some examples:

- "This story is true, as I remember it, but I've changed names and disguised identities to protect those who didn't ask to be in my story." (In a preface.)

- "I've changed the names to protect the privacy of the non-famous." (In a footnote.)

- "I met Luke Michaels (that's what I call him here) outside of Walmart." (In the text.)

Our experience has been that such gestures boost credibility and undermine nothing, as long as the markers have a light touch. The writer who keeps saying "I can't be sure," "I don't remember but. . ." again and again, must either make the struggle of remembering central to the story or find a more creative way to disclose. Otherwise you lose your readers who will naturally wonder, "Why should I spend my time reading about things you can't recall?"

Writing About Family

Kim Barnes, before she published her coming-of-age memoir, *In the Wilderness,* showed her parents the manuscript. She was nervous that her father, in particular, would be angry at her version of her rebellion against the Pentecostal religion of her parents. But his main complaint, she said in an interview in *Fourth Genre,* was about a few small facts she had wrong. Much relieved, she realized:

> One thing that we always assume, wrongly, is that if we write about people honestly they will resent it and become angry. If you come at it for the right reasons and you treat people as you would your fictional characters — you know, you don't allow them to be static — if you treat them with complexity and compassion, sometimes they will feel as though they've been honored, not because they're presented in some ideal way but because they're presented with understanding.

Her advice is an excellent guideline for writing about family, friends — and strangers too: To write honestly, but with respect. To show a fully developed character, not a caricature. To capture people — even our least favorite — with complexity and empathy, not in anger or for revenge. We all vent in our notebooks, but in stories meant to be shared, we need to get our subjects "right" — not just for the moment, but for all the days that follow.

While literature is an art, it is not a martial art . . . no place to defend yourself from an attack, real or imagined, and no place to launch an attack.

— ANNIE DILLARD

Not everyone bravely shares work with family, the way Barnes did. Some count on family members not reading it. If necessary, they may, like best-selling writer Frank McCourt, wait years. Sure that his mother would be embarrassed by tales of their poverty, he didn't publish *Angela's Ashes* until after her death.

Still others, preferring good relations to publication, let family members decide. About writing *An American Childhood,* Annie Dillard says:

> My parents are quite young. My sisters are watching the book carefully. Everybody I'm writing about is alive and well, in full possession of his faculties and possibly willing to sue. . . . Things were simpler when I wrote about muskrats. . . . As a result . . . I've promised my family that each may pass on the book. I've promised to take out anything that anyone objects to — anything at all.

To grant such power, you had best have a reasonable family — or you might never write another word.

Some writers, like James McBride, try a collaborative approach to family stories. To write *The Color of Water,* McBride taped his mother's story during hours of interviews and then wrote alternating chapters, one in his voice, one in hers. Poet Hilda Raz joined forces with her son to write a memoir called *What Becomes You,* also in alternating chapters. The power of authority, usually in the hands of one, says Raz, is shared but not diluted — and there are other perks. "By exchanging and critiquing drafts, he pushed me to greater and greater candor," she says of her son. "It's been hard but important for both of us."

There's always the option of calling our work fiction. We once taught a workshop where a student was writing a memoir about her uncle in the Mafia. "Call it fiction, please!" the whole group advised — "and be sure no one is recognizable!" Even when writing about more innocuous figures, like an admired grandmother, some writers opt to call their work fiction. Bret Lott wrote his best-selling book, *Jewel,* as fiction, even though it was 90 percent true. It gave him room to maneuver creatively, but also, he says, "It was nice to tell my grandmother, 'Oh, that was greatly exaggerated!'" when she questioned his portrayal of her. The word "fiction" satisfied her.

Some family stories, even painful ones, must be told as true. That's what Helen Fremont decided, after the research for a novel she was planning to write revealed her parents' great secret: that they were Jews and Holocaust survivors. Her grandparents, she discovered, had not died in a bombing as she'd always thought but in Auschwitz. Fiction felt wrong, not only because the real story was powerful, but because no matter what the family fallout, the truth had to be preserved: to bear witness and pay tribute. In *After the Long Silence,* Fremont writes:

> In effect, my grandparents and aunts and uncles had been wiped off the face of the earth by fascist regimes. There are no gravestones, or markers, and the generation of eyewitnesses is rapidly dwindling. Holocaust revisionists and deniers increasingly dismiss the fact of the extermination of Jews as fiction or fantasy, and I felt it important to add my voice to the record. Fiction no longer served my needs; I realized that I had to write the story, finally, as memoir.

One thing that all creative nonfiction writers agree upon: issues of ethics and obligations are decided on a case-by-case basis, after there's a solid draft. The options, as we see them, are these: To call your final draft fiction, not nonfiction. To modify what feels fictional to bring it closer to what happened (often this complicates work in good ways). To put your draft in a drawer for awhile and wait. To publish and keep your fingers crossed that those involved won't read about themselves. To show your work to "your characters" and solicit their feedback. Whatever you choose, be sure to wait until later in the writing process, so you don't stop yourself from writing true, as you recreate characters and their experiences as best you can.

Writing About Everyone Else

Writing about those we don't live with, who don't share our name, is both easier and harder. It is easier in that we can keep their identities private if we want to, by giving pseudonyms and/or changing a few details. It's harder in that we have to get them "right" without a shared history of years; we may only have a few interviews, or less, to capture the personality of someone we barely know. If we are unfair, inattentive, sloppy with facts, lacking compassion, one-sided in understanding, and just generally get them "wrong," real people get hurt, people who trust us. And unless they want to sue or write their own versions, they lack the many ways that family and friends have for making their displeasure felt.

What the Law Says

In addition to being an ethical issue, writing about real people is a legal issue. Writers need to consider the threat of a lawsuit (even though it is hard for the plaintiffs to win). Writers can be sued for libel if they say something that defames someone's character and is not true. Writers can also be sued for invasion of privacy, in which truth is no defense, according to Carol Meyer, author of *The Writer's Survival Manual*. "Even if what you say is true, you can be sued for invasion of privacy, especially under the false-light and embarrassing facts concepts." False light refers to "embellishing, fictionalizing, or distorting certain facts" to make a person look bad. Embarrassing facts refers to making disclosures the person has not given you permission to reveal. So whenever possible, lawyers usually advise, it's best not to use a person's real name without permission. If you don't have that permission and plan to publish, change the name — and let the reader know.

One Last Word

The brothers Geoffrey Wolff and Tobias Wolff both wrote coming-of-age memoirs about their lives after their parents divorced. Geoffrey, who lived with his father, wrote *The Duke of Deception*, and Tobias, who lived with his mother, wrote *This Boy's Life*. At a writers' workshop, Geoffrey recounted that their mother read both books and said both versions were wrong. "So write your own!" both sons responded.

   Most of those we write about have no such recourse. We are writing their world for them, as *we* see it. That is the great potential of the genre: to capture one person's view of real life, with clarity, passion, and grace. But we need to remember that real people are in our hands. We have the power to authenticate them, to bear witness to who they were — these mostly ordinary people who would never make the history books. We must use our power honestly, and well.

Ways In. . .

1. To see how selection and omission shape different truths, try writing a Year-Round-Up holiday letter to family and friends. Now make a list of everything important that you left out, including things you wouldn't dare to write. Ask friends or family members about what else they might add to your year and add that to the list. Now write a second Year-Round-Up holiday letter, focusing on the second list. Be interesting in both letters. How would you rate each on the "truth" scale?

2. Write two portraits of someone you feel strongly about. Write one that he or she will never read. Write another that you will share. Which one is truer? If you like some of each, write a third, and then decide whether you would use her or his real name or a pseudonym. Why?

3. Force yourself to write a first line that challenges your current mood. For example, if you're feeling low, begin with "I'm great because . . ." If you're feeling furious, begin with "It's funny that . . ." Keep writing, continuing with that premise, but don't make up events. Our experience has been that what you end up with won't be a lie, no matter how hard you try. Your imagination will find a way to tell the truth.

PART TWO

Reading Creative Nonfiction

A Preface to Our Anthology

Writers read with a bit of the scavenger in their hearts, not to imitate what others say but to study the craft that makes writing succeed (or not). What we like as readers — say, a whole story in dialogue or four pages on one small object — we might try as writers.

In this anthology, you'll find a range of forms from straight narratives, to segmented essays, to multi-genre works, to all-dialogue essays, to lyric meditations. You'll hear a variety of voices from many places, with many perspectives: by young and old, rich and poor, famous and unknown. Some readings are long; others are short. Some have multilayered themes; others focus on one subject or one moment in time. Taken collectively, they offer views of the world from many different angles, capturing the ordinary and the extraordinary in our lives. Most important, they give us permission to risk more as writers, to experiment, to try new forms, voices, and themes. The power of creative nonfiction lies in the way one voice helps another to speak. We hope that the words of these writers will lead you to your own.[1]

We've divided this anthology into seven categories: Memoir, Personal Essay, Portrait, Essay of Place, Literary Journalism, Stories of Craft, and Short Shorts. These are not hard-and-fast categories, just divisions to facilitate discussion and to ease the way toward finding springboards for more writing. Feel free to use these divisions as you

---

[1] See the Notes on Contributors section for more information about the authors.

see fit, reshuffle them freely, or make your own categories. Whatever you use, read for what inspires you and then ask, "How did the writer do that?"

Reading Like a Writer

We suggest reading a work once for pleasure and once as a writer looking at craft. It helps to star favorite parts, make comments in the margins, copy out quotes you like (with citation), and ask the same questions you ask when reading works-in-progress — about theme, characterization, narrative thrust, pacing, scene development, foreshadowing, use of dialogue, and so on. For more on specific terms, see Workshopping a Draft (Chapter 6) and Twenty Ways to Talk About Creative Nonfiction (pp. 80–84).

CHAPTER 11

Memoir

Memoir recreates a slice of one's past for the reader. Its emphasis on memory gives it its name. Memoir can focus on a single day and its effect, as in David Sedaris's "Let It Snow." Or it can capture key moments over time, as in Alice Walker's "Beauty: When the Other Dancer Is the Self" and Nora Ephron's "A Few Words about Breasts." It can be told in past tense (Sedaris), or in present tense (Walker), or shift between past and present, as in Lisa Chavez's "Independence Day, Manley Hot Springs, Alaska." It can be chronological, a memory told from beginning to end, as Sedaris does; or it can jump back and forth in segments of time as Walker does. It can even be told using an object, like a TV, as Tony Earley does in "Somehow Form a Family."

Whatever the form, these memoirists invite us into their past lives and hope we will connect and identify, even find some of ourselves in the writers' memories. The key to their success is figuring out, while writing, the answers to some hard questions: Why, of all the stories I can tell, am I telling this one? What's at stake here for me — and for my readers? To see how these memoirists do this, notice the following: how each uses detail and scene to make the past come alive; how each creates one or more appealing voices for telling his or her story; how each struggles with and reflects on the past; how each makes connections to whom they are now. Virginia Woolf's caveat to memoirists was this: "The reason so many memoirs fail is that they focus on the events of what happened and leave out the person to whom things happened." These writers know, as did Woolf, that it is not "the plot," but the "I" trying to make sense out of the plot, that makes a memoir work.

LISA D. CHAVEZ

Independence Day, Manley Hot Springs, Alaska

Independence Day, 1975. I was twelve. A little more than a month before, my mother had withdrawn me from school early, loaded up our car — a flashy but impractical Camaro with dual side-pipes — and headed north for Alaska. She brought with her everything she thought essential: daughter; dog; photos of the family she was leaving behind; a haphazard scattering of household goods; and two army surplus sleeping bags, purchased especially for the trip. What she was traveling toward was uncertain but full of promise — a mysterious box, beguilingly wrapped.

What she was leaving behind was certain; perhaps that is why she was so eager to go. A narrow rented house in southern California; a steady, if boring, secretarial job; a marriage proposal from a man she didn't love. What she was leaving behind were her everyday fears: her route to work through Watts, a place blighted and dangerous even then. The muggings in the company parking lot. The fear of being a young woman alone with her child in a decaying neighborhood, a derelict factory looming across the street. The fear, perhaps, of succumbing to a loveless marriage for the security it offered.

I was too young to really understand my mother's concerns, but I felt her tension. My mother and her women friends wore their fears like perfume, like the lingering scent of smoke from the erupting fires of those violent days. I remember the things my mother's friends talked about: the Manson murders; the serial killer who left body parts scattered on the freeway in trash bags; the man in our own town who killed five people in a movie theater. And the more personal terrors, the ones they alluded to less directly: fear of the arm slipping around the neck from behind, fear of the window breaking in the house in the middle of the night. Fear for their children in a place gone crazy. Or just the fear of being alone. And while my world was a child's world, full of long imaginative games in the park near our house, or afternoons watching Disney movies at the mall, I also heard my mother and her friends talking about getting out, moving to someplace safe. My mother was looking for sanctuary, and for a new start. She picked Alaska, as far north as she could drive.

Independence Day, 1975. We've been in Alaska less than a month and are still exploring. Now we have driven as far north as the road will take us, landed here, on the banks of the Tanana River. Manley Hot Springs. A town with no function really, except for the raw springs: two pools of hot water bubbling up out of the ground. There's a lodge with a few desultory cabins ringing it. A combination gas station/store. That is all. Down the river a half a dozen miles lies Minto, an Athabascan Indian village. Fairbanks, the biggest city in the interior, swollen to a population of 60,000 by pipeline construction, lies less than a hundred miles south, far enough away — along these rough gravel roads — to be totally insignificant.

And I am twelve. Everything new astounds me, and everything is new. My mother parks near the river and goes to find a place to stay. Instantly I am occupied, walking our dog, wetting the toes of my canvas tennis shoes in the silty current, kicking sprays of gravel into the air. Under my breath a constant stream of conversation. I narrate the scene to myself, add it to the elaborate and constant story I whisper of my adventures in Alaska. Drunk on the stories of Jack London, the poems of Robert Service, I imagine myself a lone adventurer, a sled dog driver, a saloon girl. I do not see what is in front of me: a shabby small town where people stare openly at that frivolous car — bright orange and marked by its out-of-state plates — and the young woman in white, high-heeled sandals and her daughter that have emerged from it. I do not see the men swigging out of a bottle at the picnic table by the river. I do not see the people getting out of a banged up riverboat, or the beer cans they toss in the current. No. I am in my own Alaska, and it is beautiful. I erase the people, and I am alone in my fantasy of wilderness, only graceful paper birch and the sun turning the river to tinfoil. Even when two men pull a rifle out of the boat, aim it at the sky and shoot, I am unsurprised. Only when my mother hurries me into the car do I understand I should be afraid.

There is only one place to stay, in the hulking log building that serves as a lodge. And there is only one room left, above the bar. We take it, noting the sagging double bed and rust-stained sink. The bathroom is down the hall.

Manley holds few attractions. The hot springs itself — housed in another log structure, this one with steamy windows that gaze at the road like rheumy eyes — is booked out by the hour, and we discover it is rented for the entire evening. We go for a walk with our German shepherd, but we quickly run out of road to walk on. We circle the gas station yet again.

"When does it get dark?" I ask my mother; even though I already know that it does not get dark at night in Fairbanks, I cannot be sure the rules are not different here.

"In August," my mother replies, an answer she has learned from the locals. She looks nervous, walks fast. Finally, I manage to really see around me, to note the people drinking at picnic tables, the hairy-faced men entering the store with guns in holsters. She hustles us back to our little room.

And I continue to ponder the light. If it never gets dark, I wonder, when do kids get to shoot off their fireworks? This year I have no fireworks, no magical cones of cardboard with their heady black smell of powder, cones with names like "Showers of Falling Stars" and "Golden Peacock" that spray the summer night with shivering sparks of sheer delight. Fireworks are illegal here, my mother tells me, and I feel sorely cheated.

All through the sunlit night we hear voices shout and slur from the bar, and outside gunfire and laughter. Years later I will discover that Alaska is not the only place where people discharge guns on holidays, but then I knew only my mother's fear which passed to me like a virus. I lay still on the double bed beside her, pretending to sleep. At 5:00 A.M. a shot in the bar and a shuddering silence. From the car, distant and insistent, our dog's furious barking.

Time passes. I pretend to sleep. The dog barks. My mother nudges me. "Someone needs to walk the dog." That someone is me.

Years later I recount the story. People question me. Why did she send you, a child? What they are asking, what they are telling me, is that my mother was a bad mother. Perhaps. But maybe she thought it was safe; how could she know? And she was tired, and scared herself, and perhaps she thought my childishness would protect me in a way her youth and gender might not protect her.

Perhaps it was a mark of my mother's blind innocence. I like to think that she had some of the indomitable optimism of those who made the same trek before: the stampeders to the gold rush of '98, or the others that came, like we did, lured north by the pipeline boom of '74 and '75. She wanted to believe — like so many did — that Alaska was a land of golden opportunity. Think of what she had done: left a good-paying job and man who wanted to marry her to journey to a place where she knew no one, where she had no prospects at all. For her, I think Alaska represented the possibility of the undiscovered, while California was a territory already mapped with freeways and shopping malls, mile upon mile of housing developments, and the barbed wire threat of barrio and ghetto.

That summer, we were still caught up in the romance of Alaska. We sang Johnny Horton songs on the Alcan Highway: "North to Alaska," and "When It's Springtime in Alaska It's Forty Below." I wrote "Alaska or Bust" with my finger in the dust that caked the car, and my mother smiled and let it stay. She told me that we would have our own house in the country, and I believed her, even though when we got to Fairbanks we lived in a campground next to the fairgrounds, and I stayed there all day exploring muskeg woods behind the camp while my mother worked at Dairy Queen. There were none of the expected high-paying jobs, none of the dream houses that we could afford. We knew no one. But my mother, like me, was lost in her own dream of Alaska, and she refused to be discouraged. So now, when I think back to that time, I try not to judge her too harshly. Alaska was her sanctuary, and she could not imagine, then, that anything could go wrong.

I am a child; I do what she asks. Put on my worn jean jacket. Push my straight dark hair behind my ears, then tie it back with a blue bandana. This is the look I have adopted since I arrived, Indian chic. I do not know what it means, exactly, to dress like this, but I have seen young men and women outfitted in this way — people my mother told me were Indian — and I decide I will dress that way too, because Indians are cool, aren't they? And as I am a bit Indian — a mixture of Chicana and Southwestern Indian and Norwegian that I will much later learn to call Mestiza — I am determined to dress appropriately. My attire adjusted, I move toward the door. Look pleadingly at my mother's blanketed back. I really don't want to go out. Then, in imitation of my mother, I sigh loudly, pick up the keys. Step out into the hall.

Creep down the narrow stairs. Afraid, in my childish way, of strangers, of being where I think I am not supposed to be, up late in a room above a bar. And I see a man on the landing. His back to me. And he whips around and raises a shotgun and aims it at my face. "I told all you goddamn Indians to get the fuck out of my bar."

I am twelve, and I have never seen a gun before. I am twelve, and I come from California, where night follows day in an orderly fashion, where on the Fourth of July I whirl like a comet with sparklers clutched tight in two hands. Where I place black pellets on the pavement to watch them transform into sooty snakes. I am twelve, and I am frozen on the landing of a strange staircase, with a shotgun staring in my face with its one, unblinking eye.

I am usually a silent child, but my fear makes me speak. My mouth opens and out rush words, tumbling over one another like frightened animals. My mother. California. The dog in the car, maybe already peeing on the seat. The dog is like a ship I swim to, desperately. He lowers the gun and I skitter past, fly to the door. Which I cannot open; it is locked. The man raises the latch, shoves me outside.

I stand outside on the cool grass, the early morning bright and exotic around me. I close my eyes for a moment and wish hard for home. Then open them to see revelers sway aimlessly by, laughing, cursing, swigging from bottles. I move toward the safety of the car.

And I am twelve, and I don't know what to do, can't think about what happened to me in any coherent fashion. I do not understand. I know racism exists — though I do not know what it is called — but not like this. I thought it was something else, people who called black people bad names, people who snickered when they heard my last name. Mexican, they'd sneer. I knew that. Knew shame, about my last name, which I claimed was Spanish, not Mexican, knowing that to be less shameful, although I didn't know why. But nothing more. Not then. And Indian, what was that to me? An exotic people with feathers, that had some slight relation to my father, to me. But I was not Indian. Nor Mexican. Nor Norwegian. Not really. I am just myself, a quiet girl who liked to read, to write, a girl who had always loved the Fourth of July, the night's rich promise broken by the sizzle and spark of fire.

And now I have been shaken into a world I don't understand, a cold, foreign world, where men I don't know can hate me for the way I look. I don't know what to do, so I take the dog for a walk. She sniffs desultorily, squats on the lawn to pee. I look at the new grass stains on my jeans, souvenirs from the fall I took from the man's push. Two young men pass by, say hello. They have witnessed my ejection from the lodge.

"Did he hurt you?" one asks. They are both Indian; their glossy black hair is tied back with bandanas. They wear T-shirts, jean jackets.

I am afraid to answer, but I shake my head.

"He's an asshole," the other young man says. His words are slow and strangely accented; I will soon learn to recognize this as a village accent. "Fucking white man." He shakes a fist at the lodge.

I try to smile to show my gratefulness, and watch them with head bowed as they walk away. They are drunk; I know that even then, but their words redeem me nonetheless. Later I will understand those words as my introduction into a place I will dwell for all my time in Alaska, those words which delineate me as one of them, as a Native person. For in Alaska, as I would learn, the complexity of my ethnicity was irrelevant; I looked Native, therefore I was.

For a long time I crouch beside the car with my arms around the dog's neck. What will I do? I could sleep in the car, but my mother will be mad. But can I go back in? What if the man won't let me? What if he . . . my thoughts veer away from certain subjects. The dog pulls away, shakes herself. I must go back.

I stand at the door. Through the window I can see the man watching, see the slim shadow of the gun. I am afraid. My legs shake; my hand is weak, but I push the door open.

And the man grabs my shoulder hard. Twists me toward him. Peers down into my face. He is bearded and the hair on his face makes him as frightening as a fierce animal. "All right," he says, though I have no idea what he means. For me, nothing is right. He pushes me toward the stairs and I run up them, breathless, heart somersaulting. I imagine too clearly a sudden crack, a searing pain in my spine. In our room I collapse on the bed as if shot. Tears first, then the story.

My mother waits until the next morning to confront the lodge owner. She gets the story while I mop a pancake around my plate, too scared and shamed to eat. The bearded man is the man who owns the lodge, and he tells his side calmly, reasonably, as if there is nothing unusual about pointing shotguns at twelve-year-olds. Some Indians from Minto were partying in the bar, he tells us, and wouldn't leave at closing time. So he fired a shot of tear gas, cleared the place out. As for me, "she looks like a goddamn Native," he says, and shrugs. And the other guests eating breakfast look at me, nod. There is nothing more to say, no apologies necessary. And my mother's angry words are just irritations, like BBs fired at a grizzly bear.

We left soon after that, and my mother drove as fast as she dared on that gravel road, gripping the steering wheel tight, her hands like fists clenched. I was quiet. I didn't know I should be angry. Didn't know, really, why I felt so ashamed. Even my mother's anger couldn't take that shame away, for under her anger I sensed her own fear of this place she'd brought me to, of these people. Her confusion. She repeated that the man had thought I was Indian, as if somehow that should explain it. But that confused me. Because I *was* Indian, though not Alaskan Indian, and not all Indian. Did that make what the man did excusable? My mother did not explain.

What did it mean to be Indian? Did I put it on with the clothes I wore? Why was my appearance read one way in California and another way in Alaska? In California, where everyone aimed for a tan, my skin color was something to be envied, when it could be separated from the stigma of my Mexican last name. I had grown vain of it, in a childish way. Proud that I often had the best "tan." I secretly looked down on lighter-skinned children, was sure their pink and white skin was ugly, undesirable. Otherwise why would my mother and so many others spend hours roasting themselves brown on the beach? I got it naturally; I must be superior. In Alaska, far from beaches, where the long dark winters bleached skin as pale as the long months of snow, brown skin did not mean beach and health, but it meant something else, something I would understand some people thought shameful. Native. That's what it meant, and I would discover how that word could be spit out with as much disgust as any racial slur.

Manley Hot Springs was a defining moment of my life in Alaska. It was the first time someone mistook me for an Alaskan Native — and one of the most frightening — but it would not be the last. My entire life in Alaska has been shaped by the fact that people — both white and Native — think I am Athabascan or Yupik, Tlingit or Inupiat. I reaped the benefits of that: smiles and conversation from old Yupik women on the bus, an unquestioned acceptance in villages and at Native cultural events. When I taught at the university, I connected easily with Native students. But I also reaped the pain.

When I tell this story to people, there is a coda I usually include. A few years after our trip up to Manley, a similar thing happened; again the lodge owner tried to throw some people out of the bar; again he waved a shotgun. But this time it was not at a child who looked Native. It was at a man — and while I don't know if he was white or Native, I do know he was armed, and he shot first and killed the lodge owner. As vengeful as it sounds, my mother and I were pleased by this, and when I retell it as the logical end to my own story, I smile. He infected me with his hatred, and I was — am — glad he is dead. I like this end because it is satisfying; it gives the story a sort of rough justice. It gives life — so messy and vague — an aesthetically pleasing shape, as neat as fiction. I also like the way I appear in this version: invulnerable, a tough person who can speak of death coolly. Perhaps my liking for this end is left over from my turbulent adolescence, a time so fraught with pain that my only tool of survival was the tough facade I adopted and my insistence that nothing could hurt me. Perhaps the story, ended this way, is proof of that.

The real end of the story is more complicated. Because of course I was not untouched. I learned to be afraid, learned that Alaska — as beloved as it would become — was not the sanctuary my mother had hoped for. My mother was able to close her eyes and keep hoping. For me, any possibility of sanctuary was shattered. On the drive back to Fairbanks, I had asked my mother if we could go home. She knew I didn't mean the campground. We live here now, was what she told me, and I remember crying when she said that. I think even then I wondered how I would survive.

In a few years, my mother would have what she dreamed of — the high-paying construction job, her own house. In a few years she would also slam into prejudice and violence on the job, but by then, Alaska was home, so she never seriously considered leaving.

In a few years, I would hear things and learn more: hear the smug tone of the high-school counselor as he tried to steer me into the vocational track — despite my good grades; hear, more than once, the anxiety in a white boyfriend's voice as he asked for assurance that I wasn't really Native; hear the nervous laughter at a party when a white man told how he raped "a squaw" in the back of a truck. Hear the silence that followed that laughter. I was spit at in small towns, refused service in bars. In just a few years, I could recite the litany of insults so many people of color know. But I would also learn to put a name to what was happening to me, and learn to be angry. I would learn that what happened to me was not my fault, nor was it unique to Alaska. Even later, I would learn to mold my anger into something I could use.

But I didn't know any of that then. I only knew fear, and shame.

I never wore the bandana or jean jacket again.

TONY EARLEY

Somehow Form a Family

In July 1969, I looked a lot like Opie in the second or third season of The Andy Griffith Show. I was a small boy with a big head. I wore blue jeans with the cuffs turned up and horizontally striped pullover shirts. I was the brother in a father-mother-brother-sister family. We lived in a four-room house at the edge of the country, at the foot of the mountains, outside a small town in North Carolina, but it could have been anywhere.

On one side of us lived Mr. and Mrs. White. They were old and rich. Their driveway was paved. Mrs. White was the president of the town garden club. When she came to visit Mama she brought her own ashtray. Mr. White was almost deaf. When he watched the news on television, it sounded like thunder in the distance. The Whites had an aluminum travel trailer in which you could see your reflection. One summer they hitched it to their Chrysler and pulled it all the way to Alaska.

On the other side of us lived Mack and Joan. They had just graduated from college. I thought Joan was beautiful and still do. Mack had a bass boat and a three-tray tackle box in which swam a bristling school of lures. On the other side of Mack and Joan lived Mrs. Taylor, who was old, and on the other side of Mrs. Taylor lived Mr. and Mrs. Frady, who had a fierce dog. My sister, Shelly, and I called it the Frady dog. The Frady dog lived a long and bitter life. It did not die until well after I had a driver's license.

On the far side of the Whites lived Mr. and Mrs. John Harris; Mr. and Mrs. Burlon Harris lived beyond them. John and Burlon were first cousins. John was a teacher who in the summers fixed lawn mowers, including ours, in a building behind his house. Burlon reminded me of Mr. Green Jeans on Captain Kangaroo. He kept horses and let us play in his barn. Shelly once commandeered one of his cats and brought it home to live with us. He did not mind; he asked her if she wanted another one. We rode our bicycles toward Mr. Harris's house as if pulled there by gravity. We did not ride in the other direction; the Frady dog sat in its yard and watched for us.

In July 1969 we did not have much money, but in the hierarchy of southern poor, we were the good kind, the kind you would not mind living on your road. We were clean. Our clothes were clean. We went to church. Easter mornings, Mama stood us in front of the yellow-bells bush and took our picture. We had meat at every meal — chicken and cube steak and pork chops and ham — and plenty of milk to drink. We were not trashy. Mrs. White would not sit with her ashtray in the kitchen of trashy people. Trashy people lived in the two houses around the curve past Mr. Harris's. When Daddy drove by those houses we could see that the kids in the yard had dirty faces. They were usually jabbing at something with a stick. Shelly and I were not allowed to ride our bicycles around the curve.

I knew we were poor only because our television was black and white. It was an old Admiral, built in the 1950s, with brass knobs the size of baseballs. Its cabinet was a cube of steel with a painted-on mahogany grain. Hoss on Bonanza could not have picked it up by himself. It was a formidable object, but its vertical hold was shot. We gathered around it the night Neil Armstrong walked on the moon, but we could not tell what was happening. The picture flipped up and down. We turned off the lights in the living room so we could see better. We listened to Walter Cronkite. In the distance we could hear Mr. White's color TV rumbling. We changed the channel and listened to Huntley and Brinkley. We could hear the scratchy radio transmissions coming down out of space, but we could not see anything. Daddy got behind the TV with a flashlight. He said, "Is that better? Is that better?" but it never was. Mama said, "Just be thankful you've got a television."

After the Eagle had landed, but before the astronauts opened the door and came out, Mack knocked on the door and asked us if we wanted to look at the moon. He was an engineer for a power company and had set up his surveyor's transit in the back yard. Daddy and Shelly and I went with him. We left Mama sitting in the living room in the blue light of the TV. She said she did not want to miss anything. The moon, as I remember it, was full, although I've since learned that it wasn't. I remember that a galaxy of lightning bugs blinked against the black-pine trees that grew between our yard and that of the Whites. Mack pointed the transit at the sky. Daddy held me up so I could see. The moon inside the instrument was startlingly bright; the man in the moon was clearly visible, although the men on the moon weren't. "You can't see them or anything," Mack said, which I already knew. I said, "I know that." I wasn't stupid, and did not like to be talked to as if I were. Daddy put me down. He and Mack stood for a while and talked. Daddy smoked a cigarette. In the bright yard Shelly chased lightning bugs. She did not run but instead jumped slowly, her feet together. I realized that she was pretending to walk on the moon, pretending that she was weightless. I remember these things for sure. I am tempted to say that she was beautiful in the moonlight, and I'm sure she was, but that isn't something I remember noticing that night, only a thing I need to say now.

Eight, maybe nine months later, Shelly and I rode the bus home from school. It was a Thursday, Mama's day off, Easter time. The cherry tree in the garden separating our driveway from that of the Whites was in brilliant, full bloom. We could hear it buzzing from the road. One of us checked the mailbox. We looked up the driveway at our house. Something was wrong with it, but we couldn't tell what. Daddy was adding four rooms onto the house, and we were used to it appearing large and unfinished. Black tar paper was tacked to the outside walls of the new part, but the old part was still covered with white asbestos shingles. In the coming summer, Daddy and a crew of brick masons would finish transforming the house into a split-level ranch-style, remarkably similar to the one in which the Bradys would live. I loved the words "split-level ranch-style." To me they meant "rich."

Shelly and I spotted what was wrong at the same time. A giant television antenna had attached itself to the roof. It was as shiny and tall as a young tree. It looked dangerous, as if it would bite, like a praying mantis. The antenna slowly began to turn, as if it had noticed us. Shelly and I looked quickly at each other, our mouths wide open, and then back at the antenna. We sprinted up the driveway.

In the living room, on the spot occupied by the Admiral that morning, sat a magnificent new color TV, a Zenith, with a 21-inch screen. Its cabinet was made of real wood. Gomer Pyle, U.S.M.C. was on. I will never forget that. Gomer Pyle and Sergeant Carter were the first two people I ever saw on a color television. The olive green and khaki of their uniforms was dazzling. Above them was the blue sky of California. The sky in California seemed bluer than the sky in North Carolina.

We said, "Is that ours?"

Mama said, "I'm going to kill your daddy." He had charged the TV without telling her. Two men from Sterchi's Furniture had showed up at the house that morning with the TV on a truck. They climbed onto the roof and planted the antenna.

We said, "Can we keep it?"

Mama said, "I don't know," but I noticed she had written the numbers of the stations we could get on the dial of the Channel Master, the small box that controlled the direction the antenna pointed. Mama would never have written on anything she planned on taking back to the store.

The dial of the Channel Master was marked like a compass. Channel 3 in Charlotte lay to the east; Channel 13 lay to the west. Channel 7 in Spartanburg and Channel 4 in Greenville rested side by side below them in the south. For years these cities would mark the outside edges of the world as I knew it. Shelly reached out and turned the dial. Mama smacked her on the hand. Gomer grew fuzzy and disappeared. I said, "Mama, she broke it." When the dial stopped turning, Mama carefully turned it back to the south. Gomer reappeared, resurrected. Jim Nabors probably never looked better to anyone in his whole life than he did to us right then.

Mama sat us down on the couch and laid down the law. Mama always laid down the law when she was upset. We were not to touch the TV. We could not turn it on, nor could we change the channel. Under no circumstances were we to touch the Channel Master. The Channel Master was very expensive. And if we so much as looked at the knobs that controlled the color, she would whip us. It had taken her all afternoon to get the color just right.

We lived in a split-level ranch-style house, with two maple trees and a rosebush in the front yard, outside a town that could have been named Springfield. We had a color TV. We had a Channel Master antenna that turned slowly on top of our house until it found and pulled from the sky electromagnetic waves for our nuclear family.

We watched Hee Haw, starring Buck Owens and Roy Clark; we watched All in the Family, The Mary Tyler Moore Show, The Bob Newhart Show, The Carol Burnett Show, and Mannix, starring Mike Connors with Gail Fisher as Peggy; we watched Gunsmoke, and Bonanza, even after Adam left and Hoss died and Little Joe's hair turned gray; we watched Adam-12 and Kojak, McCloud, Columbo, and Hawaii Five-O; we watched Cannon, a Quinn Martin production, and Barnaby Jones, a Quinn Martin production, which co-starred Miss America and Uncle Jed from The Beverly Hillbillies. Daddy finished the new part of the house and moved out soon thereafter. He rented a trailer in town and took the old Admiral out of the basement with him. We watched Mutual of Omaha's Wild Kingdom and The Wonderful World of Disney. After school we watched Gomer Pyle, U.S.M.C., The Beverly Hillbillies, Gilligan's Island, and The Andy Griffith Show. Upstairs, we had rooms of our own. Mama stopped taking us to church.

On Friday nights we watched The Partridge Family, The Brady Bunch, Room 222, The Odd Couple, and Love, American Style. Daddy came to visit on Saturdays. We watched The Little Rascals on Channel 3 with Fred Kirby, the singing cowboy, and his sidekick, Uncle Jim. We watched The Little Rascals on Channel 4 with Monty DuPuy, the weatherman, and his sidekick, Doohickey. Mornings, before school, we watched the Three Stooges with Mr. Bill on Channel 13. Mr. Bill worked alone. The school year Daddy moved out, Mr. Bill showed Bible-story cartoons instead of the Three Stooges and we went to school angry.

After each of Daddy's visits Mama said he was getting better. Shelly and I tried to imagine living with the Bradys but realized we would not fit in. They were richer and more popular at school. They did not have southern accents. One Saturday Daddy brought me a set of golf clubs, which I had asked for but did not expect to get. It was raining that day. I took the clubs out in the yard and very quickly realized that golf was harder than it looked on television. I went back inside and wiped the mud and water off the clubs with Bounty paper towels, the quicker picker-upper. Upstairs I heard Mama say, "Do you think he's stupid?" I spread the golf clubs on the floor around me. I tuned in Shock Theater on Channel 13 and turned it up loud.

Shelly had a crush on Bobby Brady; I had a crush on Jan. Jan had braces, I had braces. Jan had glasses, I had glasses. Their daddy was an architect. Our daddy lived in a trailer in town with a poster of Wile E. Coyote and the Road Runner on the livingroom wall. The Coyote held the Road Runner firmly by the neck. The caption on the poster said, "Beep, Beep your ass." I lay in bed at night and imagined being married to Jan Brady but having an affair with Marcia. I wondered how we would tell Jan, what Marcia and I would do then, where we would go. Greg Brady beat me up. I shook his hand and told him I deserved it. Alice refused to speak to me. During this time Mrs. White died. I heard the ambulance in the middle of the night. It sounded like the one on

Emergency! I opened the door to Mama's room to see if she was okay. She was embarrassed because our dog barked and barked.

Rhoda left The Mary Tyler Moore Show. Maude and George Jefferson left All in the Family; Florida, Maude's maid, left Maude. Daddy moved back in. He watched the news during supper, the TV as loud as Mr. White's. We were not allowed to talk during the news. This was the law. After the news we watched Rhoda or Maude or Good Times. Daddy decided that cutting the grass should be my job. We had a big yard. I decided that I didn't want to do anything he said. Mr. White remarried. The new Mrs. White's daughter died of cancer. The new Mrs. White dug up every flower the old Mrs. White had planted; she cut down every tree and shrub, including the cherry tree in the garden between our driveways. Mama said the new Mrs. White broke her heart. Mr. White mowed and mowed and mowed their grass until it was as smooth as a golf course. Mack and Joan paved their driveway.

What I'm trying to say is this: we lived in a split-level ranch-style house; we had a Zenith in the living room and a Channel Master attached to the roof. But Shelly and I fought like Thelma and J.J. on Good Times. I wanted to live in Hawaii and work for Steve McGarrett. Shelly said McGarrett would never give me a job. In all things Shelly was on Daddy's side; I lined up on Mama's. Friday evenings, when Daddy got home from work, Mama sent me out to snoop around in his car. I pretended I had a search warrant, that I was Dano on a big case. Shelly reported my snooping to Daddy. Mama said I was a good son.

Every Saturday, before he went to work, Daddy left word that I was to cut the grass before he got home. I stayed in bed until lunch. Shelly came into my room and said, "You better get up." I flipped her the bird. She said, "I'm telling." I got up in time to watch professional wrestling on Channel 3. I hated the bad guys. They did not fight fair. They hid brass knuckles in their trunks and beat the good guys until they bled. They won too often. Mama brought me tomato-and-onion sandwiches. I could hear Mack on one side and Mr. White on the other mowing their grass. I could hear John Harris and Mr. Frady and Mrs. Taylor's daughter, Lucille, mowing grass. Lucille lived outside of Charlotte but came home on weekends just to mow Mrs. Taylor's grass. We had the shaggiest lawn on the road. After wrestling, I watched the Game of the Week on Channel 4. I listened for the sound of Daddy's Volkswagen. Mama came in the living room and said, "Son, maybe you should mow some of the grass before your daddy gets home. You know what's going to happen."

I knew what was going to happen. I knew that eventually he would make me mow the grass. I knew that when I was through, Mack would come through the pine trees laughing. He would say, "Charles, I swear that is the laziest boy I have ever seen." Mack had a Snapper Comet riding mower, on which he sat like a king. I never saw him on it that I did not want to bean him with a rock. Daddy would shake his head and say, "Mack, dead lice wouldn't fall off that boy." Every Saturday night we ate out at Scoggin's Seafood and Steak House. Hee Haw came on at seven; All in the Family came on at eight.

And then Shelly and I were in high school. We watched M*A*S*H and Lou Grant, The Love Boat and Fantasy Island. We watched Dynasty and Dallas. Opie was Richie Cunningham on Happy Days. Ben Cartwright showed up in a black bathrobe on Battlestar Galactica. The Channel Master stopped working, but no one bothered to have it fixed. The antenna was left immobile on the roof in a compromised position: we could almost get most of the channels. One summer Mack built a pool in his back yard. Joan lay in a bikini beside it in the sun. The next summer Mack built a fence. This was during the late Seventies. Shelly lay in her room with the lights turned off and listened to Dark Side of the Moon. On Friday nights she asked me to go out and drink beer with her and her friends. I always said no. I did not want to miss The Rockford Files.

In those days Shelly and I watched The Guiding Light when we got home from school. It was our soap. I remember that Ed Bauer's beautiful wife, Rita, left him because he was boring. Shelly said I reminded her of Ed Bauer. She wore her hair like Farrah Fawcett-Majors on Charlie's Angels. After The Guiding Light I changed the channel and watched Star Trek. I could not stay awake in school. I went to sleep during home room. During the day I woke up only long enough to change classes and eat lunch. I watched Star Trek when I got home as if it were beamed to our house by God. I did not want to be Captain Kirk or any of the main characters. I just wanted to go with them. I wanted to wear a red jersey and walk the long, anonymous halls of the starship Enterprise as it disappeared into space. One day Star Trek was preempted by an ABC After School Special. I tried to kick the screen out of the TV. I was wearing sneakers so the glass would not break. Shelly hid in Mama and Daddy's room. I said, "Five-O. Open up." Then I kicked the door off the hinges.

Our family doctor thought I had narcolepsy. He sent me to a neurologist in Charlotte. Mama and Daddy went with me. In Charlotte, an EEG technician attached wires to my head. A small, round amber light glowed high up in the corner of the examination room. I watched the light until I went to sleep. The neurologist said that the EEG looked normal but that he would talk to us more about the results in a few minutes. He led us to a private waiting room. It was small and bare and paneled with wood. In it were four chairs. Most of one wall was taken up by a darkened glass. I could not see what was on the other side of it. I studied our reflection. Mama and Daddy were trying to pretend that the glass wasn't there. I said, "Pa, when we get back to the Ponderosa, do you want me to round up those steers on the lower forty?"

Daddy said, "What?"

I said, "Dammit, Jim. I'm a doctor."

Daddy said, "What are you talking about?"

Mama said, "Be quiet. They're watching us."

Shelly died on Christmas Eve morning when I was a freshman in college. She had wrecked Mama's car. That night I stayed up late and watched the Pope deliver the Christmas mass from the Vatican. There was nothing else on. Daddy moved out again. My college almost shut down during the week The Thorn Birds was broadcast. Professors rescheduled papers and exams. In the basement of my dorm twenty-five nineteen-year-old guys shouted at the TV when the Richard Chamberlain character told the Rachel Ward character that he loved God more. At age nineteen, it was impossible to love God more than Rachel Ward. My best friend, a guy from Kenya, talked me into switching from The Guiding Light to General Hospital. This was during the glory days of General Hospital. Laura was supposedly dead, but Luke knew in his heart she was still alive.

Going home was strange, as if the Mayberry I expected had become Mayberry, R.F.D. Shelly was gone. Daddy was gone. The second Mrs. White died, then Mr. White left. The Fradys had moved away. John Harris had a heart attack and stopped fixing lawn mowers. Mama mowed our grass by herself with a rider. I stopped going to see Burlon Harris because he teared up every time he tried to talk about Shelly. Mack and Joan had a son named Timmy. Mack and Joan got a divorce. Mack moved to a farm out in the country; Joan moved to town.

Daddy fell in love with Mama my senior year and moved back in. The Zenith began slowly dying. Its picture narrowed into a greenly tinted slit. It stared like a diseased eye into the living room where Mama and Daddy sat. They turned off the lights so they could see better. I became a newspaper reporter. With my first Christmas bonus I bought myself a television, a 19-inch GE. With my second Christmas bonus I bought Mama and Daddy one. They hooked it up to cable. When I visited them on Thursdays we watched The Cosby Show, Family Ties, Cheers, Night Court, and Hill Street Blues. Daddy gave up on broadcast TV when NBC canceled Hill Street Blues and replaced it with L.A. Law. Now he mostly watches the Discovery Channel. Mama calls it the "airplanes and animals channel." They are in the fifteenth year of their new life together. I bear them no grudges. They were very young when I knew them best.

In grad school I switched back to The Guiding Light. I had known Ed Bauer longer than I had known all but a few of my friends. It pleased me to see him in Springfield every afternoon, trying to do good. I watched The Andy Griffith Show twice a day. I could glance at Opie and tell you what year the episode was filmed. I watched the Gulf War from a stool in a bar.

Eventually I married a woman who grew up in a family that watched television only on special occasions — when Billie Jean King played Bobby Riggs, when Diana married Prince Charles. My wife was a student in a seminary. She did not want to meet Ed Bauer, nor could I explain, without sounding pathetic, why he was important to me. The first year we were married I watched the winter Olympics huddled beneath a blanket in the frigid basement of the house we had rented. This was in a closed-down steel town near Pittsburgh, during the time I contemplated jumping from a bridge into the Ohio River. My wife asked the seminary community to pray for me. Ann B. Davis, who had played Alice on The Brady Bunch, was a member of that community. One day I saw her in the cafeteria at school. She looked much the same as when she played Alice, except that her hair was white, and she wore small, gold glasses. I didn't talk to her. I had heard that she didn't like talking about The Brady Bunch, and I could not think of anything to say to her about the world in which we actually lived. I sat in the seminary cafeteria and stared at her as much as I could without anyone noticing. I don't know if she prayed for me or not, but I like to think that she did. I wanted to tell her that I grew up in a split-level ranch-style house outside a small town that could have been named Springfield, but that something had gone wrong inside it. I wanted to tell her that years ago Alice had been important to me, that my sister and

I had looked to Alice for something we could not name, and had at least seen a picture of what love looked like. I wanted to tell her that no one in my family ever raised their voice while the television was on, that late at night even a bad television show could keep me from hearing the silence inside my own heart. I wanted to tell her that Ed Bauer and I were still alive, that both of us had always wanted to do what was right. Ann B. Davis stood, walked over to the trash can, and emptied her tray. She walked out of the cafeteria and into a small, gray town near Pittsburgh. I wanted her to be Alice. I wanted her to smile as if she loved me. I wanted her to say, "Buck up, kiddo, everything's going to be all right." And what I'm trying to tell you now is this: I grew up in a split-level ranch-style house outside a town that could have been anywhere. I grew up in front of a television. I would have believed her.

NORA EPHRON

A Few Words About Breasts

I have to begin with a few words about androgyny. In grammar school, in the fifth and sixth grades, we were all tyrannized by a rigid set of rules that supposedly determined whether we were boys or girls. The episode in *Huckleberry Finn* where Huck is disguised as a girl and gives himself away by the way he threads a needle and catches a ball — that kind of thing. We learned that the way you sat, crossed your legs, held a cigarette, and looked at your nails — the way you did these things instinctively was absolute proof of your sex. Now obviously most children did not take this literally, but I did. I thought that just one slip, just one incorrect cross of my legs or flick of an imaginary cigarette ash would turn me from whatever I was into the other thing; that would be all it took, really. Even though I was outwardly a girl and had many of the trappings generally associated with girldom — a girl's name, for example, and dresses, my own telephone, an autograph book — I spent the early years of my adolescence absolutely certain that I might at any point gum it up. I did not feel at all like a girl. I was boyish. I was athletic, ambitious, outspoken, competitive, noisy, rambunctious. I had scabs on my knees and my socks slid into my loafers and I could throw a football. I wanted desperately not to be that way, not to be a mixture of both things, but instead just one, a girl, a definite indisputable girl.

As soft and as pink as a nursery. And nothing would do that for me, I felt, but breasts.

I was about six months younger than everyone else in my class, and so for about six months after it began, for six months after my friends had begun to develop (that was the word we used, develop), I was not particularly worried. I would sit in the bathtub and look down at my breasts and know that any day now, any second now, they would start growing like everyone else's. They didn't. "I want to buy a bra," I said to my mother one night. "What for?" she said. My mother was really hateful about bras, and by the time my third sister had gotten to the point where she was ready to want one, my mother had worked the whole business into a comedy routine. "Why not use a Band-Aid instead?" she would say. It was a source of great pride to my mother that she had never even had to wear a brassiere until she had her fourth child, and then only because her gynecologist made her. It was incomprehensible to me that anyone could ever be proud of something like that. It was the 1950s, for God's sake. Jane Russell. Cashmere sweaters. Couldn't my mother see that? *"I am too old to wear an undershirt."* Screaming. Weeping. Shouting. "Then don't wear an undershirt," said my mother. "But I want to buy a bra." "What for?"

I suppose that for most girls, breasts, brassieres, that entire thing, has more trauma, more to do with the coming of adolescence, with becoming a woman, than anything else. Certainly more than getting your period, although that, too, was traumatic, symbolic. But you could see breasts; they were there; they were visible. Whereas a girl could claim to have her period for months before she actually got it and nobody would ever know the difference. Which is exactly what I did. All you had to do was make a great fuss over having enough nickels for the Kotex machine and walk around clutching your stomach and moaning for three to five days a month about The Curse and you could convince anybody. There is a school of thought somewhere in the women's lib/women's mag/gynecology establishment that claims that menstrual cramps are purely psychological, and I lean toward it. Not that I didn't have them finally. Agonizing cramps, heating-pad cramps, go-down-to-the-school-nurse-and-lie-on-the-cot cramps. But unlike any pain I had ever suffered, I adored the pain of cramps, welcomed it, wallowed in it, bragged about it. "I can't go. I have cramps." "I can't do that. I have cramps." And most of all, gigglingly, blushingly: "I can't swim. I have cramps." Nobody ever used the hard-core word. Menstruation. God, what an awful word. Never that. "I have cramps."

The morning I first got my period, I went into my mother's bedroom to tell her. And my mother, my utterly-hateful-about-bras mother, burst into tears. It was really a lovely moment, and I remember it so clearly not just because it was one of the two times I ever saw my mother cry on my account (the other was when I was caught being a six-year-old kleptomaniac), but also because the incident did not mean to me what it meant to her. Her little girl, her firstborn, had finally become a woman. That was what she was crying about. My reaction to the event, however, was that I might well be a woman in some scientific, textbook sense (and could at least stop faking every month and stop wasting all those nickels). But in another sense — in a visible sense — I was as androgynous and as liable to tip over into boyhood as ever.

I started with a 28 AA bra. I don't think they made them any smaller in those days, although I gather that now you can buy bras for five-year-olds that don't have any cups whatsoever in them; trainer bras they are called. My first brassiere came from Robinson's Department Store in Beverly Hills. I went there alone, shaking, positive they would look me over and smile and tell me to come back next year. An actual fitter took me into the dressing room and stood over me while I took off my blouse and tried the first one on. The little puffs stood out on my chest. "Lean over," said the fitter. (To this day, I am not sure what fitters in bra departments do except to tell you to lean over.) I leaned over, with the fleeting hope that my breasts would miraculously fall out of my body and into the puffs. Nothing.

"Don't worry about it," said my friend Libby some months later, when things had not improved. "You'll get them after you're married."

"What are you talking about?" I said.

"When you get married," Libby explained, "your husband will touch your breasts and rub them and kiss them and they'll grow."

That was the killer. Necking I could deal with. Intercourse I could deal with. But it had never crossed by mind that a man was going to touch my breasts, that breasts had something to do with all that, petting, my God, they never mentioned petting in my little sex manual about the fertilization of the ovum. I became dizzy. For I knew instantly — as naïve as I had been only a moment before — that only part of what she was saying was true: the touching, rubbing, kissing part, not the growing part. And I knew that no one would ever want to marry me. I had no breasts. I would never have breasts.

My best friend in school was Diana Raskob. She lived a block from me in a house full of wonders. English muffins, for instance. The Raskobs were the first people in Beverly Hills to have English muffins for breakfast. They also had an apricot tree in the back, and a badminton court, and a subscription to *Seventeen* magazine, and hundreds of games, like Sorry and Parcheesi and Treasure Hunt and Anagrams. Diana and I spent three or four afternoons a week in their den reading and playing and eating. Diana's mother's kitchen was full of the most colossal assortment of junk food I have ever been exposed to. My house was full of apples and peaches and milk and homemade chocolate-chip cookies — which were nice, and good for you, but-not-right-before-dinner-or-you'll-spoil-your-appetite. Diana's house had nothing in it that was good for you, and what's more, you could stuff it in right up until dinner and nobody cared. Bar-B-Q potato chips (they were the first in them, too), giant bottles of ginger ale, fresh popcorn with melted butter, hot fudge sauce on Baskin-Robbins jamoca ice cream, powdered-sugar doughnuts from Van de Kamp's. Diana and I had been best friends since we were seven; we were about equally popular in school (which is to say, not particularly), we had about the same success with boys (extremely intermittent), and we looked much the same. Dark. Tall. Gangly.

It is September, just before school begins. I am eleven years old, about to enter the seventh grade, and Diana and I have not seen each other all summer. I have been to camp and she has been somewhere like Banff with her parents. We are meeting, as we often do, on the street midway between our two houses, and we will walk back to Diana's and eat junk and talk about what has happened to each of us that summer. I am walking down Walden Drive in my jeans and my father's shirt hanging out and my old red loafers with the socks falling into them and coming toward me is . . . I take a deep breath . . . a young woman. Diana. Her hair is curled and she has a waist and hips and a bust and she is wearing a straight skirt, an article of clothing I have been repeatedly told I will be unable to wear until I have the hips to hold it up. My jaw drops, and suddenly I am crying, crying hysterically, can't catch my breath sobbing. My best friend has betrayed me. She has gone ahead without me and done it. She has shaped up.

Here are some things I did to help:
Bought a Mark Eden Bust Developer.
Slept on my back for four years.

Splashed cold water on them every night because some French actress said in *Life* magazine that that was what *she* did for her perfect bustline.

Ultimately, I resigned myself to a bad toss and began to wear padded bras. I think about them now, think about all those years in high school and I went around in them, my three padded bras, every single one of them with different-sized breasts. Each time I changed bras I changed sizes: one week nice perky but not too obtrusive breasts, the next medium-sized slightly pointy ones, the next week knockers, true knockers; all the time, whatever size I was, carrying around this rubberized appendage on my chest that occasionally crashed into a wall and was poked inward and had to be poked outward — I think about all that and wonder how anyone kept a straight face through it. My parents, who normally had no restraints about needling me — why did they say nothing as they watched my chest go up and down? My friends, who would periodically inspect my breasts for signs of growth and reassure me — why didn't they at least counsel consistency?

And the bathing suits. I die when I think about the bathing suits. That was the era when you could lay an uninhabited bathing suit on the beach and someone would make a pass at it. I would put one on, an absurd swimsuit with its enormous bust built into it, the bones from the suit stabbing me in the rib cage and leaving little red welts on my body, and there I would be, my chest plunging straight downward absolutely vertically from my collarbone to the top of my suit and then suddenly, wham, out came all that padding and material and wiring absolutely horizontally.

Buster Klepper was the first boy who ever touched them. He was my boyfriend my senior year of high school. There is a picture of him in my highschool yearbook that makes him look quite attractive in a Jewish, hornrimmed-glasses sort of way, but the picture does not show the pimples, which were air-brushed out, or the dumbness. Well, that isn't really fair. He wasn't dumb. He just wasn't terribly bright. His mother refused to accept it, refused to accept the relentlessly average report cards, refused to deal with her son's inevitable destiny in some junior college or other. "He was tested," she would say to me, apropos of nothing, "and it came out a hundred and forty-five. That's near-genius." Had the word "underachiever" been coined, she probably would have lobbed that one at me, too. Anyway, Buster was really very sweet — which is, I know, damning with faint praise, but there it is. I was the editor of the front page of the high-school newspaper and he was editor of the back page; we had to work together, side by side, in the print shop, and that was how it started. On our first date, we went to see *April Love*, starring Pat Boone. Then we started going together. Buster had a green coupe, a 1950 Ford with an engine he had hand-chromed until it shone, dazzled, reflected the image of anyone who looked into it, anyone usually being Buster polishing it or the gas-station attendants he constantly asked to check the oil in order for them to be overwhelmed by the sparkle on the valves. The car also had a boot stretched over the back seat for reasons I never understood; hanging from the rearview mirror, as was the custom, was a pair of angora dice. A previous girl friend named Solange, who was famous throughout Beverly Hills High School for having no pigment in her right eyebrow, had knitted them for him. Buster and I would ride around town, the two of us seated to the left of the steering wheel. I would shift gears. It was nice.

There was necking. Terrific necking. First in the car, overlooking Los Angeles from what is now the Trousdale Estates. Then on the bed of his parents' cabana at Ocean House. Incredibly wonderful, frustrating necking, I loved it, really, but no further than necking, please don't, please, because there I was absolutely terrified of the general implications of going-a-step-further with a near-dummy and also terrified of his finding out there was next to nothing there (which he knew, of course; he wasn't that dumb).

I broke up with him at one point. I think we were apart for about two weeks. At the end of that time, I drove down to see a friend at a boarding school in Palos Verdes Estates and a disc jockey played "April Love" on the radio four times during the trip. I took it as a sign. I drove straight back to Griffith Park to a golf tournament Buster was playing in (he was the sixth-seeded teenage golf player in southern California) and presented myself back to him on the green of the eighteenth hole. It was all very dramatic. That night we went to a drive-in and I let him get his hand under my protuberances and onto my breasts. He really didn't seem to mind at all.

"Do you want to marry my son?" the woman asked me.

"Yes," I said.

I was nineteen years old, a virgin, going with this woman's son, this big strange woman who was married to a Lutheran minister in New Hampshire and pretended she was gentile and had this son, by her first husband, this total fool of a son who ran the hero-sandwich concession at Harvard Business School and whom for one moment one December in New Hampshire I said — as much out of politeness as anything else — that I wanted to marry.

"Fine," she said. "Now, here's what you do. Always make sure you're on top of him so you won't seem so small. My bust is very large, you see, so I always lie on my back to make it look smaller, but you'll have to be on top most of the time."

I nodded. "Thank you," I said.

"I have a book for you to read," she went on. "Take it with you when you leave. Keep it." She went to the bookshelf, found it, and gave it to me. It was a book on frigidity.

"Thank you," I said.

That is a true story. Everything in this article is a true story, but I feel I have to point out that that story in particular is true. It happened on December 30, 1960. I think about it often. When it first happened, I naturally assumed that the woman's son, my boyfriend, was responsible. I invented a scenario where he had had a little heart-to-heart with his mother and had confessed that his only objection to me was that my breasts were small; his mother then took it upon herself to help out. Now I think I was wrong about the incident. The mother was acting on her own, I think: that was her way of being cruel and competitive under the guise of being helpful and maternal. You have small breasts, she was saying; therefore you will never make him as happy as I have. Or you have small breasts; therefore you will doubtless have sexual problems. Or you have small breasts; therefore you are less woman than I am. She was, as it happens, only the first of what seems to me to be a never-ending string of women who have made competitive remarks to me about breast size. "I would love to wear a dress like that," my friend Emily says to me, "but my bust is too big." Like that. Why do women say these things to me? Do I attract these remarks the way other women attract married men or alcoholics or homosexuals? This summer, for example. I am at a party in East Hampton and I am introduced to a woman from Washington. She is a minor celebrity, very pretty and Southern and blond and outspoken, and I am flattered because she has read something I have written. We are talking animatedly, we have been talking no more than five minutes, when a man comes up to join us. "Look at the two of us," the woman says to the man, indicating me and her. "The two of us together couldn't fill an A cup." Why does she say that? It isn't even true, dammit, so why? Is she even more addled than I am on this subject? Does she honestly believe there is something wrong with her size breasts, which, it seems to me, now that I look hard at them, are just right? Do I unconsciously bring out competitiveness in women? In that form? What did I do to deserve it?

As for men.

There were men who minded and let me know that they minded. There were men who did not mind. In any case, *I* always minded.

And even now, now that I have been countlessly reassured that my figure is a good one, now that I am grown-up enough to understand that most of my feelings have very little to do with the reality of my shape, I am nonetheless obsessed by breasts. I cannot help it. I grew up in the terrible fifties — with rigid stereotypical sex roles, the insistence that men be men and dress like men and women be women and dress like women, the intolerance of androgyny — and I cannot shake it, cannot shake my feelings of inadequacy. Well, that time is gone, right? All those exaggerated examples of breast worship are gone, right? Those women were freaks, right? I know all that. And yet here I am, stuck with the psychological remains of it all, stuck with my own peculiar version of breast worship. You probably think I am crazy to go on like this: here I have set out to write a confession that is meant to hit you with the shock of recognition, and instead you are sitting there thinking I am thoroughly warped. Well, what can I tell you? If I had had them, I would have been a completely different person. I honestly believe that.

After I went into therapy, a process that made it possible for me to tell total strangers at cocktail parties that breasts were the hang-up of my life, I was often told that I was insane to have been bothered by my condition. I was also frequently told, by close friends, that I was extremely boring on the subject. And my girlfriends, the ones with nice big breasts, would go on endlessly about how their lives had been far more miserable than mine. Their bra straps were snapped in class. They couldn't sleep on their stomachs. They were stared at whenever the word "mountain" cropped up in geography. And *Evangeline*, good God what they went through every time someone had to stand up and recite the Prologue to Longfellow's *Evangeline*: ". . . stand like druids of eld . . . / With beards that rest on their bosoms." It was much worse for them, they tell me. They had a terrible time of it, they assure me. I don't know how lucky I was, they say.

I have thought about their remarks, tried to put myself in their place, considered their point of view. I think they are full of shit.   *1972*

DAVID SEDARIS

Let It Snow

In Binghamton, New York, winter meant snow, and though I was young when we left, I was able to recall great heaps of it, and use that memory as evidence that North Carolina was, at best, a third-rate institution. What little snow there was would usually melt an hour or two after hitting the ground, and there you'd be in your windbreaker and unconvincing mittens, forming a lumpy figure made mostly of mud. Snow Negroes, we called them.

The winter I was in the fifth grade we got lucky. Snow fell, and for the first time in years, it accumulated. School was canceled and two days later we got lucky again. There were eight inches on the ground, and rather than melting, it froze. On the fifth day of our vacation my mother had a little breakdown. Our presence had disrupted the secret life she led while we were at school, and when she could no longer take it she threw us out. It wasn't a gentle request, but something closer to an eviction. "Get the hell out of my house," she said.

We reminded her that it was our house, too, and she opened the front door and shoved us into the carport. "And stay out!" she shouted.

My sisters and I went down the hill and sledded with other children from the neighborhood. A few hours later we returned home, surprised to find that the door was still locked. "Oh, come on," we said. I rang the bell and when no one answered we went to the window and saw our mother in the kitchen, watching television. Normally she waited until five o'clock to have a drink, but for the past few days she'd been making an exception. Drinking didn't count if you followed a glass of wine with a cup of coffee, and so she had both a goblet and a mug positioned before her on the countertop.

"Hey!" we yelled. "Open the door. It's us." We knocked on the pane, and without looking in our direction, she refilled her goblet and left the room.

"That bitch," my sister Lisa said. We pounded again and again, and when our mother failed to answer we went around back and threw snowballs at her bedroom window. "You are going to be in so much trouble when Dad gets home!" we shouted, and in response my mother pulled the drapes. Dusk approached, and as it grew colder it occurred to us that we could possibly die. It happened, surely. Selfish mothers wanted the house to themselves, and their children were discovered years later, frozen like mastodons in blocks of ice.

My sister Gretchen suggested that we call our father, but none of us knew his number, and he probably wouldn't have done anything anyway. He'd gone to work specifically to escape our mother, and between the weather and her mood, it could be hours or even days before he returned home.

"One of us should get hit by a car," I said. "That would teach the both of them." I pictured Gretchen, her life hanging by a thread as my parents paced the halls of Rex Hospital, wishing they had been more attentive. It was really the perfect solution. With her out of the way, the rest of us would be more valuable and have a bit more room to spread out. "Gretchen, go lie in the street."

"Make Amy do it," she said.

Amy, in turn, pushed it off onto Tiffany, who was the youngest and had no concept of death. "It's like sleeping," we told her. "Only you get a canopy bed."

Poor Tiffany. She'd do just about anything in return for a little affection. All you had to do was call her Tiff and whatever you wanted was yours: her allowance money, her dinner, the contents of her Easter basket. Her eagerness to please was absolute and naked. When we asked her to lie in the middle of the street, her only question was "Where?"

We chose a quiet dip between two hills, a spot where drivers were almost required to skid out of control. She took her place, this six-year-old in a butter-colored coat, and we gathered on the curb to watch. The first car to happen by belonged to a neighbor, a fellow Yankee who had outfitted his tires with chains and stopped a few feet from our sister's body. "Is that a person?" he asked.

"Well, sort of," Lisa said. She explained that we'd been locked out of our house and though the man appeared to accept it as a reasonable explanation, I'm pretty sure it was him who told on us. Another car passed and then we saw our mother, this puffy figure awkwardly negotiating the crest of the hill. She did not own a pair of pants, and her legs were buried to the calves in snow. We wanted to send her home, to kick her out of nature just as she had kicked us out of the house, but it was hard to stay angry at someone that pitiful-looking.

"Are you wearing your *loafers?*" Lisa asked, and in response our mother raised her bare foot. "I *was* wearing loafers," she said. "I mean, really, it was there a second ago."

This was how things went. One moment she was locking us out of our own house and the next we were rooting around in the snow, looking for her left shoe. "Oh, forget about it," she said. "It'll turn up in a few days." Gretchen fitted her cap over my mother's foot. Lisa secured it with her scarf, and surrounding her tightly on all sides, we made our way back home.

ALICE WALKER

Beauty: When the Other Dancer Is the Self

It is a bright summer day in 1947. My father, a fat, funny man with beautiful eyes and a subversive wit, is trying to decide which of his eight children he will take with him to the county fair. My mother, of course, will not go. She is knocked out from getting most of us ready: I hold my neck stiff against the pressure of her knuckles as she hastily completes the braiding and beribboning of my hair.

My father is the driver for the rich old white lady up the road. Her name is Miss Mey. She owns all the land for miles around, as well as the house in which we live. All I remember about her is that she once offered to pay my mother thirty-five cents for cleaning her house, raking up piles of her magnolia leaves, and washing her family's clothes, and that my mother — she of no money, eight children, and a chronic earache — refused it. But I do not think of this in 1947. I am two-and-a-half years old. I want to go everywhere my daddy goes. I am excited at the prospect of riding in a car. Someone has told me fairs are fun. That there is room in the car for only three of us doesn't faze me at all. Whirling happily in my starchy frock, showing off my biscuit-polished patent-leather shoes and lavender socks, tossing my head in a way that makes my ribbons bounce, I stand, hands on hips, before my father. "Take me, Daddy," I say with assurance; "I'm the prettiest!"

Later, it does not surprise me to find myself in Miss Mey's shiny black car, sharing the back seat with the other lucky ones. Does not surprise me that I thoroughly enjoy the fair. At home that night I tell the unlucky ones all I can remember about the merry-go-round, the man who eats live chickens, and the teddy bears, until they say: that's enough, baby Alice. Shut up now, and go to sleep.

It is Easter Sunday, 1950. I am dressed in a green, flocked, scalloped-hem dress (handmade by my adoring sister, Ruth) that has its own smooth satin petticoat and tiny hot-pink roses tucked into each scallop. My shoes, new T-strap patent leather, again highly biscuit-polished. I am six years old and have learned one of the longest Easter speeches to be heard that day, totally un-like the speech I said when I was two: "Easter lilies / pure and white / blos-som in / the morning light." When I rise to give my speech I do so on a great wave of love and pride and expectation. People in the church stop rustling their new crinolines. They seem to hold their breath. I can tell they admire my dress, but it is my spirit, bordering on sassiness (womanishness), they se-cretly applaud.

"That girl's a little *mess*," they whisper to each other, pleased.

Naturally I say my speech without stammer or pause, unlike those who stutter, stammer, or, worst of all, forget. This is before the word "beautiful" ex-ists in people's vocabulary, but "Oh, isn't she the *cutest* thing!" frequently floats my way. "And got so much sense!" they gratefully add . . . for which thought-ful addition I thank them to this day.

It was great fun being cute. But then, one day, it ended.

I am eight years old and a tomboy. I have a cowboy hat, cowboy boots, checkered shirt and pants, all red. My playmates are my brothers, two and four years older than I. Their colors are black and green, the only difference in the way we are dressed. On Saturday nights we all go to the picture show, even my mother; Westerns are her favorite kind of movie. Back home, "on the ranch," we pretend we are Tom Mix, Hopalong Cassidy, Lash LaRue (we've even named one of our dogs Lash LaRue); we chase each other for hours rustling cattle, being outlaws, delivering damsels from distress. Then my par-ents decide to buy my brothers guns. These are not "real" guns. They shoot BBs, copper pellets my brothers say will kill birds. Because I am a girl, I do not get a gun. Instantly I am relegated to the position of Indian. Now there appears a great distance between us. They shoot and shoot at everything with their new guns. I try to keep up with my bow and arrows.

One day while I am standing on top of our makeshift "garage" — pieces of tin nailed across some poles — holding my bow and arrow and looking out toward the fields, I feel an incredible blow in my right eye. I look down just in time to see my brother lower his gun.

Both brothers rush to my side. My eye stings, and I cover it with my hand. "If you tell," they say, "we will get a whipping. You don't want that to happen, do you?" I do not. "Here is a piece of wire," says the older brother, picking it up from the roof; "say you stepped on one end of it and the other flew up and hit you." The pain is beginning to start. "Yes," I say. "Yes, I will say that is what happened." If I do not say this is what happened, I know my brothers will find ways to make me wish I had. But now I will say anything that gets me to my mother.

Confronted by our parents we stick to the lie agreed upon. They place me on a bench on the porch and I close my left eye while they examine the right. There is a tree growing from underneath the porch that climbs past the railing to the roof. It is the last thing my right eye sees. I watch as its trunk, its branches, and then its leaves are blotted out by the rising blood.

I am in shock. First there is intense fever, which my father tries to break using lily leaves bound around my head. Then there are chills: my mother tries to get me to eat soup. Eventually, I do not know how, my parents learn what has happened. A week after the "accident" they take me to see a doctor. "Why did you wait so long to come?" he asks, looking into my eye and shaking his head. "Eyes are sympathetic," he says. "If one is blind, the other will likely become blind too."

This comment of the doctor's terrifies me. But it is really how I look that bothers me most. Where the BB pellet struck there is a glob of whitish scar tissue, a hideous cataract, on my eye. Now when I stare at people — a favorite pastime, up to now — they will stare back. Not at the "cute" little girl, but at her scar. For six years I do not stare at anyone, because I do not raise my head.

Years later, in the throes of a midlife crisis, I ask my mother and sister whether I changed after the "accident." "No," they say, puzzled. "What do you mean?"

What do I mean?

I am eight, and, for the first time, doing poorly in school, where I have been something of a whiz since I was four. We have just moved to the place where the "accident" occurred. We do not know any of the people around us because this is a different county. The only time I see the friends I knew is when we go back to our old church. The new school is the former state penitentiary. It is a large stone building, cold and drafty, crammed to over-flowing with boisterous, ill-disciplined children. On the third floor there is a huge circular imprint of some partition that has been torn out.

"What used to be here?" I ask a sullen girl next to me on our way past it to lunch.

"The electric chair," says she.

At night I have nightmares about the electric chair, and about all the people reputedly "fried" in it. I am afraid of the school, where all the students seem to be budding criminals.

"What's the matter with your eye?" they ask, critically.

When I don't answer (I cannot decide whether it was an "accident" or not), they shove me, insist on a fight.

My brother, the one who created the story about the wire, comes to my rescue. But then brags so much about "protecting" me, I become sick.

After months of torture at the school, my parents decide to send me back to our old community, to my old school. I live with my grandparents and the teacher they board. But there is no room for Phoebe, my cat. By the time my grandparents decide there *is* room, and I ask for my cat, she cannot be found. Miss Yarborough, the boarding teacher, takes me under her wing, and begins to teach me to play the piano. But soon she marries an African — a "prince," she says — and is whisked away to his continent.

At my old school there is at least one teacher who loves me. She is the teacher who "knew me before I was born" and bought my first baby clothes. It is she who makes life bearable. It is her presence that finally helps me turn on the one child at the school who continually calls me "one-eyed bitch." One day I simply grab him by his coat and beat him until I am satisfied. It is my teacher who tells me my mother is ill.

My mother is lying in bed in the middle of the day, something I have never seen. She is in too much pain to speak. She has an abscess in her ear. I stand looking down on her, knowing that if she dies, I cannot live. She is being treated with warm oils and hot bricks held against her cheek. Finally a doctor comes. But I must go back to my grandparents' house. The weeks pass but I am hardly aware of it. All I know is that my mother might die, my father is not so jolly, my brothers still have their guns, and I am the one sent away from home.

"You did not change," they say.

Did I imagine the anguish of never looking up?

I am twelve. When relatives come to visit I hide in my room. My cousin Brenda, just my age, whose father works in the post office and whose mother is a nurse, comes to find me. "Hello," she says. And then she asks, looking at my recent school picture, which I did not want taken, and on which the "glob," as I think of it, is clearly visible, "You still can't see out of that eye?"

"No," I say, and flop back on the bed over my book.

That night, as I do almost every night, I abuse my eye. I rant and rave at it, in front of the mirror. I plead with it to clear up before morning. I tell it I hate and despise it. I do not pray for sight. I pray for beauty.

"You did not change," they say.

I am fourteen and baby-sitting for my brother Bill, who lives in Boston. He is my favorite brother and there is a strong bond between us. Understanding my feelings of shame and ugliness he and his wife take me to a local hospital, where the "glob" is removed by a doctor named O. Henry. There is still a small bluish crater where the scar tissue was, but the ugly white stuff is gone. Almost immediately I become a different person from the girl who does not raise her head. Or so I think. Now that I've raised my head I win the boyfriend of my dreams. Now that I've raised my head I have plenty of friends. Now that I've raised my head classwork comes from my lips as faultlessly as Easter speeches did, and I leave high school as valedictorian, most popular student, and *queen,* hardly believing my luck. Ironically, the girl who was voted most beautiful in our class (and was) was later shot twice through the chest by a male companion, using a "real" gun, while she was pregnant. But that's another story in itself. Or is it?

"You did not change," they say.

It is now thirty years since the "accident." A beautiful journalist comes to visit and to interview me. She is going to write a cover story for her magazine that focuses on my latest book. "Decide how you want to look on the cover," she says. "Glamorous, or whatever."

Never mind "glamorous," it is the "whatever" that I hear. Suddenly all I can think of is whether I will get enough sleep the night before the photography session: if I don't, my eye will be tired and wander, as blind eyes will.

At night in bed with my lover I think up reasons why I should not appear on the cover of a magazine. "My meanest critics will say I've sold out," I say. "My family will now realize I write scandalous books."

"But what's the real reason you don't want to do this?" he asks.

"Because in all probability," I say in a rush, "my eye won't be straight."

"It will be straight enough," he says. Then, "Besides, I thought you'd made your peace with that."

And I suddenly remember that I have.

I remember:

I am talking to my brother Jimmy, asking if he remembers anything unusual about the day I was shot. He does not know I consider that day the last time my father, with his sweet home remedy of cool lily leaves, chose me, and that I suffered and raged inside because of this. "Well," he says, "all I remember is standing by the side of the highway with Daddy, trying to flag down a car. A white man stopped, but when Daddy said he needed somebody to take his little girl to the doctor, he drove off."

I remember:

I am in the desert for the first time. I fall totally in love with it. I am so overwhelmed by its beauty, I confront for the first time, consciously, the meaning of the doctor's words years ago: "Eyes are sympathetic. If one is blind, the other will likely become blind too." I realize I have dashed about the world madly, looking at this, looking at that, storing up images against the fading of the light. *But I might have missed seeing the desert!* The shock of that possibility — and gratitude for over twenty-five years of sight — sends me literally to my knees. Poem after poem comes — which is perhaps how poets pray.

ON SIGHT

I am so thankful I have seen
The Desert
And the creatures in the desert
And the desert Itself.

The desert has its own moon
Which I have seen
With my own eye.
There is no flag on it.

Trees of the desert have arms
All of which are always up
That is because the moon is up
The sun is up
Also the sky
The Stars
Clouds
None with flags.

If there were flags, I doubt
the trees would point.
Would you?

But mostly, I remember this:

I am twenty-seven, and my baby daughter is almost three. Since her birth I have worried about her discovery that her mother's eyes are different from other people's. Will she be embarrassed? I think. What will she say? Every day she watches a television program called *Big Blue Marble*. It begins with a picture of the earth as it appears from the moon. It is bluish, a little battered-looking, but full of light, with whitish clouds swirling around it. Every time I see it I weep with love, as if it is a picture of Grandma's house. One day when I am putting Rebecca down for her nap, she suddenly focuses on my eye. Something inside me cringes, gets ready to try to protect myself. All children are cruel about physical differences, I know from experience, and that they don't always mean to be is another matter. I assume Rebecca will be the same.

But no-o-o-o. She studies my face intently as we stand, her inside and me outside her crib. She even holds my face maternally between her dimpled little hands. Then, looking every bit as serious and lawyerlike as her father, she says, as if it may just possibly have slipped my attention: "Mommy, there's a *world* in your eye." (As in, "Don't be alarmed, or do anything crazy.") And then, gently, but with great interest: "Mommy, where did you *get* that world in your eye?"

For the most part, the pain left then. (So what, if my brothers grew up to buy even more powerful pellet guns for their sons and to carry real guns themselves. So what, if a young "Morehouse[1] man" once nearly fell off the steps of Trevor Arnett Library because he thought my eyes were blue.) Crying and laughing I ran to the bathroom, while Rebecca mumbled and sang herself to sleep. Yes indeed, I realized, looking into the mirror. There *was* a world in my eye. And I saw that it was possible to love it: that in fact, for all it had taught me of shame and anger and inner vision, I *did* love it. Even to see it drifting out of orbit in boredom, or rolling up out of fatigue, not to mention floating back at attention in excitement (bearing witness, a friend has called it), deeply suitable to my personality, and even characteristic of me.

That night I dream I am dancing to Stevie Wonder's song "Always" (the name of the song is really "As," but I hear it as "Always"). As I dance, whirling and joyous, happier than I've ever been in my life, another bright-faced dancer joins me. We dance and kiss each other and hold each other through the night. The other dancer has obviously come through all right, as I have done. She is beautiful, whole and free. And she is also me.

---

[1] *Morehouse:* Morehouse College, a black men's college in Atlanta, Georgia.

CHAPTER 12

Personal Essay

Like memoir, the personal essay draws on one's past but does not linger there as long. Many personal essays are rooted in the here-and-now, at the intersection of present with past. Kandi Tayebi's essay "Warring Memories" begins as she and her husband are watching television. Gerald N. Callahan in "Chimera" is eating a croissant in a café. Personal essays use life experience to make larger social statements. Eric Liu in "Notes of a Native Speaker" uses his struggles as a Chinese-American to examine assimilation in our society; Scott Russell Sanders in "Under the Influence" uses his family experience to highlight the problem of alcoholism. Many also use research, near and far. Connie Wieneke in "Snakebit" calls her mother, while Brian Doyle in "Being Brians" surveys other Brian Doyles, thanks to the Internet.

The challenge is not to sound stodgy or academic. As Philip Lopate writes in *The Art of the Personal Essay,* "The hallmark of the personal essay is its intimacy. The writer seems to be speaking directly into your ear, confiding everything from gossip to wisdom." We think this holds true for most creative nonfiction, whatever the category. The assumption is this: wherever we come from, no matter how rich or poor, old or young, healthy or infirm, happy or sad, we can—if we find the right words—understand each other.

❧ GERALD N. CALLAHAN   *"Chimera"*

❧ BRIAN DOYLE   *"Being Brians"*

- ERIC LIU *"Notes of a Native Speaker"*
- SCOTT RUSSELL SANDERS *"Under the Influence"*
- KANDI TAYEBI *"Warring Memories"*
- CONNIE WIENEKE *"Snakebit"*

Note: Many of the pieces in other categories, such as Patricia Hampl's "Memory and Imagination" (Chapter 16, Stories of Craft), and Max Apple's "Roommates" (Chapter 17, Short Shorts) are also personal essays.

GERALD N. CALLAHAN

Chimera

Last Thursday, one of those gray fall days when the starlings gather up and string between the elms around here, my children's mother—dead ten years—walked into a pastry shop where I was buttering a croissant. She ignored me, which she always does, ordered a plain bagel and an almond latte, picked up her food, and, without a glance at me, walked out. The starlings chittered, the day frowned, and I went back to buttering my croissant.

Just after her suicide, I saw this woman often—in towns where she never lived, walking her Airedales in the park, eating poached eggs at Joe's Cafe, sweeping grass clippings from her walk on Myrtle Street, stepping off the Sixteenth Street bus. We get together less often now. But when we do, like this morning, her image is as vivid as it ever was—her dark eyes as bright, her odd smile just as annoying.

I'm not crazy.

I know it isn't her, this woman I see. After all, she's dead, and I myself gave her ashes to my son. So it is another, a stranger, transformed by some old film still flickering through the projector inside my head. I know that. But every time I see her, it takes all that I have to stay in my chair or my car, to hold on to myself and not run after her calling out her name.

Some of this I understand. When something or someone is suddenly stripped from us, it seems only natural that our minds would try to compensate. Minds do that. If they didn't, we might be sucked into the vortex ourselves. That part, I grasp. I'd have thought, though, that in a year or two, the films in my mind would fade and break, and the tear in my life would scar and close like any other wound. And I expected, as the fissure closed, that my first wife would disappear.

I was wrong.

All the pieces of human bodies fit (more or less) into eleven systems—endocrine, musculoskeletal, cardiovascular, hematologic, pulmonary, urinary, reproductive, gastrointestinal, integumentary, nervous, and immune. So there are a limited number of places where someone could hide something inside a human body. And so far as we know, only two of the body's systems, immune and nervous, store memories—fourth birthdays or former wives. That narrows it even further.

Most of us don't for a moment associate immune systems with hopes and fears, emotions and recollections, we don't imagine that anything other than lymph—the pale liquid gathered from the blood—is stored inside of thymuses, spleens, and lymph nodes. The business of immune systems is, after all, not hope, but immunity—protection against things like measles, mumps, whooping cough, typhus, cholera, plague, African green monkey virus, you name it.

But immune systems do remember things, intricate things that the rest of the body has forgotten. And the memories stored inside our immune systems can come back, like my first wife, at unexpected moments, with sometimes startling consequences.

My grandmother had a penchant for saving things. She had grown up in a very poor family and believed nothing should be wasted. On the plywood shelves of her closets, Mason jars that once held apple butter or pickled tomatoes were filled with buttons, snaps, paper clips and strips of cloth, seashells, rubber bands, pebbles, bobby pins, and cheap, shiny buckles—everything she'd ever come across that she thought might be useful someday.

Immune systems do that, too—believe that most everything they come across will be useful again someday. Grandmother used Mason jars, immune systems use lymph nodes. Immune systems collect bacteria, parasites and fungi, proteins, fats, sugars, and viruses—the stuff that falls through the cracks in our skin.

Human skin is like nothing else in this universe. It tastes of sea salt and the iron inside of men and women. Its touch arouses us. Skin is cream, sand, teak, smoke, and stone. But mostly, skin is what keeps us apart from everything else on this planet, especially everything that might infect, infest, pollute, putrefy, and possess us. First and foremost, it is our skin that allows us to be here as individual men and women in a hungry world. Skin keeps things out—things that would eat us for lunch. And skin keeps things in—things we couldn't live without.

But skin can break down, get punctured by knives and needles or scraped off by tree limbs and tarmac. When that happens, we'd die without our immune systems—abruptly. Immune systems deal with the things that crawl through the holes in our skin. They label the intruders as dangerous, round them up, and destroy them. And immune systems never forget the things they've seen beneath our skin because they believe that one day those things will be back.

That's how we get to be adults—immunological memory. That's also how vaccines work. Until a few years ago, children in this country were regularly injected with cowpox, also know as vaccinia virus. Vaccinia virus is very similar to the virus that causes smallpox, with one important exception. Vaccinia virus doesn't cause the disfigurement, illness, and often death caused by smallpox. But as Edward Jenner discovered in the 1700s, people (in Jenner's case, milkmaids) who have been infected with cowpox don't get smallpox. A miracle. Immunity to cowpox protects a child from smallpox. That's because, even though their personalities are very different, smallpox virus and vaccinia virus have a lot of physical features in common. Immune systems that have learned to recognize and destroy cowpox virus also recognize and destroy the look-alike smallpox virus before it can do harm.

And immune systems remember. They remember each and every miracle, and remember them for a lifetime. A child vaccinated against smallpox virus will make a much more rapid and specific response on a second encounter with that virus than will an unvaccinated child. And the rapidity and specificity of that second response is what saves the vaccinated child's life.

Immunological memory is a simple memory of a tiny virus, but a memory powerful enough to have ended the devastating disease of smallpox on this planet. In essence it is no different from the memory that pulls our hand from the flame a little faster the second time, the memory that guides the cleaver beyond the scars on our knuckles or the memory of a first love lost.

The way immune systems do this is extraordinary. Lymph nodes are little filtering stations strung throughout the human body. Lymph nodes monitor the fluids of the body—mainly lymph and plasma—for infections. When something out of the ordinary is detected, it is usually the lymph nodes that remember and initiate an immune response.

Every time we are infected, a little of the bacteria or virus that infected us is saved in the lymph node where it first arrived. By the time we're adults, lymph nodes are filled with a bit of most everything we've ever been infected by; our lymph nodes are the repositories of our infectious histories. Just like my grandmother's jars, but our immune systems sort this growing mass of memorabilia and remind themselves of what they've seen before, what they are likely to see again, and what they mustn't forget.

Mustn't forget, but mustn't hold too close to the surface, either. Because, just like some of the memories lurking in our brains, an inappropriate recollection can hurt or blind us, sometimes even kill us. Those things we suppress.

Some viruses and bacteria stored inside our bodies are intact and alive. The only thing keeping us from having the same diseases all over again is the constant vigilance of our immune systems. Through that vigilance, all of those things hanging around inside us are kept in check, are suppressed to the point where they can help us remember, but cannot cause disease. Memory with a mission, selective recollection and suppression.

Lots of things can distract immune systems, though—drugs, malnutrition, stress, age, infection. When these things happen, immune systems can forget for a moment all those deadly things packed away inside of us. Then, like minds in panic, immune systems can become confused, forget which memory to recall, which memory to suppress, and the past can flare inside of us. When that happens, our very survival depends on our ability to regain our balance, to enhance some recollections and suppress others. A particularly pernicious example of this is shingles—a severe chicken pox–like rash that usually appears across the ribs beneath the arms, but may also grow in the eyes and lungs. It is most commonly a disease of the elderly.

People can't get shingles if they weren't infected with chicken pox, usually as children. Shingles and chicken pox are caused by the same virus—varicella zoster virus. When we get chicken pox, our immune systems and (interestingly) our nervous systems store a few leftover varicella zoster viruses for future reference. Later, when age or illness or depression distracts our immune systems, the virus begins to multiply again. Then the virus may blind us, may even kill us. This is shingles—a blazing memory of chicken pox, a child-hood disease—a thing we wish we could forget.

So immune systems, like minds, are filled with memories—vivid, painful, sometimes fatal memories. The fragments of a life lived, bits and pieces of the past. And sometimes immune systems lose control of this smoldering wreckage and old flames flare anew.

Within me, then, is there a woman living in this ruin, a woman who walks and speaks exactly like my first wife? It is, of course, impossible to answer that question. No one understands nearly enough about wives and immune systems. But it isn't, as it might seem, an entirely stupid question. Among the things we regularly trade with our wives (and the rest of our families for that matter) are viruses—colds, flus, cold sores, to mention only a few.

Enveloped viruses—like those that cause flu, cold sores, and AIDS—are so called because they carry with them an "envelope" of lipids and proteins taken from the host cell (the cell they grew up inside of). And many viruses also carry within them a little of the host cell's nucleic acids—DNA or RNA—the stuff of genes. Some of that DNA or DNA made from that RNA clearly gets incorporated into our chromosomes and begins to work inside of us. That means that each time we are infected with one of these viruses, we also acquire a little of the person who infected us, a little piece of someone else. Infection as communication. Infection as chimerization. Infection as memorization.

Perhaps that seems trivial—a bit of envelope here, a little DNA there. But over the course of an intimate relationship, we collect a lot of pieces of someone else. And a little of each of those pieces is stored in our lymph nodes and in our chromosomes.

Until. Until the person we've been communicating with is gone, and we stop gathering bits of someone we love. For a few days or weeks, everything seems pretty much like it was. Then one day, a day when, for no apparent reason, our defenses slip just a little, and a ghost walks through the door and orders an almond latte.

Nervous systems don't appear to store memories in the same way immune systems do. Most neurologists and neurochemists believe that memory within the nervous system involves something called long-term potentiation or LTP—a means by which certain nerve pathways become preferred. Because of LTP a particular trigger—a picture of Aunt Helen—becomes likely to stimulate the same nerve circuit—the smell of cheap perfume—every time. But in general, how nervous systems store and recall memories isn't very well understood.

Human memory has been divided into two broad categories—declarative memory (explicit, consciously accessible memory: what was the name of the cereal I had for breakfast?) and emotional memory (often subconscious and inaccessible: why was I so frightened by that harmless snake I saw today?). But there is evidence for a third kind of memory as well, something I'll call phantom memory, memories that come from someplace beyond or beneath declarative and emotional circuits.

I'm pretty confident that declarative memory had nothing to do with my first wife walking in on me as I was buttering my croissant last Thursday. I'm less certain about emotional memory. And I am deeply intrigued by phantom memory.

People who have had arms and legs removed often experience phantom limbs—a sensation that the arm or leg is still there, sometimes a very painful sensation. This feeling is so real that people with phantom hands may try to pick up a coffee cup just as you or I would. People with phantom legs may try to stand before their declarative minds remind them they have no legs. The missing limbs seem completely real to these people and as much a part of themselves as any surviving appendage—even when the phantom limb is a foot felt to be dangling somewhere below the knee with no leg, real or phantom, between the ankle and a mid-thigh stump.

Some of those who have studied phantom-limb sensations argue that these are only recollections of sensations "remembered" from the days before amputation. But children born without limbs—children who've never experienced the sensations of a normal limb—experience phantom limbs. Clearly, these phantoms are not simple recollections of better days. Instead, the presence of phantom limbs in these children suggests that some sort of prenatal image—some template of what a human should look like—is formed inside our fetal minds before our arms and legs develop, before even our nervous systems are fully formed. If at birth our bodies don't fit this template, our minds or brains attempt to remake reality, twist it until it fits what our minds say it ought to be.

No one knows where phantom memories reside. Often, phantom limbs are exceedingly painful, so physicians have tried to locate the source of the sensations and eliminate them. Spinal cords have been severed, nerve fibers cut, portions of the brain have been removed. Some of these sometimes caused the pain to disappear, but it usually returned within a few months or years. And none of these treatments routinely caused phantom limbs to disappear.

Occasionally over time phantom limbs will disappear on their own, though almost never permanently. The limbs usually return—in a month or a year or a decade. And when they do, they are just as real as the day they first appeared, or disappeared.

Phantom memories aren't always memories of limbs either. People who've lost their sight describe phantom visions: not recollections, but detailed images of sights they've never seen—buildings, burials, forests, flowers. Similarly, some people who've lost their hearing, Beethoven being one, are haunted by complex symphonies blaring in their ears.

No one knows how much of our reality comes to us from the physical world and how much "reality" we create inside our own minds. If we were to analyze, using something like a PET scanner, all the nervous activity occurring at any given moment inside a human body, no more than a fraction of a percent of this activity would be directly due to input from the senses. That is, only a tiny portion of what our nervous systems are occupied with, and by inference only a tiny portion of our thoughts, are direct results of what we see, hear, taste, smell, or touch. The rest of it, the remainder of our mental imaging, begins and ends inside of us. How that affects our "reality" isn't clear.

But it is clear that much of what originates within us is powerful enough to fill our mental hospitals with people who see and hear things that aren't there. Among the sights and sounds that originate within us are our images of ourselves and our realities—our archetypes. Such images are powerful icons, nearly immutable. These are the images of our dreams, our poetry, our theaters, our psychoses.

If physical reality, the outside world, changes abruptly, it may not be within our power to so abruptly change such deep-rooted images of ourselves and our worlds. When that happens, reality itself becomes implausible. Then our only way out is through a phantom, a bit of virtual reality that reconciles our world and the real world.

Are the dead, then, living within my neurons—inside my own pictures of me?

Images of ourselves—some apparently older than we are—are obviously deeply etched into the stones of our minds. Powerful things that resist change, particularly sudden change. But even these archetypal portraits of ourselves aren't without seams or cracks. And inside those seams and between those cracks, small forces working over years can introduce change. Time, in an intimate and powerful relationship, may reshape even our images of ourselves. The changes would be little ones at first, a tiny fissure unmortared here or there, room to include in our self-portraits parts of other men or women, a first vision of ourselves as something more. Later, larger pieces of us might be lifted and replaced by whole chunks of another. Husband and wife begin to speak alike, know what the other is thinking, anticipate what the other will say, even begin to look alike. Until one day, what remains is truly and thoroughly a mosaic, a chimera—part man, part woman; part someone, part someone else.

And then, if that man or woman is amputated from us, clipped as quickly and as cleanly as a gangrenous leg, our minds are suddenly forced into a new reality—a reality without the other, a reality in which an essential piece of us is missing. At that point, our declarative minds would be at odds with our own pictures of ourselves. To rectify that, to reconcile the frames flickering inside with the darkness flaming outside, we conjure a phantom, a phantom to change our worlds. We force a bit of what is inside out there into the real world, to create someone or something that will help us slow the universe for a moment while we repaint our pictures of ourselves with a very small brush on a very large canvas.

There is a painting by Pierre Auguste Renoir which I first saw at the National Gallery in Washington, D.C. This painting, titled *Girl with a Watering Can*, is filled mostly with the off-whites and intense blues of the impressionist painter. But in the girl's hair, there is a blood-red bow. I've often wondered about that bow and why Renoir put it there. I've imagined the bow was a symbol of the death that begins at each of our births; I've imagined it as an omen of sexual maturity—its pain and its promise; I've even imagined it was nothing more than a schoolgirl's red bow.

But just now, I think the red bow is the other one inside of us, the red one who is probably at first mother—physically, immunologically, and psychologically. The one, too, who is later so many others—grandmother, friend, severed limb, or lost wife.

Renoir placed the bow in the girl's hair, near her brain. I don't imagine, though, that by that placement he intended for us to ignore all the other spots where bits of men and women gather in us.

Today, sitting on the redwood deck behind my house, the air smells of cinnamon and rainwater. For reasons I can't recall, those smells remind me of the Brandenburg Concertos, coffee on Sunday mornings, and the intricate paths of swallows.

Somewhere inside of me, there is a woman. But where she lives and who it was that led her into that pastry shop last Thursday, I've no way of knowing. For one part of me, that ignorance is a gnawing blindness. For another part of me, it is enough to simply know for certain that I will see her again.

BRIAN DOYLE

Being Brians

— Sometimes statistics work [carefully]

There are 215 Brian Doyles in the United States, according to a World Wide Web site called "Switchboard" (www.switchboard.com), which shows telephone numbers and addresses in America.

We live in 40 states; more of us live in New York than any other state. *["us" too/personal]* Several of us live on streets named for women (Laura, Cecelia, Chris, Nicole, Jean, Joyce). A startling number of us live on streets and in towns named for flora (Apple, Ash, Bay, Berry, Chestnut, Hickory, Maple, Oak, Palm, Poinsettia, Sandlewood and Teak) or fauna (Bee, Bobolink, Buck, Buffalo, Bull, Deer, Fox, Gibbon, Hawk, Pine Siskin, Salmon, Swift, Wildcat).

Some of us live on streets named in the peculiarly American fashion for a bucolic natural place that doesn't exist, a pastoral Eden of the imagination, the sort of name that has become de rigueur for housing developments: Bellarbor, Greenfield, Greenridge, Cresthaven, Cricklewood, Knollwood, Pleasant Hill, Shady Nook, Skyridge, Ridgewood, Spring Winds, Trailwood.

And there are Brian Doyles in uncategorizable but somehow essentially American places (Vacation Lane, Enchanted Flame Street, Freedom Road, Sugar Land) and in some places that seem to me especially American in their terse utility: Main Street, Rural Route, United States Highway, Old Route, New Road.

One of us is paralyzed from the chest down; one of us is 18 and "likes to party"; one of us played second base very well indeed for the New York Yankees in the 1978 World Series; several of us have had problems with alcohol and drugs; one of us is nearly finished with his doctorate in theology;

one of us is a 9-year-old girl; one of us works for Promise Keepers; one was married while we were working on this essay; one welcomed a new baby; one died.

The rest of us soldier on being Brian Doyle.

"Tell me a little bit about yourself," I wrote us recently:

> How did you get your name? What do you do for work? What are your favorite pursuits? Hobbies? Avocations? Have any of us named our sons Brian? What Irish county were your forebears from? Where were you born? Where did you go to college? What's your wife's name?

Brian, the doctoral student in theology at the Catholic University of America:

> I ride my bike and search for new microbrews. No children. We still have family in County Kerry. They live on a dairy farm and moved out of the thatched-roof cottage about 15 years ago, but it still stands on the property.

Brian, the New England field representative for Promise Keepers, "a Christian ministry dedicated to uniting men in vital relationships so that they might be godly influences in their world":

> My wife and I are committed to honoring Jesus Christ in our lives, marriage and in all that we do. He is Central to our daily living.

Brian of Waltham, Mass., in a handwritten note:

> I am a union iron worker in Boston and have been iron working for 23 years. I am pretty much a free spirit.

Brian, the undergraduate at the University of Kansas:

> Hiked 700 miles of the Pacific Crest Trail. Biked from Newport, Ore., to San Francisco down Highway 101. I don't know much about my name, but now you got me curious.

Brian of Red Hook, N.Y., 18 years old:

> Being 18 really is not bad. It is cool for the first couple of months but the novelty wears off after a while. I am a junior at Red Hook High School where in my class there is only about 150 kids. Red Hook is a very small hick town (in the countryside). I have two jobs one at a place called Beverage Way, a beer and soda warehouse, and my second job is at Bard College where I do catering for parties. It is not much, but it pays the bills. Since I am only 18 I am not married yet, but I have a high school sweetheart named Heather. My hobbies include basketball, quadding (four wheeling), taking care of my car and partying as any teenager loves to do. Besides that there is not much more to do up here.

Brian of Denver, Pa.:

> Our clan came from Kerry around the turn of the century. One of my uncles became chief of police in New York City.

Brian of Leicester, Mass.:

> I never realized that there are that many of us. I am 49 years old and was injured in the military back in 1969. I was wounded three times in Vietnam and got to walk off the plane, but within two months I was involved in a motor vehicle accident while home on leave and I became paralyzed from the chest down. I have worked as a police dispatcher and clerk/dispatcher for my local highway department. In the last three years I have been spending the winter months in Florida and the summer months here in Massachusetts, and eventually I will be spending all my time in Florida as there is so much more to do and a lot easier to get around. I am currently retired as I decided a few years ago that it was time to enjoy life right now as I grow older I will not be able to get around as easy as I can now. My wife Shirley is legally blind with a degenerative eye disease. So let's go for the gusto and enjoy while we can. I do not know what county my Irish forebears came from. I wish I did. I went to work at our

local highway department after my one year in college and was drafted into the Army in 1968. Hope to hear back from you.

I write back to Brian of Leicester and tell him that I am grateful for his courteous note. I think about him in his wheelchair and his wife who cannot see very well and the days and months he must have spent on his back after his car crash thinking about the irony of surviving warfare only to be savagely injured on a highway, and by then it is time to put my sons and daughter to bed, which I do with the sharp flavor of gratitude in my mouth.

Brian of Livonia, Mich.:

> I have four daughters—Nicole, Meghan, Adrienne and Stephanie. Sons? What are sons?

Brian of Livonia adds a genealogical note about our surname, which is an English translation of the Gaelic word *dubghaill,* or *dark stranger,* a word often used in early times to denote a Dane. Doyle is now the 12th most common name in Ireland. Brian of Livonia also points out that the name Brian hails from the last Irish high king, or *ard righ,* Brian Boru, slain in 1014 in the battle of Clontarf.

Brian Doyle in Poughkeepsie, N.Y.:

> I know of a few other Brian Doyles—a plumbing supply salesperson, a local restauranteur and an IBM public relations official— but have met none of them. I have been asked several times if I played second base for the New York Yankees in 1978. Of course, I confess that I am this same person who nearly won the 1978 World Series MVP Award—but later confess to this lie.

Brian from Chicago, who turns out to have been a year behind me at Notre Dame, to our mutual astonishment:

> A Doyle anecdote. Our Doyles originally settled in Brooklyn, N.Y. My great-grandfather started a business making men's dress shirts, the kind without the collar, as was the custom then. Doyle and Black was a good name in dress shirts. Black, the partner, died early on, but the name was retained as Doyle and Black. The business failed during the Depression, but during its early years

of prosperity, my great-grandfather gave rings to his sons. The rings, plain gold bands with a ruby, diamond and sapphire—red, white and blue, to remind us of how good this country has been to us—are handed down from Doyle father to Doyle son. I received my father's ring when I turned 21 and will give it to my son Trevor. My father's uncle Ed passed away without heirs, so I will have his ring also to pass on to my son Jay.

Brian Doyle in Baton Rouge, La.:

Please forgive me for not responding sooner, but I, like most Brian Doyles, am extremely important and in constant demand. I work as a probation and parole agent, but consider it a ministry. I was born again in 1983 and attended Trinity Bible College in Ellendale, N.D., and became credentialed with the Assemblies of God. Evangelism is my call and my heartbeat. Baseball is my passion. I write as a hobby. My wife and I were actors in Manhattan for over a decade, and she's a published Christian playwright. I specialize in smart-aleck letters. I've never been to Ireland other than in drunken fantasies, back before I got sober in 1979. I know I'm part Irish (the sentimental, poetic, occasionally morose part), part English (the self-righteous, self-important, frequently overbearing part), part German (just ask my son about my "Gestapo tactics") and part French (the part of me that instinctively wants to immediately surrender when I face a battle). I entered AA in NYC in 1979 where I met my lovely and wonderful wife, Christy. She was an actress; I was an actor; we were both drunks; what else could we do but get married? Which is what we did in 1982. We're still having a great time together.

Brian of Naples, Fla.:

I was also named after the great Brian Boru. Recently divorced, though very much in love again with a wonderful woman. Early life at home was very confusing, and I took refuge in hiding in mind and mood alterers, i.e., alcohol and drugs. I have not indulged in such behavior in over seven years. I have taken up long-distance running and have run 10 marathons and countless other races. I was in the air-conditioning field for 15 years, but as I became more aware it just didn't feel right.

Next morning I count up the number of letters that have come back stamped UNDELIVERABLE or NO LONGER AT THIS ADDRESS or UNDELIVERABLE AS ADDRESSED or that have the new resident's angry, scrawled HE DOESN'T LIVE HERE ANYMORE!!!! on them in large, annoyed block letters: 43. Where are those Brian Doyles? The Lost Brian Doyles, addresses gone bad, addresses rotten, addresses thrown out on the compost heap, moldering.

Denise Doyle, of Saltillo, Pa., in a handwritten letter:

> We thought your letter was very neat! Brian is self-employed in the carpenter field: building, remodeling, etc. He loves to fish and hunt. We have a daughter, Brianne, named after her daddy, age 9. Brian is a layed back sort of guy and has a lot of care for other people.

Calm, compassionate, caring—it's a Brian Doyle thing.

Brian in Houston, Texas: Likes cold beer.

Brian in Braintree, Mass.: Named for Brian Boru. Parents: Francis and Frances, both Irish natives. Brian was the goalkeeper on the University of Lowell's 1979 national championship hockey team, had a cup of coffee with the National Hockey League's Phoenix Coyotes, and once played in a high school hockey game where both goalies were named Brian Doyle.

Brian of Valley Cottage, N.Y.: Father called him Boru as a boy. Appalachian Trail nut:

> I've hiked the trail from Maine to Georgia, and I guess you could say that I'm a woodsman, eastern style.

Remembers with affection his cousin Brian Doyle who died a few years ago in Pittston, Pa., where his father's people, fleeing *An Gorta Mor,* the horrendous Irish Famine of 1845–1851, landed in America to work the coal mines.

Not unlike some of my father's ancestors, who fled Wicklow and Cork from what my grandmother called "the Horror" and became bartenders, bricklayers, cigar dealers, steelworkers, die cutters, freight clerks and bookkeepers in the 10th, 18th, 20th and 34th wards of Pittsburgh, this line eventually producing my grandfather, James Aloysius Doyle, who with Sophia Holthaus produced another James Aloysius Doyle, my father, who with Ethel Clancey produced another James Aloysius Doyle, my brother, nicknamed Seamus, who died as a baby, my mother discovering him seemingly asleep in his stroller on a bright April morning in New York in 1946, which discovery plunged my parents into a great blackness, but eventually they recovered, as much as possible, and they made a daughter and four more sons, one of whom is named for Brian Boru, high king of Ireland until his last day at Clontarf.

Obituary notice in the Morning Oregonian, Thursday, May 22:

> Brian Doyle, died May 16, age 42. Veteran, United States Army; spent last 15 years of life working as mail handler for United States Postal Service. Accomplished figure skater, competed for U.S. Olympic teams in 1976 and 1980. Gifts in his memory are to be sent to the St. Vincent de Paul Society, a Catholic organization that collects food and clothes for the poor.

What Brian died of, the article does not say. Nor, for all the facts, does it say who he was. It doesn't say who or how he loved. It doesn't report the color of his eyes. It doesn't show the shape of his ambition, the tenor of his mind, the color of his sadness, the bark of his laugh. It doesn't say with what grace or gracelessness he bore his name, how he was carved by it, how his character and personality and the bounce in his step were shaped and molded by its 10 letters, how he learned slowly and painstakingly to write as a child and so

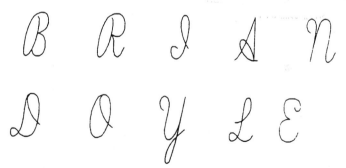

saw himself on paper, how he learned to pick the quick song of *Brian* out of the soup of sound swirling around him as an infant, how he sat in the first row at school because his surname began early in the alphabet, how other schoolchildren tried to edit and mangle and nick his name—Brian the Lion, Lying

Brian, Oily Doyle, Lace Doyley—how he was fascinated as a small boy sitting at his grandmother's knee and watching her sew a lace doily, the word doily squirming in his mouth, his tongue tumbling over *Doyle* and *doily* for days afterward. Probably as a boy he added up the letters and admired the symmetry of his first and last names, as I did. Probably he spent a few moments, once, late on a rainy summer afternoon, bored, writing *Mrs. Brian Doyle* to see what it looked like, to hold the dangerous idea of a wife on paper for a moment, as I did. Probably he saw and heard his name misspelled, as we all did, on applications and reports and documents and certificates and letters and envelopes and phone calls: Brain Doyel, Brian Dooley, Bryan Doyle, Brien Doyle, Brian Dalkey, even Brian Dahlia once, the woman at the other end of the scratchy phone doing her best to spell what she so dimly heard, to make real the faraway sound of a name.

[handwritten margin notes: "Tie Into his life", "made familiar personal", "How can you make yours part a voice?"]

ERIC LIU

Notes of a Native Speaker

Here are some of the ways you could say I am "white":

I listen to National Public Radio.
I wear khaki Dockers.
I own brown suede bucks.
I eat gourmet greens.
I have few close friends "of color."
I married a white woman.
I am a child of the suburbs.
I furnish my condo à la Crate & Barrel.
I vacation in charming bed-and-breakfasts.
I have never once been the victim of blatant discrimination.
I am a member of several exclusive institutions.
I have been in the inner sanctums of political power.
I have been there as something other than an attendant.

I have the ambition to return.
I am a producer of the culture.
I expect my voice to be heard.
I speak flawless, unaccented English.
I subscribe to *Foreign Affairs.*
I do not mind when editorialists write in the first person plural.
I do not mind how white television casts are.
I am not too ethnic.
I am wary of minority militants.
I consider myself neither in exile nor in opposition.
I am considered "a credit to my race."

I never asked to be white. I am not literally white. That is, I do not have white skin or white ancestors. I have yellow skin and yellow ancestors, hundreds of generations of them. But like so many other Asian Americans of the second generation, I find myself now the bearer of a strange new status: white, by acclamation. Thus it is that I have been described as an "honorary white," by other whites, and as a "banana," by other Asians. Both the honorific and the epithet take as a given this idea: to the extent that I have moved away from the periphery and toward the center of American life, I have become white inside. *Some are born white, others achieve whiteness, still others have whiteness thrust upon them.* This, supposedly, is what it means to assimilate.

There was a time when assimilation did quite strictly mean whitening. In fact, well into the first half of this century, mimicry of the stylized standards of the WASP gentry was the proper, dominant, perhaps even sole method of ensuring that your origins would not be held against you. You "made it" in society not only by putting on airs of anglitude, but also by assiduously bleaching out the marks of a darker, dirtier past. And this bargain, stifling as it was, was open to European immigrants almost exclusively; to blacks, only on the passing occasion; to Asians, hardly at all.

Times have changed, and I suppose you could call it progress that a Chinaman, too, may now aspire to whiteness. But precisely because the times have changed, that aspiration—and the *imputation* of the aspiration—now seems astonishingly outmoded. The meaning of "American" has undergone a revolution in the twenty-nine years I have been alive, a revolution of color, class, and culture. Yet the vocabulary of "assimilation" has remained fixed all this time: fixed in whiteness, which is still our metonym for power; and fixed in shame, which is what the colored are expected to feel for embracing the power.

I have assimilated. I am of the mainstream. In many ways I fit the psychological profile of the so-called banana: imitative, impressionable, rootless, eager to please. As I will admit in this essay, I have at times gone to great lengths to downplay my difference, the better to penetrate the "establishment" of the moment. Yet I'm not sure that what I did was so cut-and-dried as "becoming white." I plead guilty to the charges above: achieving, learning the ways of the upper middle class, distancing myself from radicals of any hue. But having confessed, I still do not know my crime.

To be an accused banana is to stand at the ill-fated intersection of class and race. And because class is the only thing Americans have more trouble talking about than race, a minority's climb up the social ladder is often willfully misnamed and wrongly portrayed. There is usually, in the portrayal, a strong whiff of betrayal: the assimilist is a traitor to his kind, to his class, to his own family. He cannot gain the world without losing his soul. To be sure, something *is* lost in any migration, whether from place to place or from class to class. But something is gained as well. And the result is always more complicated than the monochrome language of "whiteness" and "authenticity" would suggest.

My own assimilation began long before I was born. It began with my parents, who came here with an appetite for Western ways already whetted by films and books and music and, in my mother's case, by a father who'd been to the West. My parents, who traded Chinese formality for the more laissez-faire stance of this country. Who made their way by hard work and quiet adaptation. Who fashioned a comfortable life in a quiet development in a second-tier suburb. Who, unlike your "typical" Chinese parents, were not pushy, status-obsessed, rigid, disciplined, or prepared. Who were haphazard about passing down ancestral traditions and "lessons" to their children. Who did pass down, however, the sense that their children were entitled to mix and match, as they saw fit, whatever aspects of whatever cultures they encountered.

I was raised, in short, to assimilate, to claim this place as mine. I don't mean that my parents told me to act like an American. That's partly the point: they didn't tell me to do anything except to be a good boy. They trusted I would find my way, and I did, following their example and navigating by the lights of the culture that encircled me like a dome. As a function of my parents' own half-conscious, half-finished acculturation, I grew up feeling that my life was Book II of an ongoing saga. Or that I was running the second leg of a relay race. *Slap!*

I was out of the womb and sprinting, baton in hand. Gradually more sure of my stride, my breathing, the feel of the track beneath me. Eyes forward, never backward.

Today, nearly seven years after my father's death and two years after my marriage into a large white family, it is as if I have come round a bend and realized that I am no longer sure where I am running or why. My sprint slows to a trot. I scan the unfamiliar vista that is opening up. I am somewhere else now, somewhere far from the China that yielded my mother and father; far, as well, from the modest horizons I knew as a boy. I look at my limbs and realize I am no longer that boy; my gait and grasp exceed his by an order of magnitude. Now I want desperately to see my face, to see what time has marked and what it has erased. But I can find no mirror except the people who surround me. And they are mainly pale, powerful.

How did I end up here, standing in what seems the very seat of whiteness, gazing from the promontory of social privilege? How did I cover so much ground so quickly? What was it, in my blind journey, that I felt I should leave behind? And what *did* I leave behind? This, the jettisoning of one mode of life to send another aloft, is not only the immigrant's tale; it is the son's tale, too. By coming to America, my parents made themselves into citizens of a new country. By traveling the trajectory of an assimilist, so did I.

SCOTT RUSSELL SANDERS

Under the Influence

memory !
slice of life

MY father drank. He drank as a gut-punched boxer gasps for breath, as a starving dog gobbles food—compulsively, secretly, in pain and trembling. I use the past tense not because he ever quit drinking but because he quit living. That is how the story ends for my father, age sixty-four, heart bursting, body cooling and forsaken on the linoleum of my brother's trailer. The story continues for my brother, my sister, my mother, and me, and will continue so long as memory holds.

In the perennial present of memory, I slip into the garage or barn to see my father tipping back the flat green bottles of wine, the brown cylinders of whiskey, the cans of beer disguised in paper bags. His Adam's apple bobs, the liquid gurgles, he wipes the sandy-haired back of a hand over his lips, and then,

description | visual

his bloodshot gaze bumping into me, he stashes the bottle or can inside his jacket, under the workbench, between two bales of hay, and we both pretend the moment has not occurred.

"What's up, buddy?" he says, thick-tongued and edgy.

"Sky's up," I answer, playing along.

"And don't forget prices," he grumbles. "Prices are always up. And taxes."

[margin note: dialogue helps break monotony of voice]

In memory, his white 1951 Pontiac with the stripes down the hood and the Indian head on the snout jounces to a stop in the driveway; or it is the 1956 Ford station wagon, or the 1963 Rambler shaped like a toad, or the sleek 1969 Bonneville that will do 120 miles per hour on straightaways; or it is the robin's-egg blue pickup, new in 1980, battered in 1981, the year of his death. He climbs out, grinning dangerously, unsteady on his legs, and we children interrupt our game of catch, our building of snow forts, our picking of plums, to watch in silence as he weaves past into the house, where he slumps into his overstuffed chair and falls asleep. Shaking her head, our mother stubs out the cigarette he has left smoldering in the ashtray. All evening, until our bedtimes, we tiptoe past him, as past a snoring dragon. Then we curl in our fearful sheets, listening. Eventually he wakes with a grunt, Mother slings accusations at him, he snarls back, she yells, he growls, their voices clashing. Before long, she retreats to their bedroom, sobbing—not from the blows of fists, for he never strikes her, but from the force of words.

[margin note: Animal reference feel fear as well]

Left alone, our father prowls the house, thumping into furniture, rummaging in the kitchen, slamming doors, turning the pages of the newspaper with a savage crackle, muttering back at the late-night drivel from television. The roof might fly off, the walls might buckle from the pressure of his rage. Whatever my brother and sister and mother may be thinking on their own rumpled pillows, I lie there hating him, loving him, fearing him, knowing I have failed him. I tell myself he drinks to ease an ache that gnaws at his belly, an ache I must have caused by disappointing him somehow, a murderous ache I should be able to relieve by doing all my chores, earning A's in school, winning baseball games, fixing the broken washer and the burst pipes, bringing in money to fill his empty wallet. He would not hide the green bottles in his tool box, would not sneak off to the barn with a lump under his coat, would not fall asleep in the daylight, would not roar and fume, would not drink himself to death, if only I were perfect.

I am forty-two as I write these words, and I know full well now that my father was an alcoholic, a man consumed by disease rather than by

[margin note: did not begin with this | good choice why?]

[handwritten: Statistics / facts saved / till / pg 3 / good / choice / Why?]

disappointment. What had seemed to me a private grief is in fact a public scourge. In the United States alone some ten or fifteen million people share his ailment, and behind the doors they slam in fury or disgrace, countless other children tremble. I comfort myself with such knowledge, holding it against the throb of memory like an ice pack against a bruise. There are keener sources of grief: poverty, racism, rape, war. I do not wish to compete for a trophy in suffering. I am only trying to understand the corrosive mixture of helplessness, responsibility, and shame that I learned to feel as the son of an alcoholic. I realize now that I did not cause my father's illness, nor could I have cured it. Yet for all this grown-up knowledge, I am still ten years old, my own son's age, and as that boy I struggle in guilt and confusion to save my father from pain.

[handwritten: listing good tactic]

Consider a few of our synonyms for *drunk:* tipsy, tight, pickled, soused, and plowed; stoned and stewed, lubricated and inebriated, juiced and sluiced; three sheets to the wind, in your cups, out of your mind, under the table, lit up, tanked up, wiped out; besotted, blotto, bombed, and buzzed; plastered, polluted, putrified; loaded or looped, boozy, woozy, fuddled, or smashed; crocked and shit-faced, corked and pissed, snockered and sloshed. *[handwritten: humor addition]*

It is a mostly humorous lexicon, as the lore that deals with drunks—in jokes and cartoons, in plays, films, and television skits—is largely comic. Aunt *[handwritten: Is it funny?]* Matilda nips elderberry wine from the sideboard and burps politely during supper. Uncle Fred slouches to the table glassy-eyed, wearing a lamp shade for a hat and murmuring, "Candy is dandy but liquor is quicker." Inspired by *[handwritten: using humor in writing]* cocktails, Mrs. Somebody recounts the events of her day in a fuzzy dialect, while Mr. Somebody nibbles her ear and croons a bawdy song. On the sofa with Boyfriend, Daughter giggles, licking gin from her lips, and loosens the bows in her hair. Junior knocks back some brews with his chums at the Leopard Lounge and stumbles home to the wrong house, wonders foggily why he cannot locate his pajamas, and crawls naked into bed with the ugliest girl in school. The family dog slurps from a neglected martini and wobbles to the nursery, where he vomits in Baby's shoe.

It is all great fun. But if in the audience you notice a few laughing faces turn grim when the drunk lurches on stage, don't be surprised, for these are the children of alcoholics. Over the grinning mask of Dionysus, the leering mask of Bacchus, these children cannot help seeing the bloated features of their own parents. Instead of laughing, they wince, they mourn. Instead of celebrating the drunk as one freed from constraints, they pity him as one enslaved. They refuse to believe *in vino veritas*, having seen their befuddled parents skid away from truth toward folly and oblivion. And so these children bite their lips until the lush staggers into the wings.

My father, when drunk, was neither funny nor honest; he was pathetic, frightening, deceitful. There seemed to be a leak in him somewhere, and he poured in booze to keep from draining dry. Like a torture victim who refuses to squeal, he would never admit that he had touched a drop, not even in his last year, when he seemed to be dissolving in alcohol before our very eyes. I never knew him to lie about anything, ever, except about this one ruinous fact. Drowsy, clumsy, unable to fix a bicycle tire, throw a baseball, balance a grocery sack, or walk across the room, he was stripped of his true self by drink. In a matter of minutes, the contents of a bottle could transform a brave man into a coward, a buddy into a bully, a gifted athlete and skilled carpenter and shrewd businessman into a bumbler. No dictionary of synonyms for *drunk* would soften the anguish of watching our prince turn into a frog.

Father's drinking became the family secret. While growing up, we children never breathed a word of it beyond the four walls of our house. To this day, my brother and sister rarely mention it, and then only when I press them. I did not confess the ugly, bewildering fact to my wife until his wavering walk and slurred speech forced me to. Recently, on the seventh anniversary of my father's death, I asked my mother if she ever spoke of his drinking to friends. "No, no, never," she replied hastily. "I couldn't bear for anyone to know."

The secret bores under the skin, gets in the blood, into the bone, and stays there. Long after you have supposedly been cured of malaria, the fever can flare up, the tremors can shake you. So it is with the fevers of shame. You swallow the bitter quinine of knowledge, and you learn to feel pity and compassion toward the drinker. Yet the shame lingers in your marrow, and, because of the shame, anger.

For a long stretch of my childhood we lived on a military reservation in Ohio, an arsenal where bombs were stored underground in bunkers, vintage airplanes burst into flames, and unstable artillery shells boomed nightly at the dump. We had the feeling, as children, that we played in a mine field, where a heedless footfall could trigger an explosion. When Father was drinking, the house, too, became a mine field. The least bump could set off either parent.

The more he drank, the more obsessed Mother became with stopping him. She hunted for bottles, counted the cash in his wallet, sniffed at his breath. Without meaning to snoop, we children blundered left and right into damning evidence. On afternoons when he came home from work sober, we flung ourselves at him for hugs, and felt against our ribs the telltale lump in his coat. In the barn we tumbled on the hay and heard beneath our sneakers the crunch of buried glass. We tugged open a drawer in his workbench, looking for screwdrivers or crescent wrenches, and spied a gleaming six-pack among the tools. Playing tag, we darted around the house just in time to see him sway on the rear stoop and heave a finished bottle into the woods. In his good night kiss we smelled the cloying sweetness of Clorets, the mints he chewed to camouflage his dragon's breath.

Pain

I can summon up that kiss right now by recalling Theodore Roethke's lines about his own father in "My Papa's Waltz":

> The whiskey on your breath
> Could make a small boy dizzy;
> But I hung on like death:
> Such waltzing was not easy.

Such waltzing was hard, terribly hard, for with a boy's scrawny arms I was trying to hold my tipsy father upright.

For years, the chief source of those incriminating bottles and cans was a grimy store a mile from us, a cinder block place called Sly's, with two gas pumps outside and a moth-eaten dog asleep in the window. A strip of flypaper, speckled the year round with black bodies, coiled in the doorway. Inside, on rusty metal shelves or in wheezing coolers, you could find pop and Popsicles, cigarettes, potato chips, canned soup, raunchy postcards, fishing gear, Twinkies, wine, and beer. When Father drove anywhere on errands, Mother would send us kids along as guards, warning us not to let him out of our sight. And so with one or more of us on board, Father would cruise up to Sly's, pump a dollar's worth of gas or plump the tires with air, and then, telling us to wait in the car, he would head for that fly-spangled doorway.

Dutiful and panicky, we cried, "Let us go in with you!"

"No," he answered. "I'll be back in two shakes."

"Please!"

"No!" he roared. "Don't you budge, or I'll jerk a knot in your tails!"

So we stayed put, kicking the seats, while he ducked inside. Often, when he had parked the car at a careless angle, we gazed in through the window and saw Mr. Sly fetching down from a shelf behind the cash register two green pints of Gallo wine. Father swigged one of them right there at the counter, stuffed the other in his pocket, and then out he came, a bulge in his coat, a flustered look on his red face.

Because the Mom and Pop who ran the dump were neighbors of ours, living just down the tar-blistered road, I hated them all the more for poisoning my father. I wanted to sneak in their store and smash the bottles and set fire to the place. I also hated the Gallo brothers, Ernest and Julio, whose jovial faces shone from the labels of their wine, labels I would find, torn and curled, when I burned the trash. I noted the Gallo brothers' address, in California, and I studied the road atlas to see how far that was from Ohio, because I meant to go out there and tell Ernest and Julio what they were doing to my father, and then, if they showed no mercy, I would kill them.

While growing up on the back roads and in the country schools and cramped Methodist churches of Ohio and Tennessee, I never heard the word *alcoholism*, never happened across it in books or magazines. In the nearby towns, there were no addiction treatment programs, no community mental health centers, no Alcoholics Anonymous chapters, no therapists. Left alone with our grievous secret, we had no way of understanding Father's drinking except as an act of will, a deliberate folly or cruelty, a moral weakness, a sin. He drank because he chose to, pure and simple. Why our father, so playful and competent and kind when sober, would choose to ruin himself and punish his family, we could not fathom.

Our neighborhood was high on the Bible, and the Bible was hard on drunkards. "Woe to those who are heroes at drinking wine, and valiant men in mixing strong drink," wrote Isaiah. "The priest and the prophet reel with strong drink, they are confused with wine, they err in vision, they stumble in giving judgment. For all tables are full of vomit, no place is without filthiness." We children had seen those fouled tables at the local truck stop where the notorious boozers hung out, our father occasionally among them. "Wine and new wine take away the understanding," declared the prophet Hosea. We had also seen evidence of that in our father, who could multiply seven-digit numbers in his head when sober, but when drunk could not help us with fourth-grade math. Proverbs warned: "Do not look at wine when it is red, when it sparkles in the cup and goes down smoothly. At the last it bites like a serpent, and stings like an adder. Your eyes will see strange things, and your mind utter perverse things." Woe, woe.

Dismayingly often, these biblical drunkards stirred up trouble for their own kids. Noah made fresh wine after the flood, drank too much of it, fell asleep without any clothes on, and was glimpsed in the buff by his son Ham, whom Noah promptly cursed. In one passage—it was so shocking we had to read it under our blankets with flashlights—the patriarch Lot fell down drunk and slept with his daughters. The sins of the fathers set their children's teeth on edge.

Our ministers were fond of quoting St. Paul's pronouncement that drunkards would not inherit the kingdom of God. These grave preachers assured us that the wine referred to during the Last Supper was in fact grape juice. Bible and sermons and hymns combined to give us the impression that Moses should have brought down from the mountain another stone tablet, bearing the Eleventh Commandment: Thou shalt not drink.

The scariest and most illuminating Bible story apropos of drunkards was the one about the lunatic and the swine. Matthew, Mark, and Luke each told a version of the tale. We knew it by heart: When Jesus climbed out of his boat one day, this lunatic came charging up from the graveyard, stark naked and filthy, frothing at the mouth, so violent that he broke the strongest chains. Nobody would go near him. Night and day for years this madman had been wailing among the tombs and bruising himself with stones. Jesus took one look at him and said, "Come out of the man, you unclean spirits!" for he could see that the lunatic was possessed by demons. Meanwhile, some hogs were conveniently rooting nearby. "If we have to come out," begged the demons, "at least let us go into those swine." Jesus agreed. The unclean spirits entered the hogs, and the hogs rushed straight off a cliff and plunged into a lake. Hearing the story in Sunday school, my friends thought mainly of the pigs. (How big a splash did they make? Who paid for the lost pork?) But I thought of the redeemed lunatic, who bathed himself and put on clothes and calmly sat at the feet of Jesus, restored—so the Bible said—to "his right mind."

When drunk, our father was clearly in his wrong mind. He became a stranger, as fearful to us as any graveyard lunatic, not quite frothing at the mouth but fierce enough, quick-tempered, explosive; or else he grew maudlin and weepy, which frightened us nearly as much. In my boyhood despair, I reasoned that maybe he wasn't to blame for turning into an ogre. Maybe, like the lunatic, he was possessed by demons. I found support for my theory when I heard liquor referred to as "spirits," when the newspapers reported that somebody had been arrested for "driving under the influence," and when church ladies railed against that "demon drink."

If my father was indeed possessed, who would exorcise him? If he was a sinner, who would save him? If he was ill, who would cure him? If he suffered, who would ease his pain? Not ministers or doctors, for we could not bring ourselves to confide in them; not the neighbors, for we pretended they had never seen him drunk; not Mother, who fussed and pleaded but could not budge him; not my brother and sister, who were only kids. That left me. It did not matter that I, too, was only a child, and a bewildered one at that. I could not excuse myself.

On first reading a description of delirium tremens—in a book on alcoholism I smuggled from the library—I thought immediately of the frothing lunatic and the frenzied swine. When I read stories or watched films about grisly metamorphoses—Dr. Jekyll becoming Mr. Hyde, the mild husband changing into a werewolf, the kindly neighbor taken over by a brutal alien—I could not help seeing my own father's mutation from sober to drunk. Even today, knowing better, I am attracted by the demonic theory of drink, for when I recall my father's transformation, the emergence of his ugly second self, I find it easy to believe in possession by unclean spirits. We never knew which version of Father would come home from work, the true or the tainted, nor could we guess how far down the slope toward cruelty he would slide.

How far a man *could* slide we gauged by observing our back-road neighbors—the out-of-work miners who had dragged their families to our corner of Ohio from the desolate hollows of Appalachia, the tightfisted farmers, the surly mechanics, the balked and broken men. There was, for example, whiskey-soaked Mr. Jenkins, who beat his wife and kids so hard we could hear their screams from the road. There was Mr. Lavo the wino, who fell asleep smoking time and again, until one night his disgusted wife bundled up the children and went outside and left him in his easy chair to burn; he awoke on his own, staggered out coughing into the yard, and pounded her flat while the children looked on and the shack turned to ash. There was the truck driver, Mr. Sampson, who tripped over his son's tricycle one night while drunk and got so mad that he jumped into his semi and drove away, shifting through the dozen gears, and never came back. We saw the bruised children of these fathers clump onto our school bus, we saw the abandoned children huddle in the pews at church, we saw the stunned and battered mothers begging for help at our doors.

Our own father never beat us, and I don't think he ever beat Mother, but he threatened often. The Old Testament Yahweh was not more terrible in his wrath. Eyes blazing, voice booming, Father would pull out his belt and swear to give us a whipping, but he never followed through, never needed to, because we could imagine it so vividly. He shoved us, pawed us with the back of his hand, as an irked bear might smack a cub, not to injure, just to clear a space. I can see him grabbing Mother by the hair as she cowers on a chair during a nightly quarrel. He twists her neck back until she gapes up at him, and then he lifts over her skull a glass quart bottle of milk, the milk running down his forearm, and he yells at her, "Say just one more word, one goddamn word, and I'll shut you up!" I fear she will prick him with her sharp tongue, but she is terrified into silence, and so am I, and the leaking bottle quivers in the air, and milk slithers through the red hair of my father's uplifted arm, and the entire scene is there to this moment, the head jerked back, the club raised.

When the drink made him weepy, Father would pack a bag and kiss each of us children on the head, and announce from the front door that he was moving out. "Where to?" we demanded, fearful each time that he would leave for good, as Mr. Sampson had roared away for good in his diesel truck. "Someplace where I won't get hounded every minute," Father would answer, his jaw quivering. He stabbed a look at Mother, who might say, "Don't run into the ditch before you get there," or, "Good riddance," and then he would slink away. Mother watched him go with arms crossed over her chest, her face closed like the lid on a box of snakes. We children bawled. Where could he go? To the truck stop, that den of iniquity? To one of those dark, ratty flophouses in town? Would he wind up sleeping under a railroad bridge or on a park bench or in a cardboard box, mummied in rags, like the bums we had seen on our trips to Cleveland and Chicago? We bawled and bawled, wondering if he would ever come back.

He always did come back, a day or a week later, but each time there was a sliver less of him.

In Kafka's *The Metamorphosis*, which opens famously with Gregor Samsa waking up from uneasy dreams to find himself transformed into an insect, Gregor's family keep reassuring themselves that things will be just fine again, "When he comes back to us." Each time alcohol transformed our father, we held out the same hope, that he would really and truly come back to us, our authentic father, the tender and playful and competent man, and then all things would be fine. We had grounds for such hope. After his weepy departures and chapfallen returns, he would sometimes go weeks, even months without drinking. Those were glad times. Joy banged inside my ribs. Every day without the furtive glint of bottles, every meal without a fight, every bedtime without sobs encouraged us to believe that such bliss might go on forever.

Mother was fooled by just such a hope all during the forty-odd years she knew this Greeley Ray Sanders. Soon after she met him in a Chicago delicatessen on the eve of World War II, and fell for his butter-melting Mississippi drawl and his wavy red hair, she learned that he drank heavily. But then so did a lot of men. She would soon coax or scold him into breaking the nasty habit. She would point out to him how ugly and foolish it was, this bleary drinking, and then he would quit. He refused to quit during their engagement, however, still refused during the first years of marriage, refused until my sister came along. The shock of fatherhood sobered him, and he remained sober through my birth at the end of the war and right on through until we moved in 1951 to the Ohio arsenal, that paradise of bombs. Like all places that make a business of death, the arsenal had more than its share of alcoholics and drug addicts and other varieties of escape artists. There I turned six and started school and woke into a child's flickering awareness, just in time to see my father begin sneaking swigs in the garage.

He sobered up again for most of a year at the height of the Korean War, to celebrate the birth of my brother. But aside from that dry spell, his only breaks from drinking before I graduated from high school were just long enough to raise and then dash our hopes. Then during the fall of my senior year—the time of the Cuban missile crisis, when it seemed that the nightly explosions at the munitions dump and the nightly rages in our household might spread to engulf the globe—Father collapsed. His liver, kidneys, and heart all conked out. The doctors saved him, but only by a hair. He stayed in the hospital for weeks, going through a withdrawal so terrible that Mother would not let us visit him. If he wanted to kill himself, the doctors solemnly warned him, all he had to do was hit the bottle again. One binge would finish him.

Father must have believed them, for he stayed dry for the next fifteen years. It was an answer to prayer, Mother said, it was a miracle. I believe it was a reflex of fear, which he sustained over the years through courage and pride.

He knew a man could die from drink, for his brother Roscoe had. We children never laid eyes on doomed Uncle Roscoe, but in the stories Mother told us he became a fairy-tale figure, like a boy who took the wrong turning in the woods and was gobbled up by the wolf.

The fifteen-year dry spell came to an end with Father's retirement in the spring of 1978. Like many men, he gave up his identity along with his job. One day he was a boss at the factory, with a brass plate on his door and a reputation to uphold; the next day he was a nobody at home. He and Mother were leaving Ontario, the last of the many places to which his job had carried them, and they were moving to a new house in Mississippi, his childhood stomping grounds. As a boy in Mississippi, Father sold Coca-Cola during dances while the moonshiners peddled their brew in the parking lot; as a young blade, he fought in bars and in the ring, seeking a state Golden Gloves championship; he gambled at poker, hunted pheasants, raced motorcycles and cars, played semiprofessional baseball, and, along with all his buddies— in the Black Cat Saloon, behind the cotton gin, in the woods—he drank. It was a perilous youth to dream of recovering.

After his final day of work, Mother drove on ahead with a car full of begonias and violets, while Father stayed behind to oversee the packing. When the van was loaded, the sweaty movers broke open a six-pack and offered him a beer.

"Let's drink to retirement!" they crowed. "Let's drink to freedom! to fishing! hunting! loafing! Let's drink to a guy who's going home!"

At least I imagine some such words, for that is all I can do, imagine, and I see Father's hand trembling in midair as he thinks about the fifteen sober years and about the doctors' warning, and he tells himself *Goddamnit, I am a free man,* and *Why can't a free man drink one beer after a lifetime of hard work?* and I see his arm reaching, his fingers closing, the can tilting to his lips. I even supply a label for the beer, a swaggering brand that promises on television to deliver the essence of life. I watch the amber liquid pour down his throat, the alcohol steal into his blood, the key turn in his brain.

Soon after my parents moved back to Father's treacherous stomping ground, my wife and I visited them in Mississippi with our five-year-old daughter. Mother had been too distraught to warn me about the return of the demons. So when I climbed out of the car that bright July morning and saw my father napping in the hammock, I felt uneasy, for in all his sober years I had never known him to sleep in daylight. Then he lurched upright, blinked his blood-shot eyes, and greeted us in a syrupy voice. I was hurled back helpless into childhood.

"What's the matter with Papaw?" our daughter asked.

"Nothing," I said. "Nothing!"

Like a child again, I pretended not to see him in his stupor, and behind my phony smile I grieved. On that visit and on the few that remained before his death, once again I found bottles in the workbench, bottles in the woods. Again his hands shook too much for him to run a saw, to make his precious minia-ture furniture, to drive straight down back roads. Again he wound up in the ditch, in the hospital, in jail, in treatment centers. Again he shouted and wept. Again he lied. "I never touched a drop," he swore. "Your mother's making it up."

I no longer fancied I could reason with the men whose names I found on the bottles—Jim Beam, Jack Daniels—nor did I hope to save my father by burning down a store. I was able now to press the cold statistics about alco-holism against the ache of memory: ten million victims, fifteen million, twenty. And yet, in spite of my age, I reacted in the same blind way as I had in child-hood, ignoring biology, forgetting numbers, vainly seeking to erase through my efforts whatever drove him to drink. I worked on their place twelve and sixteen hours a day, in the swelter of Mississippi summers, digging ditches, running electrical wires, planting trees, mowing grass, building sheds, as though what nagged at him was some list of chores, as though by taking his worries on my shoulders I could redeem him. I was flung back into boyhood, acting as though my father would not drink himself to death if only I were perfect.

I failed of perfection; he succeeded in dying. To the end, he considered himself not sick but sinful. "Do you want to kill yourself?" I asked him. "Why not?" he answered. "Why the hell not? What's there to save?" To the end, he would not speak about his feelings, would not or could not give a name to the beast that was devouring him.

In silence, he went rushing off the cliff. Unlike the biblical swine, how-ever, he left behind a few of the demons to haunt his children. Life with him and the loss of him twisted us into shapes that will be familiar to other sons and daughters of alcoholics. My brother became a rebel, my sister retreated into shyness, I played the stalwart and dutiful son who would hold the fam-ily together. If my father was unstable, I would be a rock. If he squandered money on drink, I would pinch every penny. If he wept when drunk—and only when drunk—I would not let myself weep at all. If he roared at the Little League umpire for calling my pitches balls, I would throw nothing but strikes. Watching him flounder and rage, I came to dread the loss of control. I would go through life without making anyone mad. I vowed never to put in my mouth or veins any chemical that would banish my everyday self. I would never make a scene, never lash out at the ones I loved, never hurt a soul. Through hard work, relentless work, I would achieve something dazzling—in the classroom, on the basketball floor, in the science lab, in the pages of books—and my achievement would distract the world's eyes from his humiliation. I would become a worthy sacrifice, and the smoke of my burning would please God.

It is far easier to recognize these twists in my character than to undo them. Work has become an addiction for me, as drink was an addiction for my father. Knowing this, my daughter gave me a placard for the wall: WORKAHOLIC. The labor is endless and futile, for I can no more redeem myself through work than I could redeem my father. I still panic in the face of other people's anger, because his drunken temper was so terrible. I shrink from causing sadness or disappointment even to strangers, as though I were still concealing the family shame. I still notice every twitch of emotion in the faces around me, having learned as a child to read the weather in faces, and I blame myself for their least pang of unhappiness or anger. In certain moods I blame myself for everything. Guilt burns like acid in my veins.

I am moved to write these pages now because my own son, at the age of ten, is taking on himself the griefs of the world, and in particular the griefs of his father. He tells me that when I am gripped by sadness he feels responsible; he feels there must be something he can do to spring me from depression, to fix my life. And that crushing sense of responsibility is exactly what I felt at the age of ten in the face of my father's drinking. My son wonders if I, too, am possessed. I write, therefore, to drag into the light what eats at me—the fear, the guilt, the shame—so that my own children may be spared.

I still shy away from nightclubs, from bars, from parties where the solvent is alcohol. My friends puzzle over this, but it is no more peculiar than for a man to shy away from the lions' den after seeing his father torn apart. I took my own first drink at the age of twenty-one, half a glass of burgundy. I knew the odds of my becoming an alcoholic were four times higher than for the sons of nonalcoholic fathers. So I sipped warily.

I still do—once a week, perhaps, a glass of wine, a can of beer, nothing stronger, nothing more. I listen for the turning of a key in my brain.

↓powerful Statement
What does it mean?

Kandi Tayebi

Warring Memories

"They should take off their rings," my husband stated matter-of-factly as we watched CNN broadcasting more trouble in the Middle East. For two years he had fought in the Iran-Iraq war, but he rarely shared his experiences with me, perhaps feeling that his American-born wife might have difficulty relating to the realities of warfare in one's homeland. On the television screen, eighteen-year-old soldiers displayed their bravery, shaking rifles and shooting into the air. Faces crushed too close to the camera triumphantly spoke of victory. Without the tanks lined behind the young men, or the rifles and camouflage, one could easily think the segment centered on a basketball tournament. One young man, sweat streaked across his T-shirt, held his rifle high in the air, tilted his head back, and whooped. His golden wedding ring covered skin not yet whitened by years of being hidden. I turned slowly to my husband after my eyes focused on the wedding ring encircling the finger of a dark, soft-eyed man, the gold scraping against the side of his MG 3 and reflecting the sun into the camera lens.

My husband, mingling his words with those of the CNN announcer, said quietly, "When they die, their bodies will bloat in the heat. For gold, their fingers will be cut off." His words were almost drowned out by the victory calls of the young men on the screen.

For me, video-game graphics displaying a target and its destruction constitute war. Generals, in neatly pressed fatigues, stand in front of blackboards like coaches before the big game, explaining the strategic plans behind each assault against the enemy. Occasionally, a screaming mother, sister, or wife lies across someone's body, but the television screen separates her pain from my world, framing her in cinematic neutrality. I try to match my husband's stories with the only other versions of war I know, those from the movie screen—*Saving Private Ryan, The Green Berets, Apocalypse Now.*

An olive-skinned boy with just the beginnings of a beard across his chin pushes his way to the front of the crowd and smiles. Two gold teeth define the border of his mouth, and I laugh cautiously, "Should he remove his teeth, too?" My husband tells about men shoving the butts of their rifles against a jaw, splintering bone across the sand, to remove gold teeth for souvenirs. The boy on the television looks fragile.

I want to nullify the horror of my husband's tales by believing these acts occur only in distant lands at the hands of people unlike me, but the boy's eyes look so much like my son's. The camera turns down to show his black and white Nikes. Suddenly, the lens pans through the crowd to a building in the back. Out of the window dangles what appears at first to be a bloody white cloth or, as the camera moves in, an effigy. Standing above the lifeless form, a boy not older than sixteen or seventeen waves his bloodied hands at the camera. Blood smears his white T-shirt, making abstract patterns over the face of an unidentifiable basketball player dunking a ball. The camera zooms in on the battered, pulpy mass of the dead man, now clearly distinguishable as he falls to the ground. The crowd grabs the body—kicking, pulling, tearing. My eyes remain focused on the screen; not even this violence makes me turn away.

I realize I see war as a snapshot—moments flashed across a screen or plastered on the page. Slowly over time, bits of the war have leaked out into the conversations between my husband and me. He informs me that the worst part of war is the waiting, something the snapshots don't show. During the moments when the fighting is most intense, one doesn't have time to think or to worry. Adrenaline pushes the body to action, and the surroundings seem surreal. Yet most of the day is spent listening and waiting. Stray shots go off in the distance, planes fly over, and soldiers practice by shooting rats. After awhile, the older soldiers learn to avoid thinking by filling the air with idle talk. It is the new men, the ones who haven't yet realized where they are, the ones who still dream about normal life, who begin the taboo discussions of home and family.

Almost a year after the CNN broadcast, my husband recounts one memory from the war as we sit watching our children play in the yard under the summer sun. One young soldier, away from home for the first time, sat on the hillside next to my husband during a late-night watch. As point men, they were to listen carefully for the enemy, then stand up and shoot when the enemy crested the hill. For hours they sat, telling stories of their families—an oldest sister's trip to college, a youngest brother's business, a mother's dream for her son to become a doctor. Silence stretched the night, forcing the two men into the thickness of loneliness. Just before dawn, a shot shattered the stillness, and my husband, the wizened experienced soldier at twenty-three, stood and began firing back.

"Stand up and shoot," he hollered at his partner, who shook with fear. Grabbing the boy by a shoulder soaked with sweat, my husband tried to force him onto his feet. Finally, in resignation, he dropped the boy back down onto the soft earth.

After the battle ended and the silence returned, my husband looked down at the boy lying across his boots. That first shot had drilled a hole through his forehead—his shaking was the last sign of life, the wetness on his shoulder the blood draining from his wound. Pushing the boy off his feet, my husband turned his eyes away.

A few weeks after my husband confides this war story to me, while I am cleaning out closets before the rush of the school year begins, I run across a box of old photos he brought with him from Iran. I thumb through pictures of my husband during the war, looking at all of the wan faces for signs of the man I've come to know. I've watched him walk for hours across our bedroom floor, our son cradled against his chest. As the fevered cries of our son filled the room, my husband would patiently sing Persian lullabies and stroke the baby's back. He has deftly bandaged skinned knees, extracted splinters, and chased away scary dreams. When we were refused housing after a woman saw my husband was from the Middle East, I angrily protested while he quietly walked away. When colleagues at work have called him "camel rider," asked him about all the abusive men in his country, and even discussed how they would bomb all those "Arabs," my husband has responded with humor and reminded me that people need time to change. In contrast, I have at times come close to hitting colleagues who have asked, "How could a bright woman like you marry a man from the Middle East?"

Yet in these war pictures, the muscular body and soft eyes of my husband are camouflaged by the gaunt, grizzled look of the young man staring out. His eyes sunk deep in his head glare back in desperation. One hand grips an MG 3; the other rests gently on the front of a tank. Men no more than twenty-five years old, aged by the sights of battle, surround him. In another more haunting photo, a soldier smiles childishly, an oddity among his serious compatriots. At his feet lies a body, the head bent awkwardly to the right as a boot steps down on the face. In the soldier's hand are the dog tags of the dead man. Another soldier distractedly tosses dirt clods onto the dead man's chest, already piled with rocks and trash thrown by others. In the background, my husband shares a sandwich with another young man.

This photo wakens my husband's sharpest memory from the war. Out of all the frightening scenes of the fighting, my husband's strongest recollection is of a tomato sandwich. As his unit entered a village devastated by recent bombings, they began to search for food and shelter. Entire walls and roofs were missing from most of the houses that remained. The streets were lined with rubble, stray chickens and goats, and body parts of women, men, and children. Chunks of blackened flesh checkered the cobblestones. Two fingers, still attached to the outside of an arm blown open and swollen by the sun, lay against one wall. Occasionally, around a corner or behind some bodies, a small piece of greenery pushed its way up through the broken stones and trash.

The soldiers were lucky enough to find a few tomatoes left behind by one house's occupants and somehow untouched by the blast that had leveled all of the walls and blown off the roof. In the kitchen, a loaf of fresh-baked bread sat neatly on the counter above the body of an old woman still dressed in a white and red apron. Her arms were twisted awkwardly behind her back. The left side of her face smeared with ashes, her eyes staring at the cupboard, she seemed prepared to greet visitors—except for the large black hole ripped out of the right side of her head.

For weeks, the soldiers had had little but dried army rations to eat. Sitting on the rat-infested floor, the men devoured sandwiches, relishing the red juice streaking the white bread. The smell of yeast mixed with the stench of burnt flesh. The tomato sandwich amid the destruction was a delicacy.

Fall arrives again, bringing the frenzied activity of a new school year. I sip my last drop of tea, kiss my boys goodbye, and head off to teach at the university, where children the age of those in the photographs I looked at this past summer will struggle with their own sets of problems. One young man comes into my office to explain why he won't be able to complete my course. With vacant eyes, he explains that his two-year-old sister was killed in a drive-by shooting, and his mama needs him to help with his four- and five-year-old brothers. He apologizes for letting me down, shakes my hand, and walks out of the office wiping the nose of one of those brothers. I walk outside into the sunshine.

Fall in the South brings cool relief from the torching humidity of summer, and students sit beneath the old oak trees that line the paths winding throughout campus, taking advantage of the pleasant sun, breeze, and fragrant flowers. Walking across the landscaped lawns, I pause to enjoy the newly blossomed hibiscus, the squirrels chasing each other up one tree and around another, and the students clad in jeans and T-shirts sporting fashion designers' names. My mind drifts to scenes of my young son delighted by the pointy-nosed armadillos that dig up slugs in our yard. He and the neighborhood cats chase the armadillos, which dodge their advances while appearing nonchalantly to ignore their existence. Coming from Colorado, we marvel at these unusual spotted creatures, watching them for hours from our porch and finally resorting to the video camera to record their images for those left behind in the Rockies. Texas has exposed us to a whole new array of animals—slimy, slinking, furry, flying, wrinkled, skittering—that are unfamiliar and enticing.

Only the playful squirrels seem a familiar sight. Today, they race through the crabgrass and roll down the hills, enjoying the newly crisp air. Almost like a shooting star, seen briefly in one's peripheral vision and then gone, a squirrel falls from the tallest tree in the middle of the courtyard. Unsure what it really was, I join the increasing number of students gathered closely around the damaged body. The squirrel sits on its hind legs, at first appearing to be a movie on pause. Then, with great effort, it thrusts its front legs as if to scurry up the tree. The back legs drag for only an inch, the top half of its body collapses on the ground, and its breaths come in forced bursts. Back broken, the squirrel continues to struggle as I look away. Even after calling someone to come help the animal, I have flashbacks of the squirrel staring at me, reaching towards me with its front paws only to be pulled back against its useless rear legs.

When I return home from the university, I find my husband preparing sandwiches for a picnic in the park. Our two boys chase each other up and down the stairs, giggling and screaming. I tell my husband about the slow death of the squirrel, and after a moment of silence, he responds, "Imagine if that were a human being." For an instant I can vaguely comprehend the war he lived.

At the park, I find our neighborhood celebrating Safety Night, an event that helps citizens and local police officers come together to protect our children.

While the kids play cowboys and Indians, climb on the monkey bars, and collect police officer trading cards, the adults eat and talk. At sundown the fireworks begin, filling the sky with color. My husband cringes at the first few flashes of light and the accompanying loud booms before he can settle in. My youngest son sits on his lap, leans against his chest, and sees only beauty in the explosions.

CONNIE WIENEKE

Snakebit

As I dial my mother's phone number, I skim the first page of my story. On the computer monitor, I mouth the sentences, liking the way they roll one into the next, confident and certain.

When I was 6 years old a rattlesnake bit me.

Ask my mother and she'll say this didn't happen.

But for years now she has tried to convince me that when I was younger and we were still living in Bakersfield, California, that I passionately loved the neighbor's Irish setter. When I visit her in Seattle, she drags out the photo album and points to the half-dozen scalloped-edged, black-and-white pictures of a girl and a dog in a backyard. I don't trust those images: of a girl that could have been me — streaked with mud, being licked by this dog I do not remember.

The rattler, though, in a cemetery outside of Havre, Montana, materializes as two red marks on the skin above my ankle bone. All these years, proof that a rattle-snake bit me.

Before my mother picks up the phone, I make it through one screen of text. When I hear her voice long distance from Seattle, I work a light tone into the voice in my head before I speak. I tell her I've called to get some "facts" about the period we lived in northern Montana.

"Why do you want to know?" she says. From 500 miles away, I hear suspicion curdling her voice. I picture her on the couch: striped acrylic afghan — she made it herself and it looks it — wrapped around her legs, ash tray balanced on the couch arm, a filter cigarette inches from her mouth, and a cup with the world's weakest coffee clasped in her right hand. She is curled up on the couch, looking smaller than her 5 feet 7 inches, though the mannish cut of her coarse gray hair — she goes to a barber because it is cheap — and the determined line of her jaw speak to a bull-headed strength I know too well.

I tell her it's for a class assignment. One thousand words about childhood. "I'm just writing a story, Momma. Nothing earth-shaking." I scoot around in my chair in the small house I have rented for the school year in Missoula, repositioning myself so I can scan the computer screen better. "No skeletons will be revealed." I laugh and begin reading from the screen where I had left off before she said, "Hallstrom resident."

It was 1959. Another Montana recession. The summer between my first and second grades at Devlin Elementary School.

My father had just rented a 15-acre farm a little south of the Milk River. The property rolled away to this low spot beside the new Catholic cemetery and belonged to Bill Kimiele.

"Your father's old drinking buddy," my mother breaks in, and without waiting for me to say, "I know," she offers up more information than I need. "We were paying $50 a month rent. Part of the deal was we had to take care of Mr. Kimiele's horses."

"Yes, the horses were called Molly, Polly and Ginger," I say, proud that I know their names. "I remember riding Ginger once with Jimmy and Lyn."

"I don't remember that," she says. "Maybe you'd better let me hear what else you've written."

"This isn't supposed to be history," I remind her before I resume reading from the story.

My parents' makeshift tenant farm was bordered by the Kimieles' fields of winter wheat, an east-west dirt road and the cemetery between us and Highway 2.

"Don't forget Mr. McConnell's cows and corn," my mother interrupts. "You remember? He was on the other side. Mr. McConnell's cows were forever getting out and getting into the cemetery. One time I got a stick and I got about 30 feet up to this one cow. Oh, boy. When I saw how big it was . . ."

"I thought his name was McCoy," I say, certain I had shared this name with friends.

"That was a TV show," my mother says. "'The Real McCoys!'"

When she starts laughing like a female version of Walter Brennan, I feel embarrassed by my desire to keep the white lie of the McCoy name intact in the story. I breathe in and then continue reading.

Somehow they scraped together the money to buy a silver and blue Nashua trailer. Vintage 1955. Bedroom in the middle for my parents and another at the back to be shared by my brother, sister and me. Living room in front, the window looking south across an unpaved county road.

"Your father had to borrow the money from his brother," my mother says. "Uncle Johnny."

"It doesn't matter," I say. "That's not integral to my story."

"He didn't really want to do it. You know, your dad was in a lot of trouble as a teen-ager and your uncle could do no wrong."

"I like Uncle Johnny," I say.

"That's nice," my mother says. "I thought you'd want to know."

"OK," I say, hoping that will stop her.

"We paid $2,800 for that trailer," she says. "I still have the papers."

That figures, I think, knowing my mother keeps absolutely everything. For the proverbial rainy day, to prove her memory intact. My last trip home I made the mistake of trying to find a box of college textbooks stored in the attic. To get to the books, I first had to move hundreds of clear plastic juice jugs, the kind with orange caps; a box of advertising supplements from the Seattle Times; at least five boxes of half-gallon wine bottles, all green and with their caps screwed on tight; more boxes, these containing clean milk cartons which my mother told me later would eventually be used for freezing fish my stepfather would eventually catch, and one trash bag filled with foam packing material shaped like squashed figure-eights.

I never found the textbooks, which probably meant they had gone the way of my childhood dolls: to the Salvation Army. In her poorly lit attic, I saw her weighing my anthropology and history and dolls against the vast security and possibility of plastic and glass, the scales tipping in their favor. She had no use for my books and toys.

My parents set the trailer up on the farm, next to a well, three rundown out-buildings and a rust-colored boxcar with the Great Northern mountain goat insignia on both sides faded to little more than ghosts. Late afternoons, the cover of the well was perfect for watching sheet lightning. In that lightning, I imagined sheep and cows rushing across the horizon, followed by horses. And Indians. Always Indians. Everything galloping toward the West. Everything in such a hurry. The lightning so far to the north we never heard thunder.

"That's not right," my mother says. "It'd roll up on us and you kids would go screaming into the trailer."

"I liked the feeling," I say. "I can still feel those first drops on my face."

"They were big and usually full of dirt," my mother says.

"Well, I don't remember it that way," I say, and then ask her why she, a St. Louis city girl, and my father, who'd only done sheet metal and tended bar, decided to become farmers on the highline outside of Havre.

"We were on 'relief' at the time," she says. "You know, welfare? We got commodities, basics. You remember the powdered eggs and peanut butter, don't you? We'd get flour wrapped in brown paper and the oleo came in clear plastic. You kids used to fight over who was going to squeeze the yellow coloring into the oleo."

"I hated that margarine," I say.

"Well, it got us through," she says. "It was doodly-squat there for awhile, but that was the happiest time of my life." She pauses.

Before I ask her why, she starts telling me.

"Your father wouldn't let me take my medicine. He said the epilepsy was all in my head. The odd thing was during that year and a half we lived out there, I never had any seizures. Not one. I think it was just being on that farm."

She pauses. I don't think that's the whole story, but ask her what my father was doing at the time.

"Your dad was working for Great Northern as a switchman, but he was on call, they'd use him if they needed him which meant he wasn't working much. It was a hell of a time."

To make money, my parents decided to raise chickens in the boxcar and sell the eggs. They sold for 60 cents a dozen which was high.

"They were brown," my mother says, as if that explains the cost.

They started out with 200 chicks, which came boxed like doughnuts. One night they lost 150, because my mother forgot to turn on the heat lamps. The survivors became her exclusive property. She fed the chickens scratch in the pen they shared with the horses. She shot at hawks with an old .22 to protect them. And she chopped off their heads when we needed something to eat. Chicken-and-dumplings. Fried chicken with "smashed" potatoes as we called them. Chicken noodle soup.

"You make it sound like all we did was eat chicken," my mother says. "Your father went hunting. We had elk. One time even bear."

"Yes, but I'm telling this story, Momma. I can still see those chickens running around, blood squirting all over the place."

"It wasn't that bad," she says.

The chickens don't have a lot to do with the rattlesnake biting me, but they were connected to our living in the middle of nowhere, our closest neighbor miles down the road.

"It was only a mile, but you kids never wanted to walk that far," my mother says.

I'm thinking if she keeps interrupting, I'll never finish this story and my phone bill's going to be outrageous.

"Momma, I'd like to talk about the cemetery, and the snake."

"Well, I thought you wanted to know."

"I do, but I only have so much time and the piece is only supposed to be a thousand words."

"That should be about right." She hurries on before I can speak to tell about visiting the Simpsons down the road. "One time you got ahead of your brother and sister and me. When we caught up, you'd found a dead skunk and were sticking your fingers into it."

"That's ridiculous," I say. "You're making that up."

"I wouldn't do that," she says. "I leave that for you."

"Let me finish this. Besides, I've heard all about the Simpsons. The outside of their house was covered with tar paper."

"It was more of a shack," she says.

"OK. I know I learned to ride the Simpsons' bicycle on their gravel road."

"That wasn't there," my mother says. "You're thinking of the Keller family. Red and Ruby. They were out on the highway and had pigs. . . ."

"Not now, Mother," I say.

"You didn't like it when they butchered those pigs. They. . . ."

"Mother, I've never seen a pig killed. OK? Can I go on with this?"

"Oh, yes, do," she says, all too perky. "I don't think their name was Simpson though."

Because we didn't have any close neighbors, my brother, sister and I entertained ourselves. When bored, we'd go to the Catholic cemetery. It was a new one, meaning nobody was buried there yet. Three statues had been erected and we loved to play on them. We had to avoid the "caretakers" working there who would chase us away, especially once they started laying the sod.

My mother can't help herself. She interrupts. "No, it was still covered with sagebrush. Mr. McConnell's cows liked to eat it. That's where they were always. . . ."

"Cemeteries have grass," I say.

"Well, this one didn't," my mother says. "It was too new."

I control my voice when I continue reading.

The hottest part of the summer settled over us, and we'd gone over to the cemetery again. We were playing on a statue of Christ with children sitting and standing around him. He was obviously telling a story because the children appeared to be in rapt attention staring.

"A parable, darling." My mother again. "He was giving them a parable. You remember what a parable is?"

"Yes."

"You should come to church with me next time. You'd like the. . . ."

"Sure. I'll think about it," I say, knowing I'll never step foot in St. Thomas'.

There were several other Jesus statues, all of them carved from white marble with red marble bases. I don't know if I'd decided to go home or what, but I stepped down into the weeds behind the statue and heard this sound. You don't have to hear that sound more than the first time to know what it is.

"What was it?" my mother says, like she's talking to a toddler. "A rattlesnake?"

"Mother."

"Just teasing, darling."

After touching the snake with the toe of my shoe, I jumped straight up and ran. When I reached the ditch separating our property from the cemetery, I stopped to look where the snake had bitten me.

"Oh, hon. You shouldn't tell people that rattler bit you. They might believe you."

"Well, it did."

"You'd be dead."

"Well, I'm not. Can I continue?"

"By all means. I'm enjoying this."

I was sure I was going to die and ran home, yelling "Momma, Momma, a snake bit me!" She asked where and I pointed to my bleeding ankle, which I could see swelling. But my mother wanted to know where the snake was. I pointed toward the cemetery. She grabbed the baseball bat she had once tried to throw at a chicken hawk.

"No, I didn't," my mother said. "Don't tell people that I used the .22."

"But it's true. And you never hit a thing." I hear her taking a drag on her cigarette and decide to skip some parts.

By the time the cemetery caretakers arrived, the snake had crawled out of the weeds and was maneuvering the open ground of clods and stones. We were all running around. It was like a Laurel and Hardy movie on Saturday afternoon. Nobody knew what they were doing or why. Finally, one of the men used a long-handled hoe to chop the snake into three pieces.

"How can you remember that?" my mother says.

"What?"

"Three pieces."

"I was standing over one of the pieces, it moved and I jumped."

"Yes, that's right," she says. "I remember that. We all laughed."

"I don't remember it being all that funny," I say.

I showed everybody the two holes from the snakebite. "Look at the blood," *I said, pointing to my ankle.* "I've been bitten."

"They were just scratches from the sagebrush," my mother says. "You were always cutting yourself."

I could have died, but my mother wouldn't take me to the hospital.

"You were fine. You're making me sound like I wasn't a very good mother. Are you listening? Nobody'll believe that snake bit you."

"Look, why don't you write the story yourself."

"Maybe I should," she says.

My worst nightmare is that she will and it will get published. "Well, nobody'll print it," I say.

"No, darling, I wouldn't even try," she says. "I'll only send it to you. Keep going."

"Well, that's about all there is."

"That's not much of an ending," she says.

"I'm still working on the last paragraph," I say.

"Well, we stayed there another year," she says, "until things weren't so compatible between Mr. Kimiele and your father. Even $50 was hard to come up with."

She continues without my prompting. "We must have been a hundred bucks behind. We had to move. B.B.'d had a litter in one of the sheds out back. The kittens were wild and we couldn't. . . ."

"That's another story, Momma," I interrupt, not wanting to remember, but her words force me to think of kittens left behind on so many other occasions. "B.B." was the last of a trio, a wild black we left on that farm when we moved down the road.

On my computer screen, I scroll quickly to the last paragraph.

"Dear, are you still there?"

"Yes," I say. "I was just thinking. What happened to the snake?"

"What do you mean?" she says.

"The pieces? Of the snake?"

"I don't know. We probably just left it there."

I start keying in a new sentence. . . .

I decided to bury the snake and crawled under the trailer with it. . . .

"How did you carry it?" she says.

. . . in my pockets.

"It was a big snake," she says.

"Mother, it's just a story. Have a sense of humor."

"The dog would have dug it up that same night," she says. "Look, you were too squeamish to pick up the snake. The magpies got it or we. . . ."

"Momma, I've got to go."

She says she has a parish meeting to attend. "This has been nice," she adds. "Next time don't wait so long to call. I love you."

"Yes, me, too," I say, and hang up.

I read what I've written about the rattlesnake and one thing my mother said comes back. When I asked her about where they got the boxcar, instead of telling me, she said: "I used to go out to the boxcar with B.B. She'd never bother the chickens. I'd sit there with her in my lap and look out the window. I'd talk to the cat and cry. I couldn't talk to anybody else. You know how your father was."

I never imagined her doing that. Back then, I never knew how alone she felt. Back then, I couldn't have understood this woman forced to take comfort in one small black cat. Back then, I couldn't have taken her in my arms and explained away her tears.

I vow never again to go over a story with my mother, knowing all along that I will mail this one to her, knowing she will write immediately, inform me it wasn't an Irish setter in the backyard, but a chow, and that we never lived in Bakersfield, it was Santa Monica.

"I know," I'll have to say. "I changed a few things."

"You know what kind of people live in Bakersfield," she'll say.

"No, I don't," I'll say, "but I can imagine."

CHAPTER 13

Portrait

Portraits (or profiles) put other people on center stage, sometimes all by themselves, sometimes with others. The author may still be a main character, as in Alice Steinbach's "The Miss Dennis School of Writing." Or he may be one of a supporting cast, as in Charles Simic's "Dinner at Uncle Boris'." The author may be on the sidelines, making a few cameo appearances, as in Li-Young Lee's *The Winged Seed.* Or she may create a portrait series the way Susan Allen does in "Going to the Movies," where each of her dates appears in a separate section.

How well you know your subject often determines your role in the story. Writers rely more on emotional truth shaped by memory when writing about family or others they know from childhood (Simic, Steinbach) than when writing about someone they just met. Either way, research can be involved, as Li-Young Lee demonstrates by being the chronicler of his mother's story. To see what makes a good portrait, notice how each writer uses description and dialogue to create individualized portraits. Except for Toth, concerned with types, the others resist the urge to over-simplify, preferring to show both wonders and warts, creating characters with complexity. Notice how these writers gracefully work in back-story, so readers know the world their characters come from. And notice, too, how they convey their feelings about their characters — in either a humorous tone (Simic) or in a serious one (Lee) — so that what's important, as the writer sees it, shines through. The aim is to make readers feel as if they have met someone new, someone interesting, someone worth thinking more about.

❧ LI-YOUNG LEE   from *The Winged Seed*

❧ CHARLES SIMIC   *"Dinner at Uncle Boris'"*

❧ ALICE STEINBACH   *"The Miss Dennis School of Writing"*

❧ SUSAN TOTH   *"Going to the Movies"*

Note: For another excellent portrait, read Susan Orlean's "Meet the Shaggs" (Chapter 15, Literary Journalism).

LI-YOUNG LEE

The Winged Seed

When my mother, Jiaying, is a girl in China, she loves the summers in the mountains. The rest of the year, she lives in the city below, in the haunted mansion ruled by her father's mother, a woman as cruel as she is small and desiccated, and as selfish as her feet are twisted to fit into tiny hoof-shaped shoes of brocade. It is because of this woman, my mother insists, that drafty ghosts inhabit the countless rooms and myriad corridors of the old house, whose ceilings and rafters are so high that light never reaches them, giving Jiaying the feeling of living perpetually under a great, dark, impenetrable hood. It was from the rafters in the sewing hall, the darkest room in the entire complex, that a maid, fourteen and newly hired, hung herself after only three months of waiting on the old woman.

The sewing hall is a building whose front face is wood and whose other three walls are windowless brick. Two double-door front entrances lead into a cavernous room of stone floors and two rows of three pillars each, painted thickly red, and spaced ten feet apart. Lined with tables at which thirty women sit behind mounds of various fabrics of any color, the room whines and rings with the rapid pounding of several hand-operated sewing machines. Forbidden to wear against their bodies any piece of cloth cut or sewn by men, all the female members of the nine households have their clothes made by women in the sewing hall. Thirty seamstresses, every day all year round making and mending the clothes of births and deaths for every female Yuan, cutting and sewing from patterns handed down generation to generation without mutation for nearly a century, so that almost everyone in Tientsin knows that the less fashionable you are, the older the money you come from. Thirty indentured workers, bought or born into bondage of cloth, sew in the great hall, drinking little cups of tea that amount to green seas, gossiping and telling stories. All day long, necks bent and fingers crooked to meticulous mending or making, by machine and by hand, embroidering, and weaving, and stitching, threading endless miles of spooled thread of all different colors and thicknesses. All different ages, the workers sit according to years of servitude and age, the oldest, having been there the longest, and whose eyes see the least after years of strain, sit at the front of the room where there is the most light from the windows and doorways, while behind them in progressive densities of shadow sit the younger and younger ones less and less blind. Deepest, where the sunlight never reaches, sit the youngest ones, twelve and thirteen, the newly arrived, the tenderest with their sharp, clear eyes, sewing in shadow. Soon enough, though, they'll get to move forward more and more as the very oldest grow so blind they have to quit, just as they themselves, the younger ones, will see less and less, even as they move nearer and nearer the sunlight. By the windows sit a few women old and almost completely blind and whose hands are so twisted as to be not recognizable as hands anymore. Useless and used up by years of service, they tend to the countless cats that live in the sewing hall. Cats of all different sizes and shapes and colors, living on a gruel of rice and fish, or mice, or sometimes their own litters, they far outnumber their keepers, none of whom knows how they came to live there in the first place. Nameless and nondescript, they endlessly prowl along the walls and the legs of the tables, so that the workers sense a constant motion at their feet, a continual brushing past of fur.

Jiaying hates the sewing hall because of the cats. She hates the smell and the hundreds of little eyes behind the tables and in the shadows. She hates the countless tails curling and brushing past her when she is there on an errand. There are so many of them they can hardly be called pets. The ones who have the job of tending the brood sit by the windows sipping tea, chewing their gums, and squinting. The oldest of them, who swears she remembers having sewed the President's scholar's robe for graduation, sits absently grinning to her toothless self. Whether she is recalling better days, or smiling in the knowledge of the fate of all those young pretty girls in the back, no one can tell.

It was here one morning someone looked up into the ceiling and there, where the swallows build their high unseen nests in the dark of the rafters and brackets, was one white sock dangling in midair. It was the white-stockinged foot of someone hanging from the rafters. Screaming and turning over chairs, the women cleared the sewing hall like frantic birds sprung from a box. Members of the nine households assembled in the yard and someone took the body down. The fifth wife's new maid had hung herself. Judging by all signs, she'd done it early in the morning. It must have been just light when she climbed up on a chair set on a table and scaled the rafters and scaffolding. Everyone speculated on what insanity made her go to so much trouble to hang herself from the highest ceiling in the whole complex. For days afterward everyone kept looking into the ceilings of whatever room or corridor they were in. And then people began to see the girl walking around. Even Jiaying's grandmother, who used to make the girl stay awake entire nights rubbing her feet, and beat her pitilessly if she fell asleep, claimed to have seen her once, but just once. She said she woke from a restful afternoon nap and had the feeling someone was in the room. Furious to have an uninvited guest, she opened her eyes to find the Little Ugly, as she was fond of calling her because of her pocked face, sitting next to her. *What did you do, Nai Nai?* the granddaughters gasped who were listening to the story. *What do you think I did?* she gloated. *I told her if she didn't behave I'd make her mother who sold her to me my maid as well.* The girl never visited the old lady again, although others continued to see her.

But, *Let's not talk about old things,* is my mother's response most of the time I ask her about her childhood. *Don't make me go back there. Like those evil-smelling, greenish black potions the servants cooked and served hot to me in winter for coughs and headaches as a child, the past is all one bitter draft to me,* she says as my sister combs my mother's hair in the morning, by the window looking onto her garden. When I press her, she says, *I can't tell if your head is an empty house, or a pot of boiling glue,* and then inserts the alabaster comb into her loosely piled-up hair, a black nest, and waves a silver stray back with her hand summarily, as though to dispel so much cobweb or smoke. *Now let's go buy some fish.*

At the Beautiful Asia Market in Chicago, the refugee grocer is a bent, brown-colored man with a big black mole on his right jaw, and the fish tank is empty, except for some filthy water. The only fish I see are two carp afloat in a bucket propping a mop in it. So we'll buy the gnarled man's perfectly trimmed napa cabbages, but have to get our fish elsewhere. *Elsewhere,* my mother says, *your head is always elsewhere, in the past or in the future. Why can't you be here?* I wonder about an answer while I push a tinny cart with a crazy wheel down the fragrant lanes of tea, aisles of lemon grass and sandalwood, musty narrows of spices and medicinal herbs, rows of shelves, and shelves of jars of chopped pickled mudfish and shrimp ferment, soybean paste and preserved monkfish, eel eyes staring out from brine, sealed stacks of biscuits and cocoa from Belgium and England, and cartons of instant noodles stacked to the ceiling. I browse with my mother, each of us keeping the same things we need for dinner as different lists, Chinese and English, in our heads, and my mother, because her eyes are bad, inspecting the goods with a spyglass.

In my mother's dreams, she wanders that old ground, the family compound, and it's evening, and becoming more evening. She's on an errand to the sewing hall, and the cloth in her hands is poorly folded. And I know by her description that it's the same path I walk in my own dream. In my mother's dream, she walks in the general direction of the sewing hall, but avoids it. In mine, I'm sitting on the steps and the doors are locked. In my dream, I sometimes stand among trees the way I stood three summers ago on Fragrant Mountain, and look across the valley to another mountain face, where my wife leads our children up a winding path. Below, my grandfather's bones scattered by the People's Army.

In my mother's dream, she is again a girl of sixteen in China, where she spends summer with her family on Fragrant Mountain, making the final two-day leg of the serpentine ascent through dense forests on muleback, in a train of twenty-five mules bearing her father, her mother, her father's concubine, three aunties, one brother (the other having been banished by the grandmother), two of her sisters, fourteen and thirteen years old (the other two attending boarding school in France), her favorite cousin, the same age as her and recently orphaned, two of her brother's friends whom he met in New York while attending school there in the fall at Columbia University, three bodyguards armed with rifles and pistols, four household servants, one cook, three dogs, and various equipment and supplies. On the trip up the narrow path, while one of her sisters reads aloud from Zola or Balzac, Jiaying nibbles on fresh lychees, which they carry up the mountain. The mule bearing the burden of Jiaying's favorite fruit can't tell as that burden imperceptibly and gradually lightens, as Jiaying fills her mouth with its sweetness.

When she is a little girl in China, Jiaying's favorite food is lychee. For one brief season a year, the markets are full of that globose, hard-skinned fruit tied in pink string at the bundled stems, and her father sends the servants to buy them for her each morning. Unlike all the other fruits that smell and taste of sunlight compacted, then mellowed to sugar, lychee yields to her tongue a darker perfume, a heavy redolence damp with the mild edge of fermentation. How wonderfully fitting it seems to her that such milky, soft meat should be surrounded by a rough, brown reptilian leather of a slightly red cast when ripe, and made almost impenetrable by being covered in tiny rivets and studs. Summertime, she grows thin on nothing but lychee flesh. She waits each morning for the servants to bring bundles of it home, and rather than have the fruit peeled and served to her in a porcelain bowl that fits precisely the bowl of her hand, she prefers to peel for herself the tough skin, rough to her fingers. Using her fingernails to puncture the exterior, she splits it open and takes with her teeth the white meat slippery with nectar, the whole plump bulb of it in her mouth, and eats it to the smooth pit, which she spits out, leaving on the verandah each morning a scattering of black stones and empty husks, sticky with sugar and swarming with bees. A servant sweeps the verandah, scolding her.

Ordinarily forbidden to go out beyond the confines of their home, a complex of nine mansions and attendant satellite buildings housing the families of the nine wives of Jiaying's grandfather, Jiaying and her sisters' only contact with the rest of the world has been for years through the private school they attend, where they make friends with girls who, while their families can afford the cost of private school, do not belong to titled households of rank, and who, as a result, are not bound to traditional ways and attitudes the same way Jiaying and her sisters are so strictly bound at home. When each of the Yuan sisters distinguishes herself in her studies, and is encouraged by her parents and her grandmother to continue her education after middle school, naturally, each of them takes advantage of the opportunity by enrolling in fashionable French and British boarding schools. All five of them except Jiaying, the oldest, who decided to stay home, where everything that surrounded her was so old, she was certain it must be permanent. The poems she read were thousands of years old, the calligraphy she practiced was practiced by smart refined girls like her thousands of years ago, the house she lived in and the grounds surrounding it looked to be as old as anything else in the whole country, and as half buried. During the summer sand storms, when all the tiles, the latticed windows, the carved railings and figured eaves were packed with sand, and little dunes formed against the buildings, she knew it was sand broken off eternal mountains and then driven the whole way from the Gobi, that old fabled desert, and was on its way to that most ancient of bodies, the sea. And her grandmother, only forty-five but already walking with the aid of a cane and three or four servants, seemed to be some eternal fixture in the universe with her medicinal odors and old ways. How could she conceive of a future when everything around her felt like the end of things, the world's very culmination.

Of all the things packed onto the sweating mules, Jiaying writes in her diary dated June 6, 1939, *an individual lychee is probably the lightest. Or else the calligraphy brushes. Only the little bamboo-handled goldfish nets are as light as the brushes. Next would certainly be the butterfly nets. Then Auntie's opium in its beautiful paper wrappings. Then the pipes. The weight of the rest of the things is distributed as evenly as possible: zithers and lutes, flutes, Ba's typewriter, and tea, mirrors, telescopes, fishing poles, and jars of embalming fluids, empty bird cages, dictionaries and books in Chinese, English, and French, subjects ranging from poetry and astronomy to* The Art of War, *and magnifying glasses, boxing gloves, chess and mahjong sets, bows and arrows, slabs of salt- and sugar-cured meats, squat clay pots sealed in wax holding assorted preserved fruits and vegetables, and pages of rice paper bound in boards, ink blocks, and a monkey to grind the ink.*

They ride slowly through increasingly clearer air, making frequent stops to picnic, shoot small game, and take photographs. The cool, immense night they spend at a rest station manned by servants they sent ahead days ago to prepare for their arrival. By candlelight, Jiaying writes in her diary, which she reads to her cousin: *Miles up from the city. Many more miles to go. Here a place to rest. Ahead, another. And farther, another.*

Their last stop before reaching the summit is the ancestral graveyard. An acre of meadow bounded on three sides by woods and on the fourth by the gravekeeper's small farm, on it stand the twelve-foot-high marble headstones of various shapes. The cemetery gate is a huge nail-studded crossbeam set by wedges into twin two-story posts hewn from whole trees, the entire thing tooled and painted with patterns, symbols, and signs resembling eyes or flowers or clouds, and flanked by a set of stone mythical beasts. Half dog, half lion, half scowling, half grinning, standing on their platforms taller than the gravekeeper's house, both guardians look as though they were peering over his roof.

Once at the site, Jiaying and her family burn incense and paper money, and pray to a long line of illustrious men and women whose severe portraits hang huge and forbidding in the tall, gloomy corridors of their home in Tientsin, a city far below them now as they stand in a high meadow in the mountains.

In the whirring and clicking of grasshoppers, they walk at the feet of the white marble stele. On each is carved a poem commemorating the one who lies underground shrouded in countless layers of silk and enclosed in a box filled with money and precious jewels. As well as flowers, birds, and animals, human figures are etched in various depictions of filial piety. Even as Jiaying stands bowed at the foot of a stone slab two and a half times her height and wide as a double door, above her eternally is the figure of a young girl not unlike herself, clothed in a style hundreds of years old, paying her dutiful respects to the unanswering dead.

While Jiaying and her family linger over the names and poems, no one thinks that Jiaying's father and grandmother will be put in this ground soon. Even less would any of them believe that on an afternoon years from now, a group of student revolutionaries will casually pass through the gates of this place, and dig up the graves and rob them, dragging up the corpses of her father and grandmother to strip and tie them naked to a tree. Jiaying, who will have left the country by then, will have to hear about it almost half a century after the fact, from the gravekeeper himself, who after so many years still recognizes her, and falls to his knees to bow to her, calling her by her title, when she comes back here a woman. She'll have arrived by car then, accompanied by her own children, her husband dead, to be greeted by the man who has lived on this farm ever since the one day he climbed up the mountain to work for her family and never came down again. He'll walk with her over the ground, which has been turned into a pig farm. A few feet behind one of the sties, he'll take her through shoulder-high cannabis plants to see the few smashed and overturned monuments that haven't yet been removed. She'll stand in the glare of afternoon and squint to make out the pieces of names and poems in stone. She'll walk ahead a few feet and suddenly find herself standing dumbfounded at the gaping pits of concrete vaults of defiled graves. Then the old man will show her where he buried her father and grandmother after he untied them from the trees. He'll point to a strip of ground under three feeding troughs, apologizing that he can't remember who is under which trough. *But they've all been punished by heaven,* he assures her. One by one, he says, the looters died from wearing the silks they stripped off the corpses.

CHARLES SIMIC

Dinner at Uncle Boris'

Always plenty of good food and wine. The four of us at the table take turns uncorking new bottles. We drink out of water glasses the way they do in the old country. "More bread," somebody yells. There's never enough bread, never enough olives, never enough soup. We are eating through our second helping of thick bean soup after having already polished off a dozen smoked sausages and a couple of loaves of bread.

And we argue with mouths full. My Uncle Boris would make Mother Teresa reach for a baseball bat. He likes to make big pronouncements, to make the earth tremble with his political and artistic judgments. You drop your spoon. You can't believe your ears. Suddenly, you are short of breath and choking as if you swallowed a big fly.

"Is he kidding?" I hear myself say, my voice rising to a falsetto.

I am the reasonable type. I try to lay out the pros and cons as if I were a judge making a summation to the jury. I believe in the calming effect of an impeccable logical argument. Before I can get very far, my brother interrupts to tell me that I'm full of shit. His philosophy is: The more reasonable it sounds, the less likely it is that it's true. My father, on the other hand, always takes the Olympian view. "None of you know what the fuck you're talking about," he informs us and resumes slurping his soup.

Before we can all gang up on him, the pork roast is served. The skin is brown and crusty with a bit of fat underneath. There are potatoes and onions in the pan soaked in the drippings. We are in heaven. The new bottle of wine is even better. Nuit Saint Georges is my father's favorite wine since his name is George. That's the only one he buys when he is flush.

For a while we don't say anything. We just grunt with our faces in our plates. My aunt is carving more meat while my uncle runs into the kitchen to get those hot little red Mexican peppers he forgot all about.

Unfortunately, one of us starts on politics. Immediately, we are arguing again. In the last few years Boris has become very conservative. He loves Barry Goldwater. He loves Nixon. As for Bobby Kennedy, he's a Russian agent, if you ask him. Boris even warned The New York Times about that, but they didn't print the letter, of course. Tonight he shouts that I am a Communist, too. He has suspected it for years and now has had his final proof just two minutes ago.

I have no idea what I said to make him think that, so I ask him to please repeat it. He's appalled. "No guts," he says. "Feigning innocence, backtracking. Jesus Christ!" He calls on the heavens to witness.

"It's what you said about Hoover," my brother says guffawing. Both he and my father are enjoying themselves, while I'm debating whether to punch Boris in the mouth. He's really pissed, too. He says I even look like Trotsky with my wire rim glasses. "Get me the FBI on the phone," he yells to my aunt. He's going to speak to J. Edgar personally about me.

It's hard to tell with Boris if he's entirely serious. He loves scenes. He loves opera. It's the third act, we are all dead on the stage, and he is caterwauling. Without histrionics life is boring. This is bliss, as far as he's concerned.

Watching him rant like that, I get an inspiration. I rise from the table, walk over and solemnly kiss him on the top of his bald head. He's stunned speechless. It takes him some time to collect himself. Finally, he smiles sheepishly and embraces me in turn.

"Forget about the FBI," he yells to my aunt in the kitchen.

She comes out with enough different cheeses to open a store. We eat and drink and converse politely. The old guys are reminiscing about the war.

Is it true that one grows nostalgic even about the horrors as one grows old? Probably. I'm nostalgic about an August afternoon after the war. My mother, brother and I were being escorted at gunpoint and on foot from one prison to the other. At some point we walked past an apple orchard, and our guard let us stop and pick apples. Not a care in the world. Munching the apples and chatting with the guard.

As for my father and Boris, it seems, when they were in Trieste they used to pull this stunt. My father would invite friends to a fancy restaurant, but when the time came to pay the bill, he'd send Boris to break the news to the unsuspecting owner that they were completely broke.

"You were very good at it," my father assured him.

Boris, when he's not raving, looks like an English gentleman and has the appropriate clothes and fine manner to go along with his face. The owner of the restaurant would accept his apologies and his promise to settle the bill expeditiously, and would even permit his financially strapped guests to order another round of brandies before going off into the night.

"It's his smile," we all agree. Boris has the sweetest, shiest smile when he's happy. Old ladies, especially, adore him. Nobody knows how to bow and kiss their hands like he does. It's hard to believe he was once a guard in a maximum security penitentiary in Australia. Come to think of it, none of us, individually or collectively, make much sense. We are all composite characters, made up of a half dozen different people, thanks to being kicked around from country to country.

Boris, for instance, right now is singing. He studied opera singing for years, tried to make a career of it, and failed. Now he sings only when he's happy. He has a huge, beautiful tenor voice, but no ear. When he starts hitting the high notes, you have to run for your life. It's no use. He can be heard across the street. He has the world's loudest voice, and it's off-key.

He sings for us an aria from "Othello." We survive that somehow, but he's not through yet. We are going to hear Tristan's death scene. Across the table my father looks grim. My brother has vanished. I am lying on the floor at Tristan's feet, trying my best to keep a straight face. Boris paces up and down conducting the Berlin Philharmonic as he sings. From time to time he stops to translate for us. "Tristan is going mad," he whispers. No doubt about that. This Tristan is ready for the loony bin. His tongue is lolling, and his eyes are popping out of his head. He's standing on the sofa and leaning against the wall, arms spread, spread, as if he is about to be crucified.

"*Verflucht wer dich gebrant!*" he shrieks.

"Stop it, Boris," my aunt says calmly, coming in from the kitchen with the cake.

"Please let him sing the death scene, Auntie," I say, and now even my father has to grin.

You have to admire the man's love of the music. Boris confessed to me once that he could never sing in the real opera house. He'd get so excited on the stage, he'd jump into the orchestra pit at the conclusion of his aria.

Now we applaud him. We are thirsty and hungry again, and so is he, luckily. My brother has reappeared.

"I'm going to bed," my aunt announces after she brings back the cheese and cold cuts. She knows this is not going to end soon. We are on our favorite topic, the incredible stupidity of our family.

I don't know if all large families indulge in such orgies of self-abuse, but we make a specialty of it. I don't think it's pretense either. I mean, it's not like we believe secretly we are really superior and this is just talk. Our family is a story of endless errors of judgment, of bad situations made even worse by bickering.

"Imagine this," my father says. "There's a war on, the Nazis, the Ustashi, the Hungarians, the Rumanians, the Chetniks, the Italians, the Bulgarians, the Communists are killing us, and even the English and the Americans are dropping bombs. So, what do we do to make things really interesting? We all take different sides in that war so we can really make life miserable for each other."

We are silent with the weight of our drunkenness and the sad truth of my father's last remark. Finally, Boris looks up and says, "How about a really great bottle of wine?"

We all look at Boris, puzzled, but he explains that this wine is supposed to be very special, very old, very expensive.

"What is it?" we want to know.

He's not telling. He's going to decant it in the cellar so we can blindtaste it and guess its origins.

Very well. Off he goes, and he's gone so long we are beginning to think the bastard sneaked off to bed. Instead, he returns with an air of mystery, carrying a bottle wrapped in a towel. The last time Boris had a bottle of expensive wine he had us sip it from a teaspoon. He went around the table pouring drops of a fine old Margot into a spoon and making us all in turn say "Aaaaaahh" like a baby doctor.

This time we just get clean glasses, and he pours everybody a little taste. It's red wine. There's no doubt about that even at 3 in the morning. We twirl it in our glasses, sniff it like real pros and take a sip. I think it's a Chianti, my father says it's a Burgundy, my brother mentions Spanish wine, but is not sure.

Boris is triumphant! Here's the final proof! Serbs as a people, and the members of this family, especially, are all know-nothings, show-offs and the world's biggest phonies.

Then, to rub it in, he tells us how he found out recently that the Sicilian who pumps his gas in Brooklyn makes his own wine. "Probably in the same bathtub where he washes his ass," he adds for effect. Anyway, the man gave him a bottle for Christmas and this is what we are drinking.

It still tastes pretty good, but on second thought, we have to admit, we made complete fools of ourselves. Of course, we can barely keep our eyes open. The day is breaking. For the moment we have run out of talk. We just look at each other, yawning occasionally. The house is quiet. The city is quiet. Even the cops are catching 40 winks in their patrol car on the corner.

"How about some ice cream?" Boris asks.

ALICE STEINBACH

The Miss Dennis School of Writing

[handwritten: Beginning with dialogue]

"What kind of writing do you do?" asked the novelist sitting to my left at a writer's luncheon.

"I work for a newspaper in Baltimore," he was told.

"Oh, did you go to journalism school?"

"Well, yes."

"Columbia?" he asked, invoking the name of the most prestigious jour- *[handwritten: much better than saying Miss Dennis]* nalism school in the country.

"Actually, no," I heard myself telling him. "I'm one of the lucky ones. I am *[handwritten: was a great teacher]* a graduate of the Miss Dennis School of Writing."

Unimpressed, the novelist turned away. Clearly it was a credential that did not measure up to his standards. But why should it? He was not one of the lucky ones. He had never met Miss Dennis, my ninth-grade creative writing teacher, or had the good fortune to be her student. Which meant he had never experienced the sight of Miss Dennis chasing Dorothy Singer around the classroom, threatening her with a yardstick because Dorothy hadn't paid attention and her writing showed it.

"You want to be a writer?" Miss Dennis would yell, out of breath from *[handwritten: Switch dialogue to Miss Dennis]* all the running and yardstick-brandishing. "Then pay attention to what's going on around you. Connect! You are not Switzerland — neutral, aloof, uninvolved. Think Italy!"

Miss Dennis said things like that. If you had any sense, you wrote them down.

"I can't teach you how to write, but I can tell you how to look at things, how to pay attention," she would bark out at us, like a drill sergeant confronting a group of undisciplined, wet-behind-the-ears Marine recruits. To drive home her point, she had us take turns writing a description of what we saw on the way to school in the morning. Of course, you never knew which morning would be your turn, so — just to be on the safe side — you got into the habit of looking things over carefully every morning and making notes: "Saw a pot of red geraniums sitting in the sunlight on a white stucco porch; an orange-striped cat curled like a comma beneath a black van; a dark gray cloud scudding across a silver morning sky."

It's a lesson that I have returned to again and again throughout my writing career. To this day, I think of Miss Dennis whenever I write a certain kind of sentence. Or to be more precise, whenever I write a sentence that actually creates in words the picture I want readers to see.

Take, for instance, this sentence: Miss Dennis was a small, compact woman, about albatross height — or so it seemed to her students — with short, straight hair the color of apricots and huge eyeglasses that were always slipping down her nose.

Or this one: Miss Dennis always wore a variation of one outfit — a dark-colored, flared woolen skirt, a tailored white blouse, and a cardigan sweater, usually black, thrown over her shoulders and held together by a little pearl chain.

Can you see her? I can. And the image of her makes me smile. Still.

But it was not Miss Dennis's appearance or her unusual teaching method — which had a lot in common with an out-of-control terrier — that made her special. What set her apart was her deep commitment to liberating the individual writer in each student.

"What lies at the heart of good writing," she told us over and over again, "is the writer's ability to find his own unique voice. And then to use it to tell an interesting story." Somehow she made it clear that we were interesting people with interesting stories to tell. Most of us, of course, had never even known we had a story to tell, much less an interesting one. But soon the stories just started bubbling up from some inner wellspring.

Finding the material, however, was one thing; finding the individual voice was another.

Take me, for instance. I arrived in Miss Dennis's class trailing all sorts of literary baggage. My usual routine was to write like Colette on Monday, one of the Bronte sisters on Wednesday, and Mark Twain on Friday.

Right away, Miss Dennis knocked me off my high horse.

"Why are you telling other people's stories?" she challenged me, peering up into my face. (At 14, I was already four inches taller than Miss Dennis.) "You have your own stories to tell."

I was tremendously relieved to hear this and immediately proceeded to write like my idol, E.B. White. Miss Dennis, however, wasn't buying.

"How will you ever find out what you have to say if you keep trying to say what other people have already said?" was the way she dispensed with my E.B. White impersonation. By the third week of class, Miss Dennis knew my secret. She knew I was afraid — afraid to pay attention to my own inner voice for fear that when I finally heard it, it would have nothing to say.

What Miss Dennis told me — and I have carefully preserved these words because they were then, and are now, so very important to me — was this: "Don't be afraid to discover what you're saying in the act of saying it." Then, in her inimitably breezy and endearing way, she added: "Trust me on this one."

From the beginning, she made it clear to us that it was not "right" or "wrong" answers she was after. It was thinking.

"Don't be afraid to go out on a limb," she'd tell some poor kid struggling to reason his way through an essay on friendship or courage. And eventually — once we stopped being afraid that we'd be chopped off out there on that limb — we needed no encouragement to say what we thought. In fact, after the first month, I can't remember ever feeling afraid of failing in her class. Passing or failing didn't seem to be the point of what she was teaching.

Miss Dennis spent as much time, maybe more, pointing out what was right with our work as she did pointing out what was wrong. I can still hear her critiquing my best friend's incredibly florid essay on nature. "You are a very good observer of nature," she told the budding writer. "And if you just write what you see without thinking so much about adjectives and comparisons, we will see it through your attentive eyes."

By Thanksgiving vacation, I think we were all a little infatuated with Miss Dennis. And beyond that, infatuated with the way she made us feel about ourselves — that we were interesting people worth listening to.

I, of course, fancied having a special relationship with her. It was certainly special to me. And, to tell the truth, I knew she felt the same way.

The first time we acknowledged this was one day after class when I stayed behind to talk to her: I often did that and it seemed we talked about everything — from the latest films to the last issue of the *New Yorker*. The one thing we did not talk about was the sadness I still felt about my father's death. He had died a few years before and, although I did not know it then, I was still grieving his absence. Without knowing the details, Miss Dennis somehow picked up on my sadness. Maybe it was there in my writing. Looking back,

many students would write just this. boring [handwritten marginalia]

I see now that, without my writing about it directly, my father's death hovered at the edges of all my stories.

But on this particular day, I found myself talking not about the movies or writing, but instead pouring out my feelings about the loss of my father. I shall never forget that late fall afternoon: the sound of the vanilla-colored blinds flap, flap, flapping in the still classroom; the sun falling in shafts through the windows, each ray illuminating tiny galaxies of chalk dust in the air; the smell of wet blackboards; the teacher, small with apricot-colored hair, listening intently to a young girl blurting out her grief. These memories are stored like vintage photographs in my memory.

The words that passed between the young girl and the attentive teacher are harder to recall. With this exception. "One day," Miss Dennis told me, "you will write about this. Maybe not directly. But you *will* write about it. And you will find that all this has made you a better writer and a stronger person."

After that day, it was like Miss Dennis and I shared something. We never talked again about my father, but spent most of our time discussing our mutual interests. We both loved poetry and discovered one afternoon that each of us regarded Emily Dickinson with something approaching idolatry. Right then and there, Miss Dennis gave me a crash course in why Emily Dickinson's poems worked. I can still hear her talking about the "spare, slanted beauty" in Dickinson's unique choice of words. She also told me that, despite the rather cloistered life led by this New England spinster, Emily Dickinson knew the world as few others did. "She found her world within the word" is the way I remember Miss Dennis putting it. Of course, I could be making that part up.

That night, propped up in bed reading Emily Dickinson's poetry, I wondered if Miss Dennis, a spinster herself, identified in some way with the woman who wrote:

> "Wild Nights —Wild Nights!
> Were I with thee
> Wild Nights should be
> Our luxury!"

It seems strange, I know, but I never really knew anything about Miss Dennis's life outside of the classroom. Oh, once she confided in me that the initial "M" in her name stood for Mildred. And I was surprised when I passed by the teachers' lounge one day and saw her smoking a cigarette, one placed in a long, silver cigarette holder. It seemed an exceedingly sophisticated thing to do and it struck me then that she might be more worldly than I had previously thought.

But I didn't know how she spent her time or what she wanted from life or anything like that. And I never really wondered about it. Once I remember talking to some friends about her age. We guessed somewhere around 50 ~~personal~~ which seemed really old to us. In reality, Miss Dennis was around 40.

It was Miss Dennis, by the way, who encouraged me to enter some writing contests. To my surprise, I took first place in a couple of them. Of course, *relate* taking first place is easy. What's hard is being rejected. But Miss Dennis *bk to* helped me with that, too, citing all the examples of famous writers who'd *narrator* been rejected time and time again. "Do you know what they told George Orwell when they rejected 'Animal Farm'?" she would ask me. Then without waiting for a reply, she'd answer her own question: "The publisher told him, 'It is impossible to sell animal stories in the U.S.A.'"

When I left her class at the end of the year, Miss Dennis gave me a present: a book of poems by Emily Dickinson. I have it still. The spine is cracked and the front cover almost gone, but the inscription remains. On the inside flyleaf, in her perfect Palmer Method handwriting, she had written: "Say what you see. Yours in Emily Dickinson, Miss Dennis."

She had also placed little checks next to two or three poems. I took this to mean she thought they contained a special message for me. One of those checked began this way:

> Hope is the thing with feathers
> That perches in the soul . . .

I can remember carefully copying out these lines onto a sheet of paper, one which I carried around in my handbag for almost a year. But time passed, the handbag fell apart, and who knows what happened to the yellowing piece of paper with the words about hope.

The years went by. Other schools and other teachers came and went in my life. But one thing remained constant: My struggle to pay attention to my own inner life; to hear a voice that I would recognize finally as my own. Not only in my writing but in my life.

Only recently, I learned that Miss Dennis had died at the age of 50. When I heard this, it occurred to me that her life was close to being over when I met her. Neither of us knew this, of course. Or at least I didn't. But lately I've wondered if she knew something that day we talked about sadness and my father's death. "Write about it," she said. "It will help you."

And now, reading over these few observations, I think of Miss Dennis. But not with sadness. Actually, thinking of Miss Dennis makes me smile. I think of her and see, with marked clarity, a small, compact woman with apricot-colored hair. She is with a young girl and she is saying something. She is saying: Pay attention.

great conclusion   why?

SUSAN ALLEN TOTH

Going to the Movies

I

Aaron takes me only to art films. That's what I call them, anyway: strange movies with vague poetic images I don't understand, long dreamy movies about a distant Technicolor past, even longer black-and-white movies about the general meaninglessness of life. We do not go unless at least one reputable critic has found the cinematography superb. We went to *The Devil's Eye*, and Aaron turned to me in the middle and said, "My God, this is *funny*." I do not think he was pleased.

When Aaron and I go to the movies, we drive our cars separately and meet by the box office. Inside the theater he sits tentatively in his seat, ready to move if he can't see well, poised to leave if the film is disappointing. He leans away from me, careful not to touch the bare flesh of his arm against the bare flesh of mine. Sometimes he leans so far I am afraid he may be touching the woman on his other side instead. If the movie is very good, he leans forward too, peering between the heads of the couple in front of us. The light from the screen bounces off his glasses; he gleams with intensity, sitting there on the edge of his seat, watching the screen. Once I tapped him on the arm so I could whisper a comment in his ear. He jumped.

After *Belle de Jour*, Aaron said he wanted to ask me if he could stay overnight. "But I can't," he shook his head mournfully before I had a chance to answer, "because I know I never sleep well in strange beds." Then he apologized for asking. "It's just that after a film like that," he said, "I feel the need to assert myself."

II

Bob takes me only to movies that he thinks have a redeeming social conscience. He doesn't call them films. They tend to be about poverty, war, injustice, political corruption, struggling unions in the 1930s, and the military-industrial complex. Bob doesn't like propaganda movies, though, and he doesn't like to be too depressed either. We stayed away from *The Sorrow and the Pity*: it would be, he said, too much. Besides, he assured me, things are never that hopeless. So most of the movies we see are made in Hollywood. Because they are always very topical, these movies offer what Bob calls "food for thought." When we saw *Coming Home*, Bob's jaw set so firmly with the first half that I knew we would end up at Poppin' Fresh Pies afterward.

When Bob and I go to the movies, we take turns driving so no one owes anyone else anything. We park far away from the theater so we don't have to pay for a space. If it's raining or snowing, Bob offers to let me off at the door, but I can tell he'll feel better if I go with him while he parks, so we share the walk too. Inside the theater Bob will hold my hand when I get scared if I ask him. He puts my hand firmly on his knee and covers it completely with his own hand. His knee never twitches. After a while, when the scary part is past, he loosens his hand slightly and I know that is a signal to take mine away. He sits companionably close, letting his jacket just touch my sweater, but he does not infringe. He thinks I ought to know he is there if I need him.

One night after *The China Syndrome* I asked Bob if he wouldn't like to stay for a second drink, even though it was past midnight. He thought awhile about that, considering my offer from all possible angles, but finally he said no. Relationships today, he said, have a tendency to move too quickly.

III

Sam likes movies that are entertaining. By that he means movies that Will Jones of the *Minneapolis Tribune* loved and either *Time* or *Newsweek* rather liked; also movies that do not have sappy love stories, are not musicals, do not have subtitles, and will not force him to think. He does not go to movies to think. He liked *California Suite* and *The Seduction of Joe Tynan*, though the plots, he said, could have been zippier. He saw it all coming too far in advance, and that took the fun out. He doesn't like to know what is going to happen. "I just want my brain to be tickled," he says. It is very hard for me to pick out movies for Sam.

When Sam takes me to the movies, he pays for everything. He thinks that's what a man ought to do. But I buy my own popcorn, because he doesn't approve of it; the grease might smear his flannel slacks. Inside the theater, Sam makes himself comfortable. He takes off his jacket, puts one arm around me, and all during the movie he plays with my hand, stroking my palm, beating a small tattoo on my wrist. Although he watches the movie intently, his body operates on instinct. Once I inclined my head and kissed him lightly just behind his ear. He beat a faster tattoo on my wrist, quick and musical, but he didn't look away from the screen.

When Sam takes me home from the movies, he stands outside my door and kisses me long and hard. He would like to come in, he says regretfully, but his steady girlfriend in Duluth wouldn't like it. When the *Tribune* gives a movie four stars, he has to save it to see with her. Otherwise her feelings might be hurt.

IV

I go to some movies by myself. On rainy Sunday afternoons I often sneak into a revival house or a college auditorium for old Technicolor musicals, *Kiss Me Kate, Seven Brides for Seven Brothers, Calamity Jane,* even, once, *The Sound of Music.* Wearing saggy jeans so I can prop my feet on the seat in front, I sit toward the rear where no one will see me. I eat large handfuls of popcorn with double butter. Once the movie starts, I feel completely at home. Howard Keel and I are old friends; I grin back at him on the screen, admiring all his teeth. I know the sound tracks by heart. Sometimes when I get really carried away I hum along with Kathryn Grayson, remembering how I once thought I would fill out a formal like that. Skirts whirl, feet tap, acrobatic young men perform impossible feats, and then the camera dissolves into a dream sequence I know I can comfortably follow. It is not, thank God, Bergman.

If I can't find an old musical, I settle for Hepburn and Tracy, vintage Grant or Gable, on adventurous days Claudette Colbert or James Stewart. Before I buy my ticket I make sure it will all end happily. If necessary, I ask the girl at the box office. I have never seen *Stella Dallas* or *Intermezzo.* Over the years I have developed other peccadilloes: I will, for example, see anything that is redeemed by Thelma Ritter. At the end of *Daddy Long Legs* I wait happily for the scene where Fred Clark, no longer angry, at last pours Thelma a convivial drink. They smile at each other, I smile at them, I feel they are smiling at me. In the movies I go to by myself, the men and women always like each other.

CHAPTER 14

Essay of Place

Sometimes "the main character" is a landscape, as important to a writer's experience as any person. The landscape can be a new one we visit for several months, as in Gretchen Legler's "Moments of Being: An Antarctic Quintet." It can be a place we pass through, as in Colson Whitehead's "The Port Authority." It can be the hometown we experience every day, as in Dagoberto Gilb's "Living al Chuco." Or it can be a place we keep revisiting, as Gretel Ehrlich does in "Island." Sometimes writers interact with the landscape (Legler and Gilb); sometimes they remain an observer, describing the scene without use of the pronoun "I" (Whitehead). Whatever the stance, in close or far, the writer's presence is felt, showing readers what is special through strong sensory details. Note: For more essays of landscape and place, see those by Maureen Stanton and Bailey White (Chapter 14, Short Shorts).

- GRETEL EHRLICH   *"Island"*

- DAGOBERTO GILB   *"Living al Chuco"*

- GRETCHEN LEGLER   *"Moments of Being: An Antarctic Quintet"*

- COLSON WHITEHEAD   *"The Port Authority"*

GRETEL EHRLICH

Island

I come to this island because I have to. Only geography can frame my mind, only water can make my body stop. I come, not for solitude — I've had enough of that in my life — but for the discipline an island imposes, the way it shapes the movement of thoughts.

Humpbacked, willow-fringed, the island is the size of a boat, roughly eighty-five feet by twenty, and lies on the eastern edge of a small man-made lake on our Wyoming ranch. I call this island Alcatraz because I once mistook a rare whooping crane that had alighted in the lower field for a pelican, and that's what the Spanish *alcatraz* means: pelican. But the name was also a joking reference to the prison island I threatened to send my saddle horse to if he was bad, though in fact *my* Alcatraz was his favorite spot on the ranch to graze.

Now Blue is dead, and I have the island to myself. Some days, Rusty, my thirteen-year-old working dog, accompanies me, sitting when I sit, taking in the view. But a view is something our minds make of a place, it is a physical frame around natural fact, a two-way transmission during which the land shapes our eyes and our eyes cut the land into "scapes."

I sit to sweep the mind. Leaves, which I think of as a tree's discontinuous skin, keep falling as if mocking my attempts to see past my own skin, past the rueful, cantankerous, despairing, laughing racket in my head.

At water's edge the tiny leaves of wild rose are burned a rusty magenta, and their fruit, still unpicked by birds, hangs like drops of blood. Sun on water is bright: a blind that keeps my mind from wandering. The ripples are grooves the needle of memory makes, then they are the lines between which music is written — quintets of bird song and wind. The dam bank is a long thigh holding all restlessness in.

To think of an island as a singular speck or a monument to human isolation is missing the point. Islands beget islands: a terrestrial island is surrounded by an island of water, which is surrounded by an island of air, all of which makes up our island universe. That's how the mind works too: one idea unspools into a million concentric thoughts. To sit on an island, then, is not a way of disconnecting ourselves but, rather, a way we can understand relatedness.

Today the island is covered with duck down. It is the time of year when mallards molt. The old, battered flight feathers from the previous spring are discarded, and during the two or three weeks it takes for the new ones to grow in, they can't fly. The males, having lost their iridescent plumage, perform military maneuvers on the water, all dressed in the same drab uniform.

Another definition of the word "island" is "the small isolated space between the lines in a fingerprint," between the lines that mark each of us as being unique. An island, then, can stand for all that occurs between thoughts, feathers, fingerprints, and lives, although, like the space between tree branches and leaves, for example, it is part of how a thing is shaped. Without that space, trees, rooms, ducks, and imaginations would collapse.

Now it's January, and winter is a new moon that skates the sky, pushing mercury down into its tube. In the middle of the night the temperature drops to thirty-two below zero. Finally, the cold breaks, and soon the groundhog will cast a shadow, but not here. Solitude has become a reflex: when I look at the lake no reflection appears. Yet there are unseen presences. Looking up after drinking from a creek, I see who I'm not: far up on a rock ledge, a mountain lion, paws crossed, has been watching me.

Later in the month, snow on the lake melts off, and the dendritic cracks in ice reappear. The lake is a gray brain I pose questions to. Somewhere in my reading I come on a reference to the island of Reil. It is the name given to the central lobe of the cerebral hemisphere deep in the lateral tissue, the place where the division between left and right brain occurs, between what the neurobiologist Francisco Varela calls "the net and the tree."

To separate out thoughts into islands is the peculiar way we humans have of knowing something, of locating ourselves on the planet and in society. We string events into temporal arrangements like pearls or archipelagos. While waiting out winter, I listen to my mind switch from logic to intuition, from tree to net, the one unbalancing the other so no dictatorships can stay.

Now snow collapses into itself under bright sun with a sound like muffled laughter. My young friend Will, aged nineteen, who is suffering from brain cancer, believes in the laughing cure, the mango cure, the Molokai cure, the lobster cure — eating what pleases him when he can eat, traveling to island paradises when he can walk, astonished by the reversal of expectation that a life must last a certain number of years.

In the evening I watch six ravens make a playground of the sky. They fly in pairs, the ones on the left, for no reason, doing rolls like stunt pilots. Under them, the self-regulating planet moves and the landscape changes — fall to winter, winter to spring, suffering its own terminal diseases in such a way that I know nothing is unseasonal, no death is unnatural, nothing escapes a raven's acrobatic glee.

DAGOBERTO GILB

Living al Chuco

I am not going to tell you about the Rio Grande. I realize it's what most of you think of when you think of El Paso. You think of the Border Patrol cruising, dust trailing their off-road vehicles as they chase indocumentados who are looking for work framing houses or cleaning them once they've been occupied. I'm not going to tell you about Juárez in the day or in the night, about its danger or lack of, or which mercado is best for what, or which bar mixes the strongest margaritas. I'm not going to tell you where to find Rosa's Cantina. I'm not going to tell you about ostrich or snake or alligator boots. Though boots are cool. I like boots. I wear boots. But I ain't gonna talk about them.

First off, it's not the river at all. Those of us who live here rarely acknowledge the river you know and see in romanticized movie clips and glossy photos. We talk about the mountains. The Franklins, the bottom vertebrae of the Rockies, are what we see every day, what we drive around and over on workdays and days off. As imposing as the sky, they're outside with us, and the barbecue, on día de las madres and Memorial Day and all the others we pay attention to here. They're there when we pull the weeds — gotta have gloves because of nasty espinas. The mountains are here when we pull the car over the curb, tires across the rough topography of our dirt yards, and we've dragged the hose and soapy bucket over, or new parts and old wrenches. . . .

Which reminds me — since the police, on the complaint of some old-bag neighbor who thinks parked cars are a major problem with the neighborhood, have been nagging me about having my '62 Chevy next to my house. Does it run? a lawyer friend asks me. What's that got to do with it? I tell her. It's a '62 Chevy! A '62 Chevy is art! Which reminds me of other things that piss me off about El Paso. Like the newspapers. They really do suck. You feel like reading, you buy a paper from Juárez. No offense, El Paso newspapers, but face it, you guys are drinking the water too much (I forever hear this story about some huge quantity of natural lithium in our water supply). Or music. Man, it's painful to talk about music around here in Chuco. The station I'm recording this in, no offense, but you've made me hate jazz. Your idea of jazz reminds me of, well, Newt Gingrich. It's that bad for me now. This is a university, and your radio station is supposed to inspire the imagination, not deaden it! Whenever I go out of town, drive at least three hundred miles, other news-papers all read heavy like *The New York Times,* and contentedness for me has become hours listening to a radio station. I've lived here so long I've become a cheap date.

It ain't about gangs here. You know what? I'm tired of hearing about cholos. It's about quinceañeras and weddings and birthday parties. It's about Frank Castillo, who's pitching for the Cubs, and Butch Henry, who's pitching for the Expos, about Antonio Davis blocking a shot for the Pacers, and every-body wants Tim Hardaway back on the all-star team. It's about Little League diamonds, Ponder Park, where my boy hit a grand slam last night and struck out ten. "Echela al guante, m'ijo, al guante! . . . Don't swing at the piñatas!. . . ¡Se van los elotes, calientitos, se van los elotes!" Okay, so that last one was about the man who sells the corn getting ready to leave. He sells it on the cob, or in a cup, with both butter and chile.

So let me tell you a couple of other things I love about living in El Paso. Like when Jonathan Herrera and Daniel Pantoja come over to play Nintendo with my son Ricardo, and they get Cokes and Flaming Hot Cheetos. Or hear-ing my son Tony laughing on the phone with his partner Alex Gavina. Or just the other day, when I went to the hospital where my compa, el mero poeta loco don Ricardo Sánchez, lay, one hundred pounds less in body only, fighting off cancer. His voice is a whisper. His wife, Teresa, has been by his bed for him since they came home, and she asks him if he wouldn't want his feet rubbed. He nods. She peels off the socks. When I tell him that I saw a book of his in the window of a Taos bookstore, his eyes swagger like nothing's wrong, everything's right for him and toda la raza. Staring into death, they are El Paso's simplicity.

Or the light when the blurry sun looks balanced at the last edge of the day. Everything is so sharp, like you hadn't even realized you were near-sighted, or clear, like you've washed off the bug splats from the windshield after a long desert drive. It's white, almost blue it's so white, white like a washed and bleached cotton shirt, and a warm wind blows, puffing it out just so as you're crossing an empty street, the streets of El Paso so serene in the sensuous breeze and magic light, the city so quiet, as peaceful as the pregnant young mami, in cutoffs and sandals, long black hair, holding the hand of her firstborn as they walk, slow, along a sidewalk on Copia Street that looks the same as it did when, not so long ago, she held her own mom's hand.

GRETCHEN LEGLER

Moments of Being: An Antarctic Quintet
Essay of Place

I.

— Can you visualize it?

I had been lying on my back, taking notes, looking up into the crystals and into that blue that still amazes me — blue so blue it was as if my eyes had broken; blue so blue it was like gas that faded away into more and more intense blue violet; beauty so expansive I could not contain it — I had to break to let it in. The first time I had been in an antarctic ice cave, months earlier, the person who took me there said that often people who go down into crevasses and into ice caves are so overcome by the blue that it makes them cry. I remembered that as I lay there on my back, taking notes, trying to draw the crystals that hung like blooms of flowers above me, trying to figure out where the blue began and where it ended.

I had gone with nine others on this expedition to the ice caves that were part of the Erebus glacier tongue, a long spit of ancient ice spilling out onto the frozen Ross Sea from the base of Mt. Erebus, Ross Island's active volcano. The caves were about an hour's drive over the ice from the United States' main scientific base at McMurdo Station. We had signed up for the field trip on a sheet of paper outside McMurdo's galley — it was a jaunt of sorts, free to anyone who wished to go — electricians or galley cooks who had the afternoon off, a scientist who wanted out of her lab for a few hours, or me, a writer in Antarctica as a guest of the National Science Foundation's Artists and Writers Program. As the orange truck plodded across the frozen sea, heaving over humps in the ice, we passengers packed snugly inside rolled and bumped into one another like children at a carnival ride, smiling to one another over the great roar of the truck's engine.

We went to two caves. One of them was easy to get into. You climbed a hill of snow, wriggled through a rather large opening, and slid down a slight slope into a cavern about as big as an average living room. The other cave you would miss if you didn't know it was there. You kick-stepped your way up a steep incline, then pressed your body through an opening just large enough to fit your shoulders through. Then you slid down a thin, icy tube until you landed on a shelf of thick blue ice. Next, with the aid of a rope, you climbed up and around and through a maze of tight ice walls until you reached two larger caverns, luminous with the deep turquoise and violet of glacier ice, and still as a tomb. Standing on the cold, flat floor of this second cave I felt and heard a seal's high-pitched call bounce through the ice.

It was in the first cave that I lay upon my back, so intent upon studying the blue around me that I was startled when I realized I was alone. Suddenly everyone else was gone. I packed up my notebook, reluctantly, and rose to leave. Once I was out of my grotto, I realized that there was one person left in the blue room. It was my friend Gary Teetzel, an engineer from the Crary Lab at McMurdo. He and I had spent time together weeks earlier in the observation tube — an eighteen-foot-long tube set by scientists into the cold sea near McMurdo, which you could climb down into and sit in and watch creatures in the dark ocean around you.

"Oh, it's you," I said to Gary jokingly, as if, if there was anyone left in the ice cavern, still it would be *him* and *me*. He seemed a kindred spirit — a lover of quiet and contemplation. We stood at opposite ends of this ice cavern for another ten minutes, until we heard a voice calling us to come away and board the vehicle. As I stood, I cupped my hands around my eyes so that all I saw was the blue, and as I stared, my heart began to beat faster and my breath started to come faster and tears came to my eyes. It was that blue that made me cry. That blue. That blue violet that seems as if it is pulling you in, that makes you feel as if you are falling into it, that compels you somehow to look into it, even though it blurs your vision and confuses you. It was that blue, so enigmatic that for a moment you lose your balance in it. You don't quite know if you are in the sky or under water, or whether for an instant you might be in both places at once. The blue is like a frosty, vague, and endlessly deep hole in your heart. It has no edges, just color and depth. It is a color that is like some kind of yearning, some unfulfilled desire, or some constant, extreme joy. It just burns there, burns violet, burns blue.

II.

The helicopter hovered over the rugged, ice-carved mountaintop, whipping up gravel and sand. A hunched figure came running from a tent nearby, clutching a hat to its head. Someone handed a cookstove out of the open helicopter door, which the figure grabbed under its arm, then there were waves and nearly inaudible shouts of thanks, and we lifted up again, the tiny camp below us diminishing to no more than bright dots of color in the sweeping landscape of ice and stone.

I was with McMurdo technician Tracy Dahl on a morning helicopter ride up the Taylor Valley, in Antarctica's Dry Valleys, the world's coldest desert — a landscape so alien that it had become a testing ground for equipment the U.S. hoped one day to send to Mars. Dahl was to deliver the stove and other supplies to two graduate students who had pitched their peaked yellow canvas Scott tents on the top of a windy, gravelly, high plateau. The next stop was a pickup and delivery at Lake Bonney, further up the valley, and then, finally, Dahl and I were set down outside the three uninhabited canvas Jamesways that made up the Lake Fryxel Camp, which Dahl was preparing for a soon-to-be-arriving field party.

After the chores were complete Dahl and I sat beside the fuel stove in one of the Jamesways and warmed our feet on its metal sides, tipped back in our chairs, drinking tea, passing the time until his helicopter arrived to take him back to McMurdo; then I would be on my own. I was equipped for a small expedition: radio, backpack with tent, stove, sleeping bag, extra food, and clothes. I would make my way back on foot to Lake Hoare, the field camp where I had been staying for the week. Mine was an officially sanctioned several-hour walk. If I did not arrive at Lake Hoare by dinnertime, there would probably be a helicopter sent from McMurdo to find me. Nevertheless, it felt like an adventure — a walk in Antarctica, a walk in the wildest place I had ever been, a walk in what might still be the wildest place on earth.

Every walk, said Henry David Thoreau, that nineteenth-century American saunterer of woods and mind, is a sort of crusade — a westward going, a wildward going — a journey toward self-awareness, transformation, and the future. We should be prepared, he said, on even the shortest walk to go "in the spirit of undying adventure, never to return,— prepared to send back our embalmed hearts only as relics to our desolate kingdoms." The name itself, walker, saunterer, Thoreau wrote, may have derived from the expression used to describe a person in the Middle Ages who wandered about the land, *à la Saint Terre*, a pilgrim, heading toward the Holy Land. Or it might be rooted in the words *sans terre*, without a home, but everywhere at home.

I felt both as I set off across Lake Fryxel, my ice axe swinging like a walking stick at my side, its metal point pinging against the hard turquoise surface beneath me. The teeth of my crampons bit in as I walked — metal against ice. The blue lake ice was cut by geometric patterns of crazy white lines and rising white orbs. I felt homeless and at home in the universe, and as if I too were a pilgrim, walking not toward, but in, a holy land.

The flatness of the valley was broken on each side by distant hills swathed in shades of brown and white, the ones to my back more mountainous and sharp, and the ones facing me, softer. My way led across Lake Fryxel, so beautifully disturbed by the designs in its frozen surface, toward the edge of the Canada glacier, which spilled out of the mountains between Lake Fryxel and Lake Hoare and which I would have to go around. I paused frequently on the walk, gazing, enthralled with patterns in the snow made by wind, so delicately and improbably shaped — like letters, like words, like whole sentences written in dark brown dust on snow. Often I would stop to simply gaze about me, down the valley where it spread out wide and met the blue and white cloud-spattered sky, behind me to see the tiny Jamesways of the Fryxel camp receding and the towering glacial wall emanating coldness. Many times, when I paused, the glacier would crack and thunder and I would jump for fear that I would be smashed by a falling chunk of ice as big as a house, me like a fly beneath it.

Such openness I had never walked in, had never traveled by foot in such intimacy with. One step at a time would take me back to Lake Hoare by evening. Each step I savored, giddily feeling my strong legs hinge at the hips, feeling each stride, my lungs expanding fully, my arms swinging, my back bearing up the weight of the pack. I felt as Thoreau did when he wrote, "In my walks I would fain return to my senses." The land here was bare bones, stripped-down, elemental, and beautiful: beautiful in the way the bleak, landless, endless ocean is beautiful to fishermen, the way deserts are beautiful to Saharan nomads, beautiful in its smallness — the many-colored pebbles in my path, the ragged ice along the shore, the turquoise glass I walked upon; and beautiful in its largeness — the infinite reach of sky, the gigantic arc of the land. The land brought me back, as it did Thoreau, to my senses; back to my body, back to my self.

As I walked I pondered how the world was reached through the self, how the universal comes of the particular, the immense from the intimate. Thoreau called it "re-creating self," and for it he went to the most dismal of places; he entered the darkest of woods, the swampiest of swamps; they were his sacred places, *sanctum sanctorum*— for they were the places that were truly wild. What would he have made, I wondered, of Antarctica?

The woods and meadows of nineteenth-century New England were Thoreau's wilderness. He called it a mythic land: "You may name it America, but it is not America; neither Americus Vespucius, nor Columbus, nor the rest were discoverers of it. There is a truer account of it in mythology than in any history of America . . ." That he walked in a mythic landscape meant to him that his journey took him into all time. Thoreau walking in his woods, me walking alone from Lake Fryxel to Lake Hoare, around the booming edge of the towering Canada glacier, was humankind — womankind, mankind — walking, walking in an unknown land. You may name it Antarctica, but it is not Antarctica. All moments converge here in this place and time — all efforts at renewal, all quests for knowledge, all attempts at transformation and adventure collide here in this *solid* earth, in this *actual* world.

As I rounded the final protruding hunk of ice of the Canada glacier and came within sight of the Lake Hoare camp, I could see the tiny purple, blue, and yellow dots of the domed tents and the glint of the sun off the small metal buildings. I pulled my radio out of the bulging deep pocket of my bibbed wind pants and called in. "W-002 calling Lake Hoare," I said, giving my antarctic code-name, the *W* standing for Writer. The radio crackled and popped and then came the familiar voice of Bob Wharton, the principal investigator at the camp. "Roger, this is Lake Hoare Camp. How would you like your steak done?"

It would be good to be back among them, but it had also been good to be out alone, walking in Antarctica, feeling that magical, paradoxical diminishment of self and enlargement of spirit that such a landscape brings — that feeling that one is in the presence of something that has been in existence long before you and will continue long after you, into all time; some spirit that is larger and older than the human mind and that, in its power, comforts rather than terrifies, soothes rather than agitates.

"I believe in the forest, and in the meadow, and in the night in which corn grows," wrote Thoreau. This is what he crusaded for, what he walked for — the *common sense,* the link between spirit and body, earth and self. I believed in this too — that there was a sublime power in this land that could mysteriously help a person reconnect with that subtle magnetism in wildness that would show her the way. I believed in this vast glacier-scoured landscape, this thundering ice, and in the impossible simplicity of the thin line between the frozen earth and sky.

III.

Antarctica is famous for wind, wind that roars down the mountains from the Polar Plateau, spilling into the ocean; katabatic wind, fast wind, wind that carves ice into feathers and ferns; wind that carves rock into wind facts, ventifacts, signifiers of wind, something solid made of the workmanship of wild air.

The wind howling in around the seams in the McMurdo galley door is a sound I will remember from Antarctica. Wind screaming in on stormy days, at a higher pitch than I could sing, sounding so much like a piece of machinery gone haywire or an animal caught short, surprised or afraid. I'll remember the wind at the windows, knocking in a thick, padded, muffled kind of way, so that you might imagine there was someone out there, wanting you to open up, open up, let them in. And the wind whistling down the hollow shaft of a bamboo pole, one in a line planted out there in the middle of nowhere showing the way to safety, the way home, the way around a deadly crack in the ice. The wind whistled down the shaft, as if the pole were a bamboo flute and wind was playing on it a merry, eerie tune.

I'll remember too the sound of the small cotton flags tied to those poles — red and green for follow me this way, black for go this way and you'll die — the flags slap, slap, slapping in the wind, snapping against themselves, cracking like whips in the one hundred degrees below zero air.

I'll remember the wind whoop, whoop, whoop, whooping through the electrical and telephone wires. In one spot, behind McMurdo's two bars, the winds whipped and howled and moaned and moaned and moaned around the buildings, into nooks and out again, eddying and swirling, dancing and buzzing through the wires overhead, playing the wires as if they were the strings of a deep bass, pushing me along, pushing me, hurrying me along so forcefully that I had to lean back into the strength of the wind to stand upright.

I'll remember the almost nothing sound of wind across the ice, smooth and moving fast, blowing from nowhere to everywhere, taking with it my breath, the snow at my feet, the fur of my parka hood, and all of my heat.

IV.

The most subtle and some say the most beautiful light in Antarctica occurs during the antarctic spring, the period starting in mid-August, just after the antarctic winter, when the sun begins again to rise and set. This is the moment when the long-absent sun peeks tentatively up above the horizon, just high enough to send a few rays of brilliant warm yellow into the still dark sky.

The sun will rise and set, then, from August through October, making its way through the motions most of us find predictable and comforting: dawn, day, dusk, dark. Then comes the harsh light of Antarctica's summer. From October until February the antarctic sun never sets. There is eternal day, made blindingly bright by the white snow and ice that *are* Antarctica. The continent itself is so bright that astronauts looking down upon earth from outer space have called Antarctica a white lantern shining at the bottom of the globe.

The eternal day of the antarctic summer begins to ebb in mid-February, when the sun quits its high-in-the-sky circling and begins again to rise and set, following that familiar pattern that most of our bodily clocks are attuned to, creating day and night, morning and evening. Finally, total darkness settles in at the end of April. During the antarctic winter the only light comes from cold bright stars and the aurora australis which scatters the sky with green and pink and yellow bands of dancing light.

It is the low angle of the antarctic sun that makes the colors during springtime so vivid. Each morning and evening the mountains, the sea ice, towering Mt. Erebus, the edges of the glaciers, the one-hundred-year-old wooden explorers' huts, and the newer prefabricated metal buildings of the usually dingy town of McMurdo glowed peach and pink, nearly neon, buttery yellow, lavender, jade, and indigo. The first image I had ever seen of this light was a watercolor painted by antarctic expedition member Edward Wilson in the early 1900s, of a steaming Mt. Erebus in colors of such pale delicacy the work seemed forced. The colors seemed improbable, impossible in a natural setting — colors one would never associate with a landscape normally dressed in hues of black, white, gray, and brown. But Wilson's painting is accurate, and enchanting. The light did indeed transfigure the landscape and everything upon it, as if by sorcery.

When I first arrived in McMurdo, I could look out across the sea ice at the Transantarctic Mountains and see the peaks revealed as simple, dark, two-dimensional shapes in the distance, against skies that were lit up like fire or washed in cool blues and pinks. Once when I was out exploring ice caves near the Erebus glacier tongue as evening came on, I watched as the entire towering edge of ice lit up in a creamy gold that crept up the sides of the huge volcano, all the way to the top, where Erebus spewed plumes of sulfur-laden smoke into the sky.

As the weeks of the antarctic spring wore on, the mountains that I had seen earlier as solid, as two-dimensional dark shapes against a canvas of vibrant color, began to take on new depths because of the rising sun angle. As the light rose and stayed, I could see deeper into the Royal Society Range, the line of mountains across the frozen sea ice from McMurdo. The landscape became more complex. I could make out valleys and peaks that I had not been aware of before. The effect was much like turning on an overhead light in a room where you have been reading quietly with only your bedside lamp beside you — troubling complexities appear so plainly in the harsher light; things that may once have been charmingly disguised become visible.

At the peak of the antarctic summer season it is light twenty-four hours a day. The light is bright, sterile, technical, like the light in a hospital operating room. It is unavoidable light that actively seeks and annihilates corners of darkness and mystery. It was a shock to be out with friends, leaving McMurdo's coffeehouse near midnight, and have to blink into the brightness, shading my eyes with my hand. I might rise at 7:00 A.M. and it would be just as bright then as when I went to bed. To sleep, I put a blanket over my window to block the light. During this time of year, just to peer out my window onto the sea ice to check the weather conditions I needed sunglasses. One day I burned my eyes and had to wear, from that point on, two pairs of glasses — dense green glacier glasses and, over those, tinted ski goggles — in order to see without experiencing searing pain. Brightness began to overwhelm everything, illuminate everything. It became a light like water, washing over everything, washing everything down to its barest, clearest bones.

I am not sure which was more beautiful — the delicate, pleasing light of the antarctic spring, which painters and photographers coveted, as it made for the most aesthetically startling pictures, or the unforgiving but clearer and much more precise light of summer.

V.

Siple Dome camp was simple and spare: a small runway, a collection of tents and canvas Jamesways surrounded by mounds of snow-buried gear and supplies. Beyond that there was nothing familiar, nothing kind to human flesh or desire, only miles-thick ice and snow, only *the fresh and natural surface of the planet Earth, as it was made forever and ever.*

Thoreau's words atop Maine's Mt. Katahdin (or Ktaadn, as he spelled it) came to me then as I, like he, marveled at how *wild* the space around me was, how nobly spacious, how elemental, and how being here grounded me undeniably in my own flesh, in what Thoreau called the *actual world.* Siple Dome, a scientific field camp on the West Antarctic Ice Sheet, was a place by all accounts in the middle of absolutely nowhere, where one could turn 360 degrees and not see the horizon alter its unwaveringly straight face; where one was surrounded by a wilderness of snow and ice stretching as far as the mind could imagine; wildness so extreme it could extinguish you in a blink, as quickly as if you were being drowned, as quickly as if you had been set free in outer space with no oxygen.

Before the cooks, electricians, carpenters, and scientists at Siple Dome could even begin the work of setting up the field station and going about their research, they had to shovel the camp out from beneath yards and yards of snow that had buried it over the antarctic winter. Now this unlikely village lay atop the snow and ice, looking ever so much like a nomadic encampment in a wide, icy desert, at any moment prone to being blown away, to being buried again, to being neatly erased from the face of the earth.

Kendrick Taylor, from the Desert Research Institute in Reno, Nevada, a man who studies ice, drove out with me on a sunny Sunday, to a spot ten kilometers from the camp, following a line of green flags on bamboo poles that marked a safe route along the snow. When we reached the end of the flag line, we stopped our snowmobiles and Kendrick said to me, pointing into nowhere, at nothing, "Go ahead another two kilometers and turn off your machine and sit. I'll wait here."

I drove out into a horizon like I had never seen. I imagined that, had I kept going, I could have driven right off the edge of the planet. The only thing separating the land from the sky in this place was a thin white line and the faintest change in hue from white to pale blue. The snowy wind moved like a fog over the ground, like a slinky, elegant, snaky thing, throwing off my sense of balance, blurring the edges of my vision.

I drove for two kilometers, watching the odometer as I went. Then I stopped, turned off the machine, and sat in the quiet. I looked behind me for Kendrick and saw only a dark speck in the distance, surrounded by an immensity of blankness, sky and ground inextricably fused. I got off the snowmobile and lay down in the snow. I spread out my legs and my arms so that I looked as if I might be making a snow angel. I could feel the hard coolness of the ice all along my back and legs. *Contact!* Here it was beneath me. Here I was upon it —Thoreau's *solid* earth! *Here was no man's garden, but the unhandselled globe.* All I heard was the sharp hiss of the wind blowing crystals of snow over me, past my ears, and across my face. All I felt was my body against matter. How comical I must have looked, and how tiny: an amalgam of flesh and bone, nylon and rubber in the midst of that Titanic ice. But who would have seen? I shut my eyes and must have been lulled by the wind, hypnotized by the cold, because I was roused only when a snowmobile engine broke my reverie. It was Kendrick coming to get me. I looked down at my legs, my arms, my boots — they were covered with snow, the black of my windpants now white. The snow had begun to conceal me, as it had buried the pallets of cargo lined up around Siple Dome camp, as it had drifted over the Jamesways themselves. How easily, how effortlessly, I could have disappeared; how easily any of us could, and how inexplicably this knowledge of our smallness, of my smallness, filled me with joy.

COLSON WHITEHEAD

The Port Authority

How) we readers?
Can grab attention?

They're all broken somehow, sagging down the stairs of the bus. Otherwise they would have come here differently. The paparazzi do not wait to take their picture. Barricades do not hold back the faithful. This is the back entrance, after all.

Makes us curious

Broad outlook

In the parking berth it is anticlimactic. A man in goggles records the time of arrival. The baggage handler huffs into his palms, one job closer to punching out. Thousands of arrivals every day, they won't stop coming. Different people but all the same. They try to sneak by with different faces but it is no use. They step down the grooved steps, clutching items and the attendant lugs the bags out of the bin, looking for handles. They get excited and jostle: is someone going to steal their bags. They have all heard the stories. One of them has a cousin who came here once and was a victim of street crime. He had to have money wired so he could get home and that was the last time their clan went to New York. There is a thing called three card monte out to get you. They have all heard the stories and they all come anyway. The bags thud on concrete and get taken.   *familiar*

No matter their hometowns, no matter their reasons for sliding cash through ticket windows, on the bus they are all alike. They get on. By the driver they take stock, shoving receipts into pockets and bags. There are some seats in the back. They all want to sit alone. You have never been the first on the bus and had your pick. People have theories about window seats and aisle seats and which areas are safer in the event of a crash. He is unaware that his duffel hits each person on the head as he passes. Is this seat taken, he says, and his measure is taken by his neighbor. Scowls come easy. It only takes five minutes for them to ease into lasting discomfort. If only she could breathe through her mouth for the next thousand miles. She practices a technique. At the next stop people arrange bags and jackets on the empty seats beside them and avoid eye contact or feign sleep when the new pilgrims try to find seats. *Creative*

There is not much to occupy them on the highways except intermittent *description* foreshadowings. An industrial park, the confident skyline of a smaller city than the one named on their ripped tickets. Signs on the highway count down miles, sometimes heartening. More furtive things dart from the headlights to escape glimpses. Across three states the empty bottle of juice rolls up and down the bus between shoes and bags. No one claims ownership. Responsible parties pretend not to hear. That is surely a wig two rows up. They try out new positions for their legs. One drawn up and the other wedged into the footrest. Both feet almost in the aisle until the third person trips on them. He has long legs and deserves special rights. The tall man drives his knees into the seat in front of him, squeezing up a chimney. Hers is the only seat that won't recline. The lever has been ripped off and every inclination of her neighbors summons jealousy. Each new combination of limbs might be the one that unlocks the vault of comfort and then sleep. Instead, parts that don't matter fall asleep before their brains. Legs, feet. As they cross state lines, license plates change colors. Something happens to the bags up there in the baggage racks. When you go to get something out of them they are inexplicably heavier, as if they repacked themselves when you weren't looking. Zippers won't close, hang open in half smiles. Innocuous imperfections in the highway have consequences. The cap of the shampoo loosens itself. Shampoo oozes onto garments, a drop a mile. The smell of shampoo seeps through canvas and reminds whole rows of showers denied them. He falls asleep on the window and when he wakes notices a gray cloud of grease, indentation on a tinted pillow. She thinks she has slept a long time but it has only been ten minutes. Hardly closer.

Thank God for the white detachable headrest slipcovers, an invention that saves us from germs. Pat pending. Without gratitude the bus speeds past the factory that manufactures them. The guy in the next seat won't take a hint. She sends signals, glancing at her book, nods or grunts noncommittally but he keeps on yapping. Finally closing the book to submit to prattle. If this loaf of bread lasts for the next three days, he will have nine dollars and seventy-five cents when he gets there. Someone is eating fried chicken, there can be no mistake. The smell of fried chicken makes Rows 8 through 15 hungry and envious until someone cons open a sticky window. The bathroom disinfectant is a genie periodically loosed from its bottle, all out of wishes. Hold it for as long as possible before braving that place. For ten miles of interstate a man inspects his face in the bathroom mirror. Is he actually going to start fresh in a new place with that face of his. If you can endure the verdict of the fluorescent lighting the city will be no problem. He takes a piss and tries not to splash at every latest jolt. Occasionally self-abuse. Through the tiny window left open for ventilation the world blurs. Cool reassurances from moist towelettes. The latch slides to vacant. Then the staggering return down the aisle to find the seat shrunk while you were away.

The driver is some kind of priest, changing gears for their salvation. A blank space follows the words, The Name of Your Driver Is. More and more frequently he falls asleep at the wheel for whole seconds. If you ask him to turn the heat up, he might do it. He steers behind dark aviator glasses. He announces a ten-minute rest stop and the prisoners scramble out into the exercise yard. They scramble for fast food, the last chance to eat for who knows how many miles. She recognizes that guy over there from the bus and has a cigarette. As long as he stands there the bus hasn't left yet. Forced to prioritize, some choose food over phone calls to loved ones. Pennies accumulate. It is tense in the fast food lines, how long is ten minutes. To stand there in the parking lot with hot french fries looking at the departing red lights of the bus. Best to cut these missions short. When they get back to the bus there is still plenty of time and they stand there stupidly, too fearful to make another attempt. Everybody has forgotten napkins.

It is the biggest hiding place in the world. The inevitable runaways. The abandoned, only recently reading between the lines. After the beauty contest this is the natural next step. All the big agencies are there. He saved his tips all summer and to see them disappear into a ticket quickened his heart. Not the first in the family to make the attempt. The suitcase is the same one his father used decades before. This time it will be different. The highway twists. She will be witty and stylish there. With any luck he will be at the same address and won't it be quite a shock when he opens the door but after all he said if you're ever in town. Hope and wish. In the light of the bonfire she realized the madness of that place and was packed by morning. They will send back money when they get settled, whatever they can. A percentage. Reliving each good-bye. Practicing the erasure of her accent, she watches her jaw's reflection in the window. Wily vowels escape. No one will know the nickname that makes him mad. This is the right decision, they tell themselves. And then there is you.

They refuel between towns, gliding down ramps for gasoline. Diesel oases. After all they have been through together, the drivers switch without farewells. What is a passenger to a driver. Apparently those fingerless leather gloves are standard issue. One driver, she never saw his face, just his sure shoulders. The bus changes when you are not looking. It is possible to fall asleep and wake up and everyone is different, all the scalps and haircuts accidentally memorized over miles are transmuted. Everyone reached their destination and got off except for you and it might be the case that all these new people will reach their destinations before you and only you will remain, in this seat, the lone fool sticking for the terminus. In one seat successively sit an infant, a small child, then a teenager and the next occupant will be the next stage older, he is sure of it. But then time is a funny thing on a bus.

If they think those two words New York will fix them, who are we to say otherwise. They wait for so long to see the famous skyline but wake at the arrival gate and with a final lurch are delivered into dinginess. This first disappointment will help acclimate. The weather is always the same in there. It may be day or night outside, or sunny or rainy outside, but inside the terminal the light is always the same queasy green rays. In effect, no matter what time of day it is, everyone arrives at the same time, in the same weather, and in this way it is possible for all of them to start even. At other gates buses heave in and head out according to schedule. They roar. The fleet returns bit by bit. The buses depart with the ones who need to leave and come back with replacements from every state. The replacements are a bit dazed after the long ride and the tiny brutalities. Row after row they wait to shuffle into the aisle. On her asleep foot she stumbles. He wants to say thanks to the driver but the driver fills out the clipboard and won't look up. In front of the luggage bin they take what is theirs, move bags from hand to hand to discover what is best for the next leg of the trek. Sag on one side. Some take deep breaths. The door opens easily, they are not the first through, and they enter the Port Authority.

Word Choice description [handwritten annotation]

1st time mentioned build suspense till end. [handwritten annotation]

CHAPTER 15

Literary Journalism

Objective reportage is the basis of journalism. Reportage, combined with point of view, grace of language, and storytelling, is literary journalism. Unlike personal essayists and memoirists, literary journalists are investigating topics they do not know well—or even at all. Research is key for these writers who investigate their topics through reading books and newspapers, conducting interviews, and taking field trips. Anne Fadiman in "Do Doctors Eat Brains?" describes the clash of Eastern and Western medicine in a Hmong refugee camp in Thailand. Tracy Kidder stays closer to home in *Among Schoolchildren*, spending a year observing a fifth-grade classroom in New England. Both of these writers remain detached, not really entering the story. Susan Orlean does interact with the three sisters in "Meet the Shaggs," but the main focus is on them, not her, as she creates a portrait of a local singing group that hit the national charts.

Notice how each selection is filled with facts but never at the expense of the story. Literary journalists know how to weave together facts gleaned from research and from life experience, using description, dialogue, anecdote, character development, and a strong authorial presence to engage readers in new worlds.

🔥 ANNE FADIMAN   *"Do Doctors Eat Brains?"* from *The Spirit Catches You and You Fall Down*

🔥 TRACY KIDDER   from *"Among Schoolchildren"*

🔥 SUSAN ORLEAN   *"Meet the Shaggs"*

ANNE FADIMAN

Do Doctors Eat Brains?

Shocking facts intertwined with stories

In 1982, Mao Thao, a Hmong woman from Laos who had resettled in St. Paul, Minnesota, visited Ban Vinai, the refugee camp in Thailand where she had lived for a year after her escape from Laos in 1975. She was the first Hmong-American ever to return there, and when an officer of the United Nations High Commissioner for Refugees, which administered the camp, asked her to speak about life in the United States, 15,000 Hmong, more than a third of the population of Ban Vinai, assembled in a soccer field and questioned her for nearly four hours. Some of the questions they asked her were: Is it forbidden to use a *txiv neeb* to heal an illness in the United States? Why do American doctors take so much blood from their patients? After you die, why do American doctors try to open up your head and take out your brains? Do American doctors eat the livers, kidneys, and brains of Hmong patients? When Hmong people die in the United States, is it true that they are cut into pieces and put in tin cans and sold as food?

The general drift of these questions suggests that the accounts of the American health care system that had filtered back to Asia were not exactly enthusiastic. The limited contact the Hmong had already had with Western medicine in the camp hospitals and clinics had done little to instill confidence, especially when compared to the experiences with shamanistic healing to which they were accustomed. A *txiv neeb* might spend as much as eight hours in a sick person's home; doctors forced their patients, no matter how weak they were, to come to the hospital, and then might spend only twenty minutes at their bedsides. *Txiv neebs* were polite and never needed to ask questions; doctors asked many rude and intimate questions about patients' lives, right down to their sexual and excretory habits. *Txiv neebs* could render an immediate diagnosis; doctors often demanded samples of blood (or even urine or feces, which they liked to keep in little bottles), took X rays, and waited for days for the results to come back from the laboratory—and then, after all that, sometimes they were unable to identify the cause of the problem. *Txiv neebs* never undressed their patients; doctors asked patients to take off all their clothes, and sometimes dared to put their fingers inside women's vaginas.

Txiv neebs knew that to treat the body without treating the soul was an act of patent folly; doctors never even mentioned the soul. *Txiv neebs* could preserve unblemished reputations even if their patients didn't get well, since the blame was laid on the intransigence of the spirits rather than the competence of the negotiators, whose stock might even rise if they had had to do battle with particularly dangerous opponents; when doctors failed to heal, it was their own fault.

To add injury to insult, some of the doctors' procedures actually seemed more likely to threaten their patients' health than to restore it. Most Hmong believe that the body contains a finite amount of blood that it is unable to replenish, so repeated blood sampling, especially from small children, may be fatal. When people are unconscious, their souls are at large, so anesthesia may lead to illness or death. If the body is cut or disfigured, or if it loses any of its parts, it will remain in a condition of perpetual imbalance, and the damaged person not only will become frequently ill but may be physically incomplete during the next incarnation; so surgery is taboo. If people lose their vital organs after death, their souls cannot be reborn into new bodies and may take revenge on living relatives; so autopsies and embalming are also taboo. (Some of the questions on the Ban Vinai soccer field were obviously inspired by reports of the widespread practice of autopsy and embalming in the United States. To make the leap from hearing that doctors removed organs to believing that they ate them was probably no crazier than to assume, as did American doctors, that the Hmong ate human placentas—but it was certainly scarier.)

The only form of medical treatment that was gratefully accepted by at least some of the Hmong in the Thai camps was antibiotic therapy, either oral or by injection. Most Hmong have little fear of needles, perhaps because some of their own healers (not *txiv neebs*, who never touch their patients) attempt to release fevers and toxicity through acupuncture and other forms of dermal treatment, such as massage; pinching; scraping the skin with coins, spoons, silver jewelry, or pieces of bamboo; applying a heated cup to the skin; or burning the skin with a sheaf of grass or a wad of cotton wool. An antibiotic shot that could heal an infection almost overnight was welcomed. A shot to immunize someone against a disease he did not yet have was something else again. In his book *Les naufragés de la liberté*, the French physician Jean-Pierre Willem, who worked as a volunteer in the hospital at the Nam Yao camp, related how during a typhoid epidemic, the Hmong refugees refused to be vaccinated until they were told that only those who got shots would receive their usual allotments of rice—whereupon 14,000 people showed up at the hospital, including at least a thousand who came twice in order to get seconds.

When Foua Yang and Nao Kao Lee brought their three sick children to the hospital at Mae Jarim, they were engaging in behavior that many of the other camp inhabitants would have considered positively aberrant. Hospitals were regarded not as places of healing but as charnel houses. They were populated by the spirits of people who had died there, a lonesome and rapacious crew who were eager to swell their own ranks. Catherine Pake, a public health nurse who spent six months working at Phanat Nikhom (a camp where refugees from Laos, Vietnam, and Cambodia came for their final "processing" before they were sent to a country of permanent asylum), concluded from a study of the hospital log that "in comparison to refugees of other ethnic groups, the Hmong have the lowest per capita rate of visits." (Pake also discovered, not coincidentally, that the Hmong had an extremely "high utilization rate" of indigenous healing arts: shamanism, dermal treatments, herbalism. She published an article in the *Journal of Ethnobiology* identifying twenty medicinal plants she had collected under the tutelage of Hmong herbalists, which, in various forms—chopped, crushed, dried, shredded, powdered, decocted, infused with hot water, infused with cold water, mixed with ashes, mixed with sulphur, mixed with egg, mixed with chicken—were indicated for burns, fever, weakness, poor vision, broken bones, stomachaches, painful urination, prolapsed uterus, insufficient breast milk, arthritis, anemia, tuberculosis, rabies, scabies, gonorrhea, dysentery, constipation, impotence, and attacks by a *dab ntxaug*, a spirit who lives in the jungle and causes epidemics when he is disturbed. In this last case, the plant, *Jatropha curcas*, is crushed and its oil left in a cup, to be consumed not by the patient but by the *dab*.)

Wendy Walker-Moffat, an educational consultant who spent three years teaching and working on nutritional and agricultural projects in Phanat Nikhom and Ban Vinai, suggests that one reason the Hmong avoided the camp hospitals is that so many of the medical staff members were excessively zealous volunteers from Christian charitable organizations. "They were there to provide medical aid, but they were also there—though not overtly—to convert people," Walker-Moffat told me. "And part of becoming converted was believing in Western medicine. I'll never forget one conversation I overheard when I was working in the hospital area at Ban Vinai. A group of doctors and nurses were talking to a Hmong man whom they had converted and ordained as a Protestant minister. They had decided that in order to get the Hmong to come into the hospital they were going to allow a traditional healer, a shaman, to practice there. I knew they all thought shamanism was witch-doctoring. So I heard them tell this Hmong minister that if they let a shaman work in the medical center he could only give out herbs, and not perform any actual work with the spirits. At this point they asked the poor Hmong minister, 'Now *you* never go to a shaman, do you?' He was a Christian convert, he knew you cannot tell a lie, so he said, 'Well, yes, I do.' But then their reaction was so shocked that he said, 'No, no, no, I've never been. I've just heard that *other* people go.' What they didn't realize was that—to my knowledge, at least—no Hmong is ever fully converted."

In 1985, the International Rescue Committee assigned Dwight Conquergood, a young ethnographer with a special interest in shamanism and performance art, to design an environmental health program for Ban Vinai. He later wrote:

> I heard horror story after horror story from the refugees about people who went to the hospital for treatment, but before being admitted had their spirit-strings cut from their wrists by a nurse because "the strings were unsanitary and carried germs." Doctors confidently cut off neck-rings that held the life-souls of babies intact. Instead of working in cooperation with the shamans, they did everything to disconfirm them and undermine their authority. . . . Is it any wonder that the Hmong community regarded the camp hospital as the last choice of available health care options? In the local hierarchy of values, consulting a shaman or herbalist, or purchasing medicine available in the Thai market just outside the entrance to the camp, was much preferred and more prestigious than going to the camp hospital. The refugees told me that only the very poorest people who had no relatives or resources whatsoever would subject themselves to the camp hospital treatment. To say that the camp hospital was under-utilized would be an understatement.

Unlike the other camp volunteers, who commuted from an expatriate enclave an hour away, Conquergood insisted on living in Ban Vinai, sharing the corner of a thatched hut with seven chickens and a pig. His first day in the camp, Conquergood noticed a Hmong woman sitting on a bench, singing folk songs. Her face was decorated with little blue moons and golden suns, which he recognized as stickers the camp clinic placed on medication bottles to inform illiterate patients whether the pills should be taken morning or night. The fact that Conquergood considered this a delightful example of creative costume design rather than an act of medical noncompliance suggests some of the reasons why the program he designed turned out to be the most (indeed, possibly the only) completely successful attempt at health care delivery Ban Vinai had ever seen.

Conquergood's first challenge came after an outbreak of rabies among the camp dogs prompted a mass dog-vaccination campaign by the medical staff, during which the Ban Vinai inhabitants failed to bring in a single dog to be inoculated. Conquergood was asked to come up with a new campaign. He decided on a Rabies Parade, a procession led by three important characters from Hmong folktales—a tiger, a chicken, and a *dab*—dressed in homemade costumes. The cast, like its audience, was one hundred percent Hmong. As the parade snaked through the camp, the tiger danced and played the *qeej*, the *dab* sang and banged a drum, and the chicken (chosen for this crucial role because of its traditional powers of augury) explained the etiology of rabies through a bullhorn. The next morning, the vaccination stations were so besieged by dogs—dogs carried in their owners' arms, dogs dragged on rope leashes, dogs rolled in on two-wheeled pushcarts—that the health workers could hardly inoculate them fast enough. Conquergood's next production, a sanitation campaign in which a parade of children led by Mother Clean (a huge, insanely grinning figure on a bamboo frame) and the Garbage Troll (dressed in ragged clothes plastered with trash) sang songs about latrine use and refuse disposal, was equally well received.

During Conquergood's five months in Ban Vinai, he himself was successfully treated with Hmong herbs for diarrhea and a gashed toe. When he contracted dengue fever (for which he also sought conventional medical treatment), a *txiv neeb* informed him that his homesick soul had wandered back to Chicago, and two chickens were sacrificed to expedite its return. Conquergood considered his relationship with the Hmong to be a form of barter, "a productive and mutually invigorating dialog, with neither side dominating or winning out." In his opinion, the physicians and nurses at Ban Vinai failed to win the cooperation of the camp inhabitants because they considered the relationship one-sided, with the Westerners holding all the knowledge. As long as they persisted in this view, Conquergood believed that what the medical establishment was offering would continue to be rejected, since the Hmong would view it not as a gift but as a form of coercion.

TRACY KIDDER

Among Schoolchildren [*Literary Journalism* — handwritten]

[handwritten: ✱ Most of Piece description of her classroom]

At the beginning of the first social studies lesson of the year, Chris asked the class, "What's the name of our country?" She made her voice sound puzzled. She didn't want to shame the ones who didn't know the answer. About half of the class fell into that category.

"Holyoke?" Courtney ventured to guess.

"No-oh," said Chris. "Holyoke is our city. Our *country.*" She called on Arnie.

"Massachusetts?" said Arnie.

"No. That's the name of our state," said Chris. "Dick?"

"North America?" said Dick.

"That's our continent," said Chris. "It's even bigger than our country."

Chris carried in her mind a fifth-grade curriculum guide. It conformed roughly to the twenty-year-old official guide, which she kept in her desk and never consulted anymore. If she could help it, her students would not leave this room in June without improving their penmanship and spelling, without acquiring some new skills in math, reading, and writing, and without discovering some American history and science. At about ten of eight in the morning, before the children arrived, she stood at the chalkboard, coffee cup in her right hand, a piece of chalk in her left. One of her own grade school teachers had slapped Chris's sinister hand when she'd used it, but Chris remained a lefty. The chalk rattled, never squeaked, as she wrote down the word of the day in penmanship under the lists of children who owed her work. Her own handwriting was indeed exemplary, slanted to the right and curvaceous. Sometimes she chose a word to suit her own mood ("fancy") or the weather ("puddles"). Other days she wrote the names of historical figures whom she wanted to discuss ("Benjamin Franklin," "Martin Luther King") and once in a while a word that the children would not know ("eugenics")—she hoped thereby to train them to use the dictionary.

At eight, a high-pitched beep from the intercom announced math, which lasted an hour. Some children left her room for math, replaced by some children from the room next door. For math and reading, children were "levelized," which means the opposite of "leveled"—they were grouped by abilities. Her lower math group began the year with a review of the times tables and her top group with decimals. She would take each group as far as she could, but every child had to improve in problem solving, every member of the low group had to master long division at least, and all of the top group should get at least to the brink of geometry.

A half hour of spelling followed math. For fifteen minutes, Chris would talk to them about their spelling words. Responses were unpredictable.

"What's a cyclone? Arabella?"

"Like a ride?"

"What does 'abroad' mean? Anyone? Robert?"

"A woman," said Robert.

Then came fifteen minutes of study, during which teams of two children quizzed each other. Chris paired up good spellers with poor ones. She also made spelling an exercise in socialization, by putting together children who did not seem predisposed to like each other. She hoped that some would learn to get along with classmates they didn't think they liked. At least they'd be more apt to do some work than if she paired them up with friends. Her guesses were good. Alice raised her eyes to the fluorescent-lit ceiling at the news that she had Claude for a spelling partner. Later she wrote, "Today is the worst day of my life." Clarence scowled at the news that he had Ashley, who was shy and chubby and who didn't look happy either. A little smile collected in one corner of Chris's mouth as she observed the reactions. "Now, you're not permanently attached to that person for the rest of your life," she said to the class.

She'd tell them they could take out their snacks, often adding, "Don't you think you could bring something nutritious? An apple?" One child or another would say "Ugh!" Then, as a rule, she left the spelling partners quizzing each other, and carried her coffee cup to the Teachers' Room, where she sat down for a few minutes, the first minutes of rest for her feet since penmanship. Then she hurried back to her classroom in time to supervise the comings and goings of students for reading.

She had three different reading groups, composed of children from various fifth-grade homerooms. Two of her groups were lodged in the third-grade-level and one in the fourth-grade-level "basal" readers. The school had brand new basals. They were more than reading books. They were mountains of equipment: big charts for teaching what were called "skill lessons," and big metal frames to hold those charts erect, and workbooks for the children to practice those skills, and readers full of articles and stories that did not fairly represent the best of children's literature, and, for each grade level, a fat teacher's manual that went so far as to print out in boldface type the very words that Chris, or any other teacher anywhere, should say to her pupils, so as to *make* them learn to read. Chris didn't teach reading by the numbers, right out of the manual. She made up her own lessons from the basal's offerings.

She spoke with each of her groups for twenty-five minutes every day about skills and stories. Most of the time her reading students enjoyed those conversations, and many enjoyed the twenty-five minutes each group spent in reading whatever they liked to themselves—she let them lie on the floor if they wanted during that time. But almost every child hated the twenty-five minutes spent in the basal's workbooks. Judith, a most proficient reader, who went to another room for that period, said, "I love to read, but I hate reading-reading." Chris had many disaffected readers, and the workbooks were not improving their attitudes. They slumped over those workbooks, and some looked around for other things to do. She could make them behave, but from many she couldn't get more than halfhearted efforts. Her two lower groups weren't making up the ground between them and grade level. She couldn't quit the basal altogether, but she knew she ought to make the children see that there is more to reading than workbooks. She planned to give them breaks from the basal. She'd have them read some novels. Maybe they'd prefer that. She'd have to get Debbie, the director of the reading program, to find her multiple copies of some novels.

Chris wished she could vary the morning's timetable now and then, so that she could linger over certain lessons. But the movement of students among homerooms for math and reading meant that, in the morning, she had to quit every subject when the clock commanded, and, on occasion, had to leave some children puzzled until the next day. As her reading groups left and her homeroom reassembled, the hallway and room full of high-pitched chatter, Chris would stand in her doorway, keeping an eye on the returning Clarence, trying to read his current mood in his face.

She almost always stayed on her feet for the next hour, which belonged to social studies. After the first day they all knew the names of their city, state, and country, and could find them on the map that she pulled down like a window shade, over by the door and the social studies bulletin board. The official curriculum guide expected her to cover all of U.S. history. She had never yet gotten past Reconstruction by June, and did not expect to go further this year. She began with the pre-Columbian Indians, whom she was careful to call Native Americans. She defined the term "stereotype" for the children—that fall a visiting politician helped inadvertently by handing out to the sixth graders paper headdresses that identified the wearers as "Big Chief Friend of Congressman Conte."

Eleven-thirty was lunchtime. She ate in the Teachers' Room, a small, grubby sanctuary with three tables and a couple of orange vinyl sofas and a coffee machine. She usually sat with her best school friend, Mary Ann, and they talked about wakes and weddings, sales and husbands, and only rarely about students and lessons. Afternoon brought some freedom from the clock. She read aloud for fifteen minutes to the children, who usually came back from their recess with flushed faces. Her voice calmed them. She read novels, their favorite that fall about a boy whose toy cowboy comes to life and has adventures. Many times when she closed the book and said, "We'll find out what happens tomorrow," children would groan. "Read some more, please, Mrs. Zajac?" As often as not, she obliged them.

When she closed the novel once and for all, and said, "Okay, take out your journals, please," several children would again groan. She said, day after day, "Oh, come on. I know you have lots of interesting things to write about." They could write about anything, she told them. If they wanted, they could write that they hated Mrs. Zajac. But they must write. The fifteen minutes or so with their journals was to warm them up for an hour of more formal creative writing. They could write stories on any topic they chose. On her own Chris had read up on the so-called "process" technique of teaching writing. Most of the gurus on that subject advised that children pick their own topics, but in her experience some children would not write at all if she did not offer them freedom from complete freedom. She'd turn off the lights and pass around the room a children's book full of spooky illustrations, or she'd say they could write stories imagining how they got on the cover of *Time* magazine.

Every month the children wrote a book report, a science report, a social studies report, and several drafts of a story. They jotted down story ideas for a day or two. They composed rough drafts, which they read aloud to a couple of classmates, who were supposed to give them advice. They wrote second drafts and read those aloud to Mrs. Zajac, who gave more advice. When most had finished their final drafts, Chris would examine the stories and pick out a couple of frequent grammatical errors, and then for a week would teach formal grammar lessons—on the possessive, on verb tenses, on exclamations.

She left science for last. For several other subjects she used textbooks, but only as outlines. She taught science right out of the book; this was one of those texts that takes pains with the obvious and gives the complex short shrift. Chris didn't know much science and didn't usually enjoy teaching it. Sometimes she let creative writing encroach on science's time. About one day in ten she canceled science altogether and announced—to cheers, Felipe's the loudest—an informal art lesson. She often felt guilty about science.

A box of tissues always sat on a corner of Chris's desk—her classes went through about twenty boxes a year. All day long stacks of papers and books accumulated on the corner of her desk, on the front table, on the counter under the window. She handled about 150 pieces of paper each day—the attendance sheet, the free lunch forms, the students' many assignments. The room looked disorderly, but every category of paper had its proper place. Within a couple of weeks, the children had mastered the routines, and only rarely did Chris lose anything, except for the key to her classroom closet, which she misplaced almost daily, the only visible manifestation of the strain on her memory. Counting all her math and reading and homeroom students, she dealt with fifty children. Every morning she brought a new list of special chores, mainly concerning children who needed individual tutoring in a subject. Four or five times a day, the intercom erupted in the middle of her lessons, usually paging staff—usually the guidance counselor—and three or four times another teacher would appear in the doorway with a question or request. After many lessons—and always after ones that had gone badly—Chris paused to perform what she called a "self-evaluation," saying inwardly, "I was boring myself. I've got to think of a way to jazz that up next time."

According to one famous piece of research, a classroom teacher must manage, in a predictable enough way to make the children feel secure, about two hundred unpredictable "personal interactions" an hour. Some interactions are more difficult than others, of course. Chris managed an average of thirty disciplinary incidents during each six-hour day. Some lasted only seconds and required from her just a dark look or a snap of her fingers. Others, mostly incidents involving Clarence, went on for minutes, and some of those led to further incidents—some, in effect, lasted all day.

Some days ended in haste. The intercom would announce, "Bus one," and Chris would still be assigning homework. She wrote the assignments on the narrow chalkboard between the closets in the back of the room, and always explained three times what she expected them to do for tomorrow.

SUSAN ORLEAN

Meet the Shaggs

Things I Wonder (2:12)

Depending on whom you ask, the Shaggs were either the best band of all time or the worst. Frank Zappa is said to have proclaimed that the Shaggs were "better than the Beatles." More recently, though, a music fan who claimed to be in "the fetal position, writhing in pain," declared on the Internet that the Shaggs were "hauntingly bad," and added, "I would walk across the desert while eating charcoal briquettes soaked in Tabasco for forty days and forty nights *not* to ever have to listen to anything Shagg-related ever again." Such a divergence of opinion confuses the mind. Listening to the Shaggs' album *Philosophy of the World* will further confound. The music is winsome but raggedly discordant pop. Something is sort of wrong with the tempo, and the melodies are squashed and bent, nasal, deadpan. Are the Shaggs referencing the heptatonic, angular microtones of Chinese *ya-yueh* court music and the atonal note clusters of Ornette Coleman, or are they just a bunch of kids playing badly on cheap, out-of-tune guitars? And what about their homely, blunt lyrics? Consider the song 'Things I Wonder':

> There are many things I wonder
> There are many things I don't
> It seems as though the things I wonder most
> Are the things I never find out

Is this the colloquial ease and dislocated syntax of a James Schuyler poem or the awkward innermost thoughts of a speechless teen-ager?

The Shaggs were three sisters, Helen, Betty, and Dorothy (Dot) Wiggin, from Fremont, New Hampshire. They were managed by their father, Austin Wiggin, Jr., and were sometimes accompanied by another sister, Rachel. They performed almost exclusively at the Fremont town hall and at a local nursing home, beginning in 1968 and ending in 1973. Many people in Fremont thought the band stank. Austin Wiggin did not. He believed his girls were going to be big stars, and in 1969 he took most of his savings and paid to record an album of their music. Nine hundred of the original thousand copies of *Philosophy of the World* vanished right after being pressed, along with the record's shady producer. Even so, the album has endured for thirty years. Music collectors got hold of the remaining copies of *Philosophy of the World* and started a small Shaggs cult. In the mid-seventies, WBCN-FM, in Boston, began playing a few cuts from the record. In 1988, the songs were repackaged and re-released on compact disk and became celebrated by outsider-music mavens, who were taken with the Shaggs' artless style. Now the Shaggs are entering their third life: *Philosophy of the World* was reissued last spring by RCA Victor and will be released in Germany this winter. The new CD of *Philosophy of the World* has the same cover as the original 1969 album's photograph of the Wiggin girls posed in front of a dark-green curtain. In the picture, Helen is twenty-two, Dot is twenty-one, and Betty is eighteen. They have long blond hair and long blond bangs and stiff, quizzical half-smiles. Helen, sitting behind her drum set, is wearing flowered trousers and a white Nehru shirt; Betty and Dot, clutching their guitars, are wearing matching floral tunics, pleated plaid skirts, and square-heeled white pumps. There is nothing playful about the picture; it is melancholy, foreboding, with black shadows and the queer, depthless quality of an aquarium. Which leaves you with even more things to wonder about the Shaggs.

Shaggs' Own Thing (3:54)

Fremont, New Hampshire, is a town that has missed out on most everything. Route 125, the main highway bisecting New Hampshire, just misses the east side of Fremont; Route 101 just misses the north; the town is neither in the mountains nor on the ocean; it is not quite in the thick of Boston's outskirts, nor is it quite cosseted in the woods. Fremont is a drowsy, trim, unfancy place, rimmed by the Exeter River. Ostentation is expressed only in a few man-size gravestones in the Fremont cemetery; bragging rights are limited to Fremont's

being the home town of the eminent but obscure nineteen-twenties meteorologist Herbert Browne and its being the first place a B-52 ever crashed
without killing anyone.

In the 1960s, when the Wiggin sisters formed the Shaggs, many people in
Fremont raised dairy cows or made handkerchiefs at the Exeter textile mill or
built barrels at Spaulding & Frost Cooperage, went to church, tended their
families, kept quiet lives. Sometimes the summer light bounces off the black-
glass surface of the Exeter River and glazes the big stands of blue pine, and
sometimes the pastures are full and lustrous, but ordinary days in southern
New Hampshire towns can be mingy and dismal. "Loneliness contributed to severe depression, illness and drunkenness for countless rural families," Matthew
Thomas wrote, in his book *History of Fremont, N. H. Olde Poplin: An Independent New England Republic 1764 –1997*, which came out last year. "There may
have been some nice, pleasant times . . . but for the most part, death, sick-
ness, disease, accidents, bad weather, loneliness, strenuous hard work, insect-
infested foods, prowling predatory animals, and countless inconveniences
marked day-to-day existence."

When I was in Fremont recently, I asked Matthew Thomas, who is forty-
three and the town historian, what it had been like growing up there. He said
it was nice but that he had been bored stiff. For entertainment, there were
square dances, sledding, an annual carnival with a Beano tent, Vic Marcotte's
Barber Shop and Poolroom. (These days, there are weekend grass drags out
near Phil Peterson's farm, where the pasture is flat and firm enough to race
snowmobiles in the summer.) When the Shaggs were growing up, there were
ham-and-bean suppers, boxing matches, dog shows, and spelling bees at the
town hall. The hall is an unadorned box of a building, but its performance hall
is actually quite grand. It isn't used anymore, and someone has made off with
the red velvet curtain, but it still has a sombre dark stage and high-backed
chairs, and the gravid air of a place where things might happen. In a quiet
community like Fremont, in the dull hours between barn dances, a stage like
that might give you big ideas.

Who Are Parents? (2:58)

Where else would Austin Wiggin have got the idea that his daughters should
form a rock band? Neither he nor his wife, Annie, was musical; she much preferred television to music, and he, at most, fooled around with a Jew's harp.

He wasn't a showoff, dying to be noticed—by all accounts he was an ornery loner who had little to do with other people in town. He was strict and old-fashioned, not a hippie manqué, not a rebel, very disapproving of long hair and short skirts. He was from a poor family and was raising a poor family— seven kids on a mill hand's salary—and music lessons and instruments for the girls were a daunting expense.

And yet the Shaggs were definitely his idea—or, more exactly, his mother's idea. Austin was terribly superstitious. His mother liked to tell fortunes. When he was young, she studied his palm and told him that in the future he would marry a strawberry blonde and would have two sons whom she would not live to see, and that his daughters would play in a band. Her auguries were borne out. Annie was a strawberry blonde, and she and Austin did have two sons after his mother died. It was left to Austin to fulfill the last of his mother's predictions, and when his daughters were old enough he told them they would be taking voice and music lessons and forming a band. There was no debate: his word was law, and his mother's prophecies were gospel. Besides, he chafed at his place in the Fremont social system. It wasn't so much that his girls would make him rich and raise him out of a mill hand's dreary métier; it was that they would prove that the Wiggin kids were not only different from but better than the folks in town.

The girls liked music—particularly Herman's Hermits, Ricky Nelson, and Dino, Desi & Billy—but until Austin foretold their futures they had not planned to become rock stars. They were shy, small-town teen-agers who dreamed of growing up and getting married, having children, maybe becoming secretaries someday. Even now, they don't remember ever having dreamed of fame or of making music. But Austin pushed the girls into a new life. He named them the Shaggs, and told them that they were not going to attend the local high school, because he didn't want them travelling by bus and mixing with outsiders, and, more important, he wanted them to practice their music all day. He enrolled them in a Chicago mail-order outfit called American Home School, but he designed their schedule himself: practice in the morning and afternoon, rehearse songs for him after dinner, and then do calisthenics and jumping jacks and leg lifts or practice for another hour before going to bed. The girls couldn't decide which was worse, the days when he made them do calisthenics or the days when he'd make them practice again before bed. In either case, their days seemed endless. The rehearsals were solemn, and Austin could be cutting. One song in particular, "Philosophy of the World," he claimed they never played right, and he would insist on hearing it again and again.

The Shaggs were not leading rock-and-roll lives. Austin forbade the girls to date before they were eighteen and discouraged most other friendships. They hadn't been popular kids, anyway—they didn't have the looks or the money or the savvy for it—but being in the band, and being home-schooled, set them apart even more. Friday nights, the family went out together to do grocery shopping. Sundays they went to church, and the girls practiced when they got home. Their world was even smaller than the small town of Fremont.

This was 1965. The Beatles had recently débuted on American television. The harmony between generations—at least, the harmony between the popular cultures of those generations—was busting. And yet the sweet, lumpish Wiggin sisters of Fremont, New Hampshire, were playing pop music at their father's insistence, in a band that he directed. Rebellion might have been driving most rock and roll, but in Fremont Dot Wiggin was writing tributes to her mom and dad, with songs like "Who Are Parents?":

> Parents are the ones who really care
> Who are parents?
> Parents are the ones who are always there
> Some kids think their parents are cruel
> Just because they want them to obey certain rules. . . .
> Parents do understand
> Parents do care

Their first public performance was at a talent show in nearby Exeter, in 1968. The girls could barely play their instruments. They didn't think they were ready to appear in public, but Austin thought otherwise. When they opened, with a cover of a loping country song called 'Wheels,' people in the audience threw soda cans at them and jeered. The girls were mortified; Austin told them they just had to go home and practice more. If they thought about quitting, they thought about it very privately, because Austin would have had no truck with the idea; he was the kind of father who didn't tolerate debate. They practiced more, did their calisthenics, practiced more. Dot wrote the songs and the basic melodies, and she and Betty worked together on the chords and rhythms. Helen made up her drum parts on her own. The songs were misshapen pop tunes, full of shifting time signatures and odd meters and abrupt key changes, with lyrics about Dot's lost cat, Foot Foot, and her yearning for a sports car and how much she liked to listen to the radio.

On Halloween, the Shaggs played at a local nursing home—featuring Dot's song 'It's Halloween' in their set—and got a polite response from the residents. Soon afterward, Austin arranged for them to play at the Fremont town hall on Saturday nights. The girls worried about embarrassing themselves, but at the same time they liked the fact that the shows allowed them to escape the house and their bounded world, even if it was just for a night. At that point, the girls had never even been to Boston, which was only fifty miles away.

The whole family took part in the town-hall shows. Austin III, the older of the two sons who had been seen in Austin's future, played the maracas; the other son, Robert, played the tambourine and did a drum solo during intermission; Annie sold tickets and ran the refreshment stand. A Pepsi truck would drop off the cases of soda at their green ranch house, on Beede Road, every Friday night. Even though, according to one town-hall regular, most people found the Shaggs' music "painful and torturous," sometimes as many as a hundred kids showed up at the dances—practically the whole adolescent population of Fremont. Then again, there really wasn't much else to do in Fremont on a Saturday night. The audience danced and chatted, heckled the band, pelted the girls with junk, ignored them, grudgingly appreciated them, mocked them.

The rumor around town was that Austin forced his daughters to be in the band. There was even talk that he was inappropriately intimate with them. When asked about it years later, Betty said that the talk wasn't true, but Helen said that Austin once was intimate with her. Certainly, the family was folded in on itself; even Austin's father and Annie's mother, after they were both widowed, became romantically involved and lived together in a small house on the Wiggin property. The gossip and criticism only made Austin more determined to continue with the band. It was, after all, his destiny.

I'm So Happy When You're Near (2:12)

"Through the years, this author as town historian has received numerous requests from fans around the country looking for information on The Shaggs and the town they came from," Matthew Thomas wrote in his section about the band. "They definitely have a cult following, and deservedly so, because the Wiggin sisters worked hard and with humble resources to gain respect and acceptance as musicians. To their surprise they succeeded. After all, what other New Hampshire band has a record album worth $300–$500?"

The Beatles' arrival in America piqued Austin. He disliked their moppy hair but was stirred by their success. If they could make it, why couldn't his girls? He wanted to see the Shaggs on television, and on concert tours. Things weren't happening quickly enough for him, though, and this made him unhappy. He started making tapes and home movies of the town-hall shows. In March, 1969, he took the girls to Fleetwood Studios, outside Boston, to make a record. According to the magazine *Cool and Strange Music!*, the studio engineer listened to the Shaggs rehearse and suggested that they weren't quite ready to record. But Austin insisted on going forward, reportedly telling the engineer, "I want to get them while they're hot." In the album's liner notes, Austin wrote:

> "The Shaggs are real, pure, unaffected by outside influences. Their music is different, it is theirs alone. They believe in it, live it. . . . Of all contemporary acts in the world today, perhaps only the Shaggs do what others would like to do, and that is perform only what they believe in, what they feel, not what others think the Shaggs should feel. The Shaggs love you. . . . They will not change their music or style to meet the whims of a frustrated world. You should appreciate this because you know they are pure what more can you ask? They are sisters and members of a large family where mutual respect and love for each other is at an unbelievable high . . . in an atmosphere which has encouraged them to develop their music unaffected by outside influences. They are happy people and love what they are doing. They do it because they love it."

The Wiggins returned to Fleetwood a few years later. By then, the girls were more proficient—they had practiced hundreds of hours since the first recording session—but their playing still inspired the engineer to write, "As the day progressed, I overcame my disappointment and started feeling sorry for this family paying $60 an hour for studio time."

I once asked Annie Wiggin if she thought Austin was a dreamer, and after sitting quietly for a few moments she said, "Well, probably. Must have been." If he was, it no doubt got harder to dream as the years went on. In 1973, the Fremont town supervisors decided to end the Saturday-night concerts, because—well, no one really remembers why anymore, but there was talk of fights breaking out and drugs circulating in the crowd, and wear and tear on the town hall's wooden floors, although the girls scrubbed the scuff marks off every Sunday. Austin was furious, but the girls were relieved to end the grind of playing every Saturday night. They were getting older and had begun to chafe at his authority. Helen secretly married the first boyfriend she ever had—someone she had met at the dances. She continued living at home for three months after the wedding because she was too terrified to tell Austin what she had done. On the night that she finally screwed up the courage to give him the news, he got out a shotgun and went after her husband. The police joined in and told Helen to choose one man or the other. She left with her husband, and it was months before Austin spoke to her. She was twenty-eight years old.

The Shaggs continued to play at local fairs and at the nursing home. Austin still believed they were going to make it, and the band never broke up. It just shut down in 1975, on the day Austin, who was only forty-seven years old, died in bed of a massive heart attack—the same day, according to Helen, they had finally played a version of "Philosophy of the World" that he praised.

Philosophy of the World (2:56)

Shortly after the newest re-release of the Shaggs' album, I went to New Hampshire to talk to the Wiggin sisters. A few years after Austin died, Betty and Dot married and moved to their own houses, and eventually Annie sold the house on Beede Road and moved to an apartment nearby. After a while, the house's new owner complained to people in town that Austin's ghost haunted the property. As soon as he could afford it, the new owner built something bigger and nicer farther back on the property, and allowed the Fremont Fire Department to burn the old Wiggin house down for fire-fighting practice.

Dot and Betty live a few miles down the road from Fremont, in the town of Epping, and Helen lives a few miles farther, in Exeter. They don't play music anymore. After Austin died, they sold much of their equipment and later let their kids horse around with whatever was left. Dot hung on to her guitar for a while, just in case, but a few years ago she lent it to one of her brothers and hasn't got it back. Dot, who is now fifty, cleans houses for a living. Betty, forty-eight, was a school janitor until recently, when she took a better job, in the stockroom of a kitchen-goods warehouse. Helen, who suffers from serious depression, lives on disability.

Dot and Betty arranged to meet me at Dunkin' Donuts, in Epping, and I went early so that I could read the local papers. It was a soggy, warm morning in southern New Hampshire; the sky was pearly, and the sun was as gray as gunmetal. Long tractor-trailers idled in the Dunkin' Donuts parking lot and then rumbled to life and lumbered onto the road. A few people were lined up to buy Pick 4 lottery tickets. The clerk behind the doughnut counter was discussing her wedding shower with a girl wearing a fuzzy halter top and platform sneakers. In the meantime, the coffee burned.

That day's Exeter *News-Letter* reported that the recreation commission's kickoff concert would feature Beatle Juice, a Beatles tribute band led by "Brad Delp, former front man of 'Boston,' one of the biggest rock bands New England has ever produced." Southern New Hampshire has regular outbreaks of tribute bands and reunion tours, as if it were in a time zone all its own, one in which the past keeps reappearing, familiar but essentially changed. Some time ago, Dot and her husband and their two sons went to see a revived version of Herman's Hermits. The concert was a huge disappointment for Dot, because her favorite Hermit, Peter (Herman) Noone, is no longer with the band, and because the Hermits' act now includes dirty jokes and crude references.

The Shaggs never made any money from their album until years later, when members of the band NRBQ heard *Philosophy of the World* and were thrilled by its strange innocence. NRBQ's own record label, Red Rooster, released records by such idiosyncratic bands as Jake & the Family Jewels, and they asked the Wiggins if they could compile a selection of songs from the group's two recording sessions. The resulting album, *The Shaggs' Own Thing*, includes the second session at Fleetwood Studios and some live and home recordings. Red Rooster's reissue of *Philosophy of the World* was reviewed in *Rolling Stone* twice in 1980 and was described as "priceless and timeless." The articles introduced the Shaggs to the world.

Three years ago, Irwin Chusid, the author of the forthcoming book *Songs in the Key of Z: The Curious Universe of Outsider Music*, discovered that a company he worked with had bought the rights to the Shaggs' songs, which had been bundled with other obscure music-publishing rights. Chusid wanted to re-issue *Philosophy of the World* as it was in 1969, with the original cover and the original song sequence. He suggested the project to Joe Mozian, a vice-president of marketing at RCA Victor, who had never heard the band.

Mozian was interested in unusual ventures; he had just released some Belgian lounge music from the sixties, which featured such songs as "The Frère Jacques Conga." Mozian says, "The Shaggs were beyond my wildest dreams. I couldn't comprehend that music like that existed. It's so basic and innocent, the way the music business used to be. Their timing, musically, was . . . fascinating. Their lyrics were . . . amazing. It is kind of a bad record; that's so obvious, it's a given. But it absolutely intrigued me, the idea that people would make a record playing the way they do."

The new *Philosophy of the World* was released last March. Even though the record is being played on college radio stations and the reviews have been enthusiastic and outsider art has been in vogue for several years, RCA Victor has sold only a few thousand copies of *Philosophy* so far. Mozian admits that he is disappointed. "I'm not sure why it hasn't sold," he says. "I think people are a little afraid of having the Shaggs in their record collections."

While I was waiting for the Wiggins, I went out to my car to listen to the CD again. I especially love the song "Philosophy of the World," with its wrought-up, clattering guitars and chugging, cockeyed rhythm and the cheerfully pessimistic lyrics about how people are never happy with what they have. I was right in the middle of the verse about how rich people want what poor people have, and how girls with long hair want short hair, when Betty pulled up and opened the door of my car. As soon as she recognized the song, she gasped, "Do you like this?" I said yes, and she said, "God, it's horrible." She shook her head. Her hair no longer rippled down to her waist and no longer had a shelf of shaggy bangs that touched the bridge of her nose; it was short and springy, just to the nape of her neck, the hair of a grown woman without time to bother too much about her appearance.

A few minutes later, Dot drove in. She was wearing a flowered housedress and a Rugrats watch, and had a thin silver band on her thumb. On her middle finger was a chunky ring that spelled 'Elvis' in block letters. She and Betty have the same deep-blue eyes and thrusting chin and tiny teeth, but Dot's hair is still long and wavy, and even now you can picture her as the girl with a guitar on the cover of the 1969 album. She asked what we were listening to. "What do you think?" Betty said to her. "The Shaggs." They both listened for another minute, so rapt that it seemed as if they had never heard the song before. "I never play the record on my own anymore," Dot said. "My son Matt plays it sometimes. He likes it. I don't think I get sentimental when I hear it. I just don't think about playing it."

"I wonder where I put my copies of the album?" Betty said. "I know I have one copy of the CD. I think I have some of the albums somewhere."

The Wiggins have received fan letters from Switzerland and Texas, been interviewed for a documentary film, and inspired a dozen Web sites, bulletin boards, and forums on the Internet, but it's hard to see how this could matter much, once their childhood had been scratched out and rewritten as endless days of practicing guitar, and their father, who believed that their success was fated, died before they got any recognition. They are wise enough to realize that some of the long-standing interest in their music is ironic—sheer marvel that anything so unpolished could ever have made it onto a record. "We might have felt special at the time we made the record," Dot said uncertainly. "The really cool part, to me, is that it's thirty years later and we're still talking about it. I never thought we'd really be famous. I never thought we'd even be as famous as we are. I met a girl at the Shop'n Save the other day who used to come to the dances, and she said she wanted to go out now and buy the CD. And I saw a guy at a fair recently and talked to him for about half an hour about the Shaggs. And people call and ask if they can come up and meet us. That's amazing to me."

Yet, when I asked Dot and Betty for the names of people who could describe the town-hall shows, they couldn't think of any for days. "We missed out on a lot," Betty said. "I can't say we didn't have fun, but we missed a social life, we missed out on having friends, we missed everything except our music and our exercises. I just didn't think we were good enough to be playing in concerts and making records. At one point, I thought maybe we would make it, but it wasn't really my fantasy." Her fantasy, she said, was to climb into a car with plenty of gas and just drive—not to get anywhere in particular, just to go.

We ordered our coffee and doughnuts and sat at a table near the window. Betty had her two-year-old and eight-month-old granddaughters, Makayla and Kelsey, with her, and Makayla had squirmed away from the table and was playing with a plastic sign that read 'Caution Wet Floor.' Betty often takes care of her grandchildren for her son and her daughter-in-law. Things are tight. The little windfall from their recordings helps, especially since Dot's husband is in poor health and can't work, and Betty's husband was killed in a motorcycle accident six years ago, and Helen is unable to work because of her depression.

For the Wiggins, music was never simple and carefree, and it still isn't. Helen doesn't go out much, so I spoke with her on the phone, and she told me that she hadn't played music since her father died but that country-and-Western echoed in her head all the time, maddeningly so, and so loud that it made it hard for her to talk. When I asked Betty if she still liked music, she thought for a moment and then said that her husband's death had drawn her to country music. Whenever she feels bereft, she sings brokenhearted songs along with the radio. Just then, Makayla began hollering. Betty shushed her and said, "She really does have some kind of voice." A look flickered across her face. "I think, well, maybe she'll take voice lessons someday."

Dot is the only one who is still attached to her father's dream. She played the handbells in her church choir until recently, when she began taking care of one of Helen's children in addition to her own two sons and no longer had the time. She said that she's been writing lyrics for the last two years and hopes to finish them, and to compose the music for them. In the meantime, Terry Adams, of NRBQ, says he has enough material left from the Fleetwood Studio recording sessions for a few more CDs, and he has films of the town-hall concerts that he plans to synchronize with sound. The Shaggs, thirty years late, may yet make it big, the way Austin saw it in his dreams. But even that might not have been enough to sate him. The Shaggs must have known this all along. In "Philosophy of the World," the song they never could play to his satisfaction, they sang:

> It doesn't matter what you do
> It doesn't matter what you say
> There will always be one who wants things the opposite way
> We do our best, we try to please
> But we're like the rest we're never at ease
> You can never please
> Anybody
> In this world

CHAPTER 16

Stories of Craft

How do seasoned writers solve the issues that arise when writing creative nonfiction? In this section, four writers discuss their own experiences, offering both tips and solace. Patricia Hampl examines a struggle special to creative nonfiction writers: how to use memory and imagination and still write true. Steve Harvey shows the power of the other voices to counter or confer with your own. Sue Miller recounts her own struggles with revision until she found the story of her father that was eluding her. And Kim Stafford reveals his secrets for finding new themes in the taken-for-granted world we live in.

Here are stories that combine personal experience with comments on craft and form that will speak to others grappling with the same issues. Through their writing experiences, we can understand our own better. That is the power of creative nonfiction: to illuminate the larger concerns — the role of truth, memory, imagination, revision, risk-taking — through small, but important stories. Note: For additional stories on writers writing, see Connie Wieneke's essay (Chapter 12, Personal Essay) and Alice Steinbach's essay (Chapter 13, Portrait).

- PATRICIA HAMPL *"Memory and Imagination"*
- STEVE HARVEY *"The Art of Interruption"*
- SUE MILLER *"From a Lecture on Revision"*
- KIM STAFFORD *"The Writer as Professional Eavesdropper"*

PATRICIA HAMPL

Memory + Imagination
an still write-true?
How do we
do this?

Memory and Imagination

When I was seven, my father, who played the violin on Sundays with a nicely tortured flair which we considered artistic, led me by the hand down a long, unlit corridor in St. Luke's School basement, a sort of tunnel that ended in a room full of pianos. There, many little girls and a single sad boy were playing truly tortured scales and arpeggios in a mash of troubled sound. My father gave me over to Sister Olive Marie, who did look remarkably like an olive.

Her oily face gleamed as if it had just been rolled out of a can and laid on the white plate of her broad, spotless wimple. She was a small, plump woman; her body and the small window of her face seemed to interpret the entire alphabet of olive: Her face was a sallow green olive placed upon the jumbo ripe olive of her habit. I trusted her instantly and smiled, glad to have my hand placed in the hand of a woman who made sense, who provided the satisfaction of being what she was: an Olive who looked like an olive.

My father left me to discover the piano with Sister Olive Marie so that one day I would join him in mutually tortured piano-violin duets for the edification of my mother and brother who sat at the table spooning in the last of their pineapple sherbet until their part was called for: They put down their spoons and clapped while we bowed, while the sweet ice in their bowls melted, while the music melted, and we all melted a little into one another for a moment.

But first Sister Olive must do her work. I was shown middle C, which Sister seemed to think terribly important. I stared at middle C, and then glanced away for a second. When my eye returned, middle C was gone, its slim finger lost in the complicated grasp of the keyboard. Sister Olive struck it again, finding it with laughable ease. She emphasized the importance of middle C, its central position, a sort of North Star of sound. I remember thinking, Middle C is the belly button of the piano, an insight whose originality and accuracy stunned me with pride. For the first time in my life I was astonished by metaphor. I hesitated to tell the kindly Olive for some reason; apparently I understood a true metaphor is a risky business, revealing of the self. In fact, I have never, until this moment of writing it down, told my first metaphor to anyone.

Sunlight flooded the room; the pianos, all black, gleamed. Sister Olive, dressed in the colors of the keyboard, gleamed; middle C shimmered with meaning and I resolved never—never—to forget its location: It was the center of the world.

Then Sister Olive, who had had to show me middle C twice but who seemed to have drawn no bad conclusions about me anyway, got up and went to the windows on the opposite wall. She pulled the shades down, one after the other. The sun was too bright, she said. She sneezed as she stood at the windows with the sun shedding its glare over her. She sneezed and sneezed, crazy little convulsive sneezes, one after another, as helpless as if she had the hiccups.

"The sun makes me sneeze," she said when the fit was over and she was back at the piano. This was odd, too odd to grasp in the mind. I associated sneezing with colds, and colds with rain, fog, snow, and bad weather. The sun, however, had caused Sister Olive to sneeze in this wild way, Sister Olive who gleamed benignly and who was so certain of the location of the center of the world. The universe wobbled a bit and became unreliable. Things were not, after all, necessarily what they seemed. Appearance deceived: Here was the sun acting totally out of character, hurling this woman into sneezes, a woman so mild that she was named, so it seemed, for a bland object on a relish tray.

I was given a red book, the first Thompson book, and told to play the first piece over and over at one of the black pianos where the other children were crashing away. This, I was told, was called practicing. It sounded alluringly adult, practicing. The piece itself consisted mainly of middle C, and I excelled, thrilled by my savvy at being able to locate that central note amidst the cunning camouflage of all the other white keys before me. Thrilled too by the shiny red book that gleamed, as the pianos did, as Sister Olive did, as my eager eyes probably did. I sat at the formidable machine of the piano and got to know middle C intimately, preparing to be as tortured as I could manage one day soon with my father's violin at my side.

But at the moment Mary Katherine Reilly was at my side, playing something at least two or three lessons more sophisticated than my piece. I believe she even struck a chord. I glanced at her from the peasantry of single notes, shy, ready to pay homage. She turned toward me, stopped playing, and sized me up.

Sized me up and found a person ready to be dominated. Without introduction she said, "My grandfather invented the collapsible opera hat."

I nodded, I acquiesced, I was hers. With that little stroke it was decided between us—that she should be the leader and I the sidekick. My job was admiration. Even when she added, "But he didn't make a penny from it. He didn't have a patent" — even then, I knew and she knew that this was not an admission of powerlessness, but the easy candor of a master, of one who can afford a weakness or two. With the clairvoyance of all fated relationships based on dominance and submission, it was decided in advance: That when the time came for us to play duets, I should always play second piano, that I should spend my allowance to buy her the Twinkies she craved but was not allowed to have, that finally, I should let her copy from my test paper, and when confronted by our teacher, confess with convincing hysteria that it was I, I who had cheated, who had reached above myself to steal what clearly belonged to the rightful heir of the inventor of the collapsible opera hat. . . .

There must be a reason I remember that little story about my first piano lesson. In fact, it isn't a story, just a moment, the beginning of what could perhaps become a story. For the memoirist, more than for the fiction writer, the story seems already *there*, already accomplished and fully achieved in history ("in reality," as we naively say). For the memoirist, the writing of the story is a matter of transcription.

That, anyway, is the myth. But no memoirist writes for long without experiencing an unsettling disbelief about the reliability of memory, a hunch that memory is not, after all, *just* memory. I don't know why I remembered this fragment about my first piano lesson. I don't, for instance, have a single recollection of my first arithmetic lesson, the first time I studied Latin, the first time my grandmother tried to teach me to knit. Yet these things occurred too and must have their stories.

It is the piano lesson that has trudged forward, clearing the haze of forgetfulness, showing itself bright with detail decades after the event. I did not choose to remember the piano lesson. The experience was simply there, like a book that has always been on the shelf, whether I ever read it or not, the binding and title showing as I skim across the contents of my life. On the day I wrote this fragment I happened to take that memory, not some other, from the shelf and paged through it. I found more detail, more event, perhaps a little more entertainment than I had expected, but the memory itself was there from the start. Waiting for me.

Wasn't it? When I reread the piano lesson vignette just after I finished it, I realized that I had told a number of lies. I *think* it was my father who took me the first time for my piano lesson, but maybe he only took me to meet my teacher and there was no actual lesson that day. And did I even know then that he played the violin — didn't he take up his violin again much later as a result of my piano playing and not the reverse? And is it even remotely accurate to describe as "tortured" the musicianship of a man who began every day by belting out "Oh What a Beautiful Morning" as he shaved? More: Sister Olive Marie did sneeze in the sun, but was her name Olive? As for her skin tone — I would have sworn it was olivelike. I would have been willing to spend the better part of a morning trying to write the exact description of an imported Italian or Greek olive her face suggested: I wanted to get it right.

But now, were I to write that passage over, it is her intense black eyebrows I would see, for suddenly they seem the central fact of that face, some indicative mark of her serious and patient nature. But the truth is, I don't remember the woman at all. She's a sneeze in the sun and a finger touching middle C.

Worse: I didn't have the Thompson book as my piano text. I'm sure of that because I remember envying children who did have this wonderful book with its pictures of children and animals printed on the pages for music.

As for Mary Katherine Reilly. She didn't even go to grade school with me (and her name isn't Mary Katherine Reilly — but I made that change on purpose). I met her in Girl Scouts and only went to school with her later, in high school. Our relationship was not really one of leader and follower; I played first piano most of the time in duets. She certainly never copied anything from a test paper of mine: She was a better student, and cheating just wasn't a possibility for her. Though her grandfather (or someone in her family) did invent the collapsible opera hat and I remember that she was proud of this fact, she didn't tell me this news as a deft move in a childish power play.

So, what was I doing in this brief memoir? Is it simply an example of the curious relation a fiction writer has to the material of her own life? Maybe. But to tell the truth (if anyone still believes me capable of the truth), I wasn't writing fiction. I was writing memoir — or was trying to. My desire was to be accurate. I wished to embody the myth of memoir: to write as an act of dutiful transcription.

Yet clearly the work of writing a personal narrative caused me to do something very different from transcription. I am forced to admit that memory is not a warehouse of finished stories, not a gallery of framed pictures. I must admit that I invented. But why?

Two whys: Why did I invent and, then, if memory inevitably leads to invention, why do I — why should anybody — write memoir at all?

I must respond to these impertinent questions because they, like the bumper sticker I saw the other day commanding all who read it to QUESTION AUTHORITY, challenge my authority as a memoirist and as a witness.

It still comes as a shock to realize that I don't write about what I know, but in order to find out what I know. Is it possible to convey the enormous degree of blankness, confusion, hunch, and uncertainty lurking in the act of writing? When I am the reader, not the writer, I too fall into the lovely illusion that the words before me which read so inevitably, must also have been written exactly as they appear, rhythm and cadence, language and syntax, the powerful waves of the sentences laying themselves on the smooth beach of the page one after another faultlessly.

But here I sit before a yellow legal pad, and the long page of the preceding two paragraphs is a jumble of crossed-out lines, false starts, confused order. A mess. The mess of my mind trying to find out what it wants to say. This is a writer's frantic, grabby mind, not the poised mind of a reader waiting to be edified or entertained.

I think of the reader as a cat, endlessly fastidious, capable by turns of mordant indifference and riveted attention, luxurious, recumbent, ever poised. Whereas the writer is absolutely a dog, panting and moping, too eager for an affectionate scratch behind the ears, lunging frantically after any old stick thrown in the distance.

The blankness of a new page never fails to intrigue and terrify me. Sometimes, in fact, I think my habit of writing on long yellow sheets comes from an atavistic fear of the writer's stereotypic "blank white page." At least when I begin writing, my page has a wash of color on it, even if the absence of words must finally be faced on a yellow sheet as much as on a blank white one. We all have our ways of whistling in the dark.

If I approach writing from memory with the assumption that I know what I wish to say, I assume that intentionality is running the show. Things are not that simple. Or perhaps writing is even more profoundly simple, more telegraphic and immediate in its choices than the grating wheels and chugging engine of logic and rational intention suppose. The heart, the guardian of intuition with its secret, often fearful intentions, is the boss. Its commands are what a writer obeys — often without knowing it.

This is the beauty of the first draft. And why it's worth pausing a moment to consider what a first draft really is. By my lights, the piano lesson memoir is a first draft. That doesn't mean it exists here exactly as I first wrote it. I like to think I've cleaned it up from the first time I put it down on paper.

I've cut some adjectives here, toned down the hyperbole there (though not enough), smoothed a transition, cut a repetition — that sort of housekeeperly tidying up.

But the piece remains a first draft because I haven't yet gotten to know it, haven't given it a chance to tell me anything. For me, writing a first draft is a little like meeting someone for the first time. I come away with a wary acquaintanceship, but the real friendship (if any) is down the road. Intimacy with a piece of writing, as with a person, comes from paying attention to the revelations it is capable of giving, not by imposing my own notions and agenda, no matter how well intentioned they might be.

I try to let pretty much anything happen in a first draft. A careful first draft is a failed first draft. That may be why there are so many inaccuracies in the piano lesson memoir: I didn't censor, I didn't judge. I just kept moving. But I would not publish this piece as a memoir on its own in its present state. It isn't the "lies" in the piece that give me pause, though a reader has a right to expect a memoir to be as accurate as the writer's memory can make it.

The real trouble: The piece hasn't yet found its subject; it isn't yet about what it wants to be about. Note: What *it* wants, not what I want. The difference has to do with the relation a memoirist — any writer — has to unconscious or half-known intentions and impulses in composition.

Now that I have the fragment down on paper, I can read this little piece as a mystery which drops clues to the riddle of my feelings, like a culprit who wishes to be apprehended. My narrative self (the culprit who invented) wishes to be discovered by my reflective self, the self who wants to understand and make sense of a half-remembered moment about a nun sneezing in the sun.

We store in memory only images of value. The value may be lost over the passage of time (I was baffled about why I remembered my sneezing nun), but that's the implacable judgment of feeling: *This*, we say somewhere within us, is something I'm hanging on to. And, of course, often we cleave to things because they possess heavy negative charges. Pain has strong arms.

Over time, the value (the feeling) and the stored memory (the image) may become estranged. Memoir seeks a permanent home for feeling and image, a habitation where they can live together. Naturally, I've had a lot of experiences since I packed away that one from the basement of St. Luke's School; that piano lesson has been effaced by waves of feeling for other moments and episodes. I persist in believing the event has value — after all, I remember it — but in writing the memoir I did not simply relive the experience. Rather, I explored the mysterious relationship between all the images I could round up and the even more impacted feelings that caused me to store the images safely away in memory. Stalking the relationship, seeking the congruence between stored image and hidden emotion — that's the real job of memoir.

By writing about that first piano lesson, I've come to know things I could not know otherwise. But I only know these things as a result of reading this first draft. While I was writing, I was following the images, letting the details fill the room of the page and use the furniture as they wished. I was their dutiful servant — or thought I was. In fact, I was the faithful retainer of my hidden feelings which were giving the commands.

I really did feel, for instance, that Mary Katherine Reilly was far superior to me. She was smarter, funnier, more wonderful in every way — that's how I saw it. Our friendship (or she herself) did not require that I become her vassal, yet perhaps in my heart that was something I sought. I wanted a way to express my admiration. I suppose I waited until this memoir to begin to find the way.

Just as, in the memoir, I finally possess that red Thompson book with the barking dogs and bleating lambs and winsome children. I couldn't (and still can't) remember what my own music book was, so I grabbed the name and image of the one book I could remember. It was only in reviewing the piece after writing it that I saw my inaccuracy. In pondering this "lie," I came to see what I was up to: I was getting what I wanted. Finally.

The truth of many circumstances and episodes in the past emerges for the memoirist through details (the red music book, the fascination with a nun's name and gleaming face), but these details are not merely information, not flat facts. Such details are not allowed to lounge. They must work. Their labor is the creation of symbol. But it's more accurate to call it the *recognition* of symbol. For meaning is not "attached" to the detail by the memoirist; meaning is revealed. That's why a first draft is important. Just as the first meeting (good or bad) with someone who later becomes the beloved is important and is often reviewed for signals, meanings, omens, and indications.

Now I can look at that music book and see it not only as "a detail" but for what it is, how it acts. See it as the small red door leading straight into the dark room of my childhood longing and disappointment. That red book *becomes* the palpable evidence of that longing. In other words, it becomes symbol. There is no symbol, no life-of-the-spirit in the general or the abstract. Yet a writer wishes — certainly we all wish — to speak about profound matters that are, like it or not, general and abstract. We wish to talk to each other about life and death, about love, despair, loss, and innocence. We sense that in order to live together we must learn to speak of peace, of history, of meaning and values. The big words.

We seek a means of exchange, a language which will renew these ancient concerns and make them wholly, pulsingly ours. Instinctively, we go to our store of private associations for our authority to speak of these weighty issues. We find, in our details and broken, obscured images, the language of symbol. Here memory impulsively reaches out and embraces imagination. That is the resort to invention. It isn't a lie, but an act of necessity, as the innate urge to locate truth always is.

All right. Invention is inevitable. But why write memoir? Why not call it fiction and be done with it? And if memoir seeks to talk about "the big issues," of history and peace, death and love — why not leave these reflections to those with expert or scholarly knowledge? Why let the common or garden variety memoirist into the club? I'm thinking again of that bumper sticker: Question Authority. Why?

My answer, naturally, is a memoirist's answer. Memoir must be written because each of us must possess a created version of the past. Created: that is, real in the sense of tangible, made of the stuff of a life lived in place and in history. And the downside of any created thing as well: We must live with a version that attaches us to our limitations, to the inevitable subjectivity of our points of view. We must acquiesce to our experience and our gift to transform experience into meaning. You tell me your story, I'll tell you mine.

If we refuse to do the work of creating this personal version of the past, someone else will do it for us. That is the scary political fact. "The struggle of man against power," Milan Kundera's hero in *The Book of Laughter and Forgetting* says, "is the struggle of memory against forgetting." He refers to willful political forgetting, the habit of nations and those in power (Question Authority!) to deny the truth of memory in order to disarm moral and ethical power.

It is an efficient way of controlling masses of people. It doesn't even require much bloodshed, as long as people are entirely willing to give over their personal memories. Whole histories can be rewritten. The books which now seek to deny the existence of the Nazi death camps now fill a room.

What is remembered is what becomes reality. If we "forget" Auschwitz, if we "forget" My Lai, what then do we remember? And what is the purpose of our remembering? If we think of memory naively, as a simple story, logged like a documentary in the archive of the mind, we miss its beauty but also its function.

The beauty of memory rests in its talent for rendering detail, for paying homage to the senses, its capacity to love the particles of life, the richness and idiosyncrasy of our existence. The function of memory, while experienced as intensely personal, is surprisingly political.

Our capacity to move forward as developing beings rests on a healthy relation with the past. Psychotherapy, that widespread method for promoting mental health, relies heavily on memory and on the ability to retrieve and organize images and events from the personal past. We carry our wounds and perhaps even worse, our capacity to wound, forward with us. If we learn not only to tell our stories but to listen to what our stories tell us — to write the first draft and then return for the second draft — we are doing the work of memory.

Memoir is the intersection of narration and reflection, of storytelling and essay writing. It can present its story *and* consider the meaning of the story. The first commandment of fiction — Show, Don't Tell — is not part of the memoirist's faith. Memoirists must show *and* tell. Memoir is a peculiarly open form, inviting broken and incomplete images, half-recollected fragments, all the mass (and mess) of detail. It offers to shape this confusion — and, in shaping, of course, it necessarily creates a work of art, not a legal document. But then, even legal documents are only valiant attempts to consign the truth, the whole truth, and nothing but the truth to paper. Even they remain versions.

Locating touchstones — the red music book, the olive Olive, my father's violin playing — is satisfying. Who knows why? Perhaps we all sense that we can't grasp the whole truth and nothing but the truth of our experience. Just can't be done.

What can be achieved, however, is a version of its swirling, changing wholeness. A memoirist must acquiesce to selectivity, like any artist. The version we dare to write is the only truth, the only relationship we can have with the past. Refuse to write your life and you have no life. That is the stern view of the memoirist.

Personal history, logged in memory, is a sort of slide projector flashing images on the wall of the mind. And there's precious little order to the slides in the rotating carousel. Beyond that confusion, who knows who is running the projector? A memoirist steps into this darkened room of flashing, unorganized images and stands blinking for a while. Maybe for a long while. But eventually, as with any attempt to tell a story, it is necessary to put something first, then something else. And so on, to the end. That's a first draft. Not necessarily the truth, not even *a* truth sometimes, but the first attempt to create a shape.

The first thing I usually notice at this stage of composition is the appalling inaccuracy of the piece. Witness my first piano lesson draft. Invention is screamingly evident in what I intended to be transcription. But here's the further truth: I feel no shame. In fact, it's only now that my interest in the piece quickens. For I can see what isn't there, what is shyly hugging the walls, hoping not to be seen. I see the filmy shape of the next draft. I see a more acute version of the episode or — this is more likely — an entirely new piece rising from the ashes of the first attempt.

The next draft of the piece would have to be true re-vision, a new seeing of the materials of the first draft. Nothing merely cosmetic will do — no rouge buffing up the opening sentence, no glossy adjective to lift a sagging line, nothing to attempt covering a patch of gray writing.

I can't say for sure, but my hunch is the revision would lead me to more writing about my father (Why was I so impressed by that ancestral inventor of the collapsible opera hat? Did I feel I had nothing as remarkable in my own background?). I begin to think perhaps Sister Olive is less central to this business than she appears to be. She is meant to be a moment, not a character. I'm probably wasting my time on her, writing and writing around her in tight descriptive circles, waiting for the real subject to reveal itself. My father!

So I might proceed, if I were to undertake a new draft of the memoir. I begin to feel a relationship developing between a former self and me.

And even more important, a relationship between an old world and me. Some people think of autobiographical writing as the precious occupation of the unusually self-absorbed. Couldn't the same accusation be hurled at a lyric poet, at a novelist — at anyone with the audacity to present a personal point of view? True memoir is written, like all literature, in an attempt to find not only a self but a world.

The self-absorption that seems to be the impetus and embarrassment of autobiography turns into (or perhaps always was) a hunger for the world. Actually, it begins as hunger for *a* world, one gone or lost, effaced by time or a more sudden brutality. But in the act of remembering, the personal environment expands, resonates beyond itself, beyond its "subject," into the endless and tragic recollection that is history. We look at old family photographs in which we stand next to black, boxy Fords, and are wearing period costumes, and we do not gaze fascinated because there we are young again, or there we are standing, as we never will again in life, next to our mother. We stare and drift because there we are historical. It is the dress, the black car that dazzle us now and draw us beyond our mother's bright arms which once caught us. We reach into the attractive impersonality of something more significant than ourselves. We write memoir, in other words. We accept the humble position of writing a version, the consolation prize for our acknowledgment we cannot win "the whole truth and nothing but."

I suppose I write memoir because of the radiance of the past — it draws me back and back to it. Not that the past is beautiful. In our communal memoir, in history, the darkness we sense is not only the dark of forgetfulness. The darkness is history's tunnel of horrors with its tableaux vivants of devastation. The blasted villages, the hunted innocents, the casual acquiescence to the death camps and tiger cages are back there in the fetid holes of history.

But still, the past is radiant. It sheds the light of lived life. One who writes memoir wishes to step into that light, not to see one's own face — that is not possible — but to feel the length of shadow cast by the light. No one owns the past, though typically the first act of new political regimes, whether of the left or the right, is an attempt to rewrite history, to grab the past and make it over so the end comes out right. So their power looks inevitable.

No one owns the past, but it is a grave error (another age would have said a grave sin) not to inhabit memory. Sometimes I think it is all we really have. But that may be melodrama, the bad habit of the memoirist, coming out. At any rate, memory possesses authority for the fearful self in a world where it is necessary to claim authority in order to Question Authority.

There may be no more pressing intellectual need in our culture than for people to become sophisticated about the function of memory. The political implications of the loss of memory are obvious. The authority of memory is a personal confirmation of selfhood, and therefore the first step toward ethical development. To write one's life is to live it twice, and the second living is both spiritual and historical, for a memoir reaches deep within the personality as it seeks its narrative form and it also grasps the life-of-the-times as no political analysis can.

Our most ancient metaphor says life is a journey. Memoir is travel writing, then, notes taken along the way, telling how things looked and what thoughts occurred. Show *and* tell. But I cannot think of the memoirist as a tourist. The memoir is no guide book. This traveler lives the journey idiosyncratically, taking on mountains, enduring deserts, marveling at the lush green places. Moving through it all faithfully, not so much a survivor with a harrowing tale to tell as that older sort of traveler, the pilgrim, seeking, wondering.

Steve Harvey

The Art of Interruption

When I teach college writing, I often begin with an in-class assignment. Once the assignment is well underway — the heads all bent over pages and pens scratching — I interrupt the class by speaking while the students write. "This," I say, "is the miracle, the distinctively human miracle. The voice in your head that gives you the next word is your genius." I want them to know the value of what my teacher, James Britton, called "shaping at the point of utterance." I want them to know the joy of staking a life on that voice. "Attend to that voice in your head," I say. "It is your great friend for life. Trust it."

Of course, that is a lie — one that I will need to disabuse them of later in the semester when they write their first research papers. One voice alone is never enough. Consider the student in my class looking at a blank page praying for the miracle I'm talking about. All of us face that page eventually when our "great friend for life" sulks in the back of our stilled brains. Even when the miracle happens, that voice in our head can get carried away. Any voice — no matter how adorable, witty, brilliant, or miraculous — becomes dull over time. The miracle of utterance uninterrupted becomes the monotone of indulgence — and those of you who have suffered the long-winded, perhaps even here at AWP, know what I mean.

I am Socratic enough to believe that learning happens always and only in dialogue, not monologue. Other voices offer new words that open up possibilities for meaning for us. I think of the smart-aleck at the back of the class whose hand shoots into the air, and the way we in the class turn to that hand expectantly. If the lecture is long enough that interruption is always welcome. I think of the obscenity — language meant to be spoken in the wings — and the shock it creates when it grabs center stage. I think of the way any words — as long as they are not our own — can quicken our words. The research paper is not so much an exercise in bringing new information to bear on a subject as it is a forum in juggling contending voices — and there is always room for a shout from the back of the class.

The reason that I enjoy assigning the research paper is that it offers relief from the solitary voice that I encouraged students to trust the first day of class. What, after all, is an interruption but another word for a breakthrough. When a lone voice is compelling — even mesmerizing as it can be with so many writers — an interruption is sometimes the only way for inarticulate truths to come crashing in. Some writers search out other voices for confirmation of their views. Montaigne was given to quoting classical authors who agreed with him in order to reinforce points he made. Other writers like adversaries. I'm reading Harold Bloom now on Shakespeare, a writer who relishes his enemy's words as a goad and stimulus to his own. My point is that the nature of the interruption does not matter as much as the simple fact that it is there. Doris Smith — a writer friend who died this year — says that she would re-read her novels and at the moment she got bored, throw in some dialogue. Not bad advice, I'd say.

But it is the art of interrupting the interruption that reveals the essentially dialectical nature of writing and thought. Here, we approach the holy of holies. Increasingly, as I get older, I find myself lingering over where to place the "she said" and "he said" in quotations. Am I alone in this or have you noticed the tendency in yourself? It does make a difference — and in that difference is all meaning. "If music be the food of love," Orsino says, "play on" — and if I put the "he says" there, at the comma, I share Shakespeare's notion that his sentence is about love, the word just before the interruption. If I want to shift our attention away from love to music, I change the syntax. "If *music*," Orsino says, "be the fruit of love, play on." On days that I'm particularly fussy I might try an earlier interruption: "*If*," Orsino says, "music be the food of love, play on." And when I'm feeling downright athletic I would write the sentence this way: "If music be the food of love, *play*," Orsino says, "on."

The point is that *I* choose, *I* get to play with the words of those who have, for the moment, usurped my own. I make them my own. Choosing and placing the interruption — and interrupting *it* at my whim — is my chance to reclaim some of what I give up by inviting another voice to speak. The language is not mine — I have not invented a single word — but with a little help from my friends and enemies, I learn to wield it. Subsuming other voices, I make them mine. It is for that reason that I tell my students — without really lying to them at all — to trust their voices. That truncated instrument — the vehicle for original thought without a single original word — is what they have. It is never solitary. *E pluribus unum.* That voice is, in fact, a chorus, which is their cultural inheritance, and can indeed become a friend for life.

SUE MILLER

From a Lecture on Revision[1]

For several years after my father's death in 1991, I suffered from what I think of almost as seizures of grief — unexpected and uncontrollable bouts of sorrow and rage triggered by the memory of his helplessness in illness and my own in response to it. Sometimes I'd dream of him, dream that he was in some situation that he couldn't manage, that he needed my assistance; always, in one way or another, I failed him in these dreams.

The reasons for all this seemed clear enough to me. He'd died of Alzheimer's disease, and I was the one of his four children IN CHARGE of him through the later stages of his illness, and through his death. I was the one who knew, first hand, how little there was to be done that was of any use to him as he descended deeper and deeper into his disease. Indeed, I was the one who chose the moment of his dying, by refusing help for him when he contracted an illness we were never sure of the nature of, but which, unchecked, provided the way out I knew he would have wished from his further diminishment and loss. And I was the one who sat by him day after day until he died, until he was set free. It took ten days. The organism wants life, clings to it desperately in fact, whatever the terms; even when the intelligence has decided that there are terms so degrading that death is preferable.

---

[1] Delivered to the Master Class in Memoir Writing, November 14, 2000. This lecture was later revised to become the afterword in Miller's memoir *The Story of My Father* (New York: Knopf, 2003).

So it didn't seem startling to me that I was haunted by him. That I couldn't let him go. At some point, then, I decided it might be of use to write about it — to make an account of my father's life and of his dying. The purpose of this account would be to help someone else in my position — someone who found herself tending to a beloved parent who was slowly disappearing before her eyes; leaving behind a needier and needier husk, a kind of animated shell demanding attention and care in the memory of what and who he'd been; care which would be, in any case, finally pointless and useless — and what's more, not even registered or received with gratitude.

I got out all the boxes of papers and letters which comprised the documentation I had of my father's and my family's life. I hired a research assistant to go through the Alzheimer's literature and keep me up to date on what the current thinking was about the disease, as well as its history and symptomatology. I laid everything out and began methodically to make notes.

I'd never written non-fiction before. I had no idea even how to structure a non-fiction book, and I was well aware that the rules were utterly fluid anyway — the memoir was being reinvented daily at this time (1991 or 1992). I read perhaps eight or ten accounts of the dying and death of a parent, none of which were trying to do what I hoped to do. Still, it was my dream that by some form of literary osmosis, I would absorb a sense of alternative ways my job might be done. (It must be noted too, that this is always my answer in any difficulty. When in doubt, read a book.)

I started to write, and finished a substantial chunk by 1995. I pulled it into shape to show to my literary agent. She found some of it fascinating, some very moving; and of the rest, she said, "It strikes me that it's perhaps of most interest to the writer." How cruel. How excruciatingly truthful. How like her to be this truthful.

I gave it a few months, and then I reread what I had. Of course she was right. She's almost always right. I knew I would have to go back and essentially start again.

Somehow, though, in working myself through the material to the dead end point I'd arrived at, I'd come up with an idea for a novel, a piece of fiction. A novel, of course, about the death of a parent. The parent in this case, though, was an elderly mother. A difficult woman, a prima donna of sorts, who comes to stay with her middle-aged son for some months on her way to a retirement community. A woman who bore certain similarities to my mother — dead for many years — though she didn't have an eighth of my mother's charm.

Still, it occurred to me that it was perhaps to appease the spirit of my own mother that I was compelled to write this book. My mother was a competitive and narcissistic woman, extravagantly loving too, as narcissists can be; but she always loomed large as a goddess over my life, and over my father's too, I think. It seemed only natural that I had to cope with her first. First her book; then — only then — Dad's.

So, after I finished *The Distinguished Guest*, I went back to the memoir again. Again I hauled out the box of family papers, again I hired the assistant to find out what had been happening in Alzheimer's research — and again I hit a kind of dead end, the magic of appeasement be damned.

I began to think that a lot of my problem had to do with voice. With the fact that I was accustomed to using the first person only *fictionally* — hiding behind an imagined speaker who might be close to who I was, but who wasn't "I." I never had to own any of the thoughts and ideas and feelings I wrote in a novel; I had never had to account for myself. I had trouble figuring out in this non-fiction work how far forward I wanted to step, how much of the real "I" I wanted to expose. At least that's what I told myself and others about the source of my difficulty when they asked why the memoir was taking so long.

In any case, though, while I was struggling with the voice, along came an idea for yet another novel, a novel that rescued me again, for a while, from the memoir. But while I was writing this novel, called, aptly, *While I Was Gone*, I began to take a few journalism assignments. I thought it might be helpful to me to write a personal essay or two — to practice using a non-fictive first person voice in some shorter works that would be — that were — less difficult emotionally, less deeply intimate than the book about my father's death.

Well, it was helpful. In these short pieces, I was finally able, I think, to break down the scrim that hung between me as first-person narrator, and "the reader;" to speak comfortably and intimately, even of notions that were not all that intimate to me, as the ideas in these rather polite personal essays were not.

When I finished *While I Was Gone*, I returned once more to the memoir, this time finally with a sense of ease about the voice, and began another revision. But the problem had moved, I discovered. A shape-shifter, it was now something else. It had to do now with the point of the whole thing.

Let me explain. Among the papers I had about my father was the copy of a short eulogy given at Princeton Theological Seminary, where he'd taught and been Dean for many years. The text, written by a colleague of his, sought to explain what was unusual about him. This was difficult, for my father was a painstakingly thorough but not terribly original scholar. He was a generous, attentive teacher, but not a dynamic or exciting one. He was a loyal, faithful, hardworking colleague; but not a charming or easy-going one. He was, I think, incapable of falsity, but his truthfulness was dispassionate, disinterested. This memorial statement began: On the wall of the Office of the Academic Dean when James H. Nichols was the incumbent, there hung a framed, cross-stitched message which in a quiet way dominated the room. It seemed to set the tone. The text was from Calvin's Institutes and it read:

"We are not our own: let not our reason nor our will, therefore, sway our plans and deeds. We are not our own: let us therefore not set it as our goal to seek what is expedient for us according to the flesh. We are not our own: insofar as we can, let us therefore forget ourselves and all that is ours. Conversely, we are God's: let us therefore live for him and die for him. We are God's: let his wisdom and will therefore rule all our actions. We are God's: let all parts of our life accordingly strive toward him as our only lawful goal."

Now with that in mind, listen for a minute while I tell you a story my father loved to tell about a colleague of his at the University of Chicago, where he taught for 25 years. A colleague named Charles Hartshorne, a theologian. The story is possibly apocryphal — I've heard similar ones about other academics. It goes this way: One fine day, Hartshorne had gone for a walk, wheeling his infant daughter Emily in a carriage. He'd run into a colleague somewhere on campus and gotten into a passionate and intriguing discussion which went on for quite a while. When he returned home, his wife asked, "But Charles, where's the baby?"

Here my father's face would dramatize blankness, then a dawning horror. The baby! Charles Hartshorne had simply forgotten her when he got so involved—involved, of course, in talking about God.

The story does not end badly. In that more innocent time, they retrieved Emily without incident from wherever on the campus her father had parked her, and they all, presumably, lived happily ever after.

I had included this tale in my earlier version of the memoir, without really knowing what to do with it. I understood its meaning for me, of course. I was Emily, left in her carriage, forgotten when the excitement of the other part of his life claimed her father. It seemed a cautionary tale to me, but without my seeing what useful lesson I might derive from it. For what control did I have, did baby Emily have, over our fathers? None. How could we make our lives more real, more pressing to them? We couldn't.

The threat of that kind of forgetting, the reality of that kind of distraction, were a part of who my father was. There was a kind of impartiality, and therefore a kind of distance, even in my father's closest and most loving attention. I don't know if he ever would have done exactly what Charles Hartshorne did, but I certainly knew him to be capable of a kind of forgetfulness of what — to him, I suppose — seemed mundane or unimportant, and this occasionally included obligations he'd undertaken to one of us, or to my mother.

The Emily Hartshorne story seems to me to be the nightmare side of living with someone whose first allegiance is elsewhere, is otherworldly. You are left. You are abandoned. You have no real importance in the great scheme of things.

There is, of course, another side to living with such a person, and I'd been witness to that too. For instance, when my father first understood that something was wrong with him, he received it extraordinarily bravely. It occurred on my watch, actually, when he had, in a period of stress, a series of hallucinations one day. I'd written about it in drafts of the memoir already, about how I'd finally been able to persuade him that he hadn't seen what he thought he'd seen — little figures running around my house:

After a long pause, he said, "So I guess I was seeing things."

"I think you were," I said. "Look, you hadn't eaten or slept in a couple of days. That does things to you. Chemically. So, yes, I think you're exhausted and drained, and that you were seeing things."

We said in silence for a while. Finally he smiled ruefully and said, "Huh! I never thought I'd lose my mind."

There was an unspoken clause implicit at the start of this sentence: "I've tried to think of all the ways I might get old but . . ." and I heard it at least as clearly as I heard the part he spoke. I understood, abruptly, that he had wondered how they would come to him, old age and death, and that now he was even a little bemused that they should take this unexpected form as they approached.

I was startled at the time to realize this — that he had thought about it. But now that he is dead, and several others of his generation and the one before it in my family are dead also, it's my turn to think of it, and I do. Unlike Dad though, but largely because of him, I think often of the possibility that I may lose my mind. And when I do, I remember this moment when he seemed to be getting the news, really, about his fate, about how it would be for him; when he took it in and accepted it and was, somehow, *interested* in it, all at the same time, before my eyes. It was a moment as characteristic of him as any I can think of in his life. And as brave. Noble, really, I've come to feel.

I wasn't there when he heard his diagnosis, but my sister said it was no real surprise to him, that he heard it and took it in much as he had the notion of being hallucinatory. And never in the course of his disease did he rail against it or seem as though he was in despair. I didn't see him in every moment, of course — there may have been long periods of desperation and sorrow. But to my eyes, to my perception, he was as accepting of the idea of Alzheimer's disease — an illness which would take his intellect, his connection with other people, his ability to speak, to eat, to walk, to reason — as he was of the moment in my living room when he recognized that he'd been hallucinating.

I think the reason this was the case was that he saw himself as in God's hands, that he thought of this illness without ego, without the sense of self and grief for the loss of self that would afflict me if I found I had it. In the way in which I am very much "my own," my father was not his own; and this was the source for him of an almost unfathomable strength as he began his slow decline.

But at this point in my revising, I hadn't yet seen this, hadn't discovered it. I was still stuck writing a book with no center, constructing a story with no point.

In my first stab at constructing the memoir, I'd proceeded chronologically, starting with my father's childhood, my parents' history together, my childhood, and so on. It was this version that provoked my agent's comment. And when I reread it, I could see that many of the details I was offering of what our family's life was like would be, simply, boring to anyone but me — as details unattached to any forward momentum in a narrative are bound to be. (As Natalie Kusz says about the memoir, "Nobody cares except your mama." Unless you *make* them care.)

The second time I tried, after the appeasing novel written about the elderly mother, I completely shifted my line of attack. This time, essentially, I wrote essays, each focused on some important element in my father's life, each gathering together information or incidents from various periods of his life that connected to that element. But while some of these essays had a certain charm (I thought), they had, in the aggregate, no narrative drive either. They didn't build on each other in any way as you went through them.

What's more, neither of these versions — constructed over three or four years by now of writing and revising — worked for *me*, resolved for me any of the need to revisit and revisit the process of my father's decline and dying. They didn't relieve the tension, the anxiety that had brought me the project in the first place.

The third time around, having resolved the issue of voice, which I'd seen, falsely, as the major impediment, I decided to use tools from fiction. I told myself that fiction was what I knew, all I knew, and that I should use what tools it gave me to write this goddamned thing and get it over with.

For starters, I decided to follow Tolstoy's dictum that you should begin in the middle of things. I put a chapter I'd had mid-book in the first version of the memoir at the very front of this new version — the chapter in which the hallucinations appear, a chapter in which I dramatically describe the series of events which made it clear to me, undeniable, that something was terribly wrong with my father; and in which I step forward and tell him that he can't do what he wants to do, that I need to be responsible for him, and I can't let him drive off alone after a prolonged delusional episode. I tightened it. I focused it. The chapter ends with his diagnosis:

> That fall I had a fellowship in writing at the MacDowell Colony in New Hampshire. We didn't have phones in our studios there, so I was sitting in the public telephone booth under its single bright light when I learned from my sister what I already knew in my heart — that Dad had been diagnosed with what is called "probable Alzheimer's disease."

This is a first chapter, then, that announces what the book is about, on several levels. And which works its tail off pulling the reader in. It uses all the fictional devices — scene, dialogue, characterization, suspense — to make its points. And, I think, to assure the reader, if only subliminally, that I understand the responsibility of making this material interesting, of making it seem of consequence. I felt, rereading this chapter in its new form, in its new place, that the reader would instantly feel comfortable in my hands, would have the sense that I knew where I was going, and that I was going to competently take him along with me, which I think is important in the beginning of any work. But where was I going? This was still, really, not clear to me. What, exactly, was the point of writing this account? And if I wasn't going to proceed chronologically, or by essays, how was I going to proceed? To what purpose? How could I learn to revise, to re-see this work?

I thought of fiction again. I thought of what I would say to a fiction writer-student who handed me a long work with as little sense of motion in it as mine had, with as little sense of drive and energy. How I would start her down the path to serious revision.

What drew you here? I'd ask. What's making you want to record this? What's the point, for you? And how can you make that apparent? How can you embody that, fictionally? I remembered that I often quoted Flannery O'Connor to my writing students. In a passage from one of her beautiful essays in *Mystery and Manners,* she says:

> St. Cyril of Jerusalem, in instructing catechumens, wrote: "The dragon sits by the side of the road, watching those who pass. Beware lest he devour you. We go to the Father of Souls, but it is necessary to pass by the dragon." No matter what form the dragon may take, it is of this mysterious passage past him, or into his jaws, that stories of any depth will always be concerned to tell, and this being the case, it requires considerable courage at any time, in any country, not to turn away from the storyteller.

When I used this passage with my students, I secularized it some, which may have made O'Connor spin in her grave. I spoke of the ways in which fiction usually constructs a problem for the character or characters, and then asks them to solve it; of how fiction watches their attempt — whether they triumph (slay the dragon), whether they're defeated (are slain, devoured), whether they win but lose so much in the process that it's scarcely worth it. What is it that your character needs to struggle with? I'd ask them. What's the right dragon for the kind of person you've created? What is the nature of the conflict, implicit or explicit, that you're asking me (and taking up my time and energy) to witness?

For my father, the dragon was clear — it was his illness, and what he would make of it, *how* he would deal with it. That part of the narrative, I thought, would virtually take care of itself.

But I was present in the memoir too, of necessity. And what I hadn't asked myself was what my dragon was, what my character was struggling with in this story that she'd vanquish, or be vanquished by. That, I decided, was my task in what I hoped would be the final revision of my work. Understanding that would lead me to my point, my purpose.

It must be said that I have some confidence, by now, in the unconscious processes of writing, those processes that bring me certain scenes, certain details, to work with. I believe that it takes a fully conscious mind to do the work of writing, to bring things around, as it were; but I think there's often something deeply revelatory about the detail or the story fragment that just "occurs" to you, out of the blue — and therefore worth examining and reexamining. In fact, I would call that repeated holding up to the light, turning details and fragments this way and that, an essential part of my revision process in fiction.

So I decided to try that with this non-fiction work. Why had I picked out the elements I'd chosen for this memoir? What was the Emily Hartshorne story doing there? Why was a part of another chapter devoted to my earliest memory of my father as having been absent, gone? (He'd left Chicago for six months just after my younger brother was born to go to Germany and teach, and then to travel and do research in Europe.) Why did I keep coming back also to that Calvin quote, so far used nowhere in the memoir, as though it were the answer to some question I hadn't posed yet? What I thought was that if I kept examining and reexamining these elements I'd assembled on my desk, the meaning I was struggling for would come clear to me.

VS Naipaul has a pair of essays he's published together under the title "Finding the Center" in which he speaks of travel and writing as sharing a kind of tension, the tension that come from the wish "to understand what one has lived through or where one has been." This understanding takes thought, he says. Thought, which he describes as "a sifting of impulses, ideas and references that become more multifarious as one grows older. . . . Always, at the beginning," he says — of travel this time, but he might mean writing as well — "there was the possibility of failure — of not finding anything, not getting started on the chain of accidents and encounters, ... Always, after the tension, there came a moment when a place began to clear up, and certain incidents (some of them disregarded until then) began to have meaning."

It takes, I think, a great deal of attentiveness to the elements you've put into play in a piece of writing to figure out what you may have been meaning without intending to; and it takes a great deal of will and energy then to wrest the meaning from those elements, to restructure them so they begin to say to others what you've discovered they say to you. But this is what we owe our readers, those people who take the time, who make the effort, to read us, to try to understand our work, whether we're writing fiction or memoir. We owe them this vision; and revision.

This was my process in revision, once I had written down what I could of my father's story and mine. To find out what lay at its center — what had brought me to write it — and then to rearrange and rework what I had done in order to expose that. It's a little like certain children's puzzles, where you're given a number of objects and asked: What do these things have in common? Why do they belong together?

What does it mean or matter, for instance, that my mother railed against my father in her journals and in her poetry, railed against him for being unknowable to her, withdrawn? She wrote in one poem that she loved having lunch out with him because he had to sit opposite her and talk to her. She wanted desperately to know him, and she threw herself at him in that quest all her life to know him as she knew herself. Because of course she knew herself intimately — she was always taking her own emotional pulse, always examining herself.

What does it matter or mean that one of my dearest memories of my father — talking seriously in his study to him, in my case about the meaning of communion in my life — is a memory shared by a student of his, who spoke in a tribute after his death of his parallel generosity to all of his students?

What does it matter or mean that my earliest memory of my father is of his absence, of his being away on that trip to Germany and of trying to call him up as I sat for a picture that was going to be sent to him?

What does it matter or mean that the Emily Hartshorne story — which I do find funny — also breaks my heart?

What does it matter or mean that just as I felt I was beginning to know my father as an adult, he began to disappear into his disease?

The fact was, as I saw it at this point, that the center of all this for me was that Alzheimer's disease in a sense merely exacerbated a lifelong feeling of loss I had about my father. The colleague who wrote about the Calvin quote hanging in his office called my father "self-effacing to a fault." But I don't think that's so. That implies an action taken, a willed result: he erased himself.

My sense of my father has come to be that he simply didn't have that kind of self in the first place — the kind of post-Freudian, self-aware self most of us know all too well; the kind of self-conscious self most of us lug through life; the kind of self tortured by self-analysis that my mother had; the kind of well-developed, well-scrutinized set of feelings and sensibilities that, I confess, I take pride in myself. Painful and messed-up as it often seems, the kind of self that can offer itself to another.

My father was not his own; therefore he couldn't be my mother's — and he wasn't. I suspect that was part of why she adored him. He couldn't be mine or my siblings' either, though we acted out, we were bad in an attempt to make him claim us. Oh, he noticed. He tried to help. Always he was gentle, dispassionate, understanding, disinterested, wise. An abstract father. A father who might forget you if what he was talking about interested him too much.

This gave Alzheimer's disease a particular emotional potency for me, even beyond the tremendous power it exerts in any sufferer's family's life. It took away my father, yes. But it reminded me that my father had long since been taken. He'd been gone — gone in belief. I remember as a child being horrified by the passage in the gospel of St. Matthew in which Jesus speaks of a man's spiritual foes as being in his own household:

> "He that loveth father or mother more than me is not worthy
> of me; and he that loveth son or daughter more than me is not
> worthy of me. And he that taketh not his cross and followeth
> after me is not worthy of me. He that findeth his life shall lose
> it; and he that loseth his life for my sake shall find it."

How could this be? I had thought then. Our parents were supposed to love us best, weren't they? Wasn't that what parents were for?

Now here came Alzheimer's disease, horrifying me once more.

For a while then, in this revision, this became the shape of the story for me. I felt I'd found its center, the resolution of the tension. The dragon for me was Alzheimer's disease too — not because it took my father from me, but because it took him from me *again*. Because it seemed, in some way, so fitting, so appropriate a disease for him. And my struggle — this memoir — was an attempt to pull him back in memory from his illness, yes; to say: "This, this is the way he was before it seized him!" but also to pull him back from the way he was — from the absence, the distance that was always part of him, and to try to make him clear and palpable to a reader. To you. To pull him back, but simultaneously to honor the meaning of that distance as part of what was best about my father, painful as it may have been for me. I thought I was done revising, then.

I wasn't. For as I began to write this new version out, I discovered that the dragon for me was my very wish to tell a tale about my father's life and death. To give any narrative shape at all to that part of the memoir.

Let me explain: I think when I started with my ordinary chronology of my father's life — my first version — I was openly looking for a kind of plot for his story. Why not? That's why I chose to try a memoir. The impulse was intensely personal. Redemptive, I hoped.

At his memorial service I was assigned Psalm 103 to read. Most of you probably know this psalm, though you may not know it by number. It begins, "Bless the Lord, O my soul, and all that is within me, bless his holy name." It speaks — ironically to me as I prepared to read it at the service — of God's mercy:

> Who forgiveth all thine iniquities; who healeth all thy diseases; who redeemeth thy life from destruction; who crowneth thee with loving kindness and tender mercies; who satisfieth thy mouth with good things; so that thy youth is renewed like the eagle's.

It speaks of our inconsequence by comparison with God's goodness:

> For he knoweth our frame; he remembereth that we are dust. As for man, his days are as grass; as a flower of the field, so he flourisheth. For the wind passeth over it, and it is gone; and the place thereof shall know it no more.

I spoke these lines at the service: I who had seen my father stop eating; who had as long as he was able to swallow, fed him water from a straw, drop by drop onto his tongue, while he was dying. Who had watched him turn into a wizened, tiny form in diapers in his bed, all beaky nose and clutching hands.

Well, I think I felt I could assuage this horror and grief by insisting that he was not gone — that he was not as a flower of the field, dammit; that there was sense, meaning to be made of his life in terms of a narrative structure, an explanation of his self: *the story of my father*, as narrated by me. I would redeem him, I would snatch him back from the meaninglessness of Alzheimer's disease.

And what I came to see by "the sifting of impulses, ideas, and references" that Naipaul speaks of — by revising and revising and revising this memoir — was that there was no such narrative to be made of my father's life. No such risk of meaninglessness in his illness or his dying for him. No rescue to be performed.

The narrative, then, in this revision, is of my grief and struggle, and what it taught me. Most of the book is taken up with my father; it was what happened to him, after all, that caused me to grieve, and to struggle. And to learn. But *what* I learned, because I kept having to revise, and because revising is reseeing, rethinking, was that in this way as in so many other ways, my father didn't need me to give shape to his life. He accepted what was happening to him, the way he was fracturing and breaking apart, as he had accepted it in possibility well before it happened. For him his life and death already made sense. For him, Psalm 103 could be read through without irony to its conclusion, which goes as follows:

> But the mercy of the Lord is from everlasting to everlasting upon them that fear him, and his righteousness unto children's children; to such as keep his covenant and to those that remember his commandments to do them. . . . Bless the Lord, all his works in all places of his dominion: bless the Lord, O my soul.

I don't remember if I read this psalm to calm him when he was in one of his violent panics; I might have. And it might have been among the many psalms I read to comfort him while he was dying, but I don't remember that either; I hope it was. I think it might have comforted him: just the familiar rhythms, the old words, and the deep faith they describe. My comfort is different, but, like his, it has come from what is most central in my life. I've called him up over and over and in a variety of ways as I thought and wrote this memoir. And he's come to me over and over, and more and more clearly. I've *revised* him, as I revised my ideas about what I was doing, calling him up. For it is by writing, by the simultaneously pleasurable and painful processes of working my way through the material I collected and made over the years I labored on this memoir, that I've come to see that his consolation would always have lain beyond the reach of any story I could have made of his life. But it is by the making of the story, and by everything that changed my understanding of him and of myself as I made it, that I have been, as the writer that I am, also consoled.

KIM STAFFORD

The Writer as Professional Eavesdropper

Reading the classified section in Mexico City's *Tiempo Libre,* I came across the notice for an unusual public service:

> Hospital of the word: emergencies and preventative attention. Permanent workshop for the defense of the Spanish language . . . consultations . . . conferences . . . intensive therapy . . . clarify doubts . . . first time assistance.

This anonymous writer was nudging me toward a way of seeing my work, giving me a name for my practice OF STARTING MY OWN WRITING WITH A GIFT FROM THE WORLD. Maybe my notebook is the hospital of the word, and I practice my roving services by being what in Spanish is called *un fisgón,* a listener, eavesdropper, caretaker of gossip. Maybe I am this gatherer of treasure, shepherding words, phrases, and texts of character orphaned by the world's attention to money and fame.

How was I first recruited to this cause? As a freewheeling writer of poems and personal essays, I hold a dark secret: I was once a scholar — a medievalist. I was that awkward figure haunting libraries, poring over glossaries, thumbing my *Beowulf* and my *Pearl* to rags. I have written twenty pages on the use of the feminine pronoun in a single stanza of an obscure poem from the fourteenth century. Working sleepless through nights to dawn, I have heated cold rooms with the sheer stamina of my reading. I have internalized the nuances of suffixes in ancient texts so that my voice can recite what I no longer understand. That was a long and wonderful training for something I don't do now.

Now that I write, what do I do with that training? Now that I teach writing, how does my scholarship pertain? For both writing and teaching, I now turn that tireless scholarly attention to the flow of language that surrounds me in the world. I read talk. I annotate conversation. I catalog graffiti. I savor the traveler's fictions in bus stations, the tipsy confessions of the midnight lounge car on the train. I long for the banter of hitchhikers recounting their rides and destinations, the semipublic narratives in the booths of coffee shops. I scribble and study conversations at the White Horse Tavern in Greenwich Village, Molly's at the Market in New Orleans, the twenty-four-hour Elkhorn Café in Jackson Hole. I record fictions spoken at the Burns Brothers Truck Plaza south from Portland. I take the corner booth, hunch over my coffee, and listen both ways, tuning in to the periphery of my hearing. I revel in speeches flaunted at the Acropolis Diner, in Brooklyn, as I once absorbed the annual publications of the Early English Text Society.

I live in the modern world, but my habits are older. In the medieval period, books were so rare they were memorized. Travelers took turns reciting favorite texts. The feast of stories exchanged by the pilgrim band in Chaucer's *Canterbury Tales* exaggerates a social custom that was actual. For people living in an oral tradition were poorer in books but richer in stories. Habits of making and sharing stories were different in a way hard to appreciate since Gutenberg. Without books, newspapers, the Internet, junk mail, or radio, everybody lived by spoken stories, from sermons to ballads to jokes to proverbs to the kinds of stories Chaucer's pilgrims exchanged directly with one another.

The first book with pagination didn't appear until the fifteenth century; people *knew* the books they owned, could say them word for word. Chaucer's contemporary John Gower apparently had only eight books in his personal library; he had memorized all eight, however, and he wove quotations and adapted sentences from them throughout the three books he composed himself (one in Latin, one in French, and one in English, because no one knew which language might prevail). But as Socrates had warned his students, once we learn how to read we may forget how to remember. Gutenberg imprisoned literature, and schools maintain the tyranny. How can we join the world again — the ancient permanent human world of literature alive in public life?

As I walked past their ditch on a cold day, I overheard a steamfitter down in the earth say to his partner: "As the world around us grows colder, sincerity and honesty must be the fire to keep us warm." I was on my way to the faculty convocation and paused to jot this worker's sentence in my notebook. But when I reported these words to my colleagues, they refused to believe I had overheard them. "You're a writer," said one. "You made that up." "Where did you really hear that?" said another. "Oh," said a third, "maybe that was one of our English majors who couldn't get a real job."

As my friends honored my skill but insulted my source, I realized poetry in our culture has been exiled from daily life by the claim it is the royal prerogative of the highly educated. Only professors and their students, it would seem, know eloquence. What a shame. Wordsworth, I have been told, has said the most evocative poetry will be spoken by common people in moments of deep feeling. I think he was right.

What shall you and I make of this? As the world grows colder around us, it seems likely I will not hear anything better for some days. Sincerity and honesty — how can we live by these? How can we write and teach by these? What am I to make of my professor friends, their cynicism about language, and about humanity?

Some of my colleagues in the language-rich professions of teaching and writing admit they overhear such occasional gems, but they often explain them away. They believe literature resides in libraries, and students pay tuition to learn secret ways to consume it and perhaps to create it. Writing, in their view, is an esoteric craft to be practiced by the few; I believe such creation is a universal right and talent of my neighbors everywhere. As a writer — and eavesdropper — I know that genius lives where the language lives. Some witness it, overhearing by chance. I eavesdrop professionally, because such listening makes life a perpetual feast, and because I'm not always smart enough to invent things as powerful as what I hear.

Another way to say this: by listening to the glories of conversation around me, I am moved to write, and I am reminded to listen closely to my own most quiet thoughts and dreams. In their inventive talk, my wise neighbors give me permission to take seriously my own internal voice.

In my experience, all pleasure in writing begins with a sense of abundance — rich knowledge and boundless curiosity. A student writer, or a professional journalist, can get by with spare resources, but cannot thrive.

Anyone can begin with just enough information to fill a required writing assignment. Writing then will feel like an examination. Or, with abundance, it can feel like flight. And for me, flight begins with the fat little notebook in my pocket. I urge my students to record the hum of talk around them and to bring overheard fragments to class so we may revel together. I urge them to attend to the common muse. Chaucer delights me, but Chaucer is not my muse. Published literature is not my muse. For the muses are all around us. They seem ordinary but are very busy, very generous. I listen everywhere, hush my companion when a good story drifts into range, pull out my notebook and smile.

"Hold that thought," I whisper, "for a moment."

I make my notebooks two and three-quarters by four and a quarter inches, from two full sheets of paper folded small, slit, and sewn into brown cover stock with black thread flavored with beeswax. The little book is a plain and fragrant object. I fold it open to the next fresh page and slip it into my shirt pocket beside my pen. I make up a dozen notebooks at a time, stick my address label on the inside cover of each, and date them as I begin. A stamp decorates the outside cover, usually that old one-cent stamp with the pen and inkwell that proclaims, "The ability to write — a root of democracy." Such a notebook lasts me from a week to a month. Every few months, it's time to sit down with a stack of notebooks and glean the best stories, sayings, and thoughts, and I file these with works in progress according to their particular magnetic attractions. Or when I am given a writing task by an editor, instead of staring at a blank page to gather my thoughts, I leaf through the little notebooks to be reminded of many rich beginnings. The question then is not "What shall I write?" but rather "Which, of the many beauties in my notebook, do I wish to carry forward?" The writer thus sits down to a feast every time, and never to an empty bowl.

My own writing routine surges in a stream of notebooks, letters, and drafts of stories, songs, and essays, all in simultaneous development. A certain amount of chaos flavors the whole rush. In class, I suggest my students catalog their eavesdropping into key categories: conversations overheard, informal speeches, written texts from the street, and graffiti and short phrases. One might label sections of the notebook by these or similar categories, but in my own practice I don't. I take it down as it comes, and organize it later, selecting the best for current work and letting the rest undertake the yeasty work of time on the shelf, in the drawer, in the mind. From such external voices, my students and I move to eavesdropping on our own dreams and our fleeting thoughts. I am an informal folklorist in the world, and a forthright internal eavesdropper. I encourage my students to conduct field-work on their own cultures and themselves. Together we take dictation from the world.

Conversations Overheard

Preparing to write an essay, I find, takes a few rich days of eavesdropping, and then some writing time. The writing life has a continuing rhythm of listen and tell, listen and tell. In the world, I find myself barraged by rich conversation. I was sitting in a bar in Philadelphia, late one November evening, when I set down in my notebook this conversation from two regulars in the next booth:

"So, you're going to be a father—when?"

"March."

"You going to be a husband, too?"

"Don't know. Maybe summer."

"Maybe, huh? You don't know, or she don't?"

"I don't."

"Ah!"

What can I do with that? The characterization strikes me as very rich, very concise. Because all questions are not answered, there is room for a story to grow.

There is a similar challenge to the writing life as I savor the sentence I overheard at an education conference: "You know the old saying in surgery: The operation was a success but the patient died." I savor the line I overheard on a plane out of Cheyenne: "Danielle Steele? Oh, she's okay if you're on a cruise and the pool is full." I savor the lament by a cop at the café, as he put on his hat to go out into the rain: "Well, I guess I better get out there and fight crime, and sin, and lust, and pestilence. I keep fighting, but I never win. Oh well—God! It's raining, too!"

What I do with such fragments, again, is to wait, to ponder, to try out provisional uses in letters and postcards to friends. Either several will group themselves naturally to spark an essay, or they may open a poem, invite a story to begin, or simply enrich my abiding pleasure in the language and whet my hearing for more.

Informal Speeches

I sat on a stone bench outside the downtown library in my native city of Portland, Oregon, listening as a street musician named Gypsy Slim, who had camped between two shopping carts for some months, harangued the pedestrians.

"I been to college," he proclaimed to a woman who had paused to consider him, "majored in physics, minored in philosophy, and all the scientists will tell you the temperate zone is the most healthy — regular seasons, hot and cold. But I don't care if it's house, job, creed, ethnic group, country, institution, or sex — they *all* try to stifle what *you* can be! You want to *know* what you can be? Get outside all those categories and have a look!" Then his saxophone wrangled the air, and pigeons scattered, and the woman and several other gathered listeners tossed quarters into his hat and moved on.

On my stone bench, I put down the book I had been reading, and took out my notebook to get Slim's list. Because he had repeated this speech many times, it had developed a rhythm and an order that made it possible to remember: "house, job, creed. . . ." It all fit. If I wrote fast, and soon, I could get every word. It took him, the outsider, to tell us all something true about ourselves. And it took me to take his words down.

Several weeks later, Gypsy Slim disappeared. Now it has been years, and the pedestrians walk freely up the north side of Taylor Street. I brooded over his words, repeated them to friends. Troubled by his passing, I found myself writing a poem called "What Ever Happened to Gypsy Slim?" The poem quotes a part of his harangue. I wrote an essay called "Local Character," in which Slim's speech sets the keynote for a host of eccentrics teaching hard truths to the communities they inhabit. I wrote a short story called "A Dancer on Salmon Street," in which Gypsy Slim's words help a fugitive from office work begin to change his life. Many heard him speak; I took it down, and I study what he said by writing variations on his words again and again.

As a writer, I am aware of ethical issues involved in borrowing texts from strangers. I take these issues seriously. If I can't find Gypsy Slim to ask his permission before quoting him, am I a thief? My students ask me this, and I ask myself. It would be very wrong to use Slim's words irresponsibly. But it would also be wrong to ignore his words. I take the risk of cautious use because I believe in the importance of what he said to all of us. Sometimes my eavesdropping may get me in trouble. But if we don't listen, if we avoid the issue and borrow only from books, we are all diminished.

Gypsy Slim's speech found its way into my writing. Other speeches haven't — yet — but I live by their verve, their ready potential. Take the celebratory recollection by a gentleman I met at a nursing home:

> They ain't much difference, yes, between a square and a round dance. They ain't much difference. I been in every state in the New-nited states, and Missouri's the best one for music I was ever in — don't you worry! Why, the caller starts a-callin' and everybody dancin' and if a feller gets lost the caller goes and grabs him and starts him off again! I used to know 'em and call 'em. I ain't called one in probably ten years:

> All to your places and straighten up your faces —
> Promenade away!
> Return to your partners all —
> Swing 'em if you love 'em
> and cheat 'em if you don't!

> Yes sir, right in Missouri — don't you worry!

I accept this gift. It is one of the most breathless enthusiasms I have known. It gives me permission to stretch and listen to the next celebrations that may arise in my own voice.

Written Texts from the Street

There are private ways to publish. You can pay a printer to print your verse and then hawk your own books, which some call vanity publishing. Or you can staple your work, anonymously, to telephone poles, which I call generosity.

In Tijuana late one Halloween night, I found a ballad nailed to a pole. The song was called "Mi Tijuana Querida," a loving ballad to the city itself. I stood in the dim light taking that text down, including the sentence in small writing at the end, which I translate, "You can't pay for this — it is for you."

In Portland, I lifted a letter pasted to the sidewalk by rain beside a pile of someone's earthly possessions flung from an upper-story apartment window. The compact story in that handwritten note pleaded with my heart,

> John — Don't call Uncle Sammy anymore. Their fed up. Owe them money for phone calls. . . . You make mom cry so much she worried sick. Your driving her to an early grave. Work. Work. Work. Pray, pray, pray. Write letters. No calls.
>
> —VIOLET

What shall I do with these texts the world has sent me? There is a privacy in them, and a sufficiency to the moment of finding them. But I also feel the impulse to listen to the lives behind them, be their courier. With these two, I don't know yet. And I feel in this "not knowing — yet" the excitement of the writing life. I have a trove that might tell the world spirited things, but I keep this trove in the drawer for now, wishing to use it well. Something in my life will tell me what to do.

In Oregon, there is a group of friends who call themselves "The Homeless Waifs Holiday Club." The group was formed in the 1970s when a generation of college students realized they weren't going home for Thanksgiving, and so banded together for their own invented revelry. One of their customs is to gather at a remote place in the Oregon desert on the first Saturday following the first full moon following the fall equinox for a rousing game of Capture the Flag. No newsletter, no calls, no e-mail — just that fixed annual date.

So there they were, come from all directions (some traveling three thousand miles) to stand in a circle in the dust while the man they called Reverend Whippoorwill, who had thrown the *I Ching* in advance, read the judgment he had composed (he later sent me a copy):

> Going out and coming in without error.
> Friends come without blame.
> To and fro goes the way.
> On the seventh day comes return.
> It furthers one to have somewhere to go.
> After a time of decay comes the turning point.
> The powerful light that has been banished returns.
> There is movement, but it is not brought about by force.

He read, we stood in silence, then the piano began to play — the piano in the back of the pickup truck starting up the dusty road, with Ronald and Nancy Reagan in festive effigy tied upright against the tailgate, dogs with bandanas around their necks following our ragtag parade, and the thirty-pound cake shaped like Oregon (the west half organic flour, the east half Betty Crocker) carried on a door by four of the faithful.

> The transformation of the old becomes easy.
> The old is discarded and the new is introduced.
> Both measures accord with time.

I suddenly saw the whole spectacle through the wide eyes of a baby bouncing on his mother's hip, as she danced with the parade, shaking her tambourine.

> Walking in the midst of others, one returns alone.

My devotion to such a text is not based purely on its "poetic" quality, though that is there. I pledge allegiance to such a literary offering utterly clean of a search for money or fame. In a world where a photograph of Albert Einstein is used to sell a computer, and where jazz in the public domain sells coffee, home-grown language is restorative, and my calling is clearly to be the recording friend.

Graffiti and Short Phrases

We are surrounded by bits of wisdom and humor, puns, proverbs, jingles, little prayers, short phrases that can go suddenly deep in the midst of the passing flow. A writer takes them seriously by taking them down. It is important for me to know that someone at my college has written on the wall of a restroom stall, "How do you define success in college? Being as intelligent when you get out as when you started." I struggle with the sentence on the bedroom wall of a friend, a teenager, after his suicide: "Due to budget cuts the light at the end of the tunnel has been turned off."

What does it mean about American culture that a shirt at Nantucket proclaims, "He who dies with the most toys wins," while an Idaho bumper sticker holds, "My wife, yes, my dog, maybe, my gun never"? I live with these short texts of American literature, give them a second chance to work on my mind by copying them into my notebook and then returning to them as a basis for writerly meditation. The notebook becomes my devotional book of hours, where the hand-painted sign by a house in a poor neighborhood could launch a short story: "This is our home please dump your garbage elsewhere!" The words etched in the rearview mirror of a car could tease me into an essay about time and change: "Objects in mirror are closer than they appear."

Such passages might be the invisible ink that starts a story, never to appear verbatim in the text, but giving my writing a launch. Or they might actually appear in stories, poems, or essays. But always the prevailing habit of listening and cherishing such gifts will lie behind the solitary work of the imagination, inviting all secrets forward into the light. In daily writing practice, such phrases work like visible catalysts to bring the invisible story into being.

Sometimes I think of the work of my muse as mute elder pleading my attention: my grandparents lived with the earth in primitive ways (homesteading the high plains of Wyoming ninety years ago); my parents told me stories from that time; and my work is to tell *how* these stories have come to me. I might begin, "My mother showed me her mother's diary from 1911, which begins 'Harrison built our house today, and in the evening sawed out a nice window on the south side.'"

The text comes to me as a gift, and my work is to tell how it arrived, and what it says, and what this saying may imply or call into question. In a similar way, I might say to my students: Find an utterance from the world that seems to address you, and then write an essay telling the story of how that text arrived in your life, and what happened to you as a result of its arrival.

Gifts of rich lore surround us all. While others seem to observe these offerings on occasion and by chance, noticing and then letting them go, I make the hearing and recording of them my mission as a writer, and a key invitation to writing students. Dreams get away if we don't tell them, or write them down. Thoughts do the same. The writer's greatest chance may be devotion to the passing fragment. It is small, but it is pure, and it may hold a compact infinity. You heard it for a reason.

CHAPTER 17

Short Shorts

Short pieces provide a wealth of creative triggers. In the seven we offer below, you'll find a range of techniques to shape creative nonfiction. You'll see how Cantú writes from visual cues; how White and Danson find the extraordinary in the ordinary; how Stanton finds an unfamiliar story in a familiar place; how Norris defines a commonplace in life — rain — in an illuminating way; how Fuller renders a landscape by smell and sound alone; and how Apple writes about a beloved grandfather — without cliché. Some voices are lyrical, some are matter-of-fact; all are adept at making every word count in forms we hope will inspire and encourage experimentation.

- MAX APPLE   *"Roommates"*

- NORMA ELIA CANTÚ   *"Tino & Papi"*

- ELIZABETH DANSON   *"Lost"*

- ALEXANDER FULLER   from *Don't Let's Go to the Dogs Tonight*

- KATHLEEN NORRIS   *"Rain"*

- MAUREEN STANTON   *"Water"*

- BAILEY WHITE   *"Buzzard"*

MAX APPLE

Roommates

I came rather late to understanding myself in the cycle of life. Until three years ago, I was a boy in relation to my grandfather. He lived to 107 and remained mentally and physically capable until the end of his life. A generation after the last of his friends died, he could still mow the lawn on a hot summer afternoon, and he insisted on doing so. I usually wrestled the mower from his grip, but his extraordinary energy I took for granted. I had seen it all my life; he was my roommate.

At my birth he was 64, middle age to him, and he was not a gentle old soul. He argued with the men in the synagogue, screamed at his fellows in the bakery where he worked until his mid-80's. He was a lover of strife, even at a distance. For war news he turned up the volume on the television.

We never had to take care of each other, but as I learned to read, I voluntarily became his teacher. My grandfather came to the United States from Lithuania before World War I. He went to night school, could read and write English. Still, I, the emissary of elementary school, considered it my duty to inform him about subtle things like electricity as he got ready for bed after a 12-hour workday.

He was not too interested in my lectures. Within minutes, he fell into a deep sleep. His characteristic snoring pattern was a muted whistle that ended in a great puff of breath. But even asleep there was nothing gentle about this man. He specialized in hating his enemies, even those long dead. As he talked in his sleep, he exploded in anger. From his dreams I learned the curse words of English and Yiddish. Cushioned by his puffs of breath, visions of destruction crowded our room. Boils sprouted on the intestines of his enemies. Cholera depopulated their villages. The deep background of his life as it escaped through his lips became the chorus of my nights. I heard him the way you hear static through a radio. My young ears didn't want to listen to the uncorked anger, didn't know what to make of feelings that could stretch back 70 years. But now, I recall those staccato outbursts as music.

When I went to college, I switched to roommates my age. Then, in graduate school, I had my own apartment, and my old roommate joined me. All his friends were dead, and he had lived long enough to become, once again, a stranger in the community he had inhabited for more than half a century. It was clear to both of us that in spite of a 60-year age gap I was his most congenial companion.

So he joined me in the late 1960's at the University of Michigan. He made new friends, took care of himself, and did most of the housework. In Ann Arbor he found plenty of allies in hating Republicans, but it was even better than that. Ideologically it was the best of times. He could enjoy both the war and the anti-war movement.

He was usually asleep when I brought a girlfriend home. By then, Richard Nixon had replaced the men in the bakery at the top of my grandfather's hate list. The girls, accustomed in those days to hallucinatory experience, did not question my explanation of the snoring and the anti-Nixon ejaculations in the next room. It was just "far out."

Our only serious problem was what he called my laziness. I was studying for Ph.D. preliminary exams. My work consisted of lying on the couch with a book in my lap. Sometimes I dozed off, now and then I highlighted a significant passage. He would pick up a pencil and mockingly mark the newspaper to imitate what I was doing. I could not convince him that it was work.

But I did convince others. I finished my studies, married, fathered a daughter and a son and settled in Texas. Though reluctant to move once again, my grandfather joined us in Houston. He was exactly 100 years older than my son.

Now that I was established, a man with a career, a family, a job, I intended to help my grandfather in the last years of his life. But in the crazy irony of things, it turned out that I was the one who would need help. My solid life cracked in a matter of months, when my wife was stricken with a terrible neurologic disease. The life of the family became the life of the hospital. I lost touch with my friends, my work, even my children. I could not scream out my anger as my grandfather did in his sleep. Instead, I turned it against myself, and it settled in my bones as depression. I returned to the couch where I had studied for my Ph.D. exams, but I no longer saw anything glorious to underline.

At 103 and 104, my grandfather began to take an active role in helping me care for my children. He did not understand what had happened to my wife and had no sympathy for my depression. But he saw the work of daily life in front of him and, as always, he did it. Although by then he must have been wearing the shadow of death as an undershirt, the aroma of life stayed in his nostrils. He listened to the news, he read the paper, he took out the garbage, he played with my children, he mowed the lawn. He never offered me advice or understanding, he just kept doing things. After about two years of melancholy, I joined him, started to see how much there was to do.

Now I get up early and I stay busy. There's a lot of garbage to take out and in Texas there's always a lawn to mow. I don't talk in my sleep yet, but even if I start, nobody will hear me. Roommates like him only come along about one a century.

NORMA ELIA CANTÚ

Tino & Papi

I. Tino

In the photo, he stands to the side with his hand out as if pointing a gun or a rifle. Everyone else, sisters, cousins, friends, neighbors crowd around me; the piñata in the shape of a birthday cake sways in the wind above our heads. Everyone's there: aunts, uncles, cousins, the neighbors, my madrina, everyone, even Mamagrande Lupita from Monterrey. I'm holding the stick decorated with red, blue, yellow tissue paper that we will use to break the piñata. And at age nine he holds out the imaginary gun, like a soldier. Only ten years later, 1968, he is a soldier, and it's not a game. And we are gathered again: tías, tíos, cousins, comadres, neighbors, everyone, even Mamagrande Lupita from Monterrey, and Papi's cousin Ricardo who's escorted the body home. We have all gathered around a flag-draped coffin. Tino's come home from Vietnam. My brother. The sound of the trumpet caresses our hearts and Mami's gentle sobbing sways in the cool wind of March.

II. Papi

On the wall, the image of the Virgen de San Juan, a pale rose background, grayish black outline, shines like silver in the dark. Bueli lights candles when Tino is so sick el Doctor del Valle, the doctor across the river in Nuevo Laredo, fears he will die. He's only three. The illness has taken over. But Papi cries in front of another image of our Lady. It's a calendar from Cristo Rey Church with the image of Nuestra Señora del Perpetuo Socorro. He prays, he weeps, hits the wall with his fists, like he would hit the mesquite tree in the backyard with his head sixteen years later like a wounded animal, mourning, in pain, that morning when Tino's death came to our door. But the child Tino survives the illness; the injections, the medication, the prayers, the remedios — something works, and Papi frames the calendar image in gold leaf, builds the image a repisita — a shelf for candles. In 1968, in his pain, tears running down his face, he'll talk to the image, "For this, you spared my son," he'll take the image down from its place on the wall, cannot bear to see it, to be reminded. On the wall, a rectangle of nothing, the color of the wallpaper Mami had hung for Tio Moy's last visit three years ago, like new — lines of green fern leaves on dusty beige. The votive candle on the tiny shelf is left burning to an empty space.

ELIZABETH DANSON

Lost

It's the eggcups that keep me awake. We ate our boiled eggs from them all through our childhood, each with a preference for big end or little end up, for slicing off the crown of the egg or crazing it with the back of the spoon and picking off the resulting fragments. We dipped our buttery toast soldiers one by one into the soft yolk, then in the little mound of salt on the side of the plate. When the eggshell was empty we plunged the spoon through its base to the bottom of the eggcup, so that a witch couldn't get hold of it and use it for a boat.

This work originally appeared in *Fourth Genre,* Vol. 2, No. 1, 2002, published by Michigan State University Press.

The eggcups were well-traveled; they had started in Kashmir, crafted from walnut by the wood turners who had also made the fruit bowls and little wooden ashtrays, and the set of nesting occasional tables my parents bought. All these pieces went back and forth from India to England to China and back again. The eggcups ended up in a drawer of the dresser that stood in for a sideboard in my parents' last dining room.

I had left turning out these drawers until the night before the move that would take my widowed mother to her small "retirement flat." She was having enough trouble finding the silverware that last week, or anything else she needed, among the mess of boxes in every room. The dresser was going to my sister's house, or I wouldn't have emptied the drawers. Thinking to pack a box of table linens, I opened drawer after drawer stuffed with knitting projects, as yet unwrapped presents from past holidays, cushion covers embroidered in cross-stitch at school by my sister and me, letters and post cards and birthday cards and photos received over the last year or two, pill boxes and bottles with recent and more ancient dates on them, most of them partially full of pills that were never taken.

And the eggcups. Six of them, a more or less matched set, although one or two were dumpier than the rest, the bowls set on slightly shorter stems. I pulled them, one by one, out of a muddle of cotton serviettes and place mats. Each one had dribbles of old egg yolk down the sides, and I was scunnered by this, as my mother would have said in one of her more Scottish moments. I should have taken them into the kitchen and carefully cleaned them, but it was after midnight and there were two more drawers to go. I buried them in the bag of rubbish that was accumulating in the corner of the room, and turned to the next tangle of knitting wool and needles.

After the move, when various siblings had unpacked the boxes I packed that week, and put things away in what seemed like logical places, I heard that my mother was having a terrible time finding what she needed. My sister visited and found her eating cornflakes out of a mug with a teaspoon. The silverware had always been in the dining room drawer; why would it now be in the kitchen? The electric stove was a trial, after years of cooking with gas, and it mysteriously wouldn't light at all in the morning, after she had carefully turned off the master wall-switch the night before. Still, she could always put an egg to boil in the electric kettle, so nobody could say she wasn't cooking for herself at all.

I didn't dare ask what she was eating the boiled egg out of, or think of her fruitless search through the newly organized cabinets for the eggcups she had bought in Kashmir when I was a baby.

ALEXANDRA FULLER

Don't Let's Go to the Dogs Tonight

What I can't know about Africa as a child (because I have no memory of any other place) is her smell; hot, sweet, smoky, salty, sharp-soft. It is like black tea, cut tobacco, fresh fire, old sweat, young grass. When, years later, I leave the continent for the first time and arrive in the damp wool sock of London-Heathrow, I am (as soon as I poke my head up from the intestinal process of travel) most struck not by the sight, but by the smell of England. How flat-empty it is; car fumes, concrete, street-wet.

The other thing I can't know about Africa until I have left (and heard the sound of other, colder, quieter, more insulated places) is her noise.

At dawn there is an explosion of day birds, a fierce fight for territory, for females and food. This crashing of wings and the secret language of birds is such a perpetual background sound that I begin to understand its language. A change in the tone, an increase in the intensity of the birds' activity, will break into my everyday world and I will know that there is a snake some-where, or I will look skyward (the way a person might automatically, almost subconsciously, check their watch against the radio's announcement of time) and confirm a hovering hawk.

In the hot, slow time of day when time and sun and thought slow to a dragging, shallow, pale crawl, there is the sound of heat. The grasshoppers and crickets sing and whine. Drying grass crackles. Dogs pant. There is the sound of breath and breathing, of an entire world collapsed under the apathy of the tropics. And at four o'clock, when the sun at last has started to slide west, and cool waves of air are mixed with the heat, there is the shuffling sound of animals coming back into action to secure themselves for the night. Cows lowing to their babies, the high-honeyed call of the cattle boys singing

"Dip! Dip-dip-dip-dip" as they herd the animals to the home paddocks. Dogs rising from stunned afternoon sleep and whining for their walk.

The night creatures (which take over from the chattering, roosting birds at dusk) saw and hum with such persistence that the human brain is forced to translate the song into pulse. Night apes, owls, nightjars, jackals, hyenas; these animals have the *woo-ooping*, sweeping, land-traveling calls that add an eerie mystery to the night. Frogs throb, impossibly loud for such small bodies.

There is only one time of absolute silence. Halfway between the dark of night and the light of morning, all animals and crickets and birds fall into a profound silence as if pressed quiet by the deep quality of the blackest time of night. This is when we are startled awake by Dad on tobacco-sale day. This silence is how I know it is not yet dawn, nor is it the middle of the night, but it is the place of no-time, when all things sleep most deeply, when their guard is dozing, and when terrorists (who know this fact) are most likely to attack.

KATHLEEN NORRIS

Rain

Above all, it is a land in serious need of rain.
— WILLIAM C. SHARMAN, *Plains Folk*

Until I moved to western South Dakota, I did not know about rain, that it could come too hard, too soft, too hot, too cold, too early, too late. That there could be too little at the right time, too much at the wrong time, and vice versa.

I did not know that a light rain coming at the end of a hot afternoon, with the temperature at 100 degrees or more, can literally burn wheat, steaming it on the stalk so it's not worth harvesting.

I had not seen a long, slow rain come at harvest, making grain lying in the swath begin to sprout again, ruining it as a cash crop.

Until I had seen a few violent hailstorms and replaced the shingles on our roof twice in five years, I had forgotten why my grandmother had screens made of chicken wire for all the windows on the west side of her house.

I had not seen the whimsy of wind, rain, and hail; a path in a wheatfield as if a drunken giant had stumbled through, leaving footprints here and there. I had not seen hail fall from a clear blue sky. I had not tasted horizontal rain, flung by powerful winds.

I had not realized that a long soaking rain in spring or fall, a straight-down-falling rain, a gentle, splashing rain is more than a blessing. It's a miracle.

An old farmer once asked my husband and me how long we'd been in the country. "Five years," we answered. "Well, then," he said, "you've seen rain."

MAUREEN STANTON

Water

I see that old woman every now and then at the Y, the one who is not a lunch meat lover. She swims, as I do. She swims in a pair of black shorts and a black shirt. She is ashamed to show her loose, curdled flesh in front of the old men in the hot tub, with their big bellies and skinny legs, red faced, eyeing the teen-age girls splashing each other.

She's been coming here every day for 17 years. She swims a half-mile, I heard her tell someone. Her swimming is more like walking and treading than swimming, so slow I pass her three times before she reaches the end of the pool. Underwater, blurry and dark, she is like a manatee, slow and graceful, as if her ancestors dwelled in the water, like the water is her voice.

I, on the other hand, am fast. I am faster than any of the other swimmers. My arms are long and they easily pull the water to me. My legs are pure muscle and they push me along. I glide through the water like a slippery fish. The water flows in and out of my mouth, like a filter, separating air from water, like gills, and I feel like a fish. I am a fish.

I do a turn at the end of each length, a near, tucked somersault, efficient and powerful, propelled by my fins. I submerge and glide, scissor kick and go deeper, rise for air. I swim back and forth, one end to the other like the neon tetras in my tank at home. And each time I pass over a bobby pin at the bottom of the pool, or a Band-Aid, a rubber band. It makes me feel lonely. I stare down at the one-inch-square, dirty blue and white tiles at the bottom of the pool. Some are missing. It reminds me of when I was a child, scared of driving through Callahan Tunnel in Boston because little squares of tiles had fallen out. Water dripped from the ceiling, and I imagined more tiles popping off from the pressure and then water from Boston Harbor bursting through, rushing in, drowning us. Like a tidal wave.

I was never afraid of the ocean until I thought I could swim so well that I owned it, until once in California when I was a fearless teen-ager I swam out to some pelicans and couldn't get back in. No matter how hard I swam I still was being dragged farther and farther out to sea. I panicked. I put my face in the water and paddled my arms as hard as I could, and finally stepped down and touched soft sand on the ocean floor. I was never the same in the ocean. Never again let myself be seaweed and let the waves tumble me about until my bathing suit is full of sand, and weak and chilled fall onto the warmth of my towel to let the sun bake me.

On top of the water I am fast, like a water bug. But underneath, to myself, swimming, everything is in slow motion, dreamy. Underwater I am honest. I am left with myself. My lungs, my heart, my thoughts. When I swim I fantasize. I invent my life. Scenes are acted out in my mind. I am confident. I am witty. I am sleek and smart, and sophisticated. I am a poet of the sea. I am a painter, an athlete, a walker, a hermit on a mountain. I am dreaming. Fish water water water. I talked in my sleep once, and my friend told me I said that. Fish water water water. It has become my mantra.

After our laps, we sit in the hot tub, I and the old woman and others I don't know. Once she said to anyone, "We're blessed, ain't we?" And no one answered her. They just stared at each other. I stare too. It's because we are afraid. We are exposed. We come waddling out of the locker room. Fat hangs off our arms and legs and necks. Nipples and penises are outlined in wet bathing suits. Makeup is washed away. Hair is flattened. Baldness shows. People look like they were just born, wet and slick and ugly. They are honest.

There is a man I see often at the Y. He has broad shoulders and takes bold strokes. He has distinguished, graying hair and looks like a corporate executive. I thought he was, until one day I recognized a man in the airport and placed him as the corporate executive swimmer at the Y. His uniform pulled his shoulders down, he seemed too tall for his job, barely fit under the electronic metal detector, as he took a woman's belongings and put them in a Tupperware container, asked her to pass through again. And after that, when I saw him at the Y, I thought he could see right through me, because I can see through him. I know him now, know he is not a corporate executive, but a man who stands in the airport all day, watching people come and go, looking inside their bags and purses. But still he swims fast with strong, powerful arms that make him seem like a giant, like a great white.

There was another man who I only saw in the hot tub once. He struck up a conversation like he was lighting a cigar and puffing until he got it going, asking me if I ever listened to the radio, liked that new jazz station. I said no.

"I'm tired of listening to country, all they ever do is cry about a broken heart. I know enough about that, my wife left me two weeks ago after 18 years. She was 20 years younger than me."

"That's too bad," I said. I am not good at small talk.

"How old do you think I look?" he asked. I thought he looked 60 so I said, "55?"

He said proudly, "61."

"Nice talking to you," he said and shook my hand like we were in a business meeting, and he stepped out of the hot tub in his bathing trunks and I felt like I was acting in a movie.

It happens a lot to me, on buses and in supermarkets. Once a woman at the grocery store told me about her life, taking all the time she wanted to ring up my items, hesitating, holding my canned ham in her hand, shaking it at me when she wanted to make a point, throwing my tomatoes into the bag because she was angry about her boyfriend cheating on her and leaving her. I said, "Maybe you could start over," and she said, "Nah, too many broken promises, too many shattered dreams." And she gave me my change and picked up the tabloid she was reading with Sarah Ferguson and Lady Diana on the cover.

I take a shower after sitting in the hot tub, and the old woman is there too. Her belly falls below her pubic area so you can't see her hair there, and her skin is gathered together, stretched out from so much use, years and years of movement. Her legs are like logs, her ankles and knees are lost. She puts her dripping clothes into the new machine in the women's locker room which dries them out through centrifugal force. She turns to a lady behind her. "Ain't that wonderful?"

After her shower, she asks someone to rub lotion on her back. Her wide, white, curved back. She asks anyone who happens to be around. I've seen her. A kind stranger softens her back with lotion and she talks.

"My son and his wife are coming over today so I am making my special casserole with tomatoes and green peppers and rice and cheese."

And the other woman said, "I have a wonderful casserole that I make with peas and noodles and deli loaf."

"Oh, I'm not a lunch meat lover," the old woman says. It sounded to me like a sad poem. They talk about leftovers, what keeps, what doesn't, as the stranger kneads the old woman's back. She closes her eyes and says, "You don't know how much I appreciate that."

One day I see the woman who is not a lunch meat lover with a gadget, a towel thing with handles that lets her rub her own back, which she uses when no one is around. Some days I want to see her, with her short cropped hair, that yarn yellow of blondes when they get old, not gray or silver but like the color of her teeth. Other days I don't want to see her, cheerful and happy because we have a bathing suit dryer or a hot tub.

She looks at me and I glance away. But our eyes touch, enough for her to ask me if I would mind rubbing lotion on her back. Slowly, I put some cold lotion in my hand and touch her soft, ashy skin and she begins to talk. She says she used to be a dancer and worked on Broadway and then taught dance lessons.

"You like to swim," I said to her.

"Oh, that's not swimming," she said. "That's ballet."

I rub the lotion into her skin, and add more, basting, and coating and moving my hand all over her back without taking it off, like her back was a Ouija board and my hand, moving mysteriously, would reveal something to me. I start to cry, silently, tears streaming down my face, and she reaches around and touches my arm and says, "There, there."

BAILEY WHITE

Buzzard

> → Read whole story aloud.
> → Do you like it? why!
> → simplistic or no? why not

There was something in the road. I drove closer to it. It was a buzzard eating a dead armadillo. I got closer. It was a big buzzard. And I'd never seen a buzzard's tail feathers so bleached and pale.

That buzzard better move, I thought. I'd never had to slow down for a buzzard before. They always lope out of the way. I got closer.

The buzzard turned his head and looked at me. He stood up on his big yellow legs. His head was snow white. His eyes were gold. He wasn't a buzzard. He was a bald eagle.

Then, not until after I had brought the car to a full stop, he spread his wings and with a slow swoop lifted himself into the air. He turned his head and gave me a long look through the car windshield with his level yellow eyes. Then he slowly wheeled up into the sky until he was just a black dot against the blue.

I turned the car off. I thought about that glare he had given me: What are *you* doing here? it had said. When I got started again, I drove slower and felt smaller. I think it does us all good to get looked at like that now and then by a wild animal.

Max Apple is the author of eight books of fiction, essay, and memoir. They include the highly acclaimed *I Love Gootie: My Grandmother's Story; Roommates: My Grandfather's Story; Zip; The Oranging of America;* and *Free Agents.* His articles and stories have appeared in *Esquire, The New York Times Magazine, Atlantic Monthly;* and his screenplays have become movies such as *Bad News Bears* and *Roommates.* Apple received his B.A. and Ph.D. from the University of Michigan and is now Professor Emeritus of English at Rice University.

Gerald N. Callahan, Ph.D., is a professor of immunology at Colorado State University. His science articles have appeared in *Nature, Journal of Experimental Medicine,* and *Journal of Immunology.* A poet and essayist, Callahan also holds an appointment in the English department at Colorado State; his writing has been published by *Creative Nonfiction, Southern Poetry Review,* and *Cream City Review.*

Norma Elia Cantú earned her Ph.D. in English from the University of Nebraska, Lincoln. Her scholarly interests include folklore, Chicana literature, and borderlands studies. Her most recent work, forthcoming from Texas A&M University Press, is a study of the Matachines de la Santa Cruz, a dance group in Laredo, Texas, whose work is based on religious traditions.

Lisa D. Chavez was born in Los Angeles and raised in Fairbanks, Alaska. She has published two books of poetry, *Destruction Bay* and *In an Angry Season,* and has been included in such anthologies as *Floricanto Si! A Collection of Latina Poetry; The Floating Borderlands: 25 Years of U.S. Hispanic Literature;* and *American Poetry: The Next Generation.* She teaches in the Creative Writing Program at the University of New Mexico.

Elizabeth Danson, born to British missionaries, spent her early childhood in India and China, was educated in England, then married an American, and came to the United States. A member of U.S. 1 Poets Cooperative, Danson has published poetry and is currently working on a family memoir.

Brian Doyle is the editor of *Portland Magazine* at the University of Portland, Oregon. He is the author of four essay collections, most recently *Leaping: Revelations & Epiphanies,* published in 2003. His book *Two Voices,* co-authored with his father Jim Doyle, won the Christopher Award in 1996. Doyle's essays have appeared in *The American Scholar, The Atlantic Monthly,* and *Harper's;* three have been anthologized in *Best American Essays*— 1998, 1999, and 2003.

Tony Earley writes both fiction and nonfiction and is the author of *Somehow Form A Family: Stories that Are Mostly True; Jim the Boy;* and *Here We Are in Paradise: Stories.* A contributor to *The New Yorker* and to *Esquire,* Earley teaches at Vanderilt University in Nashville, where he lives with his wife and dogs.

Gretel Ehrlich, a native Californian, is the author of the award-winning *The Solace of Open Spaces,* as well as *John Muir: Nature's Visionary* and *This Cold Heaven: Seven Seasons in Greenland,* and other works of nonfiction, as well as fiction and poetry. In her 1994 memoir, *A Match to the Heart,* she recounts her experience of being hit by lightning in 1991 on her ranch. Severely debilitated for several years, she now travels widely, dividing her time between California and Wyoming.

Nora Ephron is an essayist, journalist, novelist, screenwriter, and director. Her columns and articles have been collected in *Wallflower at the Orgy, Crazy Salad,* and *Scribble, Scribble.* As a screenwriter, Ephron won acclaim for the Academy Award-nominated *Silkwood* and the comedy *When Harry Met Sally.* In the 1990s, Ephron turned to film directing with such works as *This Is My Life* and the romantic comedy *Sleepless in Seattle.*

Anne Fadiman is the Francis Writer-in-Residence at Yale University. She is the author of *The Spirit Catches You and You Fall Down,* an account of a Hmong family's conflicts with the American medical system that won the National Book Critics Circle Award for Nonfiction, as well as of *Ex Libris: Confessions of a Common Reader,* a collection of essays on books and reading that has or will be translated into fourteen languages. The former editor of *The American Scholar,* Fadiman is also the editor of *Best American Essays 2003* and *Rereadings: Seventeen Writers Revisit Books They Love.*

Alexandra Fuller is author of *Don't Let's Go to the Dogs Tonight,* a memoir of her childhood in Africa that's been a national bestseller. Born in England in 1969, she moved with her family to a farm in Rhodesia in 1972. After that country's civil war in 1981, the Fullers moved first to Malawi, then to Zambia. Fuller received a B.A. from Acadia University in Nova Scotia, Canada. In 1994, she moved to Wyoming, where she still lives. She has two children.

Dagoberto Gilb is the author of *Gritos, Woodcuts of Women, The Last Known Residence of Mickey Acuna,* and *The Magic of Blood,* for which he won the 1993 Hemingway/PEN Award. Gilb, who earned an M.A. degree in philosophy and religion from the University of California, spent 16 years in El Paso, making his living as a construction worker with the United Brotherhood of Carpenters.

Patricia Hampl's books include *A Romantic Education, Virgin Time, Spillville,* and *I Could Tell You Stories,* a National Book Critics Circle finalist. Her work has appeared in *The New Yorker, New York Times Book Review, Paris Review, American Poetry Review, The Sophisticated Traveler, Iowa Review,* and *Best American Short Stories.* A recipient of a 1990 MacArthur Fellowship and a Guggenheim Foundation award, Hampl teaches creative writing at the University of Minnesota.

Steven Harvey is the author of *Bound for Shady Grove,* a collection of essays about his experiences learning to sing and play the traditional music of the Appalachian mountains. The author of two other collections of personal essays, *A Geometry of Lilies* and *Lost in Translation,* Harvey teaches English at Young Harris College in northern Georgia where he lives with his family.

Tracy Kidder has won the Pulitzer Prize, the National Book Award, and the Robert F. Kennedy Award for his work in nonfiction. He received a B.A. from Harvard College and an M.F.A. from the University of Iowa. The author of *The Soul of a New Machine, House, Among School-*

children, Old Friends, and *Home Town,* Kidder lives in Massachusetts and Maine. His most recent book is *Mountains beyond Mountains,* the story of Dr. Paul Farmer who founded Zanmi Lasante, a nongovernmental organization that is the only health-care provider in the Plateau Central in Haiti.

Li-Young Lee was born in 1957 in Jakarta, Indonesia, of Chinese parents. He is the author of *Book of My Nights; The City in Which I Love You,* which was the 1990 Lamont Poetry Selection, and *Rose,* which won the Delmore Schwartz Memorial Poetry Award. His memoir, *The Winged Seed: A Remembrance,* received an American Book Award from the Before Columbus Foundation.

Gretchen Legler teaches English and Creative Writing at the University of Maine in Farmington. She has written and published widely as a freelance newspaper reporter and magazine writer. Her first book of essays, *All The Powerful Invisible Things: A Sportswoman's Notebook,* was published by Seal Press in 1995. Her essays have appeared in many anthologies, including *Uncommon Waters: Women Write about Fishing* and *American Nature Writing 1997.* She is the winner of two Pushcart Prizes.

Eric Liu is a fellow at the New America Foundation. He writes the "Teachings" column for *Slate* and is the author of *The Accidental Asian: Notes of a Native Speaker,* a New York Times Notable Book featured in the PBS documentary *Matters of Race.* Liu served as a speechwriter for President Clinton and later as White House deputy domestic policy adviser. He teaches at the University of Washington's Evans School of Public Affairs.

Sue Miller's best-selling novels include *The Good Mother* and *Inventing the Abbotts,* both of which were made into feature-length films. She also wrote *For Love, The Distinguished Guest, While You Were Gone,* and *Family Pictures,* which was nominated for a National Book Critics Circle Award. She lives in Boston and teaches creative writing at Amherst College. Her most recent publication is *The Story of My Father,* a memoir about her father's battle with Alzheimer's disease, published in 2003.

Kathleen Norris, born in Washington, D.C., and educated at Bennington College in Vermont, published her first book of poems,

Falling Off, in 1971. It was followed by three other volumes, including *How I Came to Drink My Grandmother's Piano* and *The Year of Common Things.* She has also edited *Leaving New York: Writers Look Back,* a collection of essays and poems by various New York writers. She is affiliated with Leaves of Grass, Inc., in Lemmon, South Dakota, where she lives.

Susan Orlean's books include *Saturday Night, The Orchid Thief, My Kind of Place: Travel Stories from a Woman Who's Been Everywhere,* and *The Bullfighter Checks Her Makeup,* a collection of profiles from which "Meet the Shaggs" is taken. A staff writer at *The New Yorker* since 1992, Orlean has also contributed to *Outside, Rolling Stone, Vogue,* and *Esquire.* Her book *The Orchid Thief* provided the storyline for the movie *Adaptation.*

Scott Russell Sanders, born in 1945, spent much of his youth at a military munitions base, where his father worked. This experience is the title essay of his 1987 book *The Paradise of Bombs.* Other nonfiction books include *Secrets of the Universe, The Force of Spirit, The Country of Language, Hunting for Hope, Writing from the Center,* and *Staying Put.* His fictional work includes *The Invisible Company, The Engineer of Beasts, Bad Man Ballad,* and *Terrarium.* In 1995, he received the Lannan Literary Award for Nonfiction. He teaches at Indiana University.

David Sedaris's latest book is *Dress Your Family in Corduroy and Denim.* Other work includes *Barrel Fever, Holidays on Ice, Naked,* and *Me Talk Pretty One Day,* all of which immediately became national bestsellers. Sedaris's original radio pieces can often be heard on *This American Life,* distributed nationally by Public Radio International and produced by WBEZ in Chicago. In 2001, David Sedaris became the third recipient of the Thurber Prize for American Humor and was named Humorist of the Year by *Time Magazine.*

Charles Simic, an internationally acclaimed poet, was born in Belgrade, Serbia, in 1938 and emigrated to the United States in 1953. In 1990, he received the Pulitzer Prize for Poetry for *The World Doesn't End: Prose Poems,* and in 1999, his book *Jackstraws* was named a New York Times Notable Book of the Year. Other work includes *A Wedding in Hell, Hotel Insomnia, Selected Poems: 1963–1983,* and *Unending Blues.* He has also published four books of essays, including *Orphan Factory.*

Simic has received fellowships from the Guggenheim Foundation, the MacArthur Foundation, and the National Endowment for the Arts. He is a Professor of English at the University of New Hampshire.

Kim Stafford is a poet and essayist living in Portland, Oregon. The son of writer William Stafford, the younger Stafford's books include *A Thousand Friends of Rain: New & Selected Poems; Places and Stories: A Collection of Poem; Entering the Grove; The Muses Among Us;* and *Having Everything Right: Essays of Place,* which won a citation for excellence from the Western States Book Awards in 1986. Since 1979, he has taught writing at Lewis and Clark College in Portland, and he currently serves as director and artist-in-residence at the Northwest Writing Institute.

Maureen Stanton's essays and memoirs have been published in literary magazines and anthologies, including *The Sun, Creative Nonfiction, Fourth Genre, River Teeth,* and *The Iowa Review.* Her essays have received the Penelope Niven Award from Salem College, The Mary Roberts Rinehart Award from George Mason University, and the Iowa Review Award and have been selected twice as Notable Essays in *Best American Essays.* She works as a freelance writer and editor in Georgetown, Maine.

Alice Steinbach, who was awarded the Pulitzer Prize for Feature Writing, is a freelance writer. In 1999, she began a journey to discover how to combine her three passions: learning, traveling, and writing. *Without Reservations: The Travels of an Independent Woman* was the result. Other books include *The Miss Dennis School of Writing* and *Educating Alice: Adventures of a Curious Woman.* She has taught journalism and writing at Princeton University, Washington and Lee University, and Loyola College. She lives in Baltimore.

Kandi Tayebi is Associate Professor of English and Associate Dean of Arts and Humanities at Sam Houston State University in Huntsville, Texas. Her interests range from 19th-century British literature to feminism and ecology. Tayebi recently served as the feature editor for a volume of the *Academic Exchange Quarterly* focusing on teaching environmental literature. She has published creative nonfiction in *The Georgia Review* and written the textbook *A Student's Guide to First-Year English,* which was published in 1995.

Susan Allen Toth's books include *Blooming: A Small-Town Girlhood; Ivy Day: Making My Way Out East;* and *How to Prepare for Your High-School Reunion and Other Mid-Life Musings.* She is also co-author of the *Introduction to Contemporary Literature* and has written biographies and instructional materials for contemporary nonfiction writers. She works as an adjunct professor and writer-in-residence at Macalester College in St. Paul, Minnesota.

Alice Walker, whose books have been translated into two dozen languages, attended Spelman College and received a B.A. from Sarah Lawrence College. Her collections of prose include *Anything We Love Can Be Saved: A Writer's Activism; The Same River Twice: Honoring the Difficult; Living by the Word: Selected Writings, 1973–87;* and *In Search of Our Mother's Gardens: Womanist Prose.* Her books of poetry include *Her Blue Body; Everything We Know: Earthling Poems; Complete; Revolutionary Petunias and Other Poems;* and *Once: Poems.* Among her novels and short story collections are *The Way Forward Is with a Broken Heart; By the Light of My Father's Smile; You Can't Keep a Good Woman Down;* and *The Color Purple,* which won the Pulitzer Prize and the American Book Award.

Connie Wieneke holds a Master of Fine Arts degree from the University of Montana. Her poetry, fiction, and creative nonfiction have appeared in literary journals. She lives in Jackson Hole, Wyoming.

Bailey White is the author of the national bestsellers *Mama Makes Up Her Mind, Quite a Year for Plums,* and *Sleeping at the Starlite Motel.* She is also a regular commentator on National Public Radio's *All Things Considered.* She lives in southern Georgia.

Colson Whitehead's work has appeared in *Vibe, Spin, Newsday,* and *The Village Voice,* where he was a television columnist. His first novel, *The Intuitionist,* won the QPB New Voices Award and was an Ernest Hemingway/PEN Award finalist. His second novel, *John Henry Days,* was a finalist for the Pulitzer Prize and was a New York Times Book Review Editors' Choice. *The Colossus of New York,* his most recent work of creative nonfiction, won the 2000 Whiting Writers' Award. Whitehead is a recent recipient of a MacArthur Fellowship.

APPENDIX:
RESOURCES TO KNOW ABOUT

Here is a list of some of our favorite sources for reading and publishing creative nonfiction.

For Reading

❧ Literary journals that focus exclusively on creative non-fiction: *Fourth Genre, Creative Nonfiction, River Teeth, The Sun.* Note: *Fourth Genre* also features roundtables on form, interviews with authors, and a column edited by Mimi called "Reader to Reader," in which readers write capsule reviews of their favorite creative nonfiction books available in print. To order these journals, check their websites.

❧ Literary journals that include excellent creative nonfiction along with fiction and poetry: *The Georgia Review, The Florida Review, The Missouri Review, The Gettysburg Review, Three Penny Review, Puerto del Sol,* and *The Southern Review.* The list goes on. Tip: To find others, check your library, a serious bookstore, and *Best American Essays,* which lists the periodicals in which they found the best creative non-fiction for that year.

❧ Commercial magazines: *The New Yorker, Harper's,* and *The Atlantic Monthly* all publish literary journalism and occasional personal essays; the latter can also be found in weekly columns of newspaper magazines of *The New York Times, The Washington Post,* and *The Los Angeles Times,* to name a few.

❧ Online magazines: *Brevity*, edited by Dinty Moore, features short essays and memoirs.

❧ Anthologies: *The Best American Essays*, edited by Robert Atwan, is published each year. See also *The Art of the Personal Essay*, edited by Philip Lopate; *Modern American Memoirs*, edited by Annie Dillard and Cort Conley; *In Fact*, edited by Lee Gutkind; *The Best American Travel Writing*, edited by Frances Mayes; *The Fourth Genre*, edited by Mike Steinberg and Robert Root; and *Circle of Women*, edited by Kim Barnes and Mary Clearman Blew.

❧ Essay collections by single authors: Annie Dillard's *The Writing Life;* Stephen Dunn's *Walking Light;* Patrica Hampl's *I Could Tell You Stories;* Bret Lott's *Fathers, Sons, and Brothers;* Scott Russell Sanders's *Secrets of the Universe;* Bailey White's *Mama Makes Up Her Mind.* There are, of course, so many more.

❧ 28 contemporary memoirs that are favorites of our students:

1. Andre Aciman, *Out of Egypt*— the author, now an American, grows up in a hilarious Jewish family living in exile in 20th-century Egypt.

2. Max Apple, *Roommates*— a wise curmudgeon of a grandfather shares the author's room, physically and spiritually, for 104 years, and beyond.

3. Russell Baker, *Growing Up*— a funny and poignant account of a lazy boy with a pushy mother growing up during the Depression.

4. Peter Balakian, *Black Dog of Fate*— a New Jersey boy grows up in the silences of his family's memories of the Armenian Holocaust — and sets out to uncover what happened.

5. Kim Barnes, *Out of the Wilderness*— a coming-of-age memoir about a daughter's struggle to find herself in a Pentecostal household in Idaho — and what it takes to leave that life.

6. Jung Chang, *Wild Swans: Three Daughters of China*— a story that spans three generations of women in one Chinese family: the first, a concubine; the second, an ardent Maoist; the third,

a freedom-seeking writer who leaves China to better understand all of their lives.

7. Nien Cheng, *Life and Death in Shanghai* — One woman's struggle to survive the Cultural Revolution in China with dignity and still save herself and her family.

8. Jill Ker Conway, *Road from Coorain* — a moving account of a childhood in the Australian outback and how a family, intent on doing everything right, struggles and often fails.

9. Cathy N. Davidson, *Thirty-Six Views of Mount Fuji* — an American goes to Japan to teach English for a year and brings back wonderful crosscultural insights.

10. Magda Denes, *Castles Burning* — a Hungarian family survives the Holocaust in hiding and then spends two years as displaced persons in post-war Europe.

11. Helen Epstein, *Where She Came From* — a look at three generations of Jewish women from Eastern Europe and the legacy they bequeath to the writer, their American-born descendent.

12. Lucy Grealy, *Autobiography of a Face* — a book of courage about coming to terms with issues of beauty when you've had cancer of the jaw as an eight-year-old.

13. Donald Hall, *String Too Short to Be Saved* — one of our leading poets and essayists describes summers on his grandparents' New Hampshire farm, detailing portraits of New England life and values.

14. Patricia Hampl, *A Romantic Education* — a quest to discover family roots in Prague, Czechoslovakia, and the surprising connections to past and present that can emerge on such a journey.

15. Maxine Hong Kingston, *The Woman Warrior* — a book about the legacy of the past on a Chinese-American girl who grows up in California.

16. Primo Levi, *Survival at Auschwitz* — a look at the human spirit and what it takes to survive the most inhumane of conditions, told by a survivor who became one of the key writers about the Holocaust.

17. Bret Lott, *Fathers, Sons, and Brothers* — a wonderful entrée into everyday family life told from a male perspective about fathers, sons, and brothers.

18. James McBride, *The Color of Water* — a young man's story of growing up in Harlem, one of 12 children of a white Jewish mother and a black father; told in two voices: one the son, one the mother.

19. Frank McCourt, *Angela's Ashes* — a coming-of-age story set in Limerick, Ireland; it's the rhythmic voice that makes this story of family love and dire poverty so powerful.

20. Sue Miller, *The Story of My Father* — a daughter's struggle with her father's Alzheimer's disease that offers comfort to anyone struggling with parental loss.

21. Mary Morris, *Nothing to Declare* — a travel memoir about the stress of leaving America to live alone for one year in San Miguel, Mexico.

22. Ann Patchett, *Truth and Beauty* — an honest portrayal of the competition and rocky friendship between the author and her fellow writer Lucy Grealy.

23. Richard Rodriguez, *The Hunger of Memory* — a look at what is lost and what is gained when a working-class, Spanish-speaking child adopts English and moves into mainstream American life.

24. Lauren Slater, *Welcome to My Country* — an examination of the relationships between a psychotherapist and her schizophrenic patients told with understanding by someone who has known mental illness firsthand.

25. Abraham Verghese, *My Own Country* — the story of an American-trained doctor from India who travels to Tennessee to treat AIDS patients.

26. Bruce Weigl, *The Circle of Hanh: A Memoir* — an account of how being a young soldier in Vietnam shaped the life of a poet and a man.

27. Geoffrey Wolff, *Duke of Deception* — a boy gradually finds out that the father he adores is a self-destructive con man. A great companion piece to brother Tobias Wolff's, *This Boy's Life.* You see the same family from two perspectives, a rare treat in memoir.

28. Tobias Wolff, *This Boy's Life* — After the family splits up, one son and mother leave father and brother behind and head West for a fresh start and a new identity that keeps eluding them.

For Publishing

- Reference Books: *Writer's Market; Writer's Guide to Book Editors, Publishers, and Literary Agents;* and *The International Directory of Little Magazines and Small Presses.* These books describe what individual publishers are looking for, supply names and addresses of whom to contact, and give tips on how to submit your work.

- Magazines: *The Writer's Chronicle* and *Poets & Writers* are two excellent monthly magazines filled with information about writers and the writer's craft. They also offer current information about contests, workshops, conferences, publishers' calls for submissions, and freelance editors who will critique your work for a fee.

- The Internet: In addition to many literary blogs and online magazines (some are directed at upcoming and student writers), you can also find current listings of writers' conferences and contests. A great new website to check out is the Emerging Writers Network at http://www.emergingwriters.net.

- Local Opportunities: Your library or local bookstore might know of grassroots anthologies for reading and for publishing your work. They are also a good source for finding out about open readings, poetry slams, and local writers' groups. Your local newspaper may be interested in freelance personal essays, especially those tied to holidays or current news.

CREDITS

Photo Credits

108-10 Réunion des Musées Nationalux / Art Resource, New York. Reprinted by permission. **117** Copyright © Sue Miller. Reproduced by permission. **126** Courtesy of the Franklin Delano Roosevelt Library. **127** Courtesy of the Stephen Crane Collection (#5505), Clifton Waller Barrett Library of American Literature, Special Collections, University of Virginia Library. Reprinted by permission. **130** From *Persepolis: The Story of a Childhood*, by Marjane Satrapi, translated by Mattias Ripa & Blake Ferris. Copyright © 2003 by L'Asocation, Paris, France. Used by permission of Pantheon Books, a division of Random House, Inc. **134** anonymous **136** Copyright © Gretchen Legler. Reprinted by permission. **138** From *King*, by Ho Che Anderson. Copyright © 1993 Fantagraphics Books. Reprinted by permission.

Text Credits

24 Penelope Scambly Schott is the author of *The Perfect Mother, Penelope: The Story of the Half-Scalped Woman, The Pest Maiden: A Story of a Lobotomy,* and other books. She does not drink frozen lemonade. **40** Still Life from *The First Four Books of Poems* by Louise Gluck. Copyright 1968, 1971, 1972, 1973, 1974, 1975, 1976, 1977, 1978, 1979, 1980, 1985, 1995 by Louise Gluck. Reprinted by permission of Harper Collins Publishers Inc. *Firstborn, Descending Figure, House On Marshland, Triumph Of Achilles.* Ecco Press. **114** Bukowski, Charles, "It Doesn't Always Work," originally appeared in *New York Quarterly*, no. 29, Spring 1986. Reprinted by permission of Linda Lee Bukowski and The Charles Bukowski Memorial Foundation. **278-79** "Wild nights" (4 lines); "Hope is the thing with feathers" (2 lines) are reprinted by permission of the publishers and the Trustees of Amherst College from *The Poems of Emily Dickinson,* Thomas H. Johnson, ed., Cambridge, Mass.: The Belknap Press of Harvard University Press, Copyright © 1951, 1955, 1979 by the President and Fellows of Harvard University Press, Copyright © 1951, 1955, 1979 by the President and Fellows of Harvard College. **183** Lisa Chavez, "Independence Day, Manley Hot Springs, Alaska" from *The Fourth Genre,* vol. 2, no. 1, Spring, 2002, pp. 71-78. Also reprinted in *The Fourth Genre: Contemporary Writers of/on Creative Nonfiction,* 2nd edition, Longman. Reprinted by permission of the author. **191** "Somehow Form a Family" from *Somehow Form a Family* by Tony Earley. © 2001 by Tony Earley. Reprinted by permission of Algonguin Books of Chapel Hill. **200** Nora Ephron, "A Few Words About Breasts" in *Crazy Salad: Some Things About Women,* New York: Knopf, 1975. Reprinted by permission of International Creative Management, Inc. Copyright © 1975 by Nora Ephron. **208** "Let It Snow" from *Dress Your Family in Corduroy and Denim* by David Sedaris. Copyright © 2004 by David Sedaris. By permission of Little, Brown and Co., Inc. **210** "Beauty: When the Other Dancer is the Self" from *In Search of Our Mothers' Gardens,* copyright © 1983 by Alice Walker, reprinted by permission of Harcourt, Inc. **219** Callahan, Gerald N., "Chimera," *Creative Nonfiction,* #11. Reprinted by permission. **227** Brian Doyle is the editor of *Portland Magazine* at the University of Portland, in Oregon. He is the author of five essay collections, most recently *Spirited Men,*